Outlaw Dakota

D1600006

Dedicated
to the memory of my friend
Thomas R. Kilian

Outlaw Dakota

The Murderous Times and Criminal Trials of Frontier Judge Peter C. Shannon

Wayne Fanebust

THE CENTER FOR WESTERN STUDIES
AUGUSTANA UNIVERSITY
2016

Publication made possible with funding by the Anne King Publications Endowment and Ronald R. Nelson Publications Endowment in the Center for Western Studies and by the National Endowment for the Humanities.

ISBN: 978-0-931170-56-0

Library of Congress Control Number: 2015955093

Number 16 in the Prairie Plains Series

The Center for Western Studies (CWS) at Augustana University seeks to improve the quality of social and cultural life in the Northern Plains, achieve a better understanding of the region, its heritage, and its resources, and stimulate interest in the solution to regional problems. The Center promotes understanding of the region through its archives, library, museum and art exhibitions, publications, courses, internships, conferences, and forums. It is committed, ultimately, to defining the contribution of the Northern Plains to American civilization.

The Fantle Building for the Center for Western Studies, Augustana University
2121 S. Summit Avenue, Sioux Falls, South Dakota
605-274-4007 • 605-274-4999 (fax) • cws@augie.edu
www.augie.edu/cws • Facebook • Twitter

Cover: First courthouse in Yankton, D.T., northeast corner of Fifth Street and Douglas Avenue. Courtesy Yankton County Historical Society.

Manufactured in the United States of America

CONTENTS

ACKNOWLEDGMENTS

I want to thank the South Dakota public libraries at Sioux Falls, Canton, Yankton, Mitchell, Pierre, Watertown, and Vermillion, along with the many librarians who cheerfully and patiently handled my requests for books and newspaper microfilm. I also appreciate having access to the vast resources of the libraries at Augustana University, the Center for Western Studies, and the University of South Dakota. Thank you to Ken Stewart and Matthew Reitzel at the South Dakota State Archives in Pierre for answering all my inquiries about photographs and manuscript collections. The staff at the State Historical Society of North Dakota in Bismarck was also very helpful, and I appreciate their high degree of professionalism.

I have received valuable support from my California friends and colleagues of the San Diego Independent Scholars, and I thank them all, but especially Sam Gusman and Gerry Horwitz with whom I collaborated on an essay about the frontier experience in America. Closer to home, members of the Yankton Historical Society, the Westerners, the Minnehaha Century Fund, and the Minnehaha County Historical Society have kept me in contact with fellow history buffs, many of whom provided encouragement and helpful suggestions.

Among my friends I thank attorney and local historian Bruce Blake for the many lunches we enjoyed while discussing Dakota history, including Judge Shannon. A thank you goes out to Steve Cusulos who read and commented on one of the chapters in the book, and thanks to Maxine Schuurmans Kinsley in Yankton for giving me her file on Jack McCall. Monsignor James Doyle made contacts that enabled me to visit the Shannon mansion in Yankton, for which I am grateful. And of course I thank John and Karen Harmelink, the current residents, for giving me a tour of the house.

Meeting Mike Conner, a distant relative of Judge Shannon's from Pennsylvania, was a special treat. Thanks, Mike, for your visit to South Dakota, for your enthusiasm and for sending me valuable research material.

And I thank my friends Richard Nordstrom, Byron Schmidt, David Swan, Paula Habbena, David Davis, Paul Chekola, Steve Bointe, and Matthew Dorweiller for their interest and support of my writing.

Thanks to Harry Thompson and the Publications Committee of the Center for Western Studies, at Augustana University, for taking on the publication of this book after their careful review and critique of the manuscript. I am grateful for their suggested revisions, which served to tighten the narrative and focus the book on Dakota themes.

I thank my brothers and sisters for their unfailing belief in me while the books have piled up over the years. And lastly, I thank my daughter Danae and granddaughter Angelina for their love and understanding without which I would have lost my way a long time ago.

Wayne Fanebust
Sioux Falls, South Dakota

The publisher wishes to acknowledge the assistance of South Dakota Circuit Judge (ret.) and State Senator Arthur R. Rusch, CWS Collections Assistant Elizabeth Thrond, Digital Technician Wyeth Lynch, and Hal Thompson.

INTRODUCTION

The purpose of this book is to explore the vagaries of crime and punishment in Dakota Territory through the courtroom experiences of Peter C. Shannon, Chief Justice of the Dakota Territory Supreme Court from 1873 to 1882. Years ago, when I was engaged in the private practice of law, I decided that someday I would write a book that combined my knowledge of the law with my love for the history of the American West. From that point on, I never lost sight of Judge Shannon and his times and trials.

The result is this book, a survey of crime that occurred on the frontier during the time of the outlaw—the iconic, even mythic, and always popular figure of the Old West. Although the lives of such giants among frontier figures as Jesse James, Wyatt Earp, and Wild Bill Hickok have been paraded before the eager gaze of the public repeatedly, this book concentrates on some of the less known, but no less colorful, frontier characters. The trials of the Dakota outlaws and desperadoes were much more exciting and interesting than the court work of today's lawyer. Many of the Old West trials served as great spectacles and high drama when entertainment options were otherwise limited.

The frontier life of Judge Peter C. Shannon is revealed in the pages that follow, though at times he seems to stand in the shadows cast by the villains he sought to hang or put behind bars. And except for his role on the Indian Commission in 1882-83, he emerges as the hero of this book—the man who upheld the law that he believed was the cornerstone of civilized life. For this judge, the law was the force that shaped the order of things. Knowledge of, and respect for, the law was the mark of an intelligent, cultivated person. Shannon the judge was Shannon the teacher, and he gladdened the hearts and earned the accolades of the people who listened to him pronounce judgment from the bench.

Shannon's plain judicial philosophy perseveres, but it is masked by the hypocritical reverence for the law in America today. We declare outwardly our love for peace, honor, and justice for all, while inwardly relishing the details of the outlaw life, often elevated to myth. Law and order are the bywords of every decent citizen, and yet beyond these platitudes we secretly admire the gun-toting outlaw who rejected citizenship to follow a life of crime. For most of us, reading about a desperado is far more interesting than reading about a sodbuster.

Judge Shannon's career brought him up close to both the outlaw and the law-abiding citizen. He was a brilliant lawyer and a fearless judge who believed in the majesty of the law, and through his work he urged respect for the law. But respect for the law and those who enforce it is never enough to form a complete picture of life in the Old West. We need the outlaw, too.

The ordinary frontiersman did not carry a gun to impress or intimidate or to be someone other than himself, nor did he concern himself with the Second Amendment of the Constitution. The people of the frontier did not engage in role playing; their roles were thrust upon them by the harsh demands of the wilderness, so they owned and used a pistol or rifle out of necessity. A weapon was as essential as a plow or an ax. At a time when some settlers lived in isolation with little or no police protection, a gun was used to put dinner on the table or as the "great equalizer" in a crisis. Judge Shannon probably carried a gun when he traveled on horseback or by stagecoach from town to town, conducting the business of the court. The outlaw certainly carried a gun.

In 1924 a South Dakota newspaper featured a lengthy article on Wild Bill Hickok, laying out the various details of his exciting life on the frontier, and, of course, recounting his death in Deadwood, caused by a gun fired by Jack McCall. Names are dropped freely throughout the article, and Wild Bill is falsely credited with killing "between thirty-five and forty white men." But when writing about the McCall murder trial, the reporter failed to mention Peter C. Shannon, the judge who sentenced McCall to death by hanging. Rather, Wild Bill was praised as "the greatest gunman the world has ever seen." Here, then, is the untold story of Judge Shannon and the coming of justice to outlaw Dakota.

CHAPTER 1

ORGANIZING DAKOTA TERRITORY

The organization of this great Territory opens a new field
of promise and fortune for those making homes in the West.

The Weekly Dakotian
June 6, 1861

fter a brief but spirited fight between rival townsite companies, and some persuasive lobbying, Dakota Territory joined the expanding list of new states and territories in the trans-Mississippi West. The Organic Act was passed by Congress, and on March 2, 1861, was signed into law by outgoing President James Buchanan. Along with Dakota, the territories Colorado and Nevada were created under separate but similar acts. Dakota Territory was the largest, and due to its great size, the Organic Act provided that it could be divided into two or more territories.[1]

It was probably the easiest task Buchanan had during his four beleaguered years as president, as he proved to be unable or unwilling to deal with the problems of sectionalism and slavery. With the nation gravitating toward civil war, Buchanan was eager to get out of town. He left the threat of Southern rebellion, along with naming the first Dakota territorial officials, to incoming President Abraham Lincoln. The new president wasted no time in filling in the blanks left by his predecessor.

Lincoln's appointments were more than ministerial, even though the task was miniscule compared to the decisions he was weighing as the incoming president of a divided country. He was awarding offices to men who were committed to leaving their comfortable lives and careers in the East and Midwest in favor of serving as government officials in a part of the country that was commonly referred to as the Great Northwest. Their new jobs on the wild frontier would be fraught with hardship and danger.

Dakota Territory was a vast domain of wilderness that combined elements of rich-soil prairie with great expanses of plains, wild rivers, mountains, hills, buttes, and badlands. Its human occupants were principally members of Plains Indian tribes for whom Dakota was ancestral land. White settlements were small and isolated, and except for Pembina—the oldest—near the Canadian border, were clustered in the southeastern corner of the territory.

As originally formed, the far western border of Dakota Territory was ill-defined. The territory consisted of the present-day states of North and South Dakota, Montana, a small slice of north-central Nebraska, a section of Idaho, and approximately the northern half of Wyoming. Washington Territory was on the western border of Dakota. The principal and most unifying feature of the new legal entity was the Missouri River that flowed out of the far western reaches of Dakota, cutting through much of the territory as it moved in a southeasterly direction.

The land east of the Missouri River had been attached to Minnesota Territory. When Minnesota was admitted to the Union in 1858, that land mass was unorganized but not unwanted. Townsite speculators in St. Paul, Minnesota, and Dubuque and Sioux City, Iowa, were anxious to plant towns on what they believed was soil that would produce excellent crops, flourishing cities, plentiful profits, and political plums. In 1856 the townsite of Sioux Falls was founded, followed by Flandreau, Medary, and Eminija in 1857, all on the Big Sioux River. Yankton on the Missouri River was created in 1859. All were the product of the speculators' oversized ambitions.

Aside from the harsh justice found in Native American communities, and military law that ruled soldiers serving at the various forts, lawlessness prevailed among the handful of white people, who were essentially

Fort Randall, Dakota Territory.
Courtesy Robert W. Kolbe Collection.

squatters, waiting for the federal government to bestow legitimacy on their claims. For these people the law of the gun, the mob, the claim club, or any other hastily improvised system, provided the answer to "legal" questions. For example, as early as 1858, the settlers and speculators at Sioux Falls—mostly Democrats—set up a squatter government complete with a governor and legislature.[2]

Sioux Falls and the other southeastern townsites on the Big Sioux River were positioned on land not yet ceded by the Indians. But cession was part of the grand scheme of things and in accordance with the terms of a treaty with the Yankton Sioux, forged in 1858 and approved the following year, all legal impediments were removed. The Yankton Sioux gave up approximately eleven million acres of land in exchange for a small reservation in Charles Mix County, along the east bank of the Missouri

River. The treaty allowed speculators to cling to their townsites and wait for the wagon trains that were expected to come from the East.

Other towns were founded following the exodus of the Yankton Sioux Indians. In 1859, Vermillion was located at the intersection of the Vermillion River and Missouri River, about twenty miles downriver from Yankton. The town was built on a site formerly occupied by a fur trading post.[3] Bon Homme, meaning "The Good Man" in English, got its start in 1858 when a party of young men from Dodge County, Minnesota, on their way to the gold fields of Pike's Peak in Colorado, stopped and decided to stay.[4] Elk Point was located in Cole County, (later renamed Union County) north of Sioux City, Iowa, between the Big Sioux and Missouri Rivers, in 1859, when Eli Wixson built a small shack with a dirt floor and sod roof at the townsite and called it a hotel.[5]

A powerful tide of land speculation and townsite planting was sweeping across the West in the 1850s, and the Dakota hopefuls were riding the crest of the wave. With plat maps and sales pitches at the ready, the speculators were ready to sell land by the section or by the lot. Campgrounds would become villages and then towns, which would grow into cities. With the aid of Uncle Sam and the expectation that people would come if there was something to come to, the speculators were prepared to reap their bonanza in property, money, and political power.

But none of this was likely to materialize without an organized government. To that end, President Lincoln appointed a territorial governor, Dr. William Jayne from Springfield, Illinois; a secretary, John Hutchinson from Minnesota; a U.S. attorney, William F. Gleason from Maryland; a U.S. marshal, William E. Shaffer from Missouri; and a surveyor-general, George D. Hill from Michigan. All appointees were staunch Republicans, since Lincoln and his party sought to instill as much loyalty as possible in the new territories.

In his annual message to Congress on December 3, 1861, Lincoln called attention to his official territorial selections in a manner that reflected his concern for loyalty and for his unwavering belief that slavery was to be kept out of new territories. He praised Dakota and the other new territories because "civil administration has been inaugurated therein," but warned that the "leaven of treason" had taken root "in some of the new countries when the federal officers arrived there."[6]

The Dakota governor, Dr. Jayne, was a friend and the personal physician of Lincoln and his family. He was an abolitionist, attached to the radical wing of his party, making him about as loyal as one could get. Jayne had served as the mayor of Springfield, Illinois, and was the brother-in-law of U.S. Senator Lyman Trumbull, a powerful politician. Jayne was "a clever man, a tolerably shrewd ward politician," but utterly lacking in statesmanship.[7]

Traveling by horse and wagon or by steamboat on the Missouri River, Jayne and the other officials straggled into Yankton, the temporary capital of the territory. Yankton was merely a small collection of crude log buildings hugging the banks of the Missouri River. The fledgling town was located on the site of what was once the principal Yankton Sioux village. It had been the headquarters for the fur-trade business of John Blair Smith Todd, a West Point graduate and former officer in the U.S. Army. He was also a cousin of Mary Todd Lincoln and as such, was well acquainted with the president. Todd, a Democrat, was largely responsible for the Treaty of 1858. Todd spent the winter of 1860-61 in Washington, D.C., engaged in heavy lobbying for the creation of Dakota Territory. His work paid off, for Yankton, the "Mother City" of Dakota, was called "Captain Todd's town."

Yankton could not have impressed the newcomers, all of whom felt they had been exiled to a primitive and hostile country, far from family, friends, and the comforts of civilized life. The land, however, sloped upward gently from the Missouri River, making the site an attractive place upon which to build. Moreover, the river was teeming with catfish that quickly became a dietary staple.

But it would take more than catfish and desirable land to ensure success. To facilitate the awesome task placed in the hands of the first Dakota officials, the civilizing influences of law and order were built into the Organic Act. It called for the establishment of a Supreme Court consisting of three justices to be appointed by the president for a term of four years. Each Supreme Court justice was also a trial judge, one for each of three judicial districts. The district courts had jurisdiction over violations of United States criminal laws as well as crimes against some territorial laws. Decisions made by the district courts were subject to review by the Dakota Supreme Court, which in turn, could be appealed to the U.S. Supreme Court.

To get the courts and the rest of the territorial government up and running, the Organic Act declared that the U.S. Constitution and all other laws of the states and territories applied to, and were enforceable in, Dakota Territory unless they were "locally inapplicable."[8] The Act also created such local tribunals as probate courts and justice of the peace courts.[9]

Rounding out the territorial judiciary, each district was allowed one U.S. commissioner, appointed by the district justice. Commissioners were authorized to handle a number of duties including "taking cognizance of all violations of United States laws." They were responsible for holding preliminary hearings on federal offenses to determine whether an accused should be released, held on bail, and later, turned over to a federal grand jury. In other words, they functioned much like a justice of the peace.[10]

The judicial districts were created to comply with the law but with no thought of covering the entire territory. It was just too big and wild to come under the gavels of three federal judges. Dakota Territory was suffused in a dense fog of isolation and lawlessness. As if the harsh environment itself had cast a spell, official status and dignity were often overlooked and quarrels and disputes were instead settled by violence. Governor Jayne himself was involved in a well-publicized "hair-pulling, choking, striking, blood-spitting" fistfight in Yankton with another official.[11] It would take time before the arm of the law would become long and powerful, and worthy of respect.

In the beginning, the governor was authorized by the Organic Act to draw the boundaries of the judicial districts and assign each judge to a district, where he was required to reside. After this initial effort, the territorial legislature was vested with the responsibility of organizing and altering the judicial districts, assigning judges, and designating the location of the courts.[12]

Governor Jayne was nominated by the president on March 23, 1861, and confirmed by the senate four days later. He arrived in Yankton with his private secretary, C. Fessenden, on May 27, 1861, set up his office in a log cabin, and went to work. President Lincoln gave him the job, but then stepped back and let Jayne govern without any guidance or direction. Jayne and the new government he was about to establish could, however, look to benefit from the Republican Party's liberal support of free homesteads, aid to railroads, and money for internal improvements.[13]

Sleeping accommodations in Yankton were severely limited. In lieu of an executive mansion, Governor Jayne had to bed down with U.S. Attorney Gleason, the man appointed to prosecute federal crimes. They shared a shack on the east side of what later became Broadway Street, and it was not a good arrangement. Gleason was a fussy and delicate man, accustomed to comfortable living. He resented his pushy housemate who kept him busy hauling water from the river for "toilet purposes."[14] But prosecutions were few and far between in 1861 so the disagreeable chore did not cut into Gleason's official duties.

Much of the official business in early-day Yankton was conducted in a small building erected at the corner of Walnut Street and Second Street, just a short distance from the Missouri River. In addition to holding court sessions, the structure served as the first land office and headquarters for other county business. The busy little log house became the "center of life" in the capital city in the early 1860s.[15]

By proclamation on July 13, 1861, Governor Jayne established the initial judicial districts for the territory. He decreed that the first district would consist of a slender, north-and-south portion of the extreme eastern part of the territory, from Canada to the Nebraska border, with the court located in Vermillion. The second district was an equally slender column of land that bordered the western end of the first district, with its court in Yankton. The third district consisted of the remaining territory, whose court was located in the tiny town of Bon Homme, on the Missouri River west of Yankton.[16]

It would be a great challenge for any judge to manage and administer justice over such large tracts of land, all sparsely settled and all barely penetrated—if at all—by a decree or a decision from a judge's pen. There were no courthouses so any convenient structure would have to play the part. The officials in charge of administering justice in Dakota—including the U.S. marshal, deputies, and court clerks—were tasked with making do with very little. The annual salary for a Supreme Court justice serving in Dakota in 1861 was a meager $1,800.[17]

Since Lincoln was distracted by the secessionist movement in the Southern states—and by imminent civil war—he could not be faulted if he failed to give a great deal of thought toward selecting Dakota's first federal judges. Yet he seems to have made good choices: Chief Justice Philemon Bliss and Associate Justices Lorenzo P. Williston and Joseph L. Williams.

Bliss was born in Canton, Connecticut, and raised and educated in the state of New York. He moved to Ohio and served that state in the U.S. House of Representatives. He was an abolitionist with numerous friends among both radical and moderate Republicans. Appointed on March 27, 1861, Bliss had been an attorney and judge in Ohio.[18] Arriving in Yankton in July of 1861, he was described in the *Weekly Dakotian* as a "finished gentleman, an able statesman and a distinguished jurist."[19] The chief justice was "taken in by a kind hearted citizen" who provided lodging, on the edge of town, for the "dignified jurist" and "fed him the best the market afforded."[20]

Lorenzo P. Williston,
Associate Justice, Dakota Territory Supreme Court.
Courtesy Montana Historical Society.

Williston, appointed to the Dakota bench on March 27, 1861, had been a judge in Pennsylvania and had supported the Republican presidential tickets in 1856 and 1860.[21] The youngest of the three appointees, he was said to be well qualified as a judge. But the florid and portly judge found the frontier's fleas and mosquitoes unpleasant. Williston was known to curse the insects that plagued him in the most emphatic terms.[22]

Williams, appointed on June 18, 1861, was a wealthy lawyer from Tennessee, a conscientious man of learning for whom the Dakota frontier was overwhelming.[23] He was not Lincoln's first choice as an associate justice. Allen A. Burton of Lancaster, Kentucky, was the President's original choice, but he soon changed his mind and sent Burton to New Granada, in South America, to serve as the U.S. minister, and ordered Williams to Dakota.[24] He was the last of the first three justices to arrive in Dakota.

Governor Jayne assigned Justice Williston to the first district court in Vermillion and Justice Williams to the third district court headquartered in Bon Homme. Chief Justice Bliss was given the second district in Yankton.[25] Though the first federal judges were well-qualified, they failed to distinguish themselves while serving in Dakota Territory, which generated little legal business or court intervention in these early days.

The territorial capital of Yankton, however, was the exception. When the legislature—called the "Pony Congress" because of its small size—met for the first time, it supplied enough comical antics and rough action to keep the small population entertained. For example, the Council, or upper house, engaged in "wine dinners and wine suppers, wine speeches and wine quarrels, and the hurling of bottles and glasses across tables at the bleeding heads of belligerent councilmen"[26] Booze, guns, knives and threats of bodily harm were the tools of debate, but no man was ever arrested for acts of violence committed in his "official" capacity. The legislature, however, did pass a set of criminal and civil codes.

Trouble was brewing on the western Dakota horizon. As early as 1860, prospectors roamed the far western reaches of what became Dakota Territory, now Montana and Idaho, but in the summer of 1862, gold was discovered in a stream called Grasshopper Creek. Excited gold seekers rushed into the new "gold fields" where "gold could be panned out of sagebrush."[27] Soon the town of Bannack was established on Grasshopper Creek by people who probably did not know that they were in Dakota Territory.[28]

Nor did they care. But officials in Yankton were not slow to learn of the exciting events occurring in western Dakota. The headline "Our Gold Mines" in the June 17, 1862, edition of the *Dakotian* announced that the gold discovered in the headwaters of the Missouri River had created "a perfect stampede." Anticipating that Dakota Territory would experience both a gold rush and population boom, the Yankton newspaper predicted that 100,000 new people would soon arrive.[29]

Indeed, about 13,000 prospectors did flock into far western Dakota,[30] officially a part of the third judicial district but largely unknown to those living east of the Missouri. Three federal judges could not effectively assert their authority over land 1,000 miles away. In September, the steamer *Shreveport* stopped in Yankton, filled with passengers from the gold mines who told tales of "rich diggings." To back up their boasting, they claimed to have brought with them over $100,000 in gold dust.[31] What a way to start a territory!

Then in March of 1863, Idaho Territory was created, depriving Dakota of much of its far western domain. The southeastern Dakotans would continue to reap benefits from the rapid growth in Idaho. Gold strikes encouraged migration, and the travelers needed supplies from the Yankton merchants. Unfortunately, lawlessness and violence accompanied these new arrivals. Crime went unpunished until vigilante committees and make-shift courts were set up to try, convict, and immediately hang outlaws.[32]

Freed from the kind of legal challenges Idaho Territory was facing, the Dakota Supreme Court justices frequently left the area "on business" or to visit family back East. Departing judges drew criticism from Moses K. Armstrong, an erudite Yankton journalist and politician who wrote satirical letters for a Sioux City newspaper under the *nom de plume* "Log-Roller."

Moses K. Armstrong,
Yankton journalist and Democratic politician.
Courtesy John Griffith Collection.

In one such letter, dated May 8, 1862, Armstrong noted that while the district court convened the first Monday of May, it did so without a judge. "Where are they?" he asked rhetorically. "All three judges appointed for Dakota, and paid by the government a salary of eighteen hundred a year," he answered, were "back in the states . . . carefully bagging the government's dollars."[33]

With the Civil War underway, there were worse places to pursue a career than in Dakota Territory. A frontier judgeship may have seemed like a dead-end position to someone accustomed to a busy life and an occasional dinner at a good restaurant, but all boredom was shattered when bloody chaos suddenly erupted throughout the settlements of southeastern Dakota. The U.S.-Dakota War of 1862 resulted in the death of hundreds of

Minnesota settlers but soon spilled over into Dakota. After two men were killed near Sioux Falls, panic spread among the settlers in the region and many loaded their wagons and fled for the Iowa border. Some people went to Yankton and others left the territory never to return. Sioux Falls was completely abandoned.

The people of Yankton, including refugees from other settlements, met, talked, and decided to stay. They constructed a crude fortification around some key structures in the heart of town where women and children hid and men armed themselves in the event of an Indian attack. But the group that had the courage to stay, in the main, excluded federally appointed officials.

Much to newspaperman Armstrong's bemusement, the stampede out of Dakota included "our weak-kneed, cowardly, runaway officials." They were, in fact, at or near the head of the mad procession, "governor, secretary, judges, attorney general, clerks, in one wild, panic-stricken express train of 'loyal' officials."[34] Judge Williston bailed out of a court session in Vermillion when he received word that the Indians were coming for blood. The corpulent judge jumped on a small mule and rode it all the way to Sioux City, making him one of the more comical and conspicuous travelers.[35] Armstrong was harshly critical of men who were appointed by the president to lead by example but instead ran away. Eventually, they all returned to Dakota and resumed their work, including the judges.

While the Indian threat did not result in any resignations, it seems that Judge Bliss was ready for a change. In October of 1862, he contacted Salmon P. Chase, the secretary of the treasury, asking to be appointed governor of Dakota "with the military commission of colonel."[36] Chase thought about the request but took no action.

Some months later, in August of 1863, Chase noted in his journal that he asked President Lincoln to appoint Samuel Shellberger, an Ohio congressman, governor of Dakota, unless the president wanted that office to go to Bliss. Should Bliss be named governor then Chase wanted Shellberger appointed chief justice. Once again, no action was taken on these requests.[37] For Bliss, it was either resign his judgeship or resign himself to being a frontier judge.

Although caseloads were light, criminal trials were needed for the illegal cutting of timber on federal land and for selling liquor to the Indians or selling it without a license. Judge Williams presided over one such illegal liquor sale trial during the November 1862 session of court held at Fort Randall. Arguably the most important military installation on the Missouri River, Fort Randall was built in 1856 on the west bank of the river at a site selected by General William S. Harney. The federal government invested money in Fort Randall rather lavishly, and over time it became a full-fledged community. In 1862 it was better equipped to handle trials than was Bon Homme.

In another Fort Randall court session, Williams (or one of the other judges) was remembered for an act that can only be classified as judicial misconduct. In 1862, while court was in session, the marshal, who had been sent to Yankton with a subpoena for a witness, was late in showing up for court. When he finally arrived, he flashed a wad of "greenbacks" and explained that he had won the money in a poker game at George L. Tackett's roadhouse on Choteau Creek. In an effort to extricate himself from an embarrassing situation, the marshal offered the presiding judge one-half of his winnings. The judge accepted the offer, saying, "For this, I'll let you off."[38]

In time, the third district court was moved from Fort Randall to Bon Homme. While it was well-supplied, Fort Randall was so isolated and remote that those stationed there felt like they were lost in time and space. In November of 1865, a resident of the fort started a newspaper but it lasted only a few months because there was little to report. The exasperated proprietor signed off by writing, "may you soon be discharged, and midst the peaceful pursuit of civilized life, forget there is such a country in existence as Dakota."[39]

Both Fort Randall and Bon Homme gradually gained population and respectability, but the outcome of an early trial in Bon Homme indicates how easy it was to corrupt the judicial process. Based on the recollections of "old settlers," the defendant in the trial instructed his hired man to take a jug of whiskey into the jury room ostensibly to grease the wheels of deliberation. The booze had the desired effect for the defendant received a favorable verdict.[40]

Lawyers found both refreshment and inspiration in liquor. There is a tale from the early days about a prominent and able attorney who kept a bottle in his coat pocket for easy access during trials. On one occasion in Bon Homme, he excused himself saying that he had to retire to the stable and "grease his buggy." After he returned the lawyer threw himself into a vigorous argument to the jury only to find that, in his exuberance, the bottle fell from his pocket and onto the floor. A member of the jury, an Englishman, picked it up, opened it, took a whiff, and said for all to hear: "haxle grease!"[41]

Booze was destined to play a role in the court system throughout the territorial period. At Bon Homme, the court quickly acquired a reputation where trials produced a " 'bone of contention' and is [sic] the oasis where the weary and dispairing [sic] lawyer finds refreshment . . . in the intricate and bewildering fields of litigation." The point of the coy and cumbersome remark was to remind readers that the third district had quickly become fertile ground for indicting and bringing to trial men who sold whiskey to the Indians.[42] It was a legal theme that would, over time, become a familiar refrain, keeping judges busy in all three districts.

Yet complaints about judicial misconduct emerged. Judges were required by law to reside in their districts, but not only did they maintain homes outside of Dakota, they seemed most eager to leave the territory in favor of Sioux City or points farther east. Judge Williston was taken to task by a Yankton newspaper for missing an entire court session in Vermillion in May of 1863. The editor of the *Dakotian* coyly suggested that Williston arrange his outside business interests so that he could spend at least ten to twelve days each year in Dakota attending to his official duties as a judge. It was suggested that most people would be willing to let the judges remain non-residents and collect their pay if only "they could arrange their affairs so as to be here during the few days that their personal attention to official duties is necessary."[43]

An angry citizen, with a more literal approach to the law, took to the columns of *The Dakotian* to remind judges and other officials of their obligations as defined by federal statute. Concerning judges, he quoted from Section 9 of the Organic Act, "judges *shall,* after their appointment . . . *reside in the district* which shall be assigned to them." How ironic, the writer pointed out, that the judges sent to make decisions that have the force of law failed to obey a law that was so plainly spelled out.[44]

Of the three judges, it was Williston who treated his judicial duties with a careless attitude. Judge Bliss, to his credit, seemed to like Yankton enough to take his job seriously, which was reflected in his court attendance. His ability as a trial judge, however, went untested as Bliss was never presented with a complex criminal or civil case.

Nor were the other two judges. While they may have been waiting for law officers to bring down a suspected murderer from the upriver country, it was not to be. The same could be said of civil lawsuits. The earliest civil litigation was less frequent and much less titillating than the occasional criminal case, and it often involved trespassing, lawsuits for money owed, and real property disputes. Depending upon the amount of money at stake, many civil cases were under the jurisdiction of a justice of the peace rather than a federal judge. This further cut into the business of the federal courts.

The records are sketchy, but based on available evidence, the court's three judges presided over only forty-two cases between 1861 and 1864.[45] The Supreme Court had no cases before it until 1867.[46] The Civil War, drought, the presence of Indians, and negative reports in eastern newspapers discouraged law-abiding people from coming to Dakota Territory. Furthermore, with no gold mines within its borders to inspire anger, greed, and murder, Dakota had thus far escaped the lynch mob carnage that attended the birth of Idaho and Montana territories.

Then in the spring of 1864, a small article appeared in the *Dakotian* advising farmers and merchants to prepare for lively times. The article was based on a letter from "Sojourner," who asserted that there was "more gold in the Black Hills than in the new Territory of Idaho." His bold claim was supported by an exploration led by Lieutenant Mullen who told him that "he [Mullen] found gold in such abundance in the vicinity of the Black Hills, that he was afraid to tell his men for fear they would desert him."[47]

The newly minted Yankton newspaper the *Dakota Union* disputed the claim that Mullen explored the Black Hills and chided the *Dakotian* for its lack of fact-checking. Then the *Dakota Union* jumped into the thick of the mystery, offering its own proof from actual explorers and the assertions of men such as Father Pierre-Jean de Smet to whom Indians had confirmed the existence of gold within "the hidden recesses of those mysterious Hills."[48]

While neither article resulted in an immediate stampede for the Black Hills, Dakota was destined to experience a historic rush for riches, a bonanza that would be equal to, or greater than, any previous discovery of gold in America. Of course, the golden days ahead would be tinged by varying degrees of success and failure and by the crime and tragedy that always follows dreamers to the source of their dreams.

CHAPTER 2

LAW AND LAWLESSNESS
GET OUT OF HAND

He [Papineau] has killed two men since he opened his
Missouri River ranch and is strongly suspected of numerous
lesser crimes.

Daily Press and Dakotaian
May 3, 1877

Trial by jury is the cornerstone of the American system of justice. The juror that accepts this as gospel approaches his or her duty with a serious mind-set and matching demeanor. In the early territorial days, however, all-male juries tended to treat their jobs light-heartedly and seemed eager to acquit defendants. Men who sat on juries tended to identify with defendants. They were often ordinary frontiersmen, like the jurymen themselves, struggling to survive in a harsh natural environment, in situations where men were often faced with making desperate choices.

It was hard to apprehend suspects and locate witnesses when men were scattered far and wide over great expanses, so convictions based on evidence presented in court were a rarity. Likewise it was easy to find trouble where the arm of the law was weak, and for those who acted outside of the law, it was not difficult to escape the reach of authority. Bad men found refuge and fellow travelers in the whiskey-laden roadhouses called "ranches" or "hog ranches" along the Missouri River in the "upper country." They were located at great distances from Yankton, but often close to an Indian agency.

The long and tedious journey to the "upper country" was hard on body and mind during the warm weather months, but in the winter it was described by one traveler as something dreadful and scary. A reluctant sojourner, who took the time to make a written record of his stage and wagon trip from Yankton to the Cheyenne Indian Agency, wrote: "One can go to Europe in less time than he can come here in winter." Although ocean travel was not without danger, it was nothing compared to "two hundred miles of travel in an open wagon, exposed to storms, hostile Indians," and "eating and sleeping at the ranches."[1]

William H. Hare, an Episcopal missionary, described a typical "ranche" on a visit to the Missouri River country in 1873. Calling it a vermin-infested log hut with mud-filled chinks, he found everything about it disgusting. "The food is loathsome, the men who keep them are, many of them, fugitives from justice and their ranches are the haunts of horse thieves and murderers."[2] Another "ranche" visitor called them "prairie rats," desperate men who left the "States to escape hanging." He was of the belief that these wild frontiersmen would "think no more of taking a man's life for some fancied insult than they would of shooting a coyote."[3]

The problem of lawlessness was complicated by the lack of competent, honest men to fill positions of responsibility. On June 24, 1861, Governor William Jayne appointed as a justice of the peace of Charles Mix County a Frenchman named George L. Tackett.[4] Originally from St. Louis, he was an early Sioux City resident and former sheriff of Woodbury County, Iowa. Moving further west, the unscrupulous Tackett ran a "bullet proof" roadhouse, hotel, and stage station on Choteau Creek, on the western border of Bon Homme County.[5]

Although his term of office was brief, Tackett did more than serve as a justice of the peace. As lord of his domain, he offered gambling and prostitutes and dispensed whiskey to thirsty travelers, including soldiers, settlers, and Indians, along with his own brand of justice. With no one likely to interfere, he acted as accuser, judge, jury, and executioner, with many a summary hanging at his station. It was said that Tackett carved a notch in a nearby tree (probably the hanging tree) for every luckless man he executed.[6]

Stagecoach drivers felt a certain dread when they approached Tackett's station because of the low quality of the people who patronized the place, coupled with the expectation that something bad would happen. The place reeked of violence and death that affected visitor and resident alike. Tackett had a Lakota wife who, out of fear for her safety, ran away from him with the aid of her sister and never returned.[7]

Fear, violence, and death were the lethal ingredients of life on the Dakota frontier in the 1860s, and a stop at Tackett's brought all these toxic elements into dissonant play. More than a century later, Yankton tribal elders told stories about the presence of ghosts of those shot or hanged, lurking around Tackett's old haunts.[8]

Another habitual miscreant who lived by his own law was Cuthbert DuCharme, a French Canadian. DuCharme, better known as Papineau—meaning "Pap Water" or whiskey—set up shop in 1857. His roadhouse or "ranche" was located in an area that became part of Charles Mix County, near the Missouri River, at Papineau Springs, two miles east of where the town of Wheeler was later located.[9] Papineau engaged in outrageous acts of daring and danger and was a holy terror when he was drunk. Quick to pull his pistols, he seemed to take pleasure in scaring people. Although he had a reputation for violence and bizarre behavior, his place—often referred to as "Papineau's bottom"—was designated the seat of Charles Mix County by the first territorial legislature in 1862, and remained so for years. Dakota judges, including Peter C. Shannon, would get to know him very well.

The Fort Randall military road passed by Papineau's establishment and as a result, it became a stopping point for soldiers and other wayfarers who wanted to drink, gamble, and enjoy prostitutes—all at the risk of life and limb. Since on occasion he had to shoot unruly customers, Papineau built a cemetery near his premises where unfortunate victims of violence were buried along with those who died of natural causes.

Papineau did his best to avoid contact with the law, but on occasion found himself under arrest and in court. He was tried at Bon Homme in the summer of 1869 for "giving and selling liquor" to Indians. The jury could not reach a verdict so he went free.[10] Later in the year he was arrested and hauled into court for shooting and killing a young man from upriver named John Simpson, but "Old Pap" was discharged when it was determined the killing was in self-defense. The two men were drinking at Papineau's place when an argument commenced. Simpson went for his revolver but Papineau was quicker.[11]

As time went on, criminal accusations piled up against Papineau, who was regularly charged with the illicit sale of liquor to Indians. That and other acts of bizarre and outrageous behavior only added to the Papineau legend, which flourished along the Missouri River.

At the mouth of American Creek, on the Missouri River, another wild Canadian made his Dakota home. He was Marvin H. "Jim" Somers and was every bit a desperado as was his fellow Canadian. But unlike Papineau, Somers started out as though he wanted to be respected, not feared. He came to Dakota in 1859, settling at Sioux Point in Cole County (now Union County). In 1861 he was selected as the sergeant-at-arms for the Council, the upper house of the first territorial legislature. The following year he was actually elected to the House of Representatives.[12] With an aggressive demeanor, he found that anger was a useful political tool, especially when backed up by his revolver, which he carried into the House chamber. He once attempted to settle a dispute by throwing the Speaker of the House through the window of a Yankton saloon.

Over time, Somers gained a reputation as an outlaw, a dangerous man of herculean strength with an appetite for violence. It was said that he "would rather fight than do anything else, and it was not considered safe to aggravate his feelings."[13] When he came to Yankton, people stayed inside while he would "run the town," shooting at stores and houses for amusement.[14]

How often Somers ventured to Yankton is unknown, but he was elected to the legislature again in 1868, this time from Charles Mix County, and attended the legislative session that commenced on December 7, 1868. He apparently was well-behaved at that session since a Yankton newspaper remarked that the legislators were "more friendly" than in the past. Somers took another step toward respectability when he, along with other lawmakers, donated $10 to the Lincoln National Monument fund.[15]

Then in October of 1869, Somers was back in Yankton and in the mood for some serious drinking and associated pleasures. He was about to turn from lawmaker to lawbreaker. During the drinking spree, one of his stops was at Maxwell's, a saloon on Broadway Street. After leaving the saloon, he argued with a man sitting on his horse. Somers then shot and killed the horse, although he was probably aiming at the rider. That attracted the attention of bystanders who thought the rider had been shot. One of the observers, Yankton mayor William N. Collamer, decided that the sheriff should arrest the drunken Somers, who, with his navy revolver in hand, was threatening other citizens.

At that point a man named George W. Black entered this minor frontier drama. Black had a shadowy past. In October of 1866, Black and his traveling partner, Wilford S. Stickney, both with Illinois connections, reportedly killed a man near Bridger Pass in far western Dakota Territory. The *Chicago Republican* called the crime, "one of the most atrocious and cold blooded murders ever committed on this continent." Instead of running, Black and Stickney returned to Chicago where they were arrested for the crime. Since it was discovered that the killing took place in Dakota, the U.S. marshal, Laban H. Litchfield, was contacted. He traveled to Chicago and brought the prisoners back to Yankton.[16]

Black, a Civil War veteran, confessed to the killing, but claimed it was in self-defense, and he said that Stickney had robbed the victim of about five or six thousand dollars in gold. Stickney provided a different version of the crime and insisted that he did not witness the shooting and only became aware of it when the two men reached Chicago. Because the homicide happened "on the Plains," the Chicago press played it up like a dime novel. The *Union and Dakotaian,* however, cautioned its readers not to form an opinion against either accused man.[17] Black was tried for murder in Yankton in the June 1868 term of court, Judge Ara Bartlett presiding, and was found not guilty.[18] The jury declared his innocence without ever leaving the box.[19]

Later that year, Black was elected sheriff of Yankton County, and his order of business on that October day of 1869, in response to the mayor's request, was to arrest the angry and drunken Jim Somers. Reluctantly, Sheriff Black went about his duty "in a quiet way." Somers, however, was in no mood to surrender. Making it clear he intended to kill the sheriff, he walked toward Black with his gun in hand. The gutsy sheriff jumped Somers, and in the ensuing struggle the desperado pulled the trigger shooting Black in the leg. Other men rushed in and subdued Somers, and escorted him to the "calaboose," while the wounded sheriff was taken to the International Hotel where his wound was treated. He survived, but never fully recovered, and for years was admired and cared for by the community for his brave service.

The day after the shooting, Somers was taken before the mayor, who charged him with shooting a horse. He was fined and discharged. Before he could be arrested by the U.S. marshal for shooting the sheriff, he "mounted a horse of a friend and made good his escape."[20] It was generally believed that Sheriff Black was unpopular in some Yankton circles and that due to the "connivance of some enemies of the sheriff," Somers was allowed to escape. Jim Somers was now in the up-river country and beyond the clutches of the law, but he would be heard from again.[21]

Frontier violence in early Dakota was often downplayed by the newspapers of the territory, which were interested in promoting their towns and encouraging settlement. Timid easterners were shown a rosy picture of Dakota, a "salubrious" and healthful land of rich soil, gentle rain, sunshine, good health, and great promise. Though violence was deemphasized in favor of the good life, the hanging of a man by a mob in Vermillion in February of 1866 was too shocking to be ignored by the press.

This victim of rough justice was a frontier character named James Hogan, an Irish immigrant who had claimed some land near Vermillion. After his claim shack was burned, Hogan went out looking for vengeance. He believed the culprit was a young Norwegian from Vermillion named Burgis. Hogan rode into town on February 26, confronted Burgis, and would have shot him but his revolver misfired. Hogan then angrily threatened other people with the gun in his hand.

Fortunately for his intended victims, the gun again failed to fire making him angrier. A brave citizen, Patrick Hand, confronted Hogan, seized his gun, and took it to Captain Nelson Miner who locked it in a drawer in the land office. An enraged Hogan entered the land office and demanded the return of his revolver. Miner grappled with him and tossed him out in the street. The captain then ordered a group of soldiers, quartered in Vermillion, to subdue Hogan and tie him to a tree. Later that night, vigilantes came for Hogan, and as he yelled "murder!" they strung him up on a tree beside the Vermillion River.[22]

Hogan's body was cut down the following morning and, with the aid of some of the women of the town, given a decent burial beside the hanging tree. A grand jury was empaneled to investigate Hogan's death. Some effort was made at fact finding, but the grand jury reported that it had no grounds to indict.[23]

Whether the grand jury had the names of those responsible for Hogan's death is not mentioned in any source. But the criminal code, as created by the legislature in 1865, was such that it would be difficult, under the circumstances, to prove a murder case against those who lynched Hogan. According to section 262 of the criminal code, a homicide was justifiable if "there is reasonable ground to apprehend a design to commit a felony, or to do some great personal injury and imminent danger of such design being accomplished." In other words, if a person reasonably believed that another was about to commit a felony and had the means to carry out the imminent threat, it was permissible to use deadly force to stop it. Rather than a "stand your ground" law, section 262 encouraged "shoot first and ask questions later."

When a Sioux City newspaper used the Hogan story to take a jab at lawless Dakota, the *Union and Dakotaian* fired back in anger. The paper argued that the lynch mob was merely acting in accordance with the law. Maybe, but men who participated in mob violence often experienced shame and regret, and preferred to keep it all a dirty little secret. The *Union and Dakotaian* put the seal of secrecy on the matter by saying, "it is hardly probable that a grand jury can be found in Clay County that will indict any of the parties who were engaged in the unfortunate affair."[24]

By the time of the Hogan lynching, the makeup of the Dakota Supreme Court had changed. If Hogan had faced criminal charges or his executioners been arrested, they would have appeared before Justice Jefferson P. Kidder, a native of Braintree, Vermont, who had been living in Minnesota.

On February 23, 1865, Kidder was named associate justice for the first judicial district in Vermillion.

Kidder took the place of Ara Bartlett, whom Lincoln had appointed to the first judicial district on June 22, 1864, replacing Williston, who was transferred to the Montana Territory Supreme Court.[25] Bartlett took the oath of office on October 14, 1864.[26] Then on February 23, 1865, Bartlett, formerly a mayor and county judge in Kankakee, Illinois, and a friend of the president, was designated the chief justice of the Dakota Territory Supreme Court in place of Bliss.[27]

Philemon Bliss, First Chief Justice, Dakota Territory Supreme Court.
Courtesy South Dakota State Historical Society.

Bliss left a creditable record as chief justice but did not seek reappointment. Instead he went on to a distinguished legal career in Missouri. He served as an associate justice of the Missouri Supreme Court and was a founder of the University of Missouri School of Law, where he was a professor and dean. Bliss authored a popular and widely used law book on codes of civil procedure before dying in St. Paul, on August 25, 1889.[28] Justice Joseph L. Williams was also replaced, and the new judge of the third judicial district was William F. Gleason, the U.S. district attorney for Dakota. Justice Williams was burdened by the death of his sixteen-year-old son, J. Lanier Williams, who died in Sioux City on July 31, 1863.[29] He never established a residence in Dakota and was probably glad to leave the territory. Williams returned to Tennessee where he died in Knoxville on December 14, 1865.[30]

Gleason wrote to Lincoln asking for the job of associate justice. He said he had been eyeing the governorship, but candidly told Lincoln that he wanted to be a Supreme Court justice because the position came with a higher salary than that of governor.[31] When he returned to Yankton in mid-May 1865 after an absence of eighteen months, he was warmly welcomed by the people. The *Union and Dakotaian* expressed hope that during his long absence, the improvements made in Yankton would impress the judge, for it was "no longer a city in embryo."[32]

Gleason joined his fellow justices in Yankton for a scheduled meeting of the Supreme Court. Chief Justice Ara Bartlett had recently arrived in Yankton by stage with his family, voicing his intention to make Dakota his home. The commitment was seen as further proof that Dakota Territory was on its way to becoming a prosperous destination, where federally appointed officials were not ashamed to make their homes.

Their colleague, Jefferson P. Kidder, the new associate justice for the first judicial district, had arrived in Vermillion on June 10, 1865, a passenger on the steamboat *Graham*. He began a long and distinguished career as a public official in Dakota that included the longest period of

Jefferson P. Kidder, Associate Justice, Dakota Territory Supreme Court.
Courtesy History of Minnehaha County, South Dakota, *by Dana Reed Bailey
(Sioux Falls, SD: Brown & Saenger, 1899).*

service as a federal judge in territorial history. Kidder was well suited for
the frontier and easily settled into a home in Vermillion.

Kidder had some previous connection to Dakota, having been
associated with the Dakota Land Company of St. Paul, which had
established towns on the Big Sioux River in 1857, including Sioux Falls.
Talented and politically ambitious, he was selected by the squatters at Sioux
Falls to act as a delegate to Congress in 1859. Kidder went to Washington
and launched a spirited but unsuccessful effort to obtain territorial status
for Dakota.

As a Dakotan, he was an honest, dedicated townsman and a genial,
open-minded fellow. He made the holdings of his large personal library
available to the public and even lent his credibility to stories about the
"huge river monster" in the waters of the Missouri River, near Vermillion.[33]

In July of 1865, with all three justices of the court assembled in Yankton, the *Union and Dakotaian* was proud to announce that at long last Dakota had a "resident judiciary," proving that "Dakota is coming out alright." For the first time in territorial history, "a full bench of the U.S. Supreme Court for the District of Dakota, convened in this city." An organization was effected, rules were adopted and court schedules for each district were established. All three justices then spoke with eloquence and passion about the recent assassination of President Lincoln, a crime that had cast the country into a state of sadness and anger. Their expressions of respect and admiration for the president, expressed in the remote frontier town of Yankton, reflected the mood cast over most of America.[34]

The unity of the court, however, did not last. The fastidious Justice Gleason, a non-drinker from an aristocratic Southern family, resigned after a promising start on the bench. While he was an exceptionally articulate and well-educated man, he was handicapped by what was described as being "morbidly sensitive," to the extent he was plagued by irrational suspicion.[35] He served on the court for a relatively short time, and having had enough of Dakota, he accepted the position of consul to Bordeaux, France, an office more suited to his disposition and background. On August 11, 1866, the *Union and Dakotaian* announced that President Andrew Johnson had appointed John W. Boyle from Pennsylvania to replace Gleason.[36]

Unlike the man he replaced, Boyle had ties to Dakota Territory. The son of a Pennsylvania farmer, he studied law at Jefferson College, and in 1850 he crossed the plains driving an ox-team before settling in California. In 1853, he returned to Pennsylvania, and then moved to western Texas in 1858. He came to Dakota in 1860.[37] Boyle served in the territorial legislature in 1862 and 1863, and was employed as the receiver at the U.S. Land Office in Vermillion at the time of his appointment to the Dakota Supreme Court. He was active in Republican politics and railroad promotion.[38]

The appointment of Boyle to the Dakota bench was recalled years later by a correspondent from the *Minneapolis Tribune.* As the humorous story goes, when Boyle left his position as the U.S. land officer at Vermillion, his accounts were "short." The man who held Boyle's bond was Dr. Walter A. Burleigh, who was not at all pleased at the prospect of being stiffed.[39]

Burleigh, originally from Maine, had been living in Kittaning, Pennsylvania, when he came to Dakota in 1861. He was appointed by President Lincoln as the agent to the Yankton Sioux at Greenwood Agency, effective March 28, 1861.[40] The affable doctor had stumped for Lincoln in 1860 and was not at all bashful about asking for a favor. When the president offered him the job of Indian agent, at a salary of $2,000 per year, Burleigh said that to accept the position, a man would need to steal or starve. The quick-witted Lincoln replied, "Dr. Burleigh, if I am any judge of human nature, you will not starve."[41]

Agent Burleigh prospered as Lincoln had predicted. He acquired commercial property in Yankton and came into ownership of a large amount of land in Bon Homme County, raised cattle, and lived in regal style in his well-appointed prairie mansion overlooking the Missouri River (his wife, Caroline, was an artist). Burleigh was openly proud of his sixteen miles of riverfront where his cattle, numbering in the thousands, grazed on lush grass.[42]

Both a lawyer and a doctor, the genial and pragmatic Burleigh was a man who always wanted more and was eager to get it; he loved Dakota and believed that a prosperous future awaited him. A colleague called him "a singular man" who had been an abolitionist and a "radical believer in the rights of man." While Burleigh could be vulgar, he was also a high-minded Calvinist who believed he was predestined to do great things.[43]

Great things included personal enrichment, and during his determined quest to make money, he was often suspected of cheating the Yankton

Sioux. In September of 1862, Burleigh was accused of numerous acts of fraud, including buying farm implements that did not exist, hiring his daughter to teach at a phantom school, and billing the government for workers' wages at a rate twice what was actually paid.[44]

When Lincoln was informed of the charges against Burleigh, he wanted his appointee removed from office while the matter was investigated. But at the urging of Commissioner of Indian Affairs William P. Dole, Lincoln allowed Burleigh to stay in office while his conduct was evaluated. Dole believed it would be unwise to remove Burleigh because his absence would mean that the agency would be without supervision.[45]

In 1864 Burleigh was elected delegate to Congress from Dakota Territory. By 1866 Burleigh's official conduct in his former capacity as agent to the Yankton Sioux had become a major scandal, and the House of Representatives ordered an official investigation. Testimony included that of a man who swore he saw paperwork showing that Burleigh paid himself $25,000 along with smaller amounts to other officials, including $5,000 to Commissioner Dole. It appeared that several men were feeding at the same trough.[46]

Although his methods when running for office were thought to be dubious, even scandalous, he was considered a likeable man, and accusations against his official conduct never led to criminal charges. Further, his name is forever enshrined, along with the names of other notable Americans, as a member of the National Lincoln Monument Association, formed by an act of Congress in 1867 to commemorate the author of "the great charter of emancipation and universal liberty in America."[47]

A reverence for the greatness of others sometimes comes from a deep-seated belief in one's self-worth, and Dr. Burleigh most certainly believed in himself. He had a reputation for getting what he wanted, and he used his considerable influence in Washington to get John W. Boyle appointed to the Dakota Supreme Court. As Boyle had no money to reimburse Burleigh for defaulting on the bond, the delegate came up with a clever plan to make sure he would get paid. Burleigh went to Washington with Boyle in tow to meet with his friend the U.S. attorney general. Burleigh announced that there was a vacancy on the Dakota Supreme Court and that he had just the man to fill that position. The attorney general asked if Burleigh's man was knowledgeable in the law. Burleigh is said to reply, "Law! No! But he's hell on equity."

The attorney general may have assumed that Burleigh was just trying to be funny, and decided, based on other sources, that Boyle was qualified. On the other hand, he may simply have rubber-stamped a request from a friend. Whatever the reason, as events transpired, Boyle was named by the president and approved by Congress as the new member of the Dakota Supreme Court. And to top it all off, Boyle's salary as a judge was paid directly to Burleigh, thus making up for the bond.[48]

Fortunately for all concerned, the new associate justice got off to a good start, earning the confidence of the people and praise from the press. Following Boyle's presiding over the September 1866 term of court in the third district, the *Union and Dakotaian* reported, "the people of this district owe a debt of gratitude to our present delegate [Burleigh] for the appointment of J. W. Boyle." Boyle had proved his worth as a judge, presiding with "becoming dignity and strict impartiality."[49]

Boyle and his fellow judges faced a growing list of challenges, especially in the western fringes of the territory. Congress had relieved Dakota of all the problems connected with the gold rush in the mountain west when on March 3, 1863, Idaho Territory was created out of parts of Dakota, Washington, and Nebraska territories.[50] The new territory included all of the present states of Idaho, Montana, and Wyoming. Then on May 26, 1864, an act creating Montana Territory was signed by Lincoln, saddling

Dakota again with much of the land that many were calling Wyoming.[51] The growth of this area was dramatic and sudden, and was accompanied by serious legal and political problems.

The town of Cheyenne was created on July 10, 1867, in response to the coming of the Union Pacific Railroad, symbolically reuniting the country following the Civil War, and the very embodiment of pride, profit, and progress, but most of all American ingenuity. It also brought with it the capacity for new forms of criminal behavior. The first railroad in Dakota Territory roared into Cheyenne like a storm, leaving in its wake a morass of violence and lawlessness, the likes of which seemed always to follow the rails, creating new hell holes that begged for law and order. Soon a newspaper appeared, the *Cheyenne Leader,* which, unlike its counterpart in Yankton, had little to report except fights, shootings, murders, and hangings. Each issue of the newspaper was a testament to the tawdry character of many of Cheyenne's first residents.

Eight hundred miles from the territorial capital, Cheyenne and its environs were largely ignored by the governor and legislators. While the legislature did create Laramie County, it left the matter of establishing a local government to its residents. It was part of the third judicial district but time and distance meant the judge would probably not be showing up to take the bench. As such, violence and debauchery, followed by indignant retribution, held sway in Cheyenne, Dakota Territory, where lynchings were commonplace.

In his address to the Dakota legislature on December 3, 1867, Governor Andrew J. Faulk frankly admitted the inability of government to provide law and security for the residents of Laramie County: "Our courts, as at present organized and located, at such a remote distance from their [Laramie County] settlements, can be of but little service to them in the administration of justice." Faulk acknowledged that the citizens of Laramie County would exercise vigilante justice to protect their lives and property. He said that the government was required to assist in accordance with the Organic Act, but figuratively threw up his hands, and admitted there was little or nothing the Yankton-based officials could do.[52]

Help was sought from outside Dakota Territory. In a letter to Congressman Grenville M. Dodge of Iowa, an official from the Union Pacific Railroad pleaded for help from the federal government to prevent the "building of shanties and selling whiskey along the line of the road." The "whiskey business," he complained, turned men into drunken louts who committed acts of violence and destruction, all of which threatened the progress of the railroad.[53]

Other letters followed. An angry resident of Cheyenne believed he had to do something to bring law and order to his city. O. T. B. Williams wrote a letter to President Andrew Johnson, complaining about the violence and disrespect for the law. Williams pointedly said that the judges of Dakota Territory refuse to hold court in Cheyenne and that being attached to "Dacota" was "worse than useless." He stressed the need for a territorial government for Wyoming, a part of Dakota in name only.[54]

It appears that the angry letters finally did jar the Dakota judiciary into action. The *Union and Dakotaian* reported on March 7, 1868, that Chief Justice Ara Bartlett, along with Marshal Laban Litchfield and U.S. Attorney George H. Hand, would depart for Cheyenne and hold a term of court. The trio traveled to Sioux City and then to Omaha, where they boarded a train with Pullman sleeping cars for the long journey to Cheyenne. Here they conducted the first term of court in Cheyenne, Dakota, the "Magic City."[55]

Although it was a nice effort, the discontented people of Laramie County wanted to form their own territorial government. Their eastern brethren understood the logic and most heartily agreed that a new territory was the solution to the problem of frontier violence. Councilman Wilmot W. Brookings introduced a memorial in the legislature, asking that Congress create a new territory out of western Dakota to be named "Lincoln" instead of Wyoming.[56]

On July 25, 1868, Congress created Wyoming Territory, choosing the name widely preferred by the people, but failing to appropriate the funds necessary to establish a territorial government. This obstacle was overcome, and both regions cheered when on April 12, 1869, it was announced that President Ulysses S. Grant had appointed officials to govern the new Wyoming Territory. Dakota Territory, minus its far western domain, was suddenly smaller and therefore easier to govern, and Wyoming Territory would soon have its own courts and judges.

CHAPTER 3

MUSICAL BENCHES

*Some mysterious pistol firing was heard on Broadway
on Monday night, but we have heard of no funeral on
account of it.*

The Yankton Press
December 28, 1870

Although the lynching and shooting of suspects was punishment, it was not lawful punishment. Furthermore, the impromptu executions had little impact on the problem of lawlessness on the frontier, for much of the crime committed in the far reaches of Dakota Territory went unpunished in the 1860s, leaving a trail of unsolved mysteries. Although well-intentioned officials, including the judges, usually conducted themselves with dignity and within the law, they were overwhelmed by the strength and severity of the wilderness and its ability to protect wild men who needed places to hide.

Dakota, and especially Yankton, acquired a reputation for lawlessness and violence, causing cautious easterners to stay away. The town where hogs ran free in the streets was just too dangerous and dirty for civilized people. When Rev. Joseph Ward accepted the position of pastor at the new Congregational Church at Yankton in 1868, his wife, Sarah, was apprehensive. She knew by reputation that Yankton was "the worst of the river towns" on the far border of civilization where "Indian scares" were the norm. She called Yankton a wild and wicked place that "harbored

W. W. Brookings, Associate Justice, Dakota Territory Supreme Court.
Courtesy History of Minnehaha County, South Dakota,
by Dana Reed Bailey (Sioux Falls, SD: Brown & Saenger, 1899).

many a desperate character," where "murders were not infrequent, and now and then a lynching made things lively."[1]

The 1860s were trying times for citizens, as well as for law enforcement and the courts. Dakota needed people with grit and determination who were able to stand up to the outlaws. Assistance from the federal government was also required, but would the quality of officials sent to provide law and order be equal to the needs and expectations of the law-abiding Dakotans? Or would Dakotans be left to fend for themselves?

In 1866, the legislature addressed these questions by passing a set of codes based on New York's Field Code, the first jurisdiction in the nation to take this step.[2] Then in 1868 the legislature approved a "revised" set of criminal procedure codes handed to them by a con-man, "General" J.L. Foster. Slick and suave, Foster passed himself off as a lawyer and Civil

War veteran, and impressionable men and women eagerly took to him and his "fluency of tongue." But no one was happy when the rogue left town with money he had taken from gullible citizens.[3]

One of Foster's deeds, however, bore good fruit—his drafting of a set of criminal procedure codes, which the legislature adopted. The act to establish a criminal procedure code was introduced to the legislature by Councilman Wilmot W. Brookings. A cursory review of the codes reveals that they were probably just lifted from the statute books of another state or territory. Although Foster was a fraud, the codes that he claimed to have drafted were useful, because, among other things, they divided public offenses between felonies and misdemeanors and set the ground rules for grand juries and justice-of-the-peace courts. By all accounts, the "legal fraternity" favored the new codes.[4]

Men like Foster were simply following a money trail. Since Yankton was the capital city, it was the headquarters for federally appointed office holders and their underlings, whose salaries were paid by the federal government. Federal money flowed into Yankton as did steamboats loaded with merchandise—and on occasion, a pleasant surprise such as the time in the autumn of 1866 when Madame Julia Dean, a "celebrated actress," stopped in Yankton. She was on her way to New York after a tour of the Pacific slope, and her appearance provided a moment of grace and beauty in an otherwise drab river town.[5]

While artists and actors were rare, wealthy investors and speculators made regular visits to the territorial capital, the public trough. Merchants were eager to set up shop and reap the patronage from investor capitalists, government officials, and their families. Lawyers were plentiful and on December 5, 1866, the Dakota Bar Association was created and officers elected.[6] Homesteaders, too, tended to gravitate toward Yankton, along with the usual undesirables of frontier life. The natural volatility of the transient population grating against the settled community led to disputes, disorder, and crime. Starting in the late 1860s, grand juries were kept fairly busy, with lengthy court calendars featuring both civil and criminal cases.

In 1869 the Dakota Supreme Court entered a new era when it welcomed two new members. While Chief Justice Ara Bartlett sought reappointment, it was not to be and he was replaced on April 6, 1869, by George W. French of Maine. Bartlett stayed in Dakota and practiced law in Yankton. French finally made it to Yankton on May 15. By then Associate Justice Boyle had been replaced by Wilmot W. Brookings. U.S. Marshal Laban H. Litchfield was granted another term in office as was Associate Justice Jefferson P. Kidder.

These appointments were made by Grant, the third president to put his personal stamp on Dakota.[7] In doing so he both delighted and disappointed the collection of office seekers in Washington. A correspondent for the *Union and Dakotaian* noted that most applicants went away without an office, or to their utter shock, were sent someplace they did not want to go. For example, the new Dakota governor was John A. Burbank, who had expected to be appointed the governor of Wyoming Territory. The correspondent duly noted that the nation's capital was a "sepulchre [sic] of blasted hopes. It is said that a swearing train leaves the City every evening."[8]

Among the happy faces was that of Wilmot W. Brookings, though he did not learn of his appointment until he returned to Yankton. Known as W.W. Brookings, he claimed the title of "First Pioneer." He was born and raised in Woolich, Maine, and educated at Bowdoin College. He studied law at the office of William Pitt Fessenden, a political luminary whose career included both the U.S. House of Representatives and the Senate.[9]

Disdaining all legal opportunities in Maine, Brookings headed west. He was a young lawyer living in Dubuque, Iowa, when he joined the Western Town Company as a bullwhacker, or driver of a freight wagon.

Brookings was a member of a townsite party that came to the falls of the Big Sioux River, from Dubuque, in the spring of 1857. He was instrumental in starting the town of Sioux Falls and acquired considerable land there. In October of 1862, Brookings filed one of the most important land claims in the history of Dakota Territory, claiming a quarter section that included the falls and the adjacent eleven-acre island that became known as "Brookings Island."[10]

Brookings met with a serious and debilitating accident in February 1858, which cost him both legs below the knees. Somehow he managed to survive the crude surgery performed by his friend Dr. Josiah L. Phillips, another settler from Maine also associated with the Western Town Company. Thereafter, the "miracle" patient, the indefatigable W.W. Brookings, hobbling along on squeaky artificial limbs with the aid of a cane, became both a business and political leader in Sioux Falls and later in Yankton.

The honor of presiding over the very first term of court in Sioux Falls, in 1871, went to Judge Brookings, with O. B. Iverson as the clerk of court and John Walker as sheriff. The short session of court was conducted with decorum and dignity in the "old military barracks" of Fort Dakota, situated near the banks of the Big Sioux River.[11]

More an entrepreneur and promoter than a lawyer, Brookings was appointed an associate justice on the Supreme Court, with the support of a number of powerful politicians, all Republicans. They included Senator Hannibal Hamlin, Congressman James G. Blaine, and Governor Joshua L. Chamberlain, all from Maine. He was also supported by the delegate to Congress from Dakota, Solomon L. Spink.[12] Brookings was thirty-eight years old when he took the bench, replacing John W. Boyle.

Records indicate that Brookings had a hand in getting Boyle off the Supreme Court. Among the papers of President Grant is a letter from Brookings seeking Boyle's removal. The letter claimed that Boyle was a supporter of the disruptive and unpopular Andrew Johnson administration.

Brookings declared that Boyle was not a Republican and that the "Republicans of Dakota do not desire his retention in office."[13]

The letter had the desired effect, for on May 10, 1869, Judge Brookings was presiding over the May term of court at Bon Homme in the third judicial district.[14] It was the start of a rocky road for the new judge. He had no prior judicial experience, but his leadership abilities had been tested by service in the legislature, and more important, by the rough, dispassionate hand of the frontier.

The new Chief Justice, George W. French, age forty-six, was supported by the same Maine men who were behind Brookings. He was given a boost by his boyhood friend, the irrepressible Walter A. Burleigh, former delegate to Congress from Dakota.[15] French was educated in Thomaston, Maine, the town of his birth. He read law in the office of U.S. Senator John Ruggles of Thomaston, Maine, and was admitted to the state bar.[16] Like Brookings, French was a Republican. They became political allies and were joined in their alliance by the new governor, John A. Burbank of Indiana, who replaced Andrew J. Faulk. Along with Joseph R. Hanson, Burbank and French formed a Yankton company that speculated in real estate.

As Arthur Linn of the *Union and Dakotaian* concluded, "Judge French will honor the bench, command the respect and confidence of all the people, and keep the judicial ermine unsoiled."[17] Time and circumstance would, however, prove Linn wrong and turn him against French. The new court was not an improvement over the previous one. This was due in large part to the questionable judicial ability of the new chief justice. Aside from serving as a justice of the peace in Thomaston, Maine, he had no experience as a judge.[18] Though a cultivated man, French displayed an appalling lack of knowledge of the law and legal procedure and proved to be an embarrassment to the court. He was teasingly referred to as "Old Necessity, because necessity knew no law."[19]

It was said that Judge French never made a decision from the bench on his own volition, but rather he relied on the advice of one of the attorneys arguing the case.[20] Other old timers remembered that French would make notes on "legal questions" while on the bench. He would then place the notes on the inside of his hat so that when he placed it bottom up, the notes would be in plain view.[21] French was so inept that the U.S. attorney for Dakota found it "expedient to have the chief justice granted leave of absence so that prospects would be better for convictions in criminal cases."[22]

A contemporary said that "any ordinary country justice of the peace would have made a better chief justice." He described French as "mild and harmless…having no vicious propensities, but was easily controlled by those less honest."[23] The new chief justice owed his position to the spoils system, which dominated American politics during a time when men were appointed out of friendship or favor, or as a sop to others. French was not the only unqualified man to fill a post on the frontier.

Almost from the time they took their oath of office, French and Brookings gathered political enemies who wanted them off the court. French was an easy target because he was incompetent. Brookings was more elusive. Historians have not given him high marks as a judge. He had a grating personality and was not a good speaker, but he was a wily, hard-headed politician, driven by a fierce determination to succeed. Despite his considerable efforts to promote the territory and bring in railroads, he never connected very well with the public and his enemies could be merciless. He was not well supported beyond his immediate circle of friends and political allies in Sioux Falls and Yankton, among them Chief Justice French. Brookings and French, both Maine men, came together for mutual support.

Brookings found he could rely on French's helping hand from the bench, and from time to time, the chief justice needed Brookings' help. In the fall of 1869, a U.S. grand jury indicted Judge Brookings for perjury and land fraud in connection with a homestead claim. One researcher has suggested that the indictment represented the actions of the judge's enemies who wanted to humiliate, discredit, and kick him off the bench. Lucky for Brookings, "brother" Chief Justice French intervened and quashed the indictment.[24]

By 1870 Yankton had one federal jail, one county jail, one "calaboose"—and nineteen lawyers.[25] Any white man over the age of twenty-one could expect to be named to a jury pool, and although jurors often took their jobs lightly, there were exceptions. Dan Oakes walked from Sioux Falls to Yankton in the winter of 1872-73 after he was notified that he had jury duty. It took him three days to make the trip.[26]

Lawyers were plentiful on the frontier, but the practice of law was anything but glamorous, and could be dangerous. For example, a Yankton attorney was representing a man named Bennett who had been charged with the theft of two mules. After Bennett was released on bail, the attorney sought him out to collect the fee owed. As the attorney was "seeking entrance" to his client's house of "gilt frame," Bennett fired a shotgun blast through the door. Fortunately, the attorney was not hit but he decided not to ask for his fee, believing "discretion was the better part of valor."[27]

Attorneys were versatile, out of necessity, for clients—dangerous or not—were not always easy to find. As such, attorneys were often engaged in hard physical work and were not afraid to get their hands dirty, although they preferred to wallow in the mire of trial work, both civil and criminal. For Brookings, however, court appearances came and went like a recurring nightmare because he was a party, not an advocate or a judge.

Actually he was more like an exhibit for public ridicule, for in January of 1870, another indictment against Judge Brookings was made public. It was dismissed and yet another grand jury was sworn in, and it too issued an indictment against Brookings for perjury.[28] This one was not dismissed. The foreman of the grand jury was Newton Edmunds, who had served as

Yankton Jail on Walnut Street.
Courtesy Yankton County Historical Society.

the second governor of Dakota Territory. Edmunds was a self-righteous, bulldog of a man who personally disliked Brookings.

In open court in June of 1870, Brookings, with leave from Judge French, addressed the "Court, Bar, Grand Jury and everybody else," lecturing all those present on the rights and obligations of a grand jury. In doing so, he essentially pre-empted the duty and authority of Judge French who was responsible for instructing a jury. Brookings' bizarre conduct caught the attention of the editor of the *Union and Dakotaian* who reminded him that a "guilty conscience needs no accuser." The irate editor called upon Judge French to "put his foot down firmly against this bully-raging, balderdash."[29]

The U.S. attorney, Warren Cowles, also an enemy of Brookings, was determined to bring the judge down. The specifics of the case were as follows: Brookings had filed a homestead claim on land near Vermillion, swore he built a house on it, lived in it and cultivated the soil. The grand jury said there was evidence that he did none of these things and therefore had lied under oath, committing perjury. To dress up the charges, the indictment accused Brookings of "not having the fear of God before his eyes," but was, rather, "moved and instigated by the Devil."[30]

A jury trial followed with French presiding. Brookings objected to the prosecution's evidence and went into another angry tirade, "attacking jurors, lawyers and witnesses."[31] His evidentiary objections were sustained by French, who openly took Brookings' side of the case. Court observers recalled that when stumped, French would ask: "Judge Brookings, if you were on the bench, how would you decide that question?"[32] The farce ended when Judge French instructed the jury to return a verdict of not guilty.[33] Since thousands of people throughout the West made false homestead claims, the charge against Brookings was likely selective prosecution for political purposes.

The acquittal of Brookings was one in a string of disappointments for U.S. Attorney Warren Cowles in 1870. He was struggling to get a jury to convict someone of a crime—any crime—but without success. Frustrated with the lack of success, Cowles was constrained to write to the U.S. attorney general and apologize for the lack of convictions from cases he prosecuted. He may have been thinking about the thirteen cases where defendants were charged with the illegal cutting of timber of federal land—all of which resulted in acquittals. The juries were sympathetic to men who insisted they cut trees because they needed firewood.

Cowles took office about the same time that Brookings and French were appointed. He told the attorney general that he had tried hard but he feared that convictions would only come if "there is a revolution in public sentiment."[34] From Erie, Pennsylvania, Cowles was trying to understand the frontier mentality and it was getting the best of him.

While Cowles was stumbling, Brookings was advancing toward high office, but his political aspirations had energized his enemies. Linn, of the

Union and Dakotaian, attacked Brookings with stinging editorials calling for his resignation. He argued that Brookings' career on the bench was "a long chapter of mistakes" and claimed he was a "bullying pot house politician" who had "prostituted his high calling."[35]

The reference to politics was not meant as a casual insult, for Brookings had been heavily involved in politics including the 1868 campaign for delegate to Congress. In that contest, he had supported Solomon L. Spink, the eventual winner, while Linn favored Dr. Burleigh, who wanted to get back to Congress. As the *Union and Dakotaian* was Burleigh's organ, anyone who opposed the wily doctor, including Brookings, was fair game. Hence the real reason for Linn's attack.

In these often ruthless territorial days, newspaper editors wrote frequently and furiously, with no pretense of objectivity. Dakota historian Doane Robinson admitted that when it came to editorializing, "nothing was too hideous or too ridiculous to charge to a political opponent."[36] Thus Brookings had to take a pounding and trust in his supporters to strike back. Fortunately, he had a friend in the editor of a new newspaper, the *Yankton Press,* who hammered Burleigh without mercy.

Sitting on the territorial Supreme Court was prestigious and politically important. But Brookings ached for higher office, namely that of territorial delegate to Congress. He was not a candidate in 1870, and a conviction for perjury in connection with a homestead claim would have ruined any chance he had to win that political prize in a future contest. Brookings wanted to represent Dakota in Congress, the highest, holiest, and most powerful territorial office.

As 1870 came to a close, and the territory was reeling under the effects of another bitterly fought election for delegate to Congress, news of a murder committed at Fort Sully on the Missouri River appeared in the *Union and Dakotaian*. A "special correspondent" to that newspaper could not restrain himself: "I have, in this letter, a horrible crime to report; one that will make, and has made many a stout heart quake with fear; one that makes the very flesh creep and the head dizzy."

The "cold blooded murder" occurred as a result of a quarrel between two soldiers on December 15, 1870, at the regimental band quarters at Fort Sully. The alleged perpetrator, Edward Duffy, was an eighteen-year-old soldier from New York City, who had previously used a knife and sword against others. Duffy was quarreling with a man in the Billiard Saloon when a third party, Private Patrick Pender, intervened and separated the combatants. Duffy took great offense and said he would kill Pender even if "he was sent to Stillwater [Minnesota penitentiary] for life." True to his word, Duffy attacked and stabbed Pender to death with a large butcher knife.

The "special correspondent" presumed that Duffy would be sent to Yankton for trial. He used the tragedy to lament the lack of murder convictions, noting that three killers in recent years had walked away from court as free men, having been acquitted by Yankton juries. Directing his letter to Editor Linn, he said, "we have poor hopes of him receiving his just dues which would be nothing short of the gallows."[37]

The plea played right into the thinking of Arthur Linn, who had editorialized in favor of lynching suspects in serious crimes, without benefit of due process. Linn applauded the recent mob hangings of two Montana men accused of murder, because due process was too slow.[38] A week later, after learning about incidents of horse theft, Linn called for summary justice, "according to the established rules of the frontier."[39]

When a deputy U.S. marshal went to Fort Sully to escort Edward Duffy to Yankton, Linn sounded off: "We think someone must be hung soon or life is no longer safe. Let judges and juries do their whole duty."[40] The forces of the law moved too slowly for Linn, but move they did. Duffy was finally indicted for murder and the matter was slated to be heard in the October 1871 term of court.[41]

Duffy remained locked up in jail at Yankton, and when his case finally came to trial, Judge Brookings was on the bench, French having taken a transfer to the third district in Pembina in the remote northern reaches of the territory. This left his friend, Judge Brookings, to preside over cases in the second district in Yankton where he could keep an eye on politics and business.[42] It was an arrangement that suited them both very well, and it allowed French to claim the distinction of holding the first session of court in June 1871 in the town of Pembina. [43]

Warren Cowles, the weary prosecutor, represented the government at Duffy's trial in Yankton before Judge Brookings. After four days of testimony, Cowles could finally claim victory: the jury came back with a guilty verdict of manslaughter—not murder. Unable, therefore, to issue a death sentence, Judge Brookings sentenced Duffy to fifteen years of hard labor at the federal prison in Fort Madison, Iowa.[44]

A law passed on December 14, 1870, during the ninth session of the territorial legislature, provided for imprisonment of Dakota convicts at Fort Madison. But the arrangement was not permanent, for the same law authorized the governor to "enter into a new contract with a neighboring state" if, in the interest of the territory, it was deemed prudent and necessary to do so.[45]

During all of Linn's editorial outbursts, he never brought up the issue of a territorial prison, but Governor Burbank did when he addressed the ninth session of the Dakota legislature on December 8, 1870. Burbank reminded the legislators that in accordance with an Act of Congress dated January 22, 1867, the net proceeds of internal revenue collected in Dakota during a three-year period ending June 30, 1868, was to be used to finance the building of a prison. The governor went on to say that the secretary of the treasury reported that the "expenses of collecting the revenue in the territory . . . exceeded the amount of collections made"—and for that reason, he quipped, Dakota had no prison.[46]

Nor was the territory likely to get one in the near future. That institution, which had been promised to Bon Homme, was not viewed as a priority. Dakotans were understandably concerned with the prevalence of crime, especially murder, but they were not keen on building a prison to house convicts. The average pioneer was locked in a life-and-death struggle with nature and any adversary outside of that contest could be ignored. The people did not seem to care where prisoners were incarcerated so long as they were sent away. The legislature, to its credit, acted upon the governor's advice. A deal was struck with the state of Iowa, and until new arrangements were made, all Dakota prisoners would be sent to Fort Madison.

And there were many Dakota prisoners. In Yankton men turned to drinking, gambling, and carousing, at least in part to blunt the impact of monotony and isolation. They had plenty of saloons and gambling joints to choose from, including the popular O.K. Saloon owned by Billy Try. But most drinking hangouts, especially those on the levee in lower Yankton, were dives.

The editor of the *Press* complained about the frequent displays of vulgar and violent behavior and the lax attitude of law enforcement. "Rowdyism" was becoming "altogether too prevalent in Yankton. Hideous howlings of drunken men are frequently heard in the late hours of the night in our streets; pistol firing is frequently an accompaniment of the howling."[47]

In an effort to deal with such behavior, the territorial legislature in its ninth session passed a law allowing justices of the peace to handle assaults and batteries and "affrays" in a "summary manner." Section 302 of the criminal code was added so that all such offenses "shall be prosecuted and determined . . . by a complaint made before a justice of the peace" as opposed to an indictment in district court. Convicted offenders were subjected to a fine of "not less than $5.00, nor more than $100.00, according to the nature of the offense."[48]

Well-intended laws reflected the magnitude of the problem. In Bon Homme County, a reader complained to the *Dakota Herald* about the failure of the district attorney to indict men accused of crime when evidence of criminal acts seemed so clear to ordinary citizens. "B. C." wrote, "justice has in nearly every case been perverted in our county."[49]

A man named Barus from the "upper country" had a different take on crime. He wrote to the *Press* complaining about boredom, while expecting a murder to occur. Killings and steamboat arrivals, he insisted, "are the only excitement we have worthy of the name."[50] Men like Barus feared outlaws but nevertheless had a certain curious longing for their appearance and the splash of color that was left in their wake. News of a shooting affray stirred the blood and attracted attention as nothing else could.

Bad behavior in Dakota meant the court calendar was often festooned with curious and colorful names. For example, Judge Brookings' December 1871 calendar in the second judicial district featured "Chick-a-pa-pa, alias The Twin" who was indicted for larceny.[51] On the frontier, committing a crime was one way to escape anonymity.

The first death sentence in Dakota history was handed down by Judge W.W. Brookings on August 23, 1871. The condemned man was Amiable Galineaux, a Frenchman who had operated a keelboat on the Missouri River since 1840. A contemporary described him as "a pleasant fellow when sober, but a tough character and anything but amiable when under the influence of liquor."[52]

Galineaux had spent many years among the Indians, marrying a Lakota woman of the Two Kettle tribe, the sister of Chief Four Bears. The nomadic life took Galineaux to the Black Hills several times, where he learned about places known only to his Indian companions. One such secret place was Bear Hill Creek where he found gold nuggets. In a jailhouse interview, Galineaux—who spoke primarily in a mixture of French and Lakota—described the mineral and timber wealth of the Black Hills in terms that dazzled his listeners.[53]

In the summer of 1870, Galineaux was living on Pease Island on the Missouri River, Charles Mix County, engaged in the business of chopping and stacking wood for use by steamboats. Following a quarrel with Alexander Boquelle over the ownership of some wood, a drunken Galineaux shot Boquelle in the head, killing him instantly.

He was arrested and charged with murder by a grand jury, tried in August of 1871, convicted and sentenced to be hanged on November 7, 1871.[54] An appeal was made to the Dakota Supreme Court asking for a new trial based on jury misconduct. The defense argued that a juror was drunk while deliberating and, further, that a bailiff had improperly conversed with the jury. A motion for a new trial was denied by the Supreme Court and the case remanded to Brookings for re-sentencing. The prisoner Galineaux, who was about seventy years old, was again sentenced to be hanged, the new date being April 25, 1873.[55]

Galineaux's date with the gallows coincided with the revamping of the Dakota Territory Supreme Court. The popular and competent Jefferson P. Kidder was reappointed, although his reappointment met with some opposition because he was known to use alcohol. Ex-governor Andrew J. Faulk wrote to President Grant, recommending removal, saying that Kidder was a "confirmed inebriate . . . an open, shameless, almost helpless drunkard." Grant was unmoved and Kidder was reappointed.[56]

Like Kidder, Judge Brookings wanted to stay on the court, but he was also seeking political office. In the fall of 1872, Brookings was a candidate for delegate to Congress on the "straight" Republican ticket. His former friend, lawyer Gideon C. Moody, was also in the running as a Republican. The Democratic nominee, Moses K. Armstrong from Yankton, was the third party in the bitterly fought contest, complete with the vile and libelous attacks from angry, rival newspapers.

Brookings was in the thick of the fighting and used his cane, needed after the loss of his feet, to strike a blow to Arthur Linn's head during a heated argument that occurred not long before the opening of the Yankton Republican Party convention. The *Dakota Herald* called the unkind act a "cane presentation."[57] Linn was still the editor for the *Union and Dakotaian,* the anti-Brookings, pro-Moody, newspaper. He took offense and for this incident the judge was arrested, charged with assault, and tried before the city justice of the peace. A fight broke out during the trial but was quickly dispersed by the marshal.

As if unconcerned about the outcome, Brookings ordered two kegs of beer from the brewery to be sent to the office of the city justice. When the trial was over, Brookings was found guilty, fined one dollar and released. The beer kegs were opened and the unrepentant judge invited those gathered to indulge freely and with great gusto.[58]

The prisoner, Galineaux, got a break, too. Public sentiment was strongly against hanging him. The *Dakota Herald* of Yankton offered its sympathy for the condemned man, noting Galineaux was very old and, having lived most of his life "among the lawless residents of the borders and away from the refining influences of civilization," he had little chance to avoid violent confrontations. The *Herald* predicted that the president would understand and provide executive clemency.[59]

A petition was circulated and signed eagerly by a large number of men, including every member of the Yankton bar. It was also signed by all three Supreme Court judges, meaning Judge Brookings must have had some misgivings about the death sentence. The petition for a pardon was sent to the president, who commuted Galineaux's sentence to three years in prison.[60]

The people had spoken and a man's life was saved, but the Dakota judiciary had other troubles. The federal government, which funded the territories, determined that it was not receiving a good return on its investment in Dakota Territory. In 1872, during the peak of the French era, for example, the expenses incurred by the Dakota judiciary, including both the court and marshals' office, totaled a staggering $69,474, twice the sum reported by any other territory.[61]

Still, there were special needs in the territory that were not met, such as a new jail to house prisoners awaiting trial. The old jail was so inadequate that a Yankton newspaper suggested that it be sold "for a cowshed or a hog pen."[62]

The lack of a secure structure and an expensive judiciary were only part of the problem. The territory was in dire need of a recodification of its statutes. Governor Burbank made a strong plea for recodification in his December 3, 1872, address to the legislature. He argued that a change was "imperatively demanded" and reminded the legislators that he had previously called for a recodification: "The value of law lies in its certainty, and nothing so detracts from the good effects of legislation as frequency of amendment, change, and the confusion and fragmenting character of badly arranged, illy [sic] digested and poorly expressed laws."[63] Burbank seemed to say that a bad law could get a guilty man an acquittal or an innocent man convicted.

Surely, a new chief justice for Dakota Territory was needed. Although he had expected reappointment, Justice French was destined to be replaced by Peter C. Shannon, a lawyer and former judge from Pennsylvania. Thus the erratic and often embarrassing French era ended. In its place Dakotans would get a chief justice and court system that they would look upon with pride and confidence. Dakotans were glad to see French go, although many would miss having him as the butt of their jokes.

The son of Irish immigrants, Peter C. Shannon was born in New Alexandria, Westmoreland County, Pennsylvania, on August 25, 1821. He was educated at the prestigious Greenburg Academy and read law in a judge's office. He was admitted to the Pittsburgh bar in 1846 and soon embarked on a successful career as a lawyer, serving one term also as a judge.

His first marriage, to Anna Evans, produced Sarah, born in 1849. Following his wife's death, Peter married Ann Elena Ihmsen in Pittsburgh.[64] Their marriage produced five more children, Eleanor, Elizabeth, Louis, Maria, and Christian, all born in Pennsylvania.

During the antebellum years, Shannon was an active member of the Democratic Party and through hard work and talent became an articulate and popular campaigner for party ideals and candidates. But he was at odds with many of his fellow Democrats, for Shannon was an abolitionist, a principle that over time distanced him from the Democratic Party. When the Civil War broke out, Shannon—the "War Democrat"—immediately took to the stump, endorsing President Abraham Lincoln's war policy to put down the Southern rebellion. He served for a short time in the 13th Pennsylvania Volunteer Cavalry with the rank of Lieutenant Colonel.

Throughout the remaining war years, Shannon maintained a law practice, was politically active, and continued to impress men in high places, including Lincoln whom Shannon supported for re-election in 1864. The two were personally acquainted and Lincoln once offered Shannon a position as a foreign minister. Shannon turned it down promptly, but an undismayed Lincoln went on to praise the judge in a speech at a "public reception" in Philadelphia: "Peter C. Shannon is a patriot without ambition for personal aggrandizement. I know it, for I have tried him."[65]

Peter C. Shannon may not have been eager for office at that time, but in 1873, when President Grant offered him the position of chief justice of the Dakota Territory Supreme Court, Shannon accepted, "because it was in the line of his profession and studies."[66] His decision became a turning point toward social and judicial stability in outlaw Dakota.

CHAPTER 4

JUDGE SHANNON COMES TO DAKOTA

We think that the people of Dakota have been particularly blest and the Supreme Court inherits a high token of legal ability by the appointment of Mr. Shannon as Chief Justice.

Dakota Herald
April 18, 1873

E very four years the president was required either to reappoint the sitting territorial Supreme Court justices or select new ones. Knowing this, Dakotans were expecting news from Washington, D.C. in the spring of 1873, all wondering if the president would reshuffle the deck. Judges were not the only appointees whose futures were on the table, and curious men were speculating about the appointment of a new governor and other officials.

Yankton was the headquarters for all things political, and although politics was dominated by the Republican Party, the leading men were so often divided on matters important to the development of the territory that the business of governing for the greater good was lost in a quagmire of bitter, spiteful quarreling and angry postelection contests. Throughout the 1860s, the Democrats exercised whatever clout they possessed by supporting one of the Republican factions.

By 1870 two opposing groups of Republicans had emerged, each identified by men with soaring personal ambitions and by the part of Yankton where each group set up shop. Thus history records that the "Broadway Gang" was located on Broadway Street and the "Capital Gang" was at home on Capital Street. Prominent members of the "Broadway Gang" were G. C. Moody, Walter A. Burleigh, Jake Brauch, and John Lawrence. The "Capital Gang" was led by Governor John A. Burbank, Judge W.W. Brookings, W. R. Kingsbury, and Judge George W. French. The loud and scandalous spectacle was not confined to Dakota, and alarmed observers from other states wondered if Dakotans were capable of self-government. With a famous speech by Abraham Lincoln in mind, a Sioux Falls newspaper editor said that Yankton was "a house divided against itself."[1]

Secession, the Civil War, the South, slavery, and the assassination of Lincoln vaulted the Republican Party into a position of power and dominance that it would maintain for the rest of the century. It was like being rewarded for landing on the right side of history. Unfortunately, the Dakota Territory Republicans seemed to excel in ways to neutralize that advantage.

Despite the sad state of politics, the people of Yankton and the other towns were in an optimistic frame of mind. Although immigration into Dakota was slower than expected, people were coming, the towns were growing, and more land was put under the plow. Hardships sometimes outweighed rewards, but the soil, dark and rich, provided great promise and was the well-spring for the strength needed to hang on and hope. The generous Homestead Act of 1862 offered an unprecedented incentive to come, stay, and struggle. After several years of dedicated effort, people could see that hard work was doing more than producing callused hands.

In the fall of 1870 telegraph lines were set up between Sioux City and Yankton. Vermillion's newspaper editor joyously declared a great day was coming: "When we hear the click of the telegraphic instrument," we "realize that we are in instantaneous communication with the entire world." The introduction of the new technology was hailed as the most important improvement next to the railroad.[2]

The construction of the Dakota Southern Railroad from Sioux City to Yankton was an event whose importance cannot be overstated. It was the single factor that kept the loose-knit town from completely falling apart. To the politicians who hated each other, the railroad easily trumped their differences. The coming of the "iron horse" meant that the territorial capital was connected to all points east, thus ending the era of isolation and the slow and bumpy stagecoach ride to Sioux City.

The twelve-hour, sixty-five-mile stagecoach ride from Yankton to Sioux City, however, was an experience not easily forgotten. One exasperated and tormented passenger said, "the tortures of the Spanish inquisition were tender mercies in comparison with this terrible ride of 12 hours."[3] It is no wonder that folks were relieved when the train rolled into Yankton.

A railroad quickened the pace of commerce and facilitated the ease, speed, and comfort of travel, thereby overcoming some of the bite, bang, and bounce of the stagecoach. The train was the incentive to attract stable and law-abiding people. Still, it would take more than a train to rid Yankton of its undesirables, for at any time of the day or night a drunken cowboy might ride through its dusty streets, firing his six-shooter as a noisy reminder of the persistence of the territory's lawlessness.

The completion of the Dakota Southern Railroad was, nevertheless, a powerful reason to celebrate, and on February 5, 1873, Yankton residents turned out for a big party. The railroad ball was the gala event of the winter season, and some Dakota politicos knew it would be their last hurrah.

Since the first officials arrived in 1861, Dakotans had watched a steady procession of federally appointed officials come and go. Despite the palpable hardships of life on the frontier, there seemed to be no shortage of candidates for federal jobs. A new man was usually greeted with a mixture of hope and skepticism, while many departing officials were bid good riddance. The *Dakota Herald* claimed that "political garbage, the very offal of place hunters are set down in Dakota."[4] While the *Herald* was exaggerating, the practice of sending political cronies, hacks, or otherwise unqualified men, to the territories led to widespread dissatisfaction among the people.

The term "carpetbagger" was used over the years to describe the migrating officers, many of whom exhibited a condescending attitude and acted from self-serving motives. Dakotans had grown weary of their presence and longed to hear the president appoint some worthy men from among the home-grown population.

It was not to be, however. The *Yankton Press* reported on March 19, 1873, that President U.S. Grant had once again done his duty for Dakota: and "through the medium of the telegraph, information has reached Dakota," concerning the reappointment of Governor John A. Burbank and the appointment of Peter C. Shannon, of Pennsylvania, as chief justice. The same article noted that Jefferson P. Kidder kept his place on the bench and that George W. French had become associate justice. Brookings was out and on his way to a position in Idaho.

The *Yankton Press* editorial indicated that the "new Judge [Shannon]... is said to be a lawyer of large experience and sound ability." The editorial went on to note, with pained optimism, that with the appointment of Peter C. Shannon and reappointment of Burbank, "the 'struggle' which has agitated the political waters of Dakota for a number of months, ought to, and we hope will cease." The *Press* further observed that "Judge French met only a feeble opposition from Dakota" and his reappointment will please the residents of his district. "He [French] will find a warm welcome awaiting him."[5]

The *Press* was wrong. According to official records, the Dakota Supreme Court would have two new members. Brookings was re-nominated on March 12, and on the 17th it was withdrawn. Kidder and French were re-nominated on March 13, though it appears that Grant had a sudden, partial change of heart, for French's name was withdrawn on the same day. On the 15th Shannon was nominated to replace French as chief justice, and he was quickly approved by the Senate.[6]

A few days later came more news by telegraph that A. H. Barnes of Walworth County, Wisconsin, was to be a new associate justice. A *Press* editorial noted that Barnes had been one of the "leading lawyers of southern Wisconsin for many years and will bring to the bench of Dakota a legal experience of more than a quarter of a century."[7] Barnes replaced Brookings, who was not sent to Idaho to serve, but rather was simply retired to private life, free to pursue his business and political interests. Of course, he would always be known as "Judge" Brookings.

Alanson Hamilton Barnes was born in Lewis County, New York, on April 15, 1817, and received a good education including a stint at Yale University. He studied law in the office of attorney David Bennett of New York and was admitted to the bar in 1845. He moved to Wisconsin with his wife and four children in the mid-1850s, settling in Delevan in the southeastern part of the state. Not long after, Barnes' wife died, leaving him with four young children to care for without a mother's nurturing. He developed a successful law practice and had a hand in establishing the Republican Party in Wisconsin.

Barnes was appointed, effective March 24, 1873, with the support of Wisconsin Senator Matthew H. Carpenter. Since Barnes had worked strenuously for Grant's reelection in 1872, the president no doubt felt obligated to return the favor.[8] It was not only a logical decision, it was also a good one, for over time Barnes proved to be a capable justice, bringing dignity, respect, and a good legal mind to the Dakota bench.

The popular Justice J. P. Kidder was retained on the court, much to the approval of most Dakotans. The *Dakota Republican* strongly endorsed Kidder, calling him "a prince among good judges."[9] The U.S. attorney general agreed, saying Kidder was regarded as the "very best territorial judge in the United States and we can't spare him."[10]

Two other presidential appointees are notable as well. James H. Burdick, a member of Grant's Civil War staff, living in Yankton, was appointed U.S. marshal for Dakota, and William A. Pound, also a Yankton resident, was named the new U.S. attorney. They replaced Laban H. Litchfield and Warren Cowles, both of whom died in 1872.

In May of 1871, Shannon represented Pittsburgh at the Republican Party Convention in Harrisburg, Pennsylvania. He favored the re-nomination of Grant for a second term as president. Shannon was personally acquainted with the president and was dissatisfied with the convention resolutions that were only lukewarm toward Grant. He drafted a ninth resolution containing the appropriate respect for Grant, declaring that he was in fact "our standard bearer" in 1872. The resolution was agreed to by the convention, and when the cheering stopped, both Shannon and Grant were winners.[11]

The timing and tone of Shannon's resolution brought forth some criticism and a snide suggestion that he was acting in a self-serving way. An Ebensburg, Pennsylvania, newspaper asked whether "it would be satisfactory to know what office Grant will bestow on the Judge as a suitable reward for this successful *flank movement.*"[12]

There was probably little or no connection between the resolution and the appointment. Interestingly, when the Pennsylvania state central committee of the Republican Party met in July of 1872 to select nominations for congressional house seats, Shannon was under consideration. But "according to his own request," his supporters did not "urge his name for the Congressional nomination."[13]

Did Shannon have his sights set on Dakota? As time went on his support for the appointment increased. George A. Cass, president of the Northern Pacific Railroad, which was just then under construction across northern Dakota, recommended his friend Peter C. Shannon to the president. On February 1, 1873, a delegation from Dakota Territory, in the company of Civil War General James S. Negley, met with Grant, asking that Shannon be appointed to the Dakota Supreme Court. A month later,

Grant made the appointment.[14] Peter C. Shannon would be coming to Dakota to be the next chief justice with an annual salary of $2,500.

An article in a South Dakota newspaper published after Shannon's death states that he accepted Grant's offer of the judgeship only reluctantly, and did so because he was consumptive and felt the Dakota climate would help him regain his health.[15] But he had other forms of encouragement. When the Pittsburgh press learned that Grant had sent Shannon's name to the Senate for confirmation, two newspapers came out solidly in favor

Peter C. Shannon, Chief Justice,
Dakota Territory Supreme Court (1873–1882).
Courtesy South Dakota State Historical Society.

of the appointment. The *Daily Commercial* was pleased to report that the appointment "will meet with the approval of friends of both parties [Shannon and Grant] in all parts of the state." The *Pittsburgh Morning Mail* was equally enthusiastic: "It is with unfeigned pleasure that we announce the confirmation of Hon. Judge Shannon, recently appointed Chief Justice of Dakota by the President." The new chief justice was praised as a man "with wide experience" and "rare literary attainments and knowledge of men and things."[16]

Shannon could, indeed, point to a distinguished career in law and politics, having made steady and thoughtful steps upward in professional life. He had evolved politically from Democrat to Republican, but in religious matters, he remained a Roman Catholic, despite the territory's preference for Protestants.[17] Shannon was not a man to compromise on religion or personal ethics.

As the new chief justice made his way by train to Yankton, he stopped at Vermillion for a short visit. Editor Charles H. True of the *Dakota Republican* warbled, "we had the pleasure of meeting him a moment at the cars." Shannon told the eager editor that he was very pleased with the country, on this his first trip to the West, and was especially impressed with Dakota.

Judge Barnes also stopped at Vermillion, equally impressed with the prairie and the settlements. True liked both Barnes and Shannon and concluded his article by observing, "These gentlemen both seemed to us to be men of ability and culture and we are glad to welcome them to Dakota." This sentiment was echoed at the office of the *Yankton Press,* where Shannon also stopped.[18]

When the new judges arrived at the capital city of the territory, they found themselves in distinguished company. The *Press* bade them a warm welcome and at the same time was pleased to state that "General George A. Custar [sic] famed for his service in the Army of the Potomac" was encamped on the eastern edge of Yankton with his Seventh Cavalry on their way to Fort Randall, and from there upriver to Fort Rice.

Coincident with the arrival of the new judges and soldiers, southeastern Dakota was hit by a severe and unexpected spring snowstorm. The heavy snow delayed the departure of the troops for several days, and as they were totally unprepared for the emergency, the citizens of Yankton were compelled to help out with food and shelter. After it stopped snowing, some entertainment was provided, and Lieutenant Colonel Custer served as a "referee" at a shooting match between Captain French of the Seventh and another ex-Civil War veteran, General Edwin S. McCook of Ohio, the secretary of the territory.[19]

As winter gave way to spring, a minor disturbance arose in the shape of a judicial controversy. The new justices had to be assigned to one of three districts and, as he was the chief justice, Shannon expected to work in Yankton, the capital city, in the second district. Barnes claimed the right to preside in Yankton because he was the replacement for Brookings who had held court in the second district. Kidder, of course, would remain in the first district.

The territorial legislature of 1870-71 redrew the boundaries of the three judicial districts. The first district, headquartered in Vermillion, consisted of just three southeastern counties: Clay, Union, and Lincoln. The second district, with Yankton as the principal court, consisted of seven counties including Yankton, Bon Homme, Charles Mix, and Minnehaha, along with the rest of the territory to the north and west. The third district was made up of the northeastern part of the territory, namely Pembina and Brookings counties, with the courthouse in the town of Pembina, near the Canadian border.[20]

Shannon assumed that he would be stationed in Yankton because two previous chief justices, Bliss and Bartlett, served in the capital city, in accordance with the proclamation of Governor William Jayne in 1861. When French arrived in Dakota in 1869, he too served in Yankton. Then French and Brookings muddied the judicial waters by deciding that the former would take the third district and the latter the second district. Brookings was satisfied with the third district when the court was in Bon Homme, but as he was well established in Yankton, he did not want to move hundreds of miles away to Pembina, where the legislature of 1870-71 set up a court.[21] French, on the other hand, was willing to cooperate with his friend Brookings, since the remote venue's lack of cases suited his limited judicial talent.

When the Supreme Court met in Yankton in January of 1871, the justices issued an order dated the 13th, confirming that the third district court "shall be held in the town of Pembina." It further ordered that "His Honor Geo. W. French be assigned to the Third Judicial District."[22]

The Supreme Court order was printed in the French-friendly *Yankton Press,* followed by a short editorial that sought to explain, more fully, the reason for sending French to Pembina "in accordance with his own desire." The *Press* went on to explain that the health of Mrs. French "has not been so good since her residence here [Yankton] . . . and it is thought that a change to the Red River region may result in her benefit."[23]

It is also on record that French had health problems and believed the more northern clime would be beneficial. Furthermore, he declared that he was "adventurously inclined and was anxious to get a glimpse of the wilds of the north," a region that interested him because of the coming of the Northern Pacific Railroad. His critics snidely insisted that French's "true motive" was not a desire to "exile himself to that remote region of dog trains and pemmican," but rather to escape the "intricate legal problems presented by the attorneys who practiced in the second district."[24]

Judge French dutifully spent the summer in Pembina, the "Red River District" in what is today North Dakota. He returned to Yankton on November 24, 1871, to spend the winter and to preside over the January term of the Supreme Court. He told the *Press* that he had made a study of the "agricultural capabilities of that section" and learned that the "soil is very productive." French also reported that the climate was "salubrious," the winds were not as strong as those of southern Dakota, and perhaps best of all "the air is singularly free of dust." Oh, and Mrs. French? She was living in Hampton, Illinois.[25]

The arrangement made between French and Brookings continued until April 1873 when Governor Burbank—with two new justices on the bench—tried to set it in stone. In accordance with the Organic Act, he declared that Shannon should preside in the third district, where French had worked, and Barnes, as successor to Brookings, should stay in the second district. Burbank issued a proclamation to this effect because the legislature had not exercised its right to make the assignments.[26]

Shannon was not happy with the arrangement, but as he had unknowingly become a casualty of the great political divide, he became the recipient of the governor's wrath. When Shannon arrived in Yankton, he called upon ex-governor Andrew J. Faulk, an old friend from Pennsylvania. As Faulk was part of the Broadway Street crowd, it was assumed that Shannon had come under the influence of that political faction. As such, Burbank, the titular head of the Capital Street Gang, took offense and used the power of his office to assign Shannon to the third judicial district where the new judge would work out of Pembina, far to the north, almost as if he had been banished. If the new chief justice was not willing to join the Capital Street Gang, he should be stationed in some outlying region where he could do little damage.[27]

A veteran Dakota lawyer had a slightly different slant on the Shannon banishment. He claimed that the assignment of the two justices came about because of a county seat fight in Bon Homme County between the town of Bon Homme, owned primarily by Faulk, and Springfield, owned in the main by Burbank. With much to gain if Springfield was named county seat, Burbank sent Shannon packing because the governor suspected that the new chief justice would favor Faulk, a fellow Pennsylvanian, in the pending county seat litigation.[28]

Peter C. Shannon would prove to be a careful and thoughtful man who chose duty over personal gain and reluctantly set out to preside in the third district and handle the court's business to the best of his abilities. Before he packed up for Pembina, however, he met with members of the Yankton fraternity of lawyers and paid his respects to the Chief Justice of the U.S. Supreme Court, Salmon P. Chase, who had died in May 1873. Indicative of his courtly eloquence, Shannon said of Chase, "Whilst the courts in the States of the Union are in sadness over the event, it is fit and proper that the bench and bar of this youthful territory . . . should send some funeral offering—some twig of cypress to be laid over the coffin of this illustrious man."[29]

It was a speech that foreshadowed remarks and praise that many years in the future would mark the occasion of his own death. But in 1873 Shannon was fifty-two years old and in good health and of sufficient intellectual power to fuel an admirable career on the Dakota bench. He got off to a good start in Pembina.

On May 28, 1873, Shannon and his colleagues set out for Pembina, where a member of the party noted the appearance of green grass: "I think the season is not more than a week later than at Yankton." The group consisted of the judge, U.S. Marshal James H. Burdick, Clerk of Court George I. Foster, U.S. Attorney William A. Pound, and Dr. J. Miller. The district court entourage was described as a "carpet bag affair." The building in Pembina that housed the court was described as "roomy and comfortable . . . and is blessed with a roomy and well ventilated attic." They imposed on a sympathetic resident for their meals because the food at the hotel was horrible, and they chose the attic of the courthouse for sleeping accommodations because they feared the "leading hotel" would be "pre-empted by actual settlers."

Court proceedings went smoothly, with the grand jury handing down six indictments within forty-eight hours, working at a speed that astonished everyone. Shannon made a good impression and "won golden opinions by the able manner in which he performs his duties." The judge was complimented for making careful rulings from the bench and was "most pleasant and courteous, while firm and decided whenever necessary."[30]

Having conducted a successful and busy session of eight days' duration, the party departed Pembina by steamboat on the Red River of the North, and arrived back in Yankton on June 21. The Supreme Court convened on the 23rd in Yankton, but there was nothing of importance on the docket so it adjourned until August 27. Judge Shannon had time to rest and then prepare an oration to deliver on the Fourth of July at Bon Homme.[31]

The matter of the assignment of justices lingered uneasily throughout the summer of 1873 as Shannon continued to press his claim. In September he made the 460 mile-trip to Pembina for another term of court. He also stopped at the new settlement of Fargo, where he "obtained from his old friend, George W. Cass" of the Northern Pacific Railroad a handshake agreement for lots where the Fargo courthouse was to be built. He was thinking ahead.[32]

Meanwhile, Barnes was under pressure from the governor concerning an injunction against the Dakota Southern Railroad in its suit against Yankton County. Barnes ordered the injunction, which outraged Burbank and his allies who demanded a reversal. Barnes wrote to the secretary of the interior, Columbus Delano, complaining about Burbank's conduct. He told Delano that, during a private conversation with Burbank, the governor ordered him to vacate the injunction. Barnes said that Burbank wanted Judge Shannon to handle the railroad case, and if he (Barnes) refused to vacate the injunction, he would be transferred to Pembina.[33]

At first Burbank hesitated. He was advised that to interfere with a judge's order was not only considered meddlesome but also illegal and, fearing that he might be arrested and imprisoned for contempt of court, no transfer order was issued.[34] Barnes was applauded for his strong stand in refusing to bow to the governor. He refused to order a change of venue, and the injunction stayed in effect.

Then on November 7, "acting governor" Oscar A. Whitney issued a proclamation on behalf of Governor Burbank, assigning Barnes to Pembina and Shannon to Yankton. Barnes was visiting in Wisconsin at the time. The proclamation stated that the original assignment ordering Barnes to Yankton and Shannon to Pembina was made because the U.S. attorney general ordered Barnes to replace Brookings who was holding court in the second district. It further stated that Shannon "cheerfully acquiesced in said assignment" to Pembina, but that it was a temporary arrangement only and that "courtesy and proprietary" toward the chief justice demanded that he be seated at the capital city, unless he desired to preside elsewhere.[35]

Shannon had not been brought back to Yankton out of courtesy, as the *Press* devised. The governor did not get the decision he wanted in the railroad case, so while he was safely out of the territory he arranged through Secretary Whitney to issue a proclamation sending Barnes to Pembina. The *Press,* usually sympathetic to Burbank, slammed the governor for his self-serving scheming and called the manipulation of judges an outrage: "It practically makes an Executive football of the judiciary of Dakota."[36]

When Barnes learned of the chicanery, he went to Washington, D.C., to confer with Delano and Attorney General George W. Williams. It was not that he disliked Shannon—in fact he respected the chief justice—but Barnes was suspicious of the motives of the governor and secretary of the territory and wanted the matter settled by someone at the federal level. If he had to move to Pembina, he wanted the order to come from someone other than the governor or his henchman.

Unfortunately, Barnes could have been more circumspect about his methods. A letter he had sent to Sioux Falls attorney Melvin Grigsby was published in the *Sioux Falls Pantagraph,* much to the delight of the *Dakota Herald* in Yankton. The editor of the *Herald* did not like Barnes, whom he considered a carpetbagger, and he hated Burbank, a carpetbagger and pariah, so he eagerly published a portion of the letter that revealed the judge's dislike of the governor.

In his letter to Grigsby, Barnes wrote, "I have met [R. F.] Pettigrew at Yankton. I think he is inclined to go for Burbank in your paper, perhaps ridicule the Governor and his harem." The curious but not-too-careful Judge Barnes asked that Grigsby not mention his name in connection with the letter and closed by saying, "keep the pot boiling."

The mention of the boiling pot was too tempting for Maris Taylor of the *Herald* to ignore, for he had both Barnes and Burbank in the crosshairs. Vowing to "keep the pot boiling" until Barnes' goose was cooked "tenderly but thoroughly," Taylor reminded the judge that it was unbecoming for a man of his stature and position to engage in subterfuge and suggested that he look elsewhere—for example Utah—for work.[37]

Still, Barnes' effort in Washington paid off for on December 11, Whitney retracted the proclamation of November 7 acting on federal orders. Thus it looked as though Barnes would stay in Yankton and Shannon would need to make another trip to Pembina for the spring term of court in 1874. In his latest proclamation, Whitney claimed the current arrangement "created disorder and dissatisfaction" and that he and the governor were simply acting with the "interests of the people of the territory in view," according to the *Springfield Times,* a newspaper favorable to the governor.

But "stop the press," said the *Times,* for information just in indicated that the "proclamation has been countermanded." And furthermore, the *Times* confessed that it had no authority to "give the same [the December 11 proclamation] to the public."[38]

Then, on January 10, 1874, Whitney began another round of judicial musical chairs, reinstating his order of November 7, 1873, again acting according to federal authority. Delano had changed his mind.[39] The matter was finally settled, and Chief Justice Shannon would thereafter preside over the courts of the second district in Yankton. At long last, the farce had ended, and there was no longer any "occasion for real or imaginary cartoons of a 'judiciary on wheels.'"[40]

Barnes was a good sport and had no objections to the final decision. Before departing for Pembina, Barnes was given a hearty send-off at the Merchants Hotel in Yankton by members of the bar and press, including the editor of the *Dakota Herald,* all of whom toasted and roasted the affable judge. Apparently the pot had boiled long enough and it was time to turn down the heat.[41]

Northern Dakota became a good fit for Justice Barnes, and his popularity there increased with time and the opportunity to practice his legal skills. On June 18, 1874, Barnes held the first term of court in Bismarck, Burleigh County, handling a lengthy docket of both criminal and civil cases. But first he had to swear in a crop of new lawyers, including a man known only as "Buffalo Jack,"[42] whose name suggests there was a bit of rough leather about him.

Barnes took a liking to northern Dakota and Shannon was pleased to be firmly ensconced in Yankton. As Barnes settled in at Pembina and Shannon at Yankton, some months after the dispute over judicial districts was settled, the polished and sophisticated Judge Shannon decided it was time his family joined him in Dakota. In July of 1874 he took the train to Sioux City to meet his wife and children and escort them to Yankton. Their first residence was at the Merchants Hotel.

The judge's family was accompanied by attorney Oliver Shannon and his son. Oliver Shannon was introduced to Yankton as Judge Shannon's younger, adopted brother, although Dakota historian Doane Robinson would later declare they shared the same mother and father.[43] A Springfield newspaper, however, said Oliver was the judge's friend "but not a kinsman."[44] He was certainly a Civil War veteran and had been practicing law in Butler, Pennsylvania, where he acquired a good reputation. Having been tempted to try Dakota, Oliver Shannon relocated to Yankton and set up a new law office.[45] Brothers or friends, the Shannon presence in Dakota had begun, with each man determined to make his mark.

CHAPTER 5

LYNCHING AT SNAKE CREEK

*Between 6 and 7 o'clock on Tuesday morning, the
17th inst., a party of twelve men, masked, and armed
with rifles, revolvers and knives, went to a ranch on Snake
Creek, about fifty miles above this place [Fort Randall]
and hung the proprietor, Michael Hartert, and a man named
Henry Hyer to telegraph poles.*

Dakota Herald
September 24, 1872

Free from the distractions caused by conflicting proclamations, Chief Justice Peter C. Shannon and the Dakota Supreme Court got down to business. Among the weighty matters on the agenda was a serious case left over from the French era—the killing of two men in northern Charles Mix County in the fall of 1872 that resulted in the arrest of seven suspects, all charged with murder.

The double murder was covered by territorial newspapers, but historians have concluded that the journalists were mistaken about the victims' names. Understandably, these rough men from the "up river" country were reluctant to reveal details about their activities, so articles about the crime were based largely on hearsay.

The *Dakota Republican, Springfield Times,* and *Yankton Press* reported that the victims were Michael Hartert and Henry Hyer. According to the *Republican,* Hartert operated a "ranche" on Snake Creek in Charles Mix County, about fifty miles above Fort Randall and three miles south of the Bijou Hills. Hyer was either a hired man or was associated with Hartert in some other way.

On September 17, 1872, between six and seven o'clock in the morning, a group of ten masked men, all well-armed, rode up to the Hartert house. As they approached, they encountered Hyer some distance from the house, preparing to go out hunting. He was ordered to toss his rifle away. He complied and was then seized and dragged to a telegraph post, where he was raised up on a horse. A rope was placed around his neck and "hitched to the top of the pole." The horse was slapped away, leaving Hyer strangling at the end of the rope.

Next, the party of masked men went to the house where they found their primary victim, Hartert. They called him out and ordered him to raise his hands. Hartert complied and some of the masked men escorted him to the stable where they questioned him about his alleged involvement in criminal activity. The rest of the party stayed at the house to make sure Mrs. Hartert did not attempt to interfere. Hartert was then hanged from a telegraph pole in full view of his wife, who could only watch in horror. The executioners then pillaged the house and left the area.

Mrs. Hartert cut down her dead husband and tried to drag his body into the house. She was not successful so she covered the corpse with a blanket and some boards. The next day, the mail rider from Fort Thompson stopped by the house and moved the body inside. Hyer's body was also cut down and buried.

The *Republican* article suggested the two hanged men got what they deserved, as the "ranche has long been the resort of the worst class of horse thieves and desperadoes on the river." Furthermore, the murdered men's reputations were known to be unsavory, and "horse stealing was not the worst crimes they committed." As for the group of stranglers, the writer of the article concluded that "they probably never will be discovered."[1]

An article in the *Springfield Times* declared that the victims had been warned by letters signed "vigilance committee" to leave the area, a warning that was ignored. The *Times* got its "particulars" from a party "who was on the ground but a few hours after the affair happened." According to the informant, a wagon train stopped near the Snake Creek ranche to make camp on the day of the hangings. Mrs. Hartert, described as a "prepossessing and intelligent lady," approached the wagons and received assistance in carrying the dead men into the house.

The county coroner, Bruno Conoyer, empaneled a coroner's jury to conduct an inquest. It was the opinion of the jury that "the two men came to their death by being hung to telegraph poles by persons to them unknown." The bodies were then buried.[2]

On October 2, 1872, the *Yankton Press* published an article, titled "Snake Creek Tragedy," about the lynching of Hartert and Hyer by masked men. But the *Press* claimed the advantage of having interviewed Hartert's widow, who came to Yankton to report the incident. She said she was forced to stay in the house while her husband was taken away to a telegraph pole about one-half mile from the house where he was hanged. The masked men then returned to the house, "went into the bar-room, helping themselves to the money in the drawer and to whiskey and cigars and whatever else they saw fit." They then mounted up and rode away, and after a short distance split up and went in different directions. In shock, the wife grabbed a pistol intending to shoot at the retreating riders but it failed to discharge when she pulled the trigger.

Mrs. Hartert denied that their ranch was the headquarters for horse thieves and other outlaws and claimed that they never allowed "their ranche to be used as a depot for stolen plunder." She expressed confidence that she recognized some of the riders but was reluctant to provide any names.[3]

Apparently no one in the Dakota press was eager to ask any questions or do any investigative reporting, for the matter was quickly forgotten. There were other stories to cover, including the building of the Dakota Southern Railroad and the hotly contested general election that took place on October 15, but these events did not of themselves deter investigating a double lynching.

Mrs. Hartert, herself, may have forced the issue. Perhaps acting on information she provided, in August of 1873 Sheriff Simpson of Bon Homme County and his deputy, John King, rode to the upper country in search of the men who were involved in the Snake Creek lynching. In the Bijou Hills area they arrested Jack Kincaid, Jack Sully, and George Trimmer without incident. A fourth man, the notorious Jim Somers, broke and ran when he learned he was about to be arrested. The sheriff shot at the retreating Somers and reportedly inflicted a serious wound, but the outlaw escaped.[4]

Eventually, other arrests were made and seven men appeared at the Bon Homme courthouse on the September 1873 calendar, all indicted for murder: William T. McKay, William Cunningham, Henry Walker, Jack Kinkaid, Jim Somers, George Trimmer, and Jack Sully. Two formidable Yankton attorneys, G. C. Moody and S. L. Spink, represented the defendants.[5]

McKay was the best known of the arrestees, having served in the territorial legislature from White Swan in Charles Mix County. White Swan was a rough little village on the Missouri River near Fort Randall that featured, among its attractions, two "white swans" from Missouri who offered their services to soldiers from the Fort.[6] It was the kind of place that appealed to a man like McKay, known on the frontier as "Billy" McKay. In 1872 he was in his early forties and married.[7] He was also a candidate for re-election to the legislature, but the October visit to the Snake Creek ranch was certainly not a campaign stop.

A biographical sketch in the *Black Hills Daily Times* sheds some light on the mysterious and restless life of William T. McKay. He was born in 1829 in New York State but was raised in Canada. At a young age he succumbed to a yearning to travel and explore. In 1849 he went to Howard County, Missouri, where he found work as a teamster. In 1852 he went to California and engaged in mining for eight years, both making and losing money. He moved on to Nevada and Montana and then to Salt Lake City because he wanted to "become acquainted with Brigham Young and investigate for himself the private workings of polygamy." But he found himself dissatisfied with the Mormon way of life, so in April of 1865 he headed off to Montana for more mining and prospecting.

In August of 1866, "remembering the hog and hominy of old Missouri," McKay returned to that state and got involved in railroad work. This led him to North Platte, Nebraska, where he opened a billiard saloon and made a $10,000 profit in just two months. It was there that he became acquainted with J.W. Smith and John Parker, two men who had been appointed post traders at the Spotted Tail Agency, also known as the Whetstone Indian Agency, in Dakota Territory. Smith and Parker convinced McKay to invest money in their trader business and the three-man partnership went to Dakota Territory, arriving at the agency in 1868.[8]

That same year McKay and a whiskey dealer, Lewis Obeshaw, established a saloon on the east bank of the Missouri River, opposite the Whetstone Agency. The agency was created by General William S. Harney in 1868 for the Spotted Tail band of Brulé Sioux. McKay and Obeshaw set up shop nearby so as to be ready to sell cheap whiskey to the Indians when they received their annual payments.[9] Chief Spotted Tail understood the danger to his people and strove to keep them away from the establishment of McKay and Obeshaw.

The site of McKay's saloon was at a place called Harney City. The "city" was named in honor of General Harney and, according to one report, was started about the same time as the Whetstone Agency was created, about eighteen miles upriver from Fort Randall. The report said that men were at work "making a landing for steamboats, laying out a new road to Fort Randall, in fact getting ready for winter." The correspondent predicted that in one year "you may expect to find a flourishing village with [a] church, school, stores, etc."[10]

It was a prediction that fell flat, for the fledgling community never qualified as a "city," although it boasted a post office, a steamboat landing, a few merchants, and a Chinese restaurant. It was also home to "three lady discards from Sioux City."[11] So instead of becoming a tame, respectable town with a school and churches, Harney City gained a reputation as a "famous gambling and whiskey resort," where spontaneous acts of debauchery and violence were the norm. Historian George W. Kingsbury called it the "wildest frontier town in the country."[12]

Harney City's "leading citizen," William T. McKay, was described as an intelligent and shrewd man but unscrupulous and without a conscience. A fellow frontiersman recalled that McKay was "an experienced prospector from the gold regions of California."[13] He had at least one brush with the law prior to his alleged involvement in the Snake Creek lynching, when he was indicted for "introducing spirituous liquors into Indian country."[14] In April of 1872, McKay was tried before Judge W.W. Brookings. His partner in crime, Lewis Obeshaw, was a defense witness and as a result, McKay was acquitted.[15]

McKay's saloon in Harney City was dug into the side of a hill and aptly called Rattlesnake Den. Notorious for shootings and fights, it gave rattlesnakes a bad name. Not long after they opened, McKay's partner, Obeshaw, left the business.[16] At least one shooting incident at McKay's place made the newspapers. In August of 1870, following a quarrel between Martin Markham and the Bordeaux brothers, Markham was shot and killed by one of the brothers. The trouble started over a dice game when Markham accused the brothers "about their being half-breeds." After a scuffle with one of the brothers, Markham went for a Sharp's rifle located behind the bar. But before he could arm himself, the Bordeaux brothers shot him in the head, killing him. Following an examination, the brothers were released.[17]

Regarding other suspects arrested in connection with the double lynching, Jim Somers' outlaw exploits were chronicled earlier (see Chapter 2). Avoiding trouble was never a priority for Somers and on one occasion he found it in the person of Henry Hyer. Hyer tried to kill Somers after an argument ensued while the two men played cards at Napoleon's saloon in March of 1872. Hyer pulled his pistol and aimed it at Somers. But as luck would have it, a third man, Henry Tompkins, stepped between Hyer and his intended target at the very moment Hyer pulled the trigger and thereby "received its contents." Tompkins died on the spot.[18]

Somers' Snake Creek companions, Kinkaid and Sully, came to Dakota in the 1860s and were by reputation outlaws who roamed the Missouri River country. They were reputed to be members of a gang of horse thieves called the Pony Boys. Sully's outlaw credentials were tempered somewhat by the belief that he never stole from the poor and that he gave candy to children.[19] Jack Sully eventually found himself before Judge Shannon on a charge of larceny in the fall of 1874. But he was discharged after the prosecution pleaded *nolle prosequi,* a Latin phrase meaning the prosecutor had no evidence and was throwing in the towel.[20]

William Cunningham had served as a county commissioner of Charles Mix County.[21] George Trimmer and Henry Walker were in trouble with the law following the time of their alleged involvement in the double lynching, but not much is known about them. In the May 1873 term of court at the second judicial district, both men were tried for the crime of selling liquor to Indians. Trimmer was found not guilty and in the Walker case the U.S. attorney accepted a *nollo* plea.

After a short hearing during the September 1873 court session, the murder case against Walker and Trimmer, along with McKay and four others, was continued until the March 1874 term of court.[22] They walked out of the Bon Homme County courthouse and returned to their upriver abodes, apparently without ever expecting to be tried for murder.

The March 1874 term of court in Bon Homme came and went without any mention of McKay and company. A short article in the *Springfield Times* merely states that Judge Shannon moved quickly and efficiently through the calendar of cases. The only hint offered about the infamous murder case was a reference to Moody and Spink, known to be the attorneys for the seven murder defendants.[23]

The lack of follow-up reporting about the crime caused the trail of evidence to go cold, leaving the public to accept that the murdered men were Hartert and Hyer. Or were they Holbrough and Hirl? Of interest is that latter-day historians changed the names of the Snake Creek lynching victims to William Holbrough and his hired man Henry Hirl, the latter said to have been a member of the Pony Boys Gang who quit because of an unfair distribution of profits from their criminal enterprises.[24]

As further proof that the mob hanged Hirl, and not Hyer, the Yankton court calendar for the spring of 1874 lists among its cases the matter of the U.S. vs. Henry Hyer. He was charged with larceny and conspiracy.[25] Unless there were two men by the name of Henry Hyer in Dakota, which seems unlikely, the man lynched with Holbrough was Henry Hirl.

The authors of "A Short History of Brule County," published by the South Dakota State Historical Society in 1947, claim that Holbrough was erroneously identified as Hartert by a Yankton newspaper. The essay goes on to describe Holbrough and his wife as "thrifty Germans and considered honest." He was known as the "Dutchman," who established a roadhouse in the hill country of Charles Mix County near Snake Creek and within sight of the Bijou Hills. Holbrough was aware of the presence of horse thieves in the area and on more than one occasion reported the thieves' activities and their whereabouts to the authorities in Yankton. He was promised that the matter would be investigated.[26]

Holbrough had been involved in erecting cedar poles for the telegraph line that was being extended west from Yankton to Fort Sully in 1872. According to Fred Kaufman's historical novel, based on a journal kept by Kaufman's father, Holbrough was hanged by the Pony Boys, making use of a telegraph pole, thereby adding an ironic twist to the tragedy. Rarely, if ever, in the annals of the frontier, has any man unwittingly constructed the gallows from which he was later hanged.

While the weight of evidence points to Holbrough and Hirl as the victims of the double lynching, a footnote to "A History of Dakota," by William W. Blackburn, in the *South Dakota Historical Collections*, suggests otherwise. This footnote indicates that William F. (not T.) McKay was a "leader of a vigilante committee that hung a young German named Burckman and his partner in 1871." This hanging took place on Pratt Creek, near Fort Thompson, a considerable distance from Snake Creek in Charles Mix County. The date, names, and location of the mob-inspired crime, as revealed in the footnote, are evidence that the writer was very confused, combining elements of two separate hangings, both of which were blamed on McKay and his cohorts, including "Joseph" Somers.[27]

There is, however, some corroboration for the Pratt Creek hanging. On a winter ride through the upper country in late 1873, a stagecoach driver pointed out to his passengers two telegraph poles near Fort Thompson, a considerable distance up the Missouri River from Snake Creek, that a party of stranglers employed to hang a couple of horse thieves.[28]

To add to the confusion, the *Atlas of Charles Mix County,* published in 1906, states that on January 20, 1873, the county commissioners appointed William Holbrough to fill a county vacancy, namely superintendent of schools. The same atlas also states that on September 6, 1873, Holbrough was appointed "collector and sheriff" but does not mention the Snake Creek lynching.[29] This omission suggests that the compilers thought the incident unworthy of mention, or that they were engaged in a cover up of an incident that brought shame on the county and upon those who did not wish to be reminded of the hanging of two innocent men. But then not only was Holbrough not hanged, but he was a versatile fellow to hold so many offices—and therefore his dedication to duty is noteworthy.

This writer concludes that William Holbrough was not an outlaw but a victim of the Snake Creek lynching, along with Henry Hirl. Rancher Holbrough and his wife had lived in fear of the secretive Pony Boys, a shadowy band of outlaws that included McKay, Somers, and Sully. It was said that the gang was under the leadership of the notorious Doc Middleton, from the Niobrara Valley in Nebraska. This is untrue, for in 1872 Middleton was just starting his outlaw career in Texas and would not relocate for a few years to Nebraska and Dakota, where he would become a horse thief.

Although Middleton was not part of the gang, the Holbroughs knew who the outlaws were and what they were doing when they rode down from the hills and out of the deep ravines, places made for hiding stolen horses. In short, the Holbroughs knew too much and it cost them dearly.

Holbrough was fully acquainted with McKay as both men had served in the territorial legislature from Charles Mix County. They were thoroughly caught up in the ugly carnival of Dakota politics. A South Dakota state legislature website reveals that Holbrough was born in 1847. He probably came to Dakota in the late 1860s. In 1870 Holbrough and McKay were delegates from Charles Mix County at the Republican territorial convention in Vermillion.[30] Holbrough was elected to the territorial House of Representatives from Greenwood, Charles Mix County, in 1870.

In 1870 McKay was elected to the territorial council from Charles Mix County. In May of 1872 he was a delegate from Charles Mix County to the territorial Republican Convention held in Canton.[31] In the fall of the same year, when he was allegedly involved in the hanging of a fellow member of the legislature, McKay was re-elected to the council. He was present when the legislature convened on December 4, 1872, but not for long, because McKay's seat was challenged by J. D. Flick, also of Charles Mix County, who after a contest was declared the winner.[32]

Although kicked out of the legislature, McKay decided to spend the holidays in Yankton instead of at his place of business on the Missouri River. On December 25, 1872, the *Press* reported that "Hon. W. T. McKay" was the headliner at a "Matinee," meaning a poker game at Wambole's saloon. McKay and a character known as French George were the "principal actors" in the drama, and when George won a pot worth $15, an argument broke out. McKay insulted George by "slapping his face with a pair of old drawers." George answered that insult by striking McKay, causing McKay to draw his derringer and strike his opponent, further angering George who went after McKay with a pocket knife, cutting him on the face and shoulder "in a very careless manner." No one was arrested.[33]

It may seem odd that a man who served as a lawmaker would carry on in such a lawless manner. More unusual is that such a man could put on a mask and behave like a marauder. But Billy McKay seemed to be able to cross that line at will and without pangs of conscience.

How could any man who operated a business that catered to men of violence get voted into office? The answer is that a group of border ruffians called the LaMonte organization of Charles Mix County put him in office. This obscure frontier political cartel took its name from Colin LaMonte, who directed the group's activities in his role as county register of deeds. In the 1860s and early 1870s, the organization directed or rigged elections to make sure the "right" men were voted into office. This included the "election" of outlaw Jack Sully as sheriff of Charles Mix County in 1872.[34] With 55 citizens voting, he won by a score of 61 to 1.[35]

Born at Fort Snelling, Minnesota, Colin LaMonte first came to Dakota in 1840 in the employ of the American Fur Company at Fort Pierre. He worked as an army guide and interpreter at Fort Pierre after it was purchased by the U.S. government. When the military abandoned Fort Pierre, LaMonte went to Fort Randall, then under construction. La Monte carried mail from Sioux City to Fort Randall, succeeding despite the hardships of the Dakota winters.[36] He was described as a "quarter blood Indian of French extraction" with a decent education, "modest in disposition," and a man of "sterling integrity."[37]

LaMonte's "sterling integrity" was compromised after he settled in Charles Mix County, where he became lord of his domain. The LaMonte organization operated openly and shamelessly, and their work was subject to very little official or journalistic scrutiny. Men like Moses K. Armstrong and Walter A. Burleigh courted their support because candidates for office wanted votes and were willing to look the other way when it came to voting and counting. LaMonte and his cohorts wielded political influence until Charles Mix County was officially organized in 1879. During all this time LaMonte maintained the position of register of deeds. He and his friends and allies left a legacy of self-interest and corruption along the Missouri River that was accepted behavior in Dakota Territory. Politics, backed up by bribery, threats, and other forms of coercion, were as much a part of the frontier experience as were gamblers, outlaws, and speculators.

CHAPTER 6

THE GANGS OF YANKTON AND THE MURDER OF GENERAL MCCOOK

*In a word, murder is in the atmosphere of Yankton. The air
is full of political and moral corruption and violence.*

Dakota Republican
September 18, 1873

General Edwin S. McCook and Peter P. Wintermute came to Dakota from different places in the East but for similar reasons—to take advantage of opportunities presented by the developing West. Both were educated and ambitious men who brought the remnants of successful careers to the Dakota frontier, and the two men settled into Yankton society as leaders and gentlemen. But McCook and Wintermute fell under the beguiling influence of territorial politics, and they lost their way in a whirlwind of controversy, tragedy, and death.

The general brought celebrity status with him. He was a veteran of the Civil War and a member of the nationally known and famous "Fighting McCooks" of Ohio, a family of heroes whose Civil War exploits were legendary. His father, Daniel McCook, Sr., picked up a gun and served in the army even though he was in his sixties when the war began. Three of his brothers and two cousins earned the rank of general. The four long years of fighting left four members of the family dead from battle wounds, including the elder McCook.

As a reward for his loyalty and proud service, General McCook was appointed by President Grant to the office of Secretary of Dakota Territory. In doing so the president, himself a famous Civil War general, was granting a small favor to a soldier from an Illinois regiment that had served under him in a number of campaigns, including the battles of Belmont, Fort Donelson (where McCook was seriously wounded), and Vicksburg. McCook had been living in Pekin, Illinois, since the war ended.

Edwin S. McCook, Secretary of Dakota Territory, murdered by Peter Wintermute. *Courtesy Wikimedia Commons.*

Edwin S. McCook arrived in Dakota on March 8, 1872, with his wife, Loraine, and their young son, Charles. Although the *Yankton Press* had expressed hope that an actual resident of Dakota would be chosen to be its new secretary, General McCook was looked upon with favor. His Civil War record, augmented by the heroics of his family, rendered him "honorable and decidedly creditable." Extending a warm welcome to the new secretary, the *Press* predicted, "he will fulfill his official duties to the satisfaction of the people, and with credit to himself."[1]

The general, who had just turned thirty-five, was a tall, broad-shouldered man who appeared even larger in his army uniform, which he wore with pride and honor. The Union blue was a powerful projection of his Civil War experiences. The West was filling up with veterans, but none quite like a McCook. During the war the McCooks were newsmakers, often rash and controversial, and after it ended they continued to seek the limelight. When he was about to take office as the new territorial secretary, he wanted to make certain that everyone recognized him as "General" McCook. Having drunk from the cup of ambition, he could not deny himself another serving.

With supreme confidence and celebrity status, General McCook charmed and overwhelmed the city of Yankton with his poise and gracious manner. America was in the mood to honor its Civil War heroes and Edwin S. McCook was treated with the utmost respect. The *Sioux City Journal* expressed the national sentiment: "Neither the history of our own nor that of any other country can surpass the renown of this heroic [McCook] family."[2]

Peter P. Wintermute was born in 1833 in Orange County, New York, to a family with roots in colonial America. At age fourteen Peter enrolled in Genesee College, where for three years he showed unusual talent in mathematics. He transferred to the Rensselaer Polytechnic Institute, one of the leading technical schools in New York State, and at age nineteen graduated as a civil engineer.

Wintermute found his first job as a civil engineer on the Great Western Railway in Canada and then went to work enlarging the Erie Canal. In the spring of 1856 he moved to Wisconsin, where he was employed as the chief engineer for the construction of the Lacrosse and Milwaukee Railway. Following work on another Canadian railroad, he decided to change careers. At age 26, Peter moved to Elmira, New York, where he read law and gained admission to the bar. He gravitated toward travel, however, rather than law practice, especially in the Southern states, with an occasional visit to the West.

Restless and ambitious—and now married—Wintermute moved to St. Paul. In Minnesota, Wintermute's interest turned to buying and selling real estate.[3] He must have been doing well, for in 1864 it was announced that he was planning to build a lavish home on Summit Avenue, a fourteen-room, Italian-style villa, at a cost of $15,000, said to rival anything in St. Paul.[4] But the Wintermutes left St. Paul, and after another stint in Canada, the couple moved to New York City, where Peter continued to work in real estate and railway transactions.[5]

Prospecting for business opportunities, he visited Yankton in 1871, where he was favorably impressed with the new town and its entrepreneurial climate. In August of the same year, he returned to Yankton on the steamer *Esperanza* with his family, with a view to making a home and going into business. The *Yankton Press* welcomed him as the "Hon. P. P. Wintermute from New York."[6]

His plan to open a bank was eagerly reported in the *Press* on September 27, 1871. It was announced that a company had been formed to start a "National Bank" in Yankton, with Peter P. Wintermute as president. Other stockholders included Dr. Walter A. Burleigh and former Dakota governors Andrew. J. Faulk and Newton Edmunds.[7]

The Wintermute family easily rose to the top echelon of Yankton society as Peter began spending his money, gaining influence in the manner of other rich men who flaunted their wealth, all the while gathering admirers and inspiring envy. In 1872 Wintermute built an elegant house for his family in Fowlers Addition.[8] It was a veritable jewel that stood out in stark contrast to the humble dwellings that lined the streets of Yankton. Construction costs were given at $7,000 and the furniture and fixtures were valued at $12,000, including paintings and a piano. It was considered one of the best homes in the city and included quarters for servants and a coachman.[9]

In a remote frontier town, the addition of any new dwelling place was a blessing, but a fine house was like an ornament, a beacon of light shining in the wilderness. Among the visitors at the Wintermute mansion at the corner of Eighth and Green Streets were famed Civil War General Philip H. Sheridan and Fred Grant, son of President U.S. Grant, along with other members of a party touring Dakota Territory.[10]

When the Wintermutes' infant son, George Preston, was baptized in the Episcopal Church, the reception at their elegant home was well attended by Yankton's elite, where guests were treated to a "most sumptuous entertainment."[11] Peter P. Wintermute was fast becoming one of Yankton's leading citizens.

He further ingratiated himself to the community by giving lectures that were open to the public. Literary societies were common in frontier communities as they promoted the dissemination of news and knowledge and were important social gatherings. The territorial newspapers were quick to acknowledge and thank Wintermute and others for imparting their time and expertise for the betterment of the community. The *Dakota Herald* declared, "Mr. Wintermute is an accomplished gentleman, a profound scholar and a man of superior literary culture."[12]

Many Yankton residents believed he had political ambitions, and as every knowledgeable Dakotan knew, politics could stain an otherwise unblemished reputation. There was something convulsive and villainous about Dakota politics and politicians. A man might be respected as a businessman, but vilified for his politics. Entering politics was the quickest way to make fast friends and bitter enemies.

Edwin S. McCook's job as secretary of the territory was largely ceremonial, except when he had to serve as acting governor during John A. Burbank's frequent absences. Having little else to do, McCook traveled frequently in an attempt to learn more about the territory and meet its people. In June 1872 he and his wife were members of a party of fourteen excursionists, equipped with hunting and fishing gear, who traveled to Sioux Falls to view the majestic waterfalls and see other parts of Minnehaha County, including Walled (later, Wall) Lake.[13] In July McCook and his family boarded the steamboat *Western* for a trip up the Missouri River, stopping at Fort Randall before going north to see the site of the Northern Pacific Railroad crossing.[14]

While McCook was in Pittsburgh at a meeting of the National Soldiers and Sailors Convention in September 1872, Wintermute played host to a group of distinguished visitors including Lieutenant General Philip H. Sheridan of Civil War fame and Lieutenant Fred Grant, eldest son of President Grant. The stop in Yankton was part of a tour of the military posts in Dakota. The party arrived by steamboat, was greeted by the governor and other civic leaders, and then taken by carriage to the "elegant mansion" of the Wintermutes for a reception. It was deemed a success, as "Mr. Wintermute and his accomplished lady did the honors with princely hospitality."[15]

Then things began to turn sour for the Wintermutes. In early December of 1872 the Wintermute mansion caught fire and burned down.

The family and the servants were just barely able to escape the flames, while saving very little of their personal treasures. The house whose interior matched "anything in Chicago" was destroyed.[16] It was a terrible loss to the Wintermutes and the Yankton community. Worse yet, it was a prelude to a greater tragedy for the Wintermute family.

Sioux City usually got the first look at new Dakota officials, since they often had to pass through that town before reaching Yankton. In sizing up Secretary McCook, the *Journal* of Sioux City, Iowa, could not resist taking a shot at the politics of Yankton, a rival city. While calling McCook a "man of good practical ability and fine address," the editor hinted at the possibility of future problems by mentioning the "'cliques' that infest the Territory and whose ways have been dark and vain."[17] Of course, the *Journal* felt that as a warm friend of President Grant, McCook would avoid the political snares and quicksand.

In fact, McCook, and Wintermute, too, eagerly plunged into the murky world of Dakota politics with all its temptations and potential rewards. The two men knew each other formally, of course, but they had not become friends because they went separate ways: McCook joined forces with the Capital Street Gang and Wintermute preferred the company of the Broadway Street Gang. Both groups were loud, pushy, and arrogant, and men from other parts of the territory were compelled to choose one side or the other, unless they were Democrats.

Wintermute assumed a leadership role in the business and political affairs of the Broadway Street men. He became a sharp critic of Governor Burbank and when the governor was up for reappointment or removal, Wintermute and others conducted an "indignation meeting" at a private location for the purpose of blasting the chief executive. McCook learned of the secret meeting and made an appearance. He and Wintermute exchanged some unpleasant remarks that only furthered their mutual hatred.[18]

Prior to his arrival in Dakota, McCook had sent a letter to Walter A. Burleigh, along with a copy of a Pekin, Illinois, newspaper. The letter communicated nothing of substance to the doctor and closed with, "Hoping that you may never be taken for a sardine." Burleigh sent the letter on to Burbank with a pithy endorsement. "The enclosed speaks for itself. Take good care of Ed—he will not disappoint you."[19]

Burleigh's recommendation of McCook to the governor was warmly received. Burbank's clique, the Capital Street Gang, became a natural fit for McCook, who, like the governor, was a federally appointed official. A man like McCook, large in size and with military experience, could only benefit Burbank's group. The two men became close and in time the new secretary became a hatchet man for the governor. When charm failed, intimidation was just the ticket.

Among his enemies, Governor Burbank was thought of as a scheming, self-serving man, not at all devoted to his office. This sentiment was shared by a number of Dakotans who were not part of the political landscape, but they did have a voice. They used it rather boldly in 1873 by sending a petition to President Grant, signed by over 1,000 men, demanding that Burbank be replaced.[20]

Grant, however, was unmoved and took no action to replace the governor. Burbank's negatives increased, however, and tended to rub off on his associates, including McCook. McCook found that he was increasingly disliked by much of the public and especially by those who favored the Broadway Street Gang.

Additionally, the *Dakota Herald*, published in Yankton by staunch Democrats, was harsh in its criticism of McCook. While the editors of the *Herald* gleefully picked on all Republicans, in McCook they found one of their favorite targets. They characterized him as "unfit in every respect" to be the secretary of Dakota, calling him an "illiterate boor," an insolent bully, and a drunk. He was "fonder of gazing at the bottom of a glass than he is of the people's interests."[21] When it came to insulting McCook, the *Herald* never seemed to lack for creative ways to harass, calling him a "tumble bug" and a "bellowing demagogue."[22]

Yet McCook had a strong following throughout the territory. In Springfield, L. D. F. Poore, publisher of the *Springfield Times*, was an unabashed admirer of McCook, calling him "prompt, efficient and courteous" and a "most companionable gentleman" who was "never afraid to do his duty."[23] Others in the territory liked him, too. Residents of Big Sioux Station in Union County, along the line of the new railroad, changed the name of their station to McCook to honor the secretary.[24] The town of McCook is still on the map of South Dakota.

In January of 1873, while the legislature was in session, McCook was a party to a brawl with R.F. Pettigrew of Sioux Falls, a Republican allied with G. C. Moody and the Broadway Street Gang. Pettigrew was a bright, young firebrand plagued by fierce political demons and ambitions, and though he had been elected to the legislature in 1872, his seat was contested and he was ousted. But he refused to retreat to Sioux Falls like a beaten man, and the defeat did nothing to dampen his political plans. He stayed in Yankton, and while attending an event at the Capitol building collided with McCook following an argument over seating arrangements.[25] A brief but vigorous fist fight took place in which Pettigrew bested McCook, much to the delight of the *Dakota Herald*, which reported that the fight proved that McCook was an "arrogant braggart and a coward."[26]

The incident only added to the political tension and deepened the chasm between the two rival Republican groups. Nowhere was this great divide more evident than in campaigns, but the ultimate expression of the warring elements was seen, as always, in the election results. The election of 1872 was in some respects a repeat of the election of 1870. The Republicans could not set aside their jealousy and hatred and unite behind a candidate for the office of territorial delegate to Congress. Therefore, in both elections, with the Republican candidates splitting their party's votes, Moses K. Armstrong, a Democrat from Yankton, emerged as the winner of the biggest political prize of all.

Although he served the territory in Congress with credibility and loyalty, no Democrat, including the likeable and talented Armstrong, could have beaten a united Republican machine in post-Civil War Dakota, where the party of Abraham Lincoln dominated in number and popularity. But once again, the Republicans imploded, leaving many wounded careers and sore egos in the carnage and intensifying the hate and anger that flowed in and out of both camps.

The two Yankton Republican newspapers—the *Yankton Press* and the *Union and Dakotaian*—did nothing to break the tension, nor did they attempt to bring the warring factions together. George W. Kingsbury ran the *Press*, which favored the Capital Street Gang, and Arthur Linn's *Union and Dakotaian* was the mouthpiece of the Broadway Street Gang. The rival editors kept busy by contributing to the madness, leveling blasts at each other and fanning the flames of anger and discord. With a blind eye toward reconciliation, the opposing newsmen eagerly and viciously tore an enemy down while building up an ally.

Newspapers from other Dakota towns viewed the spectacle with a mixture of alarm and bemusement. Editors used their columns to chide and criticize "Brother Kingsbury" and "Brother Linn," for their unbrotherly antics. When Minnesota Senator Alexander Ramsey came to Yankton in July 1873, stopping at the Capital Street headquarters of Governor Burbank, no one from Broadway Street stopped by to greet the visiting dignitary. The editor of the *Dakota Republican* in Vermillion spotted the insult and lambasted both groups, saying "no wonder that the politics of Dakota is . . . a laughing stock all over the land."[27]

Since 1873 was an "off" year (no election), there would be no nasty campaigning and therefore no slanderous accusations hurled back and forth by the Yankton politicians and their territorial allies. Newspaper columns would feature articles about crops or territorial prospects, rather than angry tirades. In fact, 1873 was a relatively quiet year, with no reported shootings or murders in southern Dakota.

Yankton and other Dakota towns to the east were becoming accustomed to having a railroad, something to brag about but also a boon to business. It attracted attention right along with visitors. While Bismarck and the newer towns to the north struggled with crime, the capital city of Dakota Territory, it seemed, was moving beyond its outlaw past.

On September 9 members of the St. Paul Chamber of Commerce and a gaggle of Sioux City men were on their way to Yankton, setting off a flurry of activity among the leading men at the capital city. A proper reception was in order and a meeting was convened in the schoolhouse to plan for the arrival of the visitors. Ex-governor Newton Edmunds opened the proceedings. P. P. Wintermute was to serve on the Committee of Arrangements and Edwin S. McCook on the Committee of Ways and Means as well as taking on responsibility for music and a salute. The guests were scheduled to arrive at 1 p.m. on the 10th and attorney Bartlett Tripp was prepared to deliver a welcoming address at the depot. This was a chance to show off Yankton—and its new railroad—at its best and every effort was put forth to succeed. The citizens of Yankton believed that it was imperative that there be unity on this occasion.[28]

There was one obvious blemish on Yankton's happy face. The Dakota Southern Railroad and Yankton County managed to find themselves on opposite sides of a lawsuit. It was decided, therefore, that a meeting of Yankton's citizens was necessary to discuss the pending litigation and to explore an out-of-court settlement. While the reception for the visiting dignitaries from St. Paul and Sioux City was cordial and dignified, the mood over the railroad controversy was tense and ugly.

The railroad meeting was held on the evening of September 11 in the courtroom on the second floor of the Morrison block, adjacent to the St. Charles Hotel. The hotel was either "one of the best hotels west of Chicago"[29] or as an army officer called it, a "slovenly outrage they call a hotel."[30] Although notorious for bed bugs, it was fairly new and the pride of Yankton. The St. Charles was also the headquarters of the Capital Street Gang.

The railroad meeting was well-attended, drawing in most of the leading men of Yankton, including McCook and Wintermute, all of whom had a stake in the outcome of the lawsuit. Provocative speeches were made by W. W. Brookings, S. L. Spink and others. At some point Wintermute interjected angrily with a motion that the "meeting had no confidence in the railroad company." To all appearances sober when he spoke, Wintermute then left the meeting, brushing past McCook, and the two men exchanged "rather harsh words."

Not long after the angry exchange, both men showed up at the bar in the basement of the St. Charles Hotel, where more argumentative conversation took place concerning Wintermute's request that McCook give him money for a cigar. To the denial of that request, Wintermute threatened to whip McCook—and if he could not do that, he would shoot him. This insolence was more than McCook could bear. The former general grabbed the much smaller Wintermute and roughed him up. Governor Burbank pulled McCook away and the two left the bar.

Wintermute also departed, cleaned himself up, and still fuming went back to the railroad meeting, his face showing evidence of a beating. While Dr. Walter A. Burleigh was speaking, Wintermute shouted, "I have been licked out of my boots by General McCook . . . and I've got this to show for it," gesturing to his face. No one paid particular attention to Wintermute, even though he told a man standing near him that he would shoot McCook on sight.[31]

James C. Moody was a small boy of three or four years old when he entered the meeting room with his father, lawyer G. C. Moody, the two having taken an evening stroll. Young James was placed in the care of a "big Englishman near the door," while his father went into the hall to inquire about a "pending motion." The elder Moody was talking when little James saw the "slim, consumptive" Wintermute enter and sit down on a chair "where he kept an eye on the door."[32]

S. L. Spink was speaking to the gathering emitting both cheers and hisses when McCook entered the courtroom. Upon seeing McCook walk in, Wintermute stepped forward with a pistol in his hand and fired at McCook, who stood just a short distance away. McCook was not hit but the shot unleashed pandemonium among the crowd, many of whom were worked up by alcohol and fiery speeches. Justice of the Peace Charles F. Rossteuscher sprang toward Wintermute in an attempt to disarm and arrest him. Suddenly, McCook charged into Wintermute and the two men grappled. At least three more shots were fired during the struggle, one of which hit McCook. In a state of excitement, men tried to intervene as chairs were scattered and a stove was toppled. J. R. Hanson managed to get his hands on Wintermute's pistol and wrest it away.[33] It was later identified as a Smith & Wesson revolver.[34]

Badly wounded and bleeding profusely, the stricken McCook continued to fight. He seemed to possess superhuman strength, and at one point attempted to throw Wintermute out of a second-story window. During the brief struggle, voices pleaded with McCook to stop, but he replied, "No, don't you see I am shot!" Soon after the effects of the wound had weakened the general, the two men, covered in McCook's blood, were separated.

Wintermute was arrested and taken away to a room in the Merchants Hotel and held under lock and key while a mortally wounded McCook was carried to his room in the St. Charles Hotel. There he was examined by Dr. Burleigh, who had hurried to the hotel. The doctor determined that a single bullet had struck McCook in the left rib cage, then severed the subclavian vein and artery before exiting his body through the shoulder.[35] Burleigh told the secretary that the wound was fatal. Several hours later, as his blood dripped through the mattress onto the floor, General Edwin S. McCook died in the presence of his wife, his son, and the doctors who attended him. It was a courageous death by all accounts, as he declared that he would die like a soldier—like a McCook—and that "my accounts will be found correct and straight."[36] The next day, Governor Burbank sent a terse dispatch to President Grant in Washington, D.C.: "Gen. Edwin S. McCook was assassinated last night in a public meeting by P. P. Wintermute, banker at this place."[37]

As a public figure, McCook's death was deemed an assassination, not merely a homicide. By the time the *Yankton Press* published a detailed report of the tragedy, the telegraph had already transmitted the news across the United States, setting off shockwaves of disbelief and anger. Just when Yankton had achieved an air of respectability, the town was once again branded an outlaw community. George Kingsbury of the Press, sadly and accurately, expressed the sense of horror and shame that was Yankton's fate to endure: "A pistol shot has gained for Yankton a notoriety greater and more widespread, than could have been achieved in years through ordinary course of events."[38]

The body of General Edwin S. McCook, dressed in his uniform, was placed in a hermitically sealed casket ordered from Sioux City and sent home to Ohio on a special train from Yankton, a city draped in mourning and buzzing with excitement over the assassination. Governor Burbank and other officials accompanied the body and the grieving widow to Cincinnati, where McCook was buried at Spring Grove Cemetery, next to his father and brothers.

Outraged, many Yankton citizens talked of lynching Wintermute. One rumor that circulated was that Dr. Burleigh, of all people, was gathering a lynch mob. Justice Rossteuscher deputized four men to stand guard at Wintermute's house to prevent this. Within a short time, however, calm settled over Yankton, and townspeople seemed willing to let the law take its course, believing Wintermute would be executed.

Yet everyone wanted to know why a respected member of the community would kill, in apparent cold blood, another upright citizen at a public gathering. The *Clay County Register* blamed intoxication because both parties were drinking. Without excusing drunken conduct, the article in the *Register* blamed "bad blood" caused by "worse whiskey."[39]

The *Yankton Press* was not of the same opinion. But the *Press* was quick to clear up one lingering theory: that the railroad meeting was the trigger. Kingsbury pointed out that the shooting was not "the sequel of the railroad and county difficulty." Rather it stemmed from politics. The "unfriendly feeling between the parties . . . dates back to last winter commencing in Washington," which led to a confrontational meeting the following spring in Yankton. Kingsbury reasoned that after McCook roughed up Wintermute, the banker felt he had no choice but to retaliate by playing the role of assassin.[40]

The *Dakota Republican* saw far more sinister forces at work. The shooting was not an isolated incident, or a crime of passion. Rather, it was part of a series of inter-connected events, deep and complex, with the potential for further violence. Corrupt men headquartered at Yankton, so long engaged in bitter political feuding, had brought scandal and shame upon Dakota Territory. Throughout America, Dakota, and especially Yankton, was seen as hopelessly mired in dirty politics. With roots deep in territorial history, the strain of corruption was likened to a fatal disease with only one cure—remove the capital from Yankton. Calling for capital removal, and an end to political quarrels "with murder in them," the *Republican* made an appeal to all Dakotans to reject the "shabby handful of men at Yankton," who had held power for far too long.[41]

The *Sioux City Journal* took an editorial stance that made the Dakota newspapers seem restrained by comparison. In anger and indignation, the *Journal* called for the immediate lynching of Wintermute. "In former days murderers of the Wintermute stamp received summary punishment at the end of the hangman's rope." Due process was a "mawkish" waste of time, roared the editorial—there was no "escape from the death penalty."[42]

The Dakotans who held Wintermute's fate in their hands waved off the ranting of their neighbor to the east and went about the business of dispensing judgment. The immediate problem, of course, was the disposition of Wintermute, now a prisoner in the federal jail on Walnut Street in Yankton. He waived a preliminary examination and was charged with murder. He was returned to jail to await a territorial grand jury investigation in October. Judge Peter C. Shannon had been on an extended visit to eastern and northern Dakota and western Minnesota at the time of the shooting and did not return to Yankton until October 10, 1873.[43] Judge A. H. Barnes, still presiding in the second district, was therefore in charge of the case.

At the time the Wintermute case was entering the judicial system, a financial panic was gripping the nation. In New York, the failure of the banking house of Jay Cooke and Company, which was heavily invested in railroad construction, along with the bankruptcy of nineteen other firms, caused a run on the banks, "a general raid, so to speak."[44] Disaster followed disaster as the failures piled up in rapid succession. Factory production screeched to a halt and the stock market crashed, closing for ten days in an effort to stop the downward spiral. Inspired moralists and preachers saw the hand of a punishing God in the desperate state of affairs. The unprecedented collapse became known as the "Panic of 1873" and was the beginning of several years of severe economic depression, civil unrest, high unemployment, and widespread suffering. While those who had the least were destined to suffer the most, stunned capitalists and entrepreneurs were forced to face the smoldering debris of a once-thriving economy.

Whether this panic affected Wintermute's banking business is conjecture. What is known is that Wintermute was a rich man who would likely use his money and influence to fight conviction. His legal team included G. C. Moody, S. L. Spink, and William Tripp. Along with his brother Bartlett, William Tripp was one of the best criminal defense attorneys in Dakota. The prosecution party consisted of county attorney Philip K. Faulk, the one-armed Civil War veteran, and attorneys H. A. Copeland and George H. Hand.[45]

A grand jury met in October, and after a week of deliberation, returned an indictment for manslaughter, meaning a conviction would not result in the death penalty. Wintermute, no doubt relieved, was set free after posting bond in the amount of $50,000. He was at liberty until the March 1874 session of court, at which time Chief Justice Peter C. Shannon would be presiding at the second district.

While the *Press* reported the manslaughter indictment without comment, it was greeted with outrage in other parts of the territory. The *Springfield Times* issued a scathing indictment of its own—against the grand jury for committing an "outrage on justice" and a "crime within itself." The enraged *Times* editor declared, "The whole world knows Wintermute murdered McCook . . . deliberately and with malice aforethought." He excoriated the jurors for "torturing murder into manslaughter" and warned that their ungodly act placed their souls in peril.[46]

One scorching editorial was insufficient to express the rage that the *Times* felt over the action of the grand jury. An editorial in the *St. Paul Press* was included in the columns of the Times—just one of "hundreds that have been published condemning . . . the jury," which acted in a manner "without parallel in all history." The St. Paul paper suggested that the grand jury reached its decision with "the assistance of the prisoner's counsel, with whom they are said to have been in free communication." Lashing out at Dakota justice, the *St. Paul Press* declared that the grand jury's decision about "Wintermute's desperate crime will endanger life and property in Dakota" and "encourage desperadoes."[47]

Wintermute was not a desperado, but the case stirred the blood of Dakotans far more vigorously than had previous events. Dakotans were accustomed to brawlings, shootings, and other incidents of violence, usually involving strangers. Since both Wintermute and McCook were prominent citizens, the shooting constituted a personal affront.

CHAPTER 7

THE PEOPLE VS. PETER WINTERMUTE, BANKER AND ASSASSIN

My province is, to the best of my judgment, and in the solemn performance of my duty, to give you [the jury] the law of this Territory as I solemnly believe it to be.

Peter C. Shannon
Chief Justice, Supreme Court of D.T.
June 2, 1874

While Dakota Territory and the nation waited for the Wintemute trial to begin, two startling events of great interest and importance occurred. First, the *Yankton Press* announced that it had merged with the *Union and Dakotaian*, resulting in the publication of the *Press and Dakotaian*. In the final edition of the *Press,* on November 12, 1873, the publisher stated that the entire community was in favor of combining the two newspapers, which should be seen as bringing to an end the great political division that had for so long plagued the Republican Party in the territory. Arthur Linn of the *Union and Dakotaian* was in accord. He agreed to the merger "because we find the chance to unite all Republicans . . . in one common cause."[1]

Second, Governor John A. Burbank resigned his office and left Dakota. At the time of the newspaper merger, Burbank was in Hot Springs, Arkansas, on a "protracted stay."[2] Just before leaving for Hot Springs, he issued a proclamation creating federal courts in Fargo and Bismarck in accordance with power vested in the chief executive by the Organic Act.[3] Creating courts in two fast growing northern Dakota towns was one of his last official acts.

On December 9, 1873, a telegram from Washington arrived in Yankton with news that Burbank had resigned. He had grown increasingly unpopular with the people and therefore left office under pressure from the public. Burbank had, over time, been criticized for spending too much time away from Dakota and for using his office for personal gain.

The Clay County town of Green Point, on the Dakota Southern Railroad, was renamed "Burbank City" after the governor.[4] Burbank was also instrumental in promoting the town of Springfield in Bon Homme County, where he held property. Originally named Wanari, meaning "enchanted ground,"[5] Springfield was treated like a stepchild by resentful Yankton men who were heavily invested in the town of Bon Homme. They stood to lose out to Burbank's new town—a "paper city of seven steeples and three railroads." Burbank was accused of secretly plotting to move the territorial capital to Springfield.[6]

While Burbank had some allies, he made enemies at a pace that exceeded all other federally appointed officials. As a measure of his unpopularity in Dakota, there is an old story about the time a group of men, led by Jacob Baruch, came up with a plan to banish Burbank. He was ushered to the banks of the Missouri River and placed on an unworthy "skiff with orders to leave Dakota and never again set foot upon the soil." The rabble rousers even made him pay for the skiff. According to the story, the sullen governor floated across to Nebraska and escaped to Sioux City, where he remained until the anger died down.[7] Upon learning the good news of Burbank's resignation, the new *Press and Dakotaian* declared that the honor of being the next Dakota governor should be bestowed on the respected and able Peter C. Shannon. But President Grant appointed John L. Pennington, a North Carolinian living in Alabama at the time.

The men in charge of the *Press and Dakotaian* swallowed the bitter pill and wished him well. They were forced to admit that the new governor possessed an "agreeable address" and was "qualified to fill the position."[8] Pennington and his family arrived in Yankton, without fanfare, on January 20, 1874, a frosty greeting to an incoming carpetbagger replacing an outgoing carpetbagger.

Since most Dakotans were glad to be rid of Burbank, they could not have been displeased to learn that while he was a passenger on a stagecoach in Arkansas, a band of five masked outlaws stopped the stage near Hot Springs and robbed it, including the passengers. Burbank was forced "to part with a valuable gold watch, a diamond breast pin," and about $800 in cash.[9] The "ringleader" of the gang questioned the passengers carefully, asking for names, professions, and traveling plans. He threatened to shoot Burbank, thinking the ex-governor was a detective. No one, however, was harmed.[10]

In a letter from Hot Springs, Arkansas, to Clarence Van Tassel of Yankton, Burbank said the thieves took his "watch, chain and the last cent I had with me, amounting to $860." He arrived at his destination, he wrote, "without even a nickel."[11] Burbank had left Dakota but could not quite escape the Wild West.

Years later, news came to Yankton that Burbank's watch was recovered from the possessions of Jesse James, the "noted outlaw" and desperado killed by Robert Ford on April 3, 1882. Burbank was living in Richmond, Indiana, when he received a telegram from the sheriff in St. Joseph, Missouri, informing him that during the examination of Jesse James' body, a watch inscribed with Burbank's name was found.[12] Burbank received his watch and his breast pin, too, but was never able to redeem himself among the people of Dakota.[13] Nor were they willing to forget about him, for the town of Burbank City was for many years referred to as "Morton's Brother-in-Law."[14] This was a tongue-in-cheek reminder that the unpopular and scheming former governor got his Dakota appointment through the influence of his powerful brother-in-law, Senator Oliver P. Morton of Indiana.

The departure of Burbank and the merger of the two Yankton newspapers were understood as signaling the end of the bitter political feuding among Republicans and a harbinger of better relations—and election results—in the future. Many felt that constant rancor and hateful rhetoric had reached a terrible climax in the killing of McCook. Guilty and fearful minds realized it was time for a change, not only to win elections but restore peace to the territory, too long subjected to the ravages of partisan politics. This renewed emphasis on cooperation among the Dakota Republicans was bad news for the Democratic Party, assigned to a perpetual and powerless minority.

The focus soon returned to the Wintermute case. The judiciary, the bar, the press, and the entire community realized they had a duty to perform. The celebrity murder had shocked the nation, but the people of Yankton sensed a chance to redeem themselves and their community with proper judicial action. While some would have eagerly participated in lynching Wintermute, the majority was ruled by the notion of fair play and the desire to see justice done. Free on bond, Wintermute traveled to New York City in February 1874 to arrange his business affairs, as he too was eager to get on with the trial.[15]

On March 4, 1874, the Yankton County attorney, Philip K. Faulk, moved the district court for a new grand jury, arguing that the original grand jury had proceeded under a law that was repealed. The outdated law referred to by Faulk was from the criminal code passed by the legislature of 1862-63, which had been superseded by subsequent legislation. Judge Shannon sided with the prosecution. In his written opinion, Shannon stated that all acts of the first grand jury were void as it had been "improperly empanneled [sic]." He ordered that Wintermute be returned to jail. The banker complied but he was freed on a $35,000 bond to await the decision of a new grand jury and the renewed possibility that he might eventually be hanged.[16]

The new grand jury was sworn in on April 29, and after receiving instructions from Judge Shannon to speak to no one about the case, was dismissed. The following morning the grand jury reconvened and received a lengthy set of instructions and a stern lecture from the judge on the importance of the work to be conducted under oath and in strict compliance with the law. The jurymen would hear evidence from the prosecution only, and from that evidence alone, they would reach a decision as to whether Wintermute would be charged with a crime, and if so, what crime.

Judge Shannon took extra care and time to instruct the grand jury, knowing that in the past a lackadaisical attitude and a failure to follow the law had resulted in many poorly adopted indictments.[17] Dakota was the site of a homicide case that had attracted national attention so public scrutiny would be intense. It would be Shannon's first, big test as a territorial judge. He did not want to embarrass himself or the Dakota judiciary, and most important, he wanted Wintermute to get a fair trial.

The deliberation with which the grand jury worked indicated that Shannon had struck the right chord. After asking for and receiving further instructions from the court, the grand jury returned with an indictment for murder. As there was no bail for a defendant charged with such a heinous crime, Wintermute was committed to jail to await trial.

The spring term of court for the second district, with Judge Peter C. Shannon presiding, featured a rather lengthy calendar. Before he was required to devote all his energy and attention to the Wintermute case, Shannon dealt with a long list of other matters, including another round with Cuthbert DuCharme, aka Papineau, from the upriver country. The usual suspect was tried for the usual sort of crime: "dealing in liquor without a license." He was acquitted by a jury—again.[18] Papineau returned to his "bottom" to celebrate with the boys, while the judge turned his attention to what promised to be one of the most celebrated murder cases in the West.

G. C. Moody, Associate Justice, Dakota Territory Supreme Court.
Courtesy History of Dakota Territory, *by George W. Kingsbury*
(Chicago: S. J. Clarke Publishing Co., 1915).

The trial of Peter P. Wintermute for the murder of Edwin S. McCook commenced on May 14, 1874. Representing the people were Yankton County attorney, Philip K. Faulk, George H. Hand, and Jason B. Brown, the secretary of Wyoming Territory, whose expertise and experience made him an invaluable member of the government's team. The defense coterie of eight attorneys included G. C. Moody, S. L. Spink, William and Bartlett

Tripp, N. J. Cramer from Yankton, and Leonard Swett, a hired gun in the form of a nationally known attorney from Illinois. Spink and William Tripp were also witnesses who gave testimony at the trial.

Swett had been a friend and colleague of the late Abraham Lincoln. During the 1850s the two lawyers rode the circuit in Illinois, making appearances in the various county courts. In 1865, following the president's assassination, Swett moved to Chicago to set up a law practice. He acquired a reputation among the public and press for his exceptional skill in successfully representing defendants in murder cases. Swett rarely lost a case.[19]

As a result of a motion made by Moody for the defense, John Gray, a professional stenographer from Chicago, was appointed to be the reporter for the trial proceedings. Moody and Swett urged the court to order the appointment "as a means of expediting the business of the court, shortening the trial and saving great expense to the county."[20] The judge agreed.

Jury selection was the next item on the agenda and it took three full days, because many of the men on the panel had formed opinions as to guilt or innocence. With both sides looking for an edge, men who indicated the slightest prejudice or favoritism were subjected to challenges and then excused.

The following men were selected to serve on the jury: Hiram G. Derby, James Connell, Emory P. Truesdale, John A. Haas, Jonathan Reiner, George Shearer, Willis Arnold, Iver Bagstadt, Charles Van Epps, Olus L. Grimsrud, Thomas Royster, and William Ingraham. The *Press and Dakotaian* called them "substantial, intelligent men of property" and of "grave and sober demeanor." All were farmers except Grimsrud, who was a saloon keeper, and Arnold, who operated a meat market. The jurymen were lauded for having avoided poisonous contact with either of the two political factions in Yankton. When they were not in the jury box, they were sequestered in rooms over Stone's Hall, opposite the courthouse.[21]

The first day of testimony was Monday, May 18. Among those in attendance at court was George W. McCook of Ohio, the older brother of the deceased secretary. Also present was the late Edwin S. McCook's father-in-law (and new territorial secretary), Oscar A. Whitney, Governor John L. Pennington, the wife, son, and father of the defendant, and about "a dozen lady spectators." Following an opening statement by Faulk, twenty-six witnesses for the prosecution were sworn in. Since all the witnesses lived in or near Yankton, the government's case was made easier because there was no need to send out deputy marshals on horseback to find and subpoena witnesses in remote parts of the territory.

The prosecution led with Dr. Walter A. Burleigh, who offered testimony about the nature of McCook's wounds and the doctor's treatment of the dying secretary. Burleigh also testified that he heard McCook's dying declaration: "He [Wintermute] shot me down like a dog without giving me a chance to defend myself." Burleigh's testimony was followed by other doctors and then by key eyewitnesses who testified to hearing Wintermute threaten to shoot McCook and to seeing the defendant pull a pistol and fire at the secretary in the courtroom. Burleigh and other prosecution eyewitnesses recalled hearing three or more shots fired in rapid sequence during the chaotic struggle that followed the first shot, although not all of them could swear that they saw Wintermute fire all the shots. Other men offered evidence about the events in the bar at the St. Charles Hotel preceding the shooting.

On May 19 the first order of business was to admit Oliver Shannon, member of the Pennsylvania bar, to the Dakota bar. Then the court got back to the Wintermute trial and the prosecution's case. Charles F. Rossteuscher, justice of the peace, was sworn in and testified that he saw McCook standing in the doorway, looking in at the meeting. Wintermute, his "face bruised and peeled," rose from his chair, advanced toward McCook, and fired a shot. The witness then said that he attempted to arrest Wintermute but was pushed aside by McCook. Rossteuscher testified that a second shot was fired by Wintermute "under my raised left arm." He went on to say that during the struggle, McCook took hold of the muzzle of Wintermute's pistol. The struggling men fell to the floor by the stove.

On cross-examination, Rossteuscher recalled that after the initial struggle, the men were parted, but McCook again fell upon Wintermute, knocking over the stove as they fell to the floor. Wintermute fired another shot and the pistol was taken away from him by J. R. Hanson. They were then separated but McCook, although wounded, refused to quit. He tackled Wintermute, forced him toward the window, knocked out the pane, and was trying to toss him out when the two men were parted for the final time. Rossteuscher then arrested Wintermute.

During the afternoon session, George P. Waldron, after describing the courtroom melee, said that he confronted Wintermute after the arrest by Rossteuscher. Waldron asked, "who fired the shots?" Wintermute replied that he was the shooter. J. R. Hanson testified that he put his foot on Wintermute's arm and took the pistol away from him. Hanson said he kept the pistol, minus the cylinder, in his possession and produced it while he was giving testimony. C. H. Bates, the next prosecution witness, said he picked up the cylinder from the floor and maintained custody until, in the witness chair, he showed it to the court and inserted it in the pistol.

The next day, C. L. Bancroft, a Yankton boot maker, testified that he was in the bar when Wintermute and McCook arrived with their companions. Bancroft swore that he heard Wintermute angrily say to McCook, "If I can't whip you, I can shoot you. By God I will shoot you!" He also saw McCook hit Wintermute, "beat him over the bar," then take him by the collar and throw him "on his hands or knees or elbows on the floor." McCook hit Wintermute two or three more times while taunting, "You'll shoot me, will you!" Then McCook left the bar. It was Bancroft's testimony that the blows to Wintermute by McCook were not as hard as he would have expected to see under the circumstances.

Bancroft went on to testify that Wintermute stayed in the bar and washed his face. He recalled hearing the bartender, William Cowan, suggest that Wintermute go home. But Wintermute was in no mood to simply go home and forget about what happened. Bancroft recalled that Wintermute said he would return to the railroad meeting and break it up, insisting that he had the men to do it. Then, in a reference to the two opposing political groups and their headquarters, Wintermute said this was the worst thing that ever happened to Capital Street, and if McCook ever came over to Broadway Street, he would be shot.[22] Other witnesses gave similar testimony about the activity in the bar.

The prosecution closed its case with the very emotional testimony of McCook's widow, Loraine, and his mother-in-law, Mrs. Oscar Whitney. Both women recalled the secretary's last words, recounting his final moments of life, when he told them that he had been shot by Wintermute and that he was dying. McCook said, "I have seen too many people shot to expect that I will ever get well. I am not afraid to die. I go to my God with clean hands."[23]

The prosecution rested its case on a high note. Furthermore, the team undoubtedly felt confident of success. They had established that Wintermute threatened to kill McCook while in the bar and at the meeting; that Wintermute was waiting in the meeting room for McCook to show up and in a position to see all who entered the room; that when McCook entered, Wintermute approached him with a gun in hand and fired a shot; and finally, that during the struggle between the two men, more shots were fired, one of which proved to be fatal.

The defense team, led by Leonard Swett, had its own array of eyewitnesses, all of whom were men the prosecution decided not to call. Swett began with a meticulous discussion of the law of homicide and then carefully laid out the facts the defense intended to prove. The aim of the defense was to prove that someone other than Wintermute fired the first shot, and that this unknown party therefore set off the excitement, causing the struggle. After that, more shots were fired, which ultimately resulted in the death of McCook. Under this scenario, the killing was the result of self-defense, or at the most, manslaughter. Swett and his allies planned to use the chaos surrounding the shooting to their advantage. They wanted to prove, or suggest, that McCook was armed and therefore Wintermute feared for his life. If they could confuse the jury sufficiently, and raise reasonable doubt, the verdict would not likely be murder.

On May 22 the first witness for the defense was John J. Thompson, a resident of Yankton County since 1860. He testified that Wintermute's "face and cheeks were scarred, his eyes swollen and some blood on his face." Thompson testified that he did not know who fired the first shot, and since the second shot was fired immediately after the first, he declared that in his view no single person could have fired both shots. Then, in a dramatic departure from previous testimony, Thompson said that "McCook was standing in the door way, leaning against the left door jamb, when the second was fired." He stuck to his testimony on cross-examination.

Another witness, A. M. English, a carpenter and builder who had lived in Yankton since 1860, recalled that Wintermute's face was bruised and swollen. He testified that the first shot seemed to come from the hallway and that Wintermute fired the second shot just as McCook was rushing toward him, with both hands up and open. He recalled hearing five shots in all. English did not hear McCook call out that he had been shot by Wintermute but did hear McCook say that he wanted to shoot Wintermute. English said he came to the meeting "from Broadway" with Wintermute, Spink, and H. C. Ash. Like Thompson, his sympathies were with the defendant.

Carl C. P. Meyer, a fourteen-year resident of Yankton was the third defense witness. He remembered seeing Wintermute's badly bruised and swollen face and said that no other person sat between him and the defendant at the railroad meeting. This implied that he was in a position to see anything that Wintermute might do. Then Meyer said, "the first I knew of the shooting was a shot fired from the outside of the room." Next he saw Wintermute stand up and at about the same time saw McCook and

Rossteuscher rush toward the defendant. After that, he recalled that two more shots were fired in rapid sequence and that he saw the blaze from each shot in the darkened room. When McCook seized Wintermute near the stove, "the third shot was fired that killed McCook." He insisted that he heard five shots fired in the courtroom that night. He closed his direct examination by claiming to have had forty years of firearms use and that he was positive that the first shot did not sound like the rest and therefore the shots must have been fired from different guns.

On cross-examination Meyer's testimony crumbled. He said he was an expert in firearms but could not state under oath that he could determine, by the sound of a gun, its caliber or how its sound would be distinct from another gun. Still he insisted that a shot fired in the hall would sound "sharper" than a shot fired in the courtroom. All this meant very little for the defense because Meyer's trial testimony was impeached when he was reminded that at the grand jury hearing he had testified that Wintermute admitted to firing the first shot.

If the defense had been hoping for better results from its next witness, Silas C. F. Norman, they were disappointed. Norman recalled seeing Wintermute stand up and then heard two shots in rapid succession, "spat, spat." McCook closed on Wintermute, Norman continued, and crushed him "down to the floor just like you would crack a bed bug." At that time he heard two more shots and saw a revolver pointed toward him. He said that it might have been in McCook's hand, but it could have been "a wooden imitation of a revolver." Two more shots were then fired, but he could not say who fired them. He testified that he believed a total of six shots were fired.

On cross-examination Norman testified that Wintermute's face was a mess: "I never saw a man's face worse pounded." Unlike previous witnesses, he admitted that Wintermute was very drunk. He also hurt the defense by repeating that Wintermute fired the first shot toward the door, but he was not positive. Norman said that he saw the blaze of one of the shots coming from Wintermute's gun and that one shot sounded "outside the door." He stated that he thought two shots were fired when McCook put his hands on Wintermute and, like Meyer, Norman said that five or six shots were fired.

Norman was pressed by the prosecution about his testimony as it pertained to the sequence and number of shots. The witness seemed confused and said that he heard two at the door and a third when he thought he saw a pistol in McCook's hand. He insisted that Wintermute fired the third shot but he could not state that it hit McCook. The fourth shot was "when they hit the floor." He could not say what happened to McCook's pistol, just that McCook probably "handed it to a friend." He also said that McCook might have fired it two or three times. When asked about whether he was drinking that night, Norman said he had a glass of ale and two beers.

In closing the cross-examination, a prosecutor asked Norman, "Did you tell the bar keeper that you drank 29 glasses of beer that day?" Norman answered, "If I did, I wasn't under oath. I was not under the influence of alcohol at all." Quite likely the defense was glad to see him step down from the witness stand for his jumbled testimony added nothing of value to their case.

Peter Hackney was the surprise witness for the defense, offering the most astonishing testimony of the entire trial. He was from Rushville, Wisconsin, but had lived in Yankton for two years and four months. He had been working on Broadway Street as a carpenter for three or four months prior to the shooting. Known as "English Pete," he attended the railroad meeting and testified that after hearing the first shot he saw McCook, with pistol in hand, enter the room and advance toward Wintermute. He heard shots fired at about the same time and saw a blaze of fire from McCook's pistol. Hackney further testified that he tackled McCook, trying to get the pistol from him. McCook fired a round into the ceiling and then fired a shot that hit Hackney in the right hand. At this point, Hackney "called for assistance" and, after some men responded, he "delivered McCook to them." He said he showed his wounded hand to several men including

Spink. Later, he removed the bullet himself with a jackknife, after returning to Wisconsin.

On cross-examination he answered several questions about his hand wound, then testified that at no time did he see Wintermute with a gun. Wintermute, he said, was on the floor but he had no idea as to how he got there. He did state that McCook had a pistol that looked very much like the one in court that day, and he repeated his direct examination testimony about trying to force the pistol from McCook's hand. He testified to hearing five shots that night, with the fifth one hitting his right hand.

When asked, "English Pete" denied ever saying that he told someone he was willing to help hang Wintermute or that he said his hand wound was caused by a struggle with the defendant. The cross-examiner was attempting to set Hackney up for impeachment through the testimony of other witnesses.

Finally, Henry C. Ash was called to the witness stand. Ash was one of the original Yankton settlers and had built the first hotel on the west side of Broadway Street in 1859. He testified that he was present in the bar in the basement of the St. Charles Hotel, having gone there in the company of Wintermute. Ash watched as McCook brutally beat Wintermute after the latter asked the former for a cigar or money to buy one. Ash said that McCook "knocked him against the wall, breaking a picture, and pounded him on the floor, with his fists, fifteen or twenty times." Ash said that in all his years on the frontier, he had never seen a man beaten so badly.

Testimony resumed on May 23 with witnesses essentially confirming details of the beating and shooting as related by prior witnesses for the defense. Among them was Newton Edmunds, former governor of Dakota. He testified that the audience was restive due to a "violent" speech by Burleigh. He also recalled that "persons in liquor" were noisier than the others in the audience. His son, W. H. Edmunds, followed the ex-governor, and said that the first shot was so close to him that he felt the burn of the powder. When asked on cross-examination if McCook fired the shot, W. H. Edmunds said, "I think not."

On May 24 more witnesses were called by the defense. Dr. Robert Thomas provided testimony about his treatment of Wintermute for several days following September 11, 1873. On the Friday morning following the shooting incident, Thomas said that Wintermute was "half-conscious and stupid from an internal difficulty caused by external injuries. He had a partial concussion or contusion of the brain." Dr. Thomas also testified that he attended the wounded McCook until the general died. The doctor commented on McCook's muscle structure. He said that comparing McCook to Wintermute was like comparing a giant to a pygmy.

On redirect examination the defense asked Dr. Thomas whether Wintermute's injuries, namely the brain concussion, could have excused him from responsibility for shooting McCook. The doctor said that if his "mental faculties were so disturbed by the concussion as to result in this injury, I think he would not be able to discern right from wrong." On re-cross examination, a hypothetical question concerning Wintermute's ability to discern right from wrong was put to the doctor and he answered, with some equivocation, that Wintermute might be able to know right from wrong.

Clearly, the defense was not serious about offering an insanity defense. But their strategy was to show that Wintermute had been beaten so badly that he was either justified in retaliating or that the effects of the beating altered his thinking to the extent that he lacked the capacity to commit premeditated murder. To that end two more doctors testified and the defense called a lay witness, Alexander Hughes, who told of seeing Wintermute in a "stupid" and insensible condition on the day after the shooting.

On May 26 the defense team refocused on "English Pete" Hackney and his injured hand. Witnesses were asked to confirm that they saw Hackney's right hand and that it was bleeding and wrapped. Very little in the way of cross-examination was pursued over this matter. The defense finally rested its case and the prosecution began its rebuttal.

One rebuttal witness, Charles H. Greno, swore that he saw Hackney about ten or twelve days after the shooting. Greno recalled overhearing Hackney say that it was Wintermute that he (Hackney) wrestled with over the gun and that he had an injured hand to show for it. Next John O. Bates was sworn in. He recalled seeing Hackney at the bar in the St. Charles Hotel after the shooting incident. Bates heard Hackney say that he was trying to take the revolver out of Wintermute's hand and that McCook was also trying to take it away. Three other witnesses testified in essentially the same manner. The prosecution had done well with its rebuttal witnesses.

But the defense had one more kick at the cat and they used it in an attempt to shore up the shaky testimony of Peter Hackney. On the 27th the Swett team recalled a number of witnesses who testified that Hackney told them he received the injury to his hand while trying to take a pistol away from McCook. They also called witnesses who vouched for Hackney's good reputation for honesty.

It was at this point that Judge Shannon locked horns with a defense witness. John Lawrence, who had known Hackney for three years, was asked whether he "knew his [Hackney's] general reputation for truth and veracity among the people?" Lawrence gave a fumbling answer and Shannon interjected by saying, "Do you or do you not know his general reputation?" When Lawrence continued to be evasive, Shannon insisted he give a "yes" or "no" answer. But Lawrence was stubborn and would not answer as instructed so Shannon told him to step down. The testimony was stricken. A few other character witnesses did testify that Hackney's reputation in the community was good, and with that both sides rested.[24]

With all the testimony taken, it was up to the attorneys for both sides to argue their case to the jury. On May 28 George H. Hand began the long and tortuous exercise by arguing for the people, delivering an "able and dignified speech." He spoke for two hours and twenty minutes before a large and attentive audience, but it was just the beginning. Next S. L. Spink argued for the defense, speaking an hour longer than Hand. He was followed by Bartlett Tripp, also for the defense, who spoke for an hour and forty minutes. Court was adjourned.

The next day, closing arguments resumed with prosecutor Faulk leading the verbal assault on the weary ears of the jury. He talked for two and one-half hours. Following a break, G. C. Moody countered for the defense, with a speech of three and one-half hours.

On the third day of summations, Saturday, May 30, Leonard Swett, easily the best known attorney on the case, held center stage for seven and one-half hours. Although the sheer volume of words had to strain and tax the jury's ability to concentrate and absorb, a reporter for the *Press and Dakotaian* noted that Swett's argument received "unflagging interest and silent attention." The "eloquence and pathos" flowing from Swett's mind and heart was so overwhelming that it "caused some hearers to give vent to their partisan enthusiasm by an effort to applaud when he closed." But the judge would have none of it, and after a sharp rebuke, the court fell silent.[25]

When Swett was finished with his summation, he spoke quietly to the court audience about Judge Shannon. He said that in all his years as a trial attorney he never experienced greater "fairness, kindness and impartiality displayed by a judge, or a more faithful and conscientious exercise of judicial power" than was shown by Judge Shannon. Following his final words, and to confirm his respect, Swett bowed to the judge.[26]

The jury was sequestered on Sunday and the final arguments recommenced on Monday. Jason B. Brown of Wyoming spoke for six hours for the prosecution with a "logical review of the law and evidence of the case." Judge Shannon adjourned court early because he was not feeling well. It seems that the gravity of the case, the high volume of emotionally charged evidence, and the forceful and passionate arguments of the attorneys for both sides were overwhelming, even for Judge Shannon.

On June 2 Brown resumed his long argument for the prosecution, starting a 9 a.m. and concluding at 11 a.m., consuming a total of eight hours in two days. Amazingly, Brown's marathon summation held the attention of the audience and those who stood outside in the hallway. It was hailed by the *Press and Dakotaian* as a magnificent effort, one of the most "successful ever heard in a western hall of justice; it was not only eloquent but systematic, thorough, and powerfully sustained by facts and authorities."[27]

The emotionally draining trial was, at long last, over and it was time for Judge Shannon to speak to the jury and provide the necessary instructions to use in their deliberations. Like any good judge, he reminded them of their oath. He then carefully and thoughtfully explained the territorial law of homicide in its various forms, including justifiable homicide and manslaughter. The judge explained that a homicide committed after planning and premediation was different than a killing done while in the heat of passion. He stressed that while it was his solemn duty to explain the law, it was solely up to the jury to decide the issue of innocence or guilt. Moreover, it was the sole province of the jury to determine what crime Wintermute committed, if in fact he violated any law at all.

Shannon implored the jury to weigh carefully the evidence and the credibility of the witnesses and to do so without fear or prejudice. Just as he "can pay no heed to the tears of the widow, or the agonizing sobs of the living wife or living children," the members of the jury must set aside all personal views and feelings and do their full duty, though it may cause them torment or loss. Shannon made it clear that there was no higher moral obligation in the law than that of a jury deciding a criminal case where the fate of the defendant hangs in the balance. Driving the point home, Shannon said, "neither you nor I are to look to the right hand nor to the left in the honest pursuit of our duty. This is a place to which corrupt gold shall never enter, into which sympathy shall not come in the performance of our duty; into which even friendship and love are ignored, and justice and the law alone preside." The earth may crumble and the heavens may fall, and all the wreckage may be hurled into the void, but justice and the law will prevail. So sayeth Judge Peter C. Shannon.[28]

After Judge Shannon finished his exhaustive admonitions, the case was placed in the hands of the jury. Twelve men would decide who was telling the truth and who was lying. The verdict was not too long in coming. On June 3 the jury brought back a conviction of manslaughter in the first degree. Wintermute's money was well spent; his defense team had saved him from the gallows. Not long after their verdict, the jury posed for a photograph that was to appear in an eastern publication.[29]

Before the sentencing phase, Shannon went to Sioux Falls to preside over the regular term of court. The stress of the Wintermute trial on the weary judge was evident as he went north to handle the business before the court.[30]

The Minnehaha County calendar of forty-five cases was handled and disposed of in five days, showing that Shannon's mental energy had not been completely drained by the Wintermute trial. The judge's work drew high praise from the *Sioux Falls Independent*. The paper applauded the manner in which the cases were decided, declaring that Shannon's decisions were "well received and on every hand we hear expressions of satisfaction that the judicial affairs of our county have fallen into such able and fearless hands."[31]

As Shannon made the stagecoach trip to Sioux Falls, he was able to survey the damage done by grasshoppers, for the summer of 1874 marked the return of the flying fiends. Clouds of the insects visited Dakota and the surrounding states and territories, eating crops down to the dirt while leaving settlers destitute. The losses were horrendous and staggering, foreshadowing a gaunt and hungry winter for those who chose to stay, or had no choice but to stay, in Dakota. Hundreds of families would need assistance in order to survive and plant a new crop in the spring. Suddenly, Dakota did not seem like a land of promise to the unsuspecting victims of nature's wrath.

But the disaster failed to stop the wheels of justice, and July 1, 1874, was the day set for pronouncing sentence on Peter P. Wintermute, a former banker, now a convicted felon. Judge Shannon began by overruling

Yankton, Dakota Territory, 1875.
Courtesy Yankton County Historical Society.

a defense motion for a new trial. Then in open court the judge ordered Wintermute to stand up and receive his sentence:

> You were indicted for the crime of murder. The jury sworn to try that indictment on your plea came into court on June 3rd and declare you are not guilty of murder but guilty of man- slaughter in the first degree…. It is needless for me to say to a person of your intelligence what the law demands of you. I can say, looking to God for approval, that I have sought to give you a fair trial. If I have erred, you have the Supreme Court for appeal. I could sentence you to be imprisoned for the rest of your life, but my purpose is to be as merciful to you as in my opinion is consistent with justice and the law.

Shannon then sentenced Wintermute to ten years confinement at the Fort Madison, Iowa, penitentiary.[32] Wintermute was escorted to the Yankton jail while his defense team prepared for an appeal. Judge Shannon was not finished with Peter P. Wintermute.

CHAPTER 8

SHOOTINGS, STABBINGS, AND SOLICITINGS, OH, MY!

An affray occurred on Second Street, in this city, on Saturday evening last, which may result in terminating the life of a good citizen of Yankton.

Dakota Herald
June 10, 1873

Yankton struggled throughout the 1870s to mitigate its reputation for violence. Then on July 16, 1874, news of another "shooting affray" captured the public's attention. About two weeks after the sentencing of Peter P. Wintermute, while the Dakota Supreme Court was in session, residents of the capital city were shocked to read in the *Press and Dakotaian* details of another shooting: "another of those sickening and murderous tragedies so plentiful in all parts of the country." The shooter was Daniel Hackenberg, a violent, quarrelsome man with a weary wife and grudges against his neighbors. Hackenberg, about forty years of age, lived north of Yankton near Beaver Creek. He boasted of killing a man in Illinois where he served a term in prison. His wife had filed for a divorce, but she withdrew it and returned to him.

Hackenberg shot and seriously wounded two of his neighbors, Thomas Killbride and Nelson Learned. The shooting was a direct result of a dispute over a patch of meadowland with Killbride and money allegedly owed by Learned. Hackenburg left the area on a stolen horse and easily outdistanced the pursuing sheriff and his posse. His victims survived.

Yankton County Courthouse, 1876.
Courtesy W. H. Over Museum.

The Hackenberg shootings, although shocking, were eventually forgotten as was the shooter. Attention was drawn to the opening of the new courthouse, completed in the capital city in December 1874. It was heralded as "evidence of the prosperity and progress of this portion of the territory of Dakota." The courthouse was a two-story brick building that featured a commodious, well-lit courtroom on the second floor, jury quarters and anterooms, all topped by a tower. The first floor was devoted to county offices while the basement featured "six strongly constructed cells," suggesting that the comedy of the easy jail break was a thing of the past. The entire cost to the county was $10,000 and the *Press and Dakotaian* pronounced it fit for service, a veritable jewel to the community.[1]

The courthouse was designed not only for trials, but for the territorial House and Council where both bodies could take up the noisy business of lawmaking. The Republicans had settled their differences, and with only token resistance from the Democrats were in a position to push through whatever legislation suited the party or its individual members.

An interesting addition to the work of the legislators, and an odd reflection on the Dakota judiciary, came up in the form of a contest between two members of the House of Representatives from the fifth district. One of the contestants, William T. McKay, a veteran legislator, had prior experience in this kind of fight.

McKay had moved to Bismarck in Burleigh County, a rough town on the Northern Pacific Railroad where its residents spent their time "gambling, drinking and shooting."[2] The aggressive and unscrupulous McKay found the environment to his liking and having been elected again to the legislature, the former saloon operator from Harney City was challenged by Edmund Hackett, also of Bismarck, who claimed the same seat in the House.

The roster of House members listed McKay's occupation as a "miner." He was forty-six years old, originally from New York, having resided in Nebraska before coming to Dakota. In politics he was a Republican, and in religion he was "neutral," a stance consistent with his free-spirited nature and proclivity to vice.[3]

Although still under an indictment for his alleged complicity in the 1872 Snake Creek lynching of William Holbrough and Henry Hirl, Billy McKay maintained his popularity among the voters on the Missouri River frontier all the way up to Bismarck. He was on a winning streak, which had begun in the summer of 1874 when McKay was attached to the Black Hills exploratory expedition led by George A. Custer. He and another miner found gold. Success as a miner was probably sufficient in itself to get him elected, but could it keep him elected?

During the early stages of the election contest, when the vote from Burleigh County was being reviewed, the *Dakota Herald* chided the "ironical McKay." The *Herald* reminded its readers that, although McKay was strenuously defending his election to the House, he seemed to be more concerned about "gold in the grassroots in the Black Hills, than the doubtful honors of a Dakota legislator."[4]

McKay won the first round of the contest against Hackett, for on December 7, 1874, the committee on elections' majority report concluded that McKay tallied forty-one more votes. The committee did caution, however, that the register of deeds of Charles Mix County, the notorious Colin LaMonte, was guilty of "gross irregularities." Although the work of the committee was not yet finished, McKay "came forward and was sworn in."[5]

The irrepressible McKay and his fellow mob-members had yet to be tried for murdering the two men at Snake Creek, and doubtless the public had some lingering questions about the lack of prosecution. The election contest did, however, bring the matter under sharp public and newspaper scrutiny. While the committee on elections was trying to determine which votes counted and for whom, so that one of the "two gentlemen from Dakota's uttermost wilds" could take his seat, the law intervened.[6]

With the contest going back and forth, Representative McKay was arrested under an order issued by Judge Shannon for "complicity in the hanging of Hartert [Holbrough] near White Swan, some three years ago," and was taken to the Yankton County jail. The startling article went on to say that "McKay, with a number of others, was indicted for murder, about 18 months since at a term of court in Bon Homme County." Although under arrest, McKay was permitted to attend meetings of the election committee in the company of the sheriff.[7]

After several sessions, vote reviews, and application of statutes and case law precedent, the election committee decided that "W. T. McKay's seat be declared vacant, and that Edmund Hackett be sworn in." This gave the editor of the *Press and Dakotaian* cause to reflect on the entire business, noting "it is a little curious that McKay should have been arrested and placed in jail" when the contest was proceeding and yet released from custody after a decision had been made. The editor made light of the murderous cloud over McKay's head and concluded that "to a man up a tree, it looks as though Mr. McKay's chief offense was that he aspired to a seat in the legislature."[8]

The *Dakota Herald* called it a "Legislative Outrage." In a heated editorial that favored Hackett over McKay, editor Maris Taylor claimed that the former won by a margin of about 150 votes, as acknowledged by the register of deeds in Burleigh and Sully Counties. He slammed McKay for "hunting up returns from wild-cat precincts," while counting on a friendly Republican legislature, including G. C. Moody, speaker of the house, to back his claim. It galled Taylor that McKay, "a man under the custody of the Sheriff, with an indictment pending against him for the perpetuation of the highest crime known to the law—murder" should for one minute occupy a seat in the legislature.[9]

A German newspaper in Yankton, the *Dakota Frie Presse,* was equally angry. Mincing no words, the editor condemned the "Honorable? McKay," reminding his readers that "this pure legislator is indicted as one of the main leaders of the gang who murdered Michael Hartert, a German." The column declared that McKay had up to now avoided arrest and that he sought to use the House seat as a means to "corrupt public opinion in his favor."[10] But the editor was wrong, for the public did not seem to care.

As if the lynching were old news and not worth pursuing, McKay and the rest of his cohorts were never brought to trial. He was eventually handed over to the sheriff of Bon Homme County, who released him from custody.[11] The prosecutor did not act on the indictments and the case was dismissed.[12] There was no public outcry, no indignation meetings over the lack of prosecution. Peter Shannon was a judge, not a prosecutor or an angry moralist, so he did nothing. The matter seemed to die a quiet death, not unlike the way a man lost in the wilderness would perish, his trials of nature and misfortune remaining unknown. The Snake Creek lynching remains a curious and unsolved mystery.

In an esoteric article on justice in Dakota Territory, the *Bismarck Tribune* mentioned that there was an occasion when "nine big strapping fellows" were indicted for murder. Some of the men were prominent

Dakotans and Black Hills promoters. At the arraignment each man was heavily armed and demanded an immediate trial. The judge (not named in the article) ordered the sheriff to disarm the men, but the man with the badge simply said that there were not enough men in the county to do so. Their cases were continued and "have been continued to this day."[13]

A St. Paul newspaper commenting on Dakota's "wide open" days offered another version. On the day of the trial, all of the accused showed up for court in Bon Homme and demanded to be tried. Each man was equipped "with his navy revolver and Bowie knife conspicuously displayed." The show of force was such that both the judge (unnamed) and the prosecuting attorney were unable to work up enough nerve to call the trial.[14]

Neither article mentions the names of the defendants, and each has the ring of a tall tale, but both reveal enough to suggest that whoever wrote them was referring to McKay and his crowd and their brief court appearance in Bon Homme. Whether true or not, it is an appropriate epitaph for the Snake Creek mystery.

Two of McKay's associates, accused of murdering the two men near Snake Creek, were arrested on different charges. In the November 1874 term of court in Yankton, John Kinkaid and John "Jack" Sully were both charged with larceny involving the theft of a mule at the Whetstone Agency.[15]

Of the others implicated in the lynching incident, Jim Somers' outlaw career took an even more surprising turn. When Buffalo County was organized at a mass convention, Somers was nominated as a candidate for sheriff.[16] Amazingly, and without a whimper of protest in the Dakota press, Somers went from being a desperado who shot the sheriff of Yankton County (in 1869) to a good citizen aspiring to become the sheriff of new Buffalo County. Somers was known on the Missouri River for his ability to perform "magic tricks," for example, making a watch disappear down his throat, but the switch from outlaw to sheriff was a sleight-of-hand performance without peer.

In addition to settling the McKay election contest, the legislature of 1874-75 reconfigured the boundaries of the three judicial districts. Under a new law, the first district was altered to include fifteen eastern and southeastern counties along with the Sisseton and Wahpeton Indian reservation on the extreme north end of the district. The third district was changed to include, essentially, all of what eventually became the state of North Dakota, and the second district consisted of the Black Hills and all the counties that were not included in the first and third districts. The law required each judge to reside in the district to which he was assigned, but it also gave the judge the ability to try cases in each of the other judicial districts. Finally, the legislature declared that should a judge be absent from the territory due to sickness or incapacity, one of the other judges must handle the caseload of the absent judge.[17]

Judge Shannon was a man who sought clarity, so he undoubtedly approved of the new law redefining the borders of the judicial districts. But he was never able to get his hands around the baffling Snake Creek crime. There were no indictments, no trial, no justice, but there were killers running free. Clearly, the Dakota system of justice was ailing, and the distinguished judge had not yet found the restorative balm. In his search for a cure, he continued to lecture at his court sessions, as if strong words and a stern demeanor could bring about the desired change. He took up the challenge as if he were the only man who could do so, as if he were the lone sentinel standing between order and chaos.

In a court session at Sioux Falls in October 1874, Shannon spoke to the entire assembly while instructing the jury on the importance of the oath taken by each juryman. The oath was solemn and sacred; it formed an unbreakable commitment between the juryman and the duty he owed to the public. By taking an oath, a man swore to cast aside all forms of prejudice and favoritism. The oath was a command to reach inside of himself and look for the truth though it may cause him pain or loss. Perjury was evil, a scourge upon the land and a stain upon the reputation of good people everywhere. It stood between men of conscience and the law they were sworn to uphold. Shannon believed it with all his mind and heart and sought to impart this knowledge to the public. To make his point, Shannon shared a letter with the jury from Washington, D.C., indicating that "the expenses of the courts in Dakota exceeded those of any other territory." The time to reform the system for the sake of truth had come.[18]

Just a few days before the new Wintermute indictment was issued, Shannon was served up with another murder case, one that was terminated with a speed that must have seemed surprising to most court observers. The accused men were two Santee Sioux Indians named Crooked Legs and One Road. They were charged with the murder of a Ponca Indian named Fork. Speaking through an interpreter, both men pled not guilty. One Road raised his hand and exclaimed, "The Great Spirit knows it is not true!"[19]

Their attorneys, Oliver Shannon and Philip K. Faulk, had another, less spiritual strategy. They moved to quash the indictment because the court lacked jurisdiction. Federal law barred the territorial court from hearing a case where both victim and killer were Indians. Judge Shannon agreed and promptly ordered the indictment quashed and the men were released.

Although it was the proper course to take, the *Press and Dakotaian* decried the fact that two murderers could simply walk away unpunished. The federal law, it said, was outdated and needed to be changed, unless, of course, "white man's justice" meant that the "great white father approves of shooting Poncas."[20] The story of the murderers who went unpunished received widespread attention.

The unusual case was an interesting diversion for Judge Shannon, who doubtless needed a respite from all the stress of the Wintermute mess. While relaxation was in order, he was suddenly called east on account of

Philip K. Faulk, attorney, with Oliver Shannon,
for Santee Sioux defendants Crooked Legs and One Road.
Courtesy Carl Bennett Collection.

the illness of his mother. She was dying and he rushed to Pittsburgh to be at her side. Shannon was gone for two weeks.[21]

Upon his return to Dakota, Shannon decided to move his family to a better home. While any house would probably have been nicer than living in a hotel, the Shannon family moved into a large house built in 1871 by C. H. McIntyre, a Yankton businessman. The local newspaper for May 11, 1875, recorded that Judge Shannon had rented the McIntyre house.[22]

Their new home was an elegant Victorian mansion that represented the best that had been built in Yankton or in Dakota Territory, for that matter. The large house on Green Street was constructed on what was called

Shannon residence on Magazine Hill, Yankton, Dakota Territory.
Courtesy Yankton Historical Society.

"Magazine Hill," where the land sloped gently up to the west, offering a dazzling view of the Missouri River. It was three stories of luxury and magnificence. The first floor, built of Dakota granite, was ten feet high; the second and third floors were made of chalkstone, and the whole edifice stood thirty-three feet "from the ground to the naves."

The interior, including the basement, a spacious dining room, a parlor, and servants' quarters, was "carefully studied with an eye to comfort and convenicnce." It featured a grand staircase that led to the third floor and the commodious bedrooms. It was topped by a large cupola, fifteen-feet high, from which one could see Frankfort, Nebraska, nine miles to the west, Turkey Ridge, fifteen miles to the east, and the "sinuosities [sic] of our great river."[23]

The house could not have failed to impress Ann Elena Shannon who, coming west for the first time, was probably not expecting something so large and luxurious. Instead, she found herself and her family in a veritable palace on the prairie—a one-of-a-kind mansion that still graces the city of Yankton.

In their grand house, the Shannons could entertain a large group of people or just a few ladies for afternoon tea. In coming to Dakota, Ann Elena Shannon found that she was not required to do without any luxury, even though the house, created with a Venetian flair, was just a small beacon of light shining in a frontier town, where the stillness of night might be disturbed by a church bell, a train whistle, or a gunshot.

While the Shannons were beginning to enjoy their opulent home, new criminal charges were working their way through the judicial process. George Beck of Yankton was arrested and charged with mayhem after he bit the nose off the face of Mr. Millett. Beck was released after posting a $200 bail.[24]

Beck was not, however, free from further trouble. Soon after the nose-biting incident, the *Press and Dakotaian* reported a "stabbing affray" that involved George Beck and Tom Fletcher, both men "notorious in the police annals of Yankton." They became engaged in a furious fight on First Street, with Fletcher getting the worst of it. The combatants were disrupted by a witness, Jim McCormick, who decided that they should quit. But Fletcher was not satisfied. Once freed from the entanglement, Fletcher drew a pocket knife and stabbed Beck in the bowels "just below the umbilicus, the blade penetrating about two or three inches."

As a result of the attack, the wounded Beck was taken to Hardin's saloon where he received medical attention. Fletcher was arrested and jailed. Both men had a "hard name" in Yankton and both were familiar with "the inside appearance of the jail walls."[25]

When Fletcher was arraigned before the justice of the peace, his attorney, the reliable Oliver Shannon, filed a complaint against Beck on behalf of his client. Beck was charged with assault and battery, with intent to injure, and larceny. All those present, including the sheriff, were of the opinion that Yankton would be better off if both men "took leg bail," meaning they should both just leave town and never come back.[26]

When Judge Shannon sentenced Charles E. Porter to two years in prison, he was dealing with another, very unsympathetic defendant. Porter was convicted of assault with a dangerous weapon, following a shooting incident in Yankton. He had shot at his wife, striking her ear lobe and taking off an earring in the process. Shannon gave Porter a stern lecture on the evils of drinking, "keeping bad company and the crime of carrying dangerous weapons," and then sent him off to Fort Madison, Iowa, to serve two years at hard labor.[27]

It was the duty of Yankton County Sheriff Millard A. Baker to escort prisoners, including Porter, to the territorial prison. Usually referred to by his nickname "Ole," the sheriff was a native of New York State and a veteran of the Civil War. When the voters elected him sheriff, they made an excellent choice, for Baker applied a strong, steady hand to his duties. He was fearless and devoted to protecting the public from outlaws, and he did so as sheriff for a total of six years.[28]

While it was never advisable to challenge "Ole" Baker, Charles E. Porter attempted to escape on the way to Fort Madison. The prisoner somehow managed to get his hands on a small saw and "was making movements which indicated a desire to get rid of the shackles" when the sheriff interrupted him. The *Press and Dakotaian* made light of the incident, noting that the sheriff delivered Porter to the prison gates "and it is probable that his wife's ears are safe from molestation during the balance of the season."[29]

A prison sentence for shooting off an ear lobe made for an odd case, indeed. But the prize for the strangest arrest in the spring of 1875 belongs to Sarah Bloxom. She lived at a place "down in the willows," but she apparently did not stay there all the time. Sarah was arrested by a deputy marshal and charged with being an unfit person "for the neighborhood by which she was surrounded." It was noted that two Wisconsin men were "hanging around" her place and that "they will be taken in before the grass is much higher."[30]

The article in the "Local Laconics" section of the *Press and Dakotaian* did not attempt to connect her "offense" to the criminal code of the territory. She was simply a disreputable woman, probably a prostitute or a "madame," who was looked upon as a bad influence on young Yankton men. Had she confined her improper behavior to her abode and simply stayed there, the public anger and shame might not have been so blatant. Scandalous activity behind closed doors, though still odious, was easier to ignore or deny. But Sarah was seen soliciting in broad daylight for food in respectable neighborhoods. She left Yankton of her own accord, or at the insistence of the authorities, but Sarah did leave. The *Sioux City Journal* recorded her arrival, calling the ex-Yankton resident a "seductive madam."[31]

A few crimes on Broadway Street also garnered newspaper attention. One of them especially promised to dress up the next court calendar. The incident, called a "Street Duel," was initiated by Charley Allen, a well-known Yankton resident who had just returned from the Black Hills. In the early morning of August 27, while the sun was just beginning to remind night owls that it was time to get some sleep, Allen was patronizing Charley Wambole's saloon on Broadway.

A quarrel between the two Charleys caused Allen to step outside, draw his revolver, and shoot at Wambole. The bullet, alas, went astray. At that point Wambole "called for his ordinance and appeared at the door, when Allen again opened his batteries in two or three shots at long range." Wambole ducked behind his "fortifications" and returned fire, nearly hitting Allen, who found that he was out of ammunition. Wishing to continue the gun battle, Allen broke into Wagner's gun shop, ordered the proprietor to replenish his supply of shells, "after which he again advanced to the attack." Wambole, however, "got the drop on him" and Allen laid down his gun as ordered. He was arrested and charged with assault with intent to kill.[32]

Wambole's saloon was generally thought to be a respectable place, unlike the sleazy liquor joints "in the willows, below the town." And gunplay in Yankton was certainly not an everyday occurrence, but it erupted from time to time, usually fueled by excessive drinking. Violent affrays were not always taken seriously, but more serious offenses did help Peter Shannon and his fellow judges create their legacies in Dakota Territory.

CHAPTER 9

THE SECOND WINTERMUTE MURDER TRIAL

This case, which has caused so much excitement, not only in
Dakota, but throughout the country, was brought to a
conclusion at 8 o'clock last Saturday night.

Semi-Weekly Register, Vermillion, D.T.
September 14, 1875

Yankton seemed fated to bear a heavy load over a rough trail. Years of political strife among aggressive men with violent tendencies had culminated in the death of a Civil War hero from a legendary Ohio family. The killing of General Edwin S. McCook in Yankton raised the specter of homicide to new heights. The bullets from Peter P. Wintermute's pistol left an indelible image of a smoking gun on the map of Dakota Territory. Sadness, anger, and regret descended on the entire territory but especially on the participants in the dramatic trial that resulted in a conviction of manslaughter.

Unfortunately, the exhausted city was denied closure, and all attention was drawn to the inevitable appeal. Although many negative sentiments were exchanged in the aftermath of the first trial, Wintermute's legal team was not one to rest, promising the public some type of judicial explosion.

Mrs. Wintermute decided that she did not want to stay in Yankton and bear witness to the next eruption. Opinion and sentiment were decidedly against her husband, and she too was forced to bear a measure of shame and blame. With her social standing diminished, she auctioned off all her household goods, rented their house, and with her children moved to Chicago.[1]

While preparing an appeal to the Dakota Supreme Court, Wintermute's counsel filed for a writ of *habeas corpus* in the district court at Vermillion. With Wintermute present in court, Judge J. P. Kidder considered the arguments by both sides of the question. After stating he had "serious doubts both as to the legality and propriety of the action applied for," he declined to grant the relief requested and simply referred the matter to the whole Supreme Court, when it next met in Yankton.[2] Wintermute did not gain his freedom, pending the appeal.

Justice Kidder was in a unique position when he made the ruling, for his days as a judge were numbered. He had been a successful candidate as delegate to Congress in the general election of 1874 and would soon be off to Washington, D.C. That summer the Republicans had gathered in convention at Elk Point, where genuine harmony replaced the rancor of the past. Old antagonists, including W. W. Brookings and G. C. Moody, spoke of unity and cooperation while they settled on a qualified and non-partisan candidate. Judges P. C. Shannon and A. H. Barnes were mentioned as possible candidates, but the nomination went to Kidder. The choice was more than symbolic; it was real unity, for Kidder had always remained "aloof from all the factions."[3]

In the fall election campaign of 1874, Kidder came under attack for his intemperance, and the *Press and Dakotaian* cried foul, insisting that Kidder had not imbibed since being nominated.[4] This charge had been made before to no avail and it mattered very little, if at all, to the voters.

The *Dakota Herald,* a strong supporter of the incumbent, Moses K. Armstrong, made a shrill but feeble attempt to place Kidder in an unfavorable light. First, it repeated the alcohol abuse charge, noting Kidder was a "confirmed inebriate" and "an open and shameless drunkard." Then, taking another approach, the only Democratic newspaper in Dakota accused Kidder of using his influence to "defend the cold-blooded murderer of the lamented McCook."[5]

The accusation of judicial misconduct was serious but Kidder ignored the baseless claim. So strong was his support among the voters that the popular and affable judge easily defeated Armstrong—also a drinker—who was seeking a third term. The joining of the Capital Street Gang with the Broadway Street Gang enabled the Republican Party to enhance its political dominance in Dakota. More important for Dakota, the voters sent a well-qualified man to Washington.

Prior to resigning his judgeship, Justice Kidder, along with Justice Barnes and Chief Justice Shannon, heard arguments on the Wintermute appeal during the January 1875 term of the Supreme Court. The prosecution consisted of J. R. Gamble and Jason R. Brown. Wintermute was represented by Leonard Swett, G. C. Moody, Bartlett Tripp, and S. L. Spink.

The court heard two days of oral argument from Swett and Brown. Then on January 30, 1875, the court made a ruling that stunned all observers. "It is now here ordered, adjudged and determined that said judgment of conviction of Peter P. Wintermute of manslaughter aforesaid be arrested and reversed." Next, counsel for Wintermute argued in favor of bail which was granted in the amount of $20,000.[6] He walked away from jail facing a new trial and more uncertainty.

It was Justice Kidder who wrote the opinion for the majority, having been joined in his decision by Justice Barnes, Chief Justice Shannon dissenting. The issue on appeal was whether the grand jury had been empaneled in accordance with the laws of the territory. The old argument concerning the efficacy of the 1862-63 statute was again raised. The defense team argued that the 1862-63 criminal code, section 107, #13, provided that "a person held to answer a charge for a public offense, may challenge the panel of the grand jury, or any individual grand juror, before they retire, after being drawn and charged by the court." Grounds for challenge included the question of whether a juror could act impartially and without prejudice.[7]

In his decision, Kidder noted that the criminal statute of 1862-63 had in fact been repealed by the Dakota legislature of 1868-69. He went on to rule that the 1868 statute had been repealed by the legislature of 1872-73. The effect of this second repeal was to restore the 1862-63 statute, so under that statute Wintermute should have been permitted to challenge the grand juror in question. Lacking that challenge, he was denied an important right. Citing numerous legal authorities, including William Blackstone, Kidder ruled that a "disqualified grand juror tainted the whole panel." Failing to comply with the procedural requirements for a grand jury, the case was reversed and remanded.[8]

Shannon's dissent was vigorous and lengthy. He argued that Wintermute had been granted all his rights and safeguards under statutory and common law. Since the focus of the majority opinion was on a disqualified grand juror, the main thrust of Shannon's dissent was addressed to that aspect of the case. He went to great pains to show that the selection of the grand jury was proper and lawful and that it was sworn in without a challenge by the defense. Because the challenge to the particular juror, George W. Delamater, also the foreman of the grand jury, came after the panel was sworn in, Shannon reasoned that the challenge had occurred too late. He provided ample case law and other legal authority to support his argument.

Almost lecturing his fellow justices, Shannon insisted that if the right to challenge a juror does not close after the panel is sworn, then what reason would a party have to challenge a juror before the swearing in? He acknowledged that a challenge launched after the grand jury is sworn in would be subject to the judge's discretion and could be denied or granted after considering the merits of the untimely objection. Furthermore, the challenge under consideration was one without substance or evidence to support it; nothing was offered by the defendant's counsel to explain why and how the juror in question was disqualified. Shannon concluded: "When empaneled and sworn they became and were pronounced to be, the lawfully constituted grand inquest of the county."

The chief justice addressed the statute of 1862-63 and agreed that it was partially repealed by the subsequent legislation, but he stated that had the statute remained in full force and effect Wintermute still received the full protection of that old law. He reasoned that "even if the statute of 1862-63 was then in force, it is firmly maintained that, by the true interpretation of it, the defendant's *right* to challenge Mr. Delamater ceased when he was sworn in as foreman, and when the grand inquest was organized according to the law." The respected chief justice concluded that the objection was not timely and that Wintermute should be denied a new trial.[9]

Shannon's frustration with the Wintermute decision was palpable, but he never strayed from the path of courtesy toward his fellow judges, nor did he join the public outrage over the decision. Besides, Kidder would soon be off to Congress to assume duties as delegate for Dakota Territory and a new justice would take his place. Although Kidder was respected by the people, he was the author of the hated court decision and became the target of public wrath. He heard more than an earful from the people he angered.

But he received support from a separate opinion by Justice Barnes, who in turn was endorsed by the *Bismarck Tribune.* Although that newspaper believed Wintermute deserved hanging, the *Tribune* also wanted him to have a fair trial, and after considering the opinions of Kidder and Barnes concluded that "Judge Shannon with all his legal lore and logic is wrong."[10]

When the Wintermute decision was published, Yankton erupted in white-hot anger and disbelief. A meeting was held in Stone's Hall "to give an expression of the indignation on the part of the participants over the recent ruling." One after another, many leading political and business men from Yankton and other parts of the territory gave vent to their frustration and anger. Dr. Burleigh, an erstwhile political opponent of Kidder with an obvious ax to grind, stated that he "came to Dakota fourteen years ago and had assisted with his time and money in transforming it from savage to civilized" only to learn that a couple of federal judges wrote appellate decisions that resulted in a miscarriage of justice, likely freeing a killer.

Dakota and Iowa newspapers also expressed their disapproval. An editorial in the *Press and Dakotaian* blasted the judicial system that resulted in freeing Wintermute, noting that "a little less of law and a little more of common sense would better subserve the ends of justice." The angry editor also wrote that "law which retards or prevents the punishment of crime is but a poor protection to society." The editorial in the *Press and Dakotaian* echoed the ugly sentiments of men who were livid because Wintermute—"guilty of a heinous crime"—was freed on a "technicality."

In the religion-infused nineteenth century, the role of government, the law, and the courts was to define sin, assign guilt, and administer punishment. As sure as evil is in the world, good men had to devote their lives to its eradication. People observed ever so keenly that in the Wintermute case the government of Dakota Territory and its courts had failed to measure up to these time-honored standards.

At the conclusion of the indignation meeting a resolution was adopted condemning the actions of Barnes and Kidder. It was further resolved that "a copy of these proceedings be sent to the President of the United States, to the heads of the several departments, and to each senator and member of the house of representatives of Washington, with the eternal prayer that these two unfaithful judges be at once removed from the position which they now disgrace, and that honest and capable judges be named to fill their separate places."[11]

Another report noted that the "indignators" wanted to burn the Supreme Court in effigy. About two hours after the meeting adjourned, a fire broke out in the "lower part of town" near "certain houses of prostitution." Some believed the flames arose from a fire set by the "indignators," but upon closer observation it was discovered that Platt's carriage works and blacksmith shop was on fire and soon reduced to ashes.[12]

The antics of the "indignators" were not appreciated by all Dakotans. The *Bismarck Tribune* was harshly critical of anyone who would resort to extreme protests against able judges who were following the law. Calling the Yankton gathering a "mob tribunal," the newspaper coyly advised its readers that the "judges have been able to stand it thus far, and their judicial ermine remains unsoiled notwithstanding these onslaughts."[13]

In due course, but not because of a resolution adopted at the indignation meeting, Jefferson P. Kidder's replacement on the Dakota Supreme Court was named. President Grant appointed Granville Gaylord Bennett, from Iowa, on February 5, 1875. Bennett brought his family to Vermillion in March, where he settled in to be the next associate justice from the first judicial district.[14] Bennett was an Ohioan by birth and a Civil War veteran. He had been educated in Ohio and Illinois schools and admitted to the Iowa bar in 1859. Bennett served in the Iowa legislature from 1865 to 1871 and was active in the re-election campaign of President Grant in 1872. He had no prior judicial experience but had practiced law for sixteen years.[15]

By the time Bennett got to Dakota, the anti-Wintermute anger had subsided. If an indignation meeting had any worthy purpose, it was that hateful energy was channeled toward a non-violent result. The *Sioux Falls Independent* noted that "interest in the case has much abated" and concern was now directed to the cost to Yankton County, which was said to have been at least $9,000.[16]

The cost of a new trial would add to the expenses. On May 7, 1875, it was announced in the *Press and Dakotaian* that another grand jury had indicted Wintermute on a charge of murder. The article also informed its readers that the accused man was "confined to his bed by sickness, and cannot be arraigned for trial."[17]

The prosecution eventually brought a motion before the court on May 8 for the purpose of a murder arraignment, but Wintermute was still too sick to appear and his counsel got a continuance. His recovery was slow, and on May 22 it was announced that the defense would ask for a change of venue. Finally, on June 8 Wintermute appeared before Judge Shannon and was charged with murder, although he was said to be "suffering from a cancer that is eating into his side."[18]

On June 12 counsel for Wintermute argued a motion for a change of venue. Affidavits from a number of Yankton men were submitted to the court in an effort to show that Wintermute could not get a fair trial in Yankton. The press was accused of biased reporting, which was highly prejudicial against Wintermute. Judge Shannon was convinced and ordered a change of venue to the first district court at Vermillion. Judge Bennett would sink his honorable teeth into the Wintermute case. Until then, the accused would have to languish in his cell, hoping his talented legal team could pull off a judicial miracle.

In the meantime, Yankton remained in the spotlight. A group of Minneapolis businessmen visiting Yankton were in accord with the locals who desired a guilty verdict followed by execution. When they arrived, the visiting dignitaries were greeted and feted by the leading men of Yankton, and after being wined, dined, and treated to carriage rides, they visited the courtroom where Wintermute fired the fatal bullet—and out of curiosity, examined a bullet hole in the wall. Some of them visited the jail under the courthouse and peeked into Wintermute's cell. There they found the sullen prisoner, sick and under doctors' care and in no mood to be made a sideshow attraction. When he discovered he was being watched, Wintermute pulled the curtain shut.[19]

As Wintermute's second date with destiny drew near, people gravitated to Vermillion to bear witness to the second trial. The crowd of the curious was probably smaller than the gathering for the first trial. Among those present was George W. McCook, brother to the deceased general, there to represent his family. Edwin's widow, Loraine McCook, and son, Charlie, came to attend the trial but also to visit their friends at Yankton and Sioux Falls. Loraine's parents, Oscar and Mrs. Whitney, returned for the trial and to see old friends and acquaintances. They all wanted a guilty verdict for murder and the satisfaction of seeing Wintermute hanged for his crime.

The second Wintermute trial opened on August 30, 1875. In the first order of business, Judge Bennett listened to a defense motion that struck at the heart of the case. G. C. Moody argued that Wintermute should be discharged because he had been acquitted of murder in the first trial. Bennett overruled the motion because Wintermute had been convicted of manslaughter instead of murder. Had he been acquitted altogether, trying him again would have constituted double jeopardy.

Next, the jury was selected after a lengthy session of *voir dire*. A group of forty-eight men were brought into court and questioned. The attorneys ran through the group rather quickly, and Judge Bennett ordered the Vermillion County sheriff to go out and get forty-eight more in court by ten o'clock the next morning. The sheriff was up "the greater portion of the night, scouring the country east of Vermillion in order to find the requisite number."[20] He was successful. Finally, twelve "good and true" men were seated: David Powell, Frank Dennison, J. D. Tucker, Charles Chausee, Richard Odell, Ole Highland, A. Scott Wright, Ezra Harrington, Jesse Shriner, Ole Byronson, Bernard Burke, and G. W. Woodruff.[21] The jury was ordered to be sequestered under the charge of the bailiffs.

The *Clay County Register* predicted a short session: "it is hardly possible for the case to occupy anything like the time taken up in the first trial."[22] Testimony of witnesses began on September 2, with Wintermute's wife present, having arrived in Vermillion from Chicago on the 1st. Many of the witnesses were those who testified in the first trial, including Dr. W. A. Burleigh, Charles F. Rossteuscher, William Tripp, Peter Hackney, and Loraine McCook.

Historian George W. Kingsbury states in his mammoth *History of Dakota Territory* that there were no surprises in the second trial and no new facts presented to the jury.[23] This is true to the extent that both sides essentially repeated their strategies of the first case.

The prosecution did, however, score major points when it called Dr. Frank Etter to the witness chair. In the first trial it was the defense who called him to testify about his examination of Wintermute on the night of the shooting. Now testifying for the prosecution, Etter recalled that while he was examining the defendant, Wintermute asked him to find a wound. Etter told Wintermute that finding a wound would be impossible for he (Wintermute) was not wounded. Etter went on to say that Wintermute offered him $500 to find a wound which he refused to do.[24] No such testimony had been elicited at the first trial.

The summary of the evidence in the retrial, much of it compelling, strongly points to guilt beyond a reasonable doubt—guilt of either murder or manslaughter. The general consensus of the court observers was that the prosecution had triumphed once again. Anyone who sat through the proceedings and left believing that Wintermute would walk away a free man would have been considered insane; therefore, when the verdict of "not guilty" came back on September 11, after seven hours of deliberation, the immediate reaction in all quarters was of shock and outrage in the extreme. The jury's decision was utterly baffling. How could any group of twelve men of reasonable intelligence conclude that Wintermute was not guilty in view of the testimony of several witnesses who saw him fire his pistol at McCook while the two men stood just a few feet apart? These witnesses, coupled with those who heard more shots and saw the struggle between Wintermute and a wounded and bleeding McCook, along with his dying declarations, constituted direct evidence of the crime, often lacking in homicide cases.

The *Dakota Herald* editorial page reflected the mind-boggling anger of its Yankton readers. The same newspaper that had criticized and insulted McCook at every opportunity, calling him a demagogue and other vile names, rose to defend his honor and memory while condemning the verdict in harshest terms. The *Herald* saw the "power of money" in the result, a luxury unavailable to most defendants. Surely, declared the *Herald*, "mob law" will "hereafter supplant the legal tribunal of our territory."[25]

The *Corning Journal*, a newspaper in upstate New York where the Wintermute family had lived, expressed puzzlement upon learning the verdict: "This result makes it difficult to determine what would be considered a clear case of murder in that section."[26] It was a mild rebuke compared to the reaction in Dakota Territory.

The *Times* of Springfield, where McCook was appreciated, mocked the "honest jury" that acquitted Wintermute. The editorial pointed out that the jury did not acquit because of justifiable homicide but rather the twelve "intelligent" men declared Wintermute was innocent. In other words, the editorial insisted that the jury ignored the evidence and the instructions of Judge Bennett in finding Wintermute not guilty in causing McCook's death. "Everybody who knows anything about the history of this case, knows the declaration to be a wicked, willful, barefaced lie," and the jurors would have to answer to a higher authority for their perfidy and wickedness. For reasons that might later be revealed, the jury ignored the common sense adage, "Two wrongs can never make a right."[27]

The *Sioux Falls Independent* was slow to editorialize on the verdict, but having examined the record of the trial, the paper blazed forth with an editorial condemning the verdict: "How any twelve men of ordinary common sense could find a verdict of 'Not Guilty' when the evidence was so direct and the law so plain goes beyond our ability to conceive." The *Independent* hinted that money was a factor in the case, all the while expressing the belief that juries in Dakota were, all too frequently, moved more by personal feelings than by the law.[28]

In Vermillion the response was far less shrill and wholly lacking in condemnation. The *Semi-Weekly Register* urged everyone to accept the verdict and move on. While acknowledging that many would be angry and disappointed, the editorial pointed out, rather weakly, that after two years it was difficult to "get all the particulars of such an affray before a jury." It was, undoubtedly, "conflicting testimony" that planted reasonable doubt in the minds of the jurors. At any rate, Wintermute, "after a spirited contest of two years, has been acquitted by a jury of his peers," and the *Register* declared that "all good men, will quietly acquiesce in this decision." The editor was, however, constrained to say that when the verdict was announced, "the ringing of the bell on the Baptist Church and the firing of the cannon…was in very bad taste."[29]

Vermillion's other newspaper displayed a different take on the verdict and the reaction of the townspeople. Believing that the jury was honest and did its whole duty, The *Dakota Republican* felt a celebration of acquittal was appropriate. "In fact," an editorial declared, "nearly the whole town was in favor of rejoicing." This newspaper, which had insisted that it did not take sides in the "famous Wintermute" case, also had no objection to ringing the church bell or firing the cannon.[30]

The *Dakota Republican* raised acquittal and the celebration like a victory banner and shook it wildly and in derision at Yankton, a town it considered populated by shameful and evil men. F. N. Burdick, editor and proprietor for the *Dakota Republican,* was positively gleeful in his condemnation of Yankton, reminding his readers of the old Republican Party split that had caused widespread consternation and was responsible for its scandal, corruption, and crime. Burdick all but declared that the Wintermute win was a guilty verdict for Yankton, a town that was "defeated in every encounter; beaten before the public; humiliated before the just tribunal of the people," a city that "is supported by a tax on prostitution." Yankton now stood in abject humiliation in spite of its wealth and power and of the support of the Dakota Southern Railroad. Indeed, the "clique in Yankton" had been handed a defeat that it richly deserved.[31]

The self-righteousness that oozed from the Burdick editorial was in tune with the strong support Wintermute enjoyed among Dakotans who were elated that at long last their friend was acquitted. Not so for the majority. For them the unpopular verdict—entered into the record precisely two years from the day that the shooting occurred—was a foul stench in the nostrils of respectable folks and a scandal of national proportion. Crime had triumphed and "law and order are cringing in the dust." The verdict was likened to "a cloud of ill-omen upon the hopes of those who had plumed their faith in justice's skirts."[32] Worse yet for the twelve men held in high contempt was a report that Wintermute celebrated his acquittal over drinks with some members of the jury.[33]

A juror anonymously denied the drinking incident in a letter to the *Dakota Republican*,[34] but the denial was for naught since in the public's eye the jury in the Wintermute case had utterly failed to do its duty. The shock that emanated from the "Not Guilty" verdict caused a letter writer from Springfield to declare that the jury was "packed first and bought afterwards." Twelve men had covered themselves with dishonor so great that "neither good deeds nor time will ever efface" the record they left for all to see.[35]

Although he most certainly appreciated the jury's decision, Wintermute could not wait to get out of Dakota, where he would never again be able to live without fear of retribution. Ironically, Wintermute returned to Yankton and checked into the Merchants Hotel only to find that the sheriff, his deputy, and a "small *posse* of citizens" had been called to the hotel to "quell the disturbance." An article in the *Press and Dakotaian* expressed great surprise that Wintermute would show up in Yankton immediately after his acquittal, suggesting it was done in "open defiance of a public sentiment that believed he deserved the severest punishment for his crime."[36]

But Wintermute would not tarry long in Yankton where "Judge Lynch" might intervene at the slightest provocation. He was broke and seriously ill when he departed Yankton with his family for Chicago two days after the trial ended. In February 1876 an eastern newspaper revealed that a suffering Wintermute was about to move to Florida, "where he expects to die."[37] The man who came to personify the arch-villain of the West—the killer of a Civil War hero who never paid for his crime—died at his father's home in Horseheads, Chenango County, New York, on January 27, 1877, less than two years after his acquittal.[38]

Although the tragedy was something that the McCook and Wintermute families wanted to put behind them, the story of the crime lingered long in the public memory. When writing his book *Almanac of World Crime,* Jay Robert Nash included the Wintermute murder case in a chapter entitled "Courts and Trials": "For years, the McCook-Wintermute case was the most hotly debated murder trial in the Dakotas."[39] Doubtless it was also the topic of discussion at dinner tables all over America.

The Wintermute trials were a significant development in the evolution of the Dakota judiciary. The wealth of the defendant resulted in the creation of a "dream team" of lawyers, a first in Dakota. The young territory had now proved it was more than a collection of rough, frontier towns. It was home to sophistication and talent. The Dakota lawyers who worked for one side or the other, as well as many of the trial witnesses, constitute a "Who's Who" of territorial luminaries. Most of them had made, or would make, history in other ways, but it was the Wintermute trials that showcased their personalities and abilities on a national stage in 1874 and 1875. If only for a brief time, their names were on the lips of people all across America.

That the long legal ordeal eventually resulted in an acquittal is also of significance. Acquittals were not rare in Dakota, of course but a finding of "not guilty" was stunning in view of the facts of the case. Surely, the power of great lawyering cannot be denied, but the average citizen took note that money also mattered. Another rich man got away with homicide because there were, indeed, two systems of justice: one for the rich and one for everyone else. Class warfare, so common in eastern cities, had invaded the Dakota frontier.

Notwithstanding, the most important feature of the Wintermute case is the work product of the judges who handled the hearings, trials, and appeals. There were murder trials in Dakota prior to Wintermute's, but none exhibits such a high level of legal expertise from the bench. Whether one agrees or disagrees with the final outcome, one must admire the determination and dedication to duty of P. C. Shannon, J. P. Kidder, A. H. Barnes, and G. G. Bennett. Each justice a shining example of judicial skill and integrity, they set aside personal feelings and intense pressure from the press and public and did their duty in accordance with the rule of law. They may or may not have agreed with the outcome, but they accepted the jury's decision because due process of law had run its course.

CHAPTER 10

MORE THAN A JUDGE

An innocent man's case is perfectly safe in his [Shannon's]
hands and it is said his justice leans to mercy.

Dakota Pantagraph
November 28, 1877

Peter C. Shannon had more than convinced Dakotans of his judicial skills through the handling of the Wintermute murder case. Although he had to deal with a prominent defendant and a celebrity victim, whose stature was enlarged by newspapers, Shannon—a strong man of high personal ethics—was not intimidated. He had become the complete judge: fair, fearless, dignified, and in control. Judge Shannon's knowledge of the law was thorough and his integrity undisputed; lawyers respected him and made sure they were well prepared when they appeared before him in court. Frontier lawyers could be testy and argumentative, but Shannon knew how to handle them, and they learned much by listening to him.

The same could be said of the general public, as in every town where he appeared, often to a packed courtroom, Judge Shannon was thought of as a fair and fearless dispenser of justice. He was, moreover, a gifted speaker. He possessed a commanding presence and stood out among the leaders of Dakota as one who applied common sense to difficult situations. He is credited for guiding the Dakota judicial system from the frontier period to the pre-statehood era.[1]

R. F. Pettigrew, attorney, surveyor, and politician.
Courtesy Siouxland Heritage Museums.

Judge J. P. Kidder believed that a jocular remark "relieved the tedium and kept the machinery of justice oiled,"[2] but Shannon was serious, even somber by comparison. He was far from dull, however, and when he spoke in court the audience listened with rapt attention. Shannon believed that in the criminal misadventures of others there were important lessons to be learned by the public, and he used his position as judge to caution his listeners to resist the beguiling influence of immorality and thereby avoid the damnable consequences of a life of crime.

In the 1870s a trial was a public forum where curious people gathered to be informed. They also came for entertainment, although Shannon was a stickler for decorum and formality in his court. Levity and angry outbursts were out of bounds, but these theatrics crept into the proceedings from time to time. On one such occasion, Shannon was holding court in Sioux Falls, where one of the attorneys was R. F. Pettigrew, known for his quick temper and the zealous representation of his clients. At some point civility and respect unraveled, and in a jaw-to-jaw confrontation with Judge Shannon, Pettigrew became "sarcastic and the court irascible."

During a break in the action Pettigrew left the courthouse in anger, went to his office and grabbed some cash. When asked what he was going to do with the money, Pettigrew told his law partner, Melvin Grigsby, that he would use it to pay a fine for contempt of court. Pettigrew declared that he would make the "old **** understand that he can't run over me." He returned to the courthouse and unleashed another impolite verbal barrage, causing Shannon to impose a ten-dollar fine. This was followed by more abuse from Pettigrew which led to another fine of fifty dollars. Shannon told Pettigrew, "I'll have it understood that this court is a gentleman!" Pettigrew suddenly calmed down and asked the judge to give him an "exception to that last ruling of court." Shannon laughed and said, "remit the fine, Mr. Clerk." After that it all went smoothly.[3]

Although a Dakota court session was often a time and place to expect the unexpected, Shannon believed in a serious and thoughtful approach to the dispensation of justice. He also recognized that a region with an increasing population needed more courts. In August 1875 he ordered a term of court for Hutchinson, Armstrong, Hanson, and Davison counties to be held at the town of Olivet, in Hutchinson County.[4] These areas were attracting a steady flow of settlers and rather than require citizens to travel to Yankton for the resolution of legal matters, he held a term of court in the midst of the new settlements.

The first-ever term of court held in Olivet convened in October 1875, and eager townspeople turned out to greet Shannon and ex-Governor Andrew J. Faulk, the court clerk. The two men were greatly impressed by the state of affairs in the little town on the James (Jim) River. Their visit, however, was probably a short one for there was only one case on the court calendar: *Maxwell v. Maxwell,* a trespassing matter.[5]

During the last week of June 1876, Shannon and his official entourage returned to Olivet, Hutchinson County, to handle more legal business. The judge took up lodging in a private home. Court was held in the schoolhouse and folks came from miles around to attend the session and witness the dispensation of justice first hand, even though there were no sensational criminal cases to watch. Still, it was a busy time with twelve cases on the docket.[6]

In his memoir of his Dakota experiences, attorney Robert Dollard related an interesting Olivet anecdote that escaped the Yankton newspapers. It concerned Judge Shannon and a court session held in an Olivet church. As the story goes, Shannon was examining potential jurymen when he became bogged down in some procedural mud. While questioning one man about his citizenship, the man declared that he was not born in the United States. When Shannon asked where he was born, the recalcitrant member of the jury pool said, "In Michigan." Another stubborn man said he was born "In ould Ireland be Jesus." In the presence of a number of esteemed members of the Dakota bar, Judge Shannon, not known for humorous displays from the bench, said, "Gentlemen, what shall we do with this Irishman?"[7]

Shannon, also an Irishman, established and maintained a good reputation in Olivet and other Dakota towns. A correspondent for the *Press and Dakotaian* heaped praise on the esteemed chief justice, saying, "frankly...our territory has never had his equal as a judge." The article closed with the prayer "that he may long continue to live and enjoy and honor his position."[8]

Shannon presided over the first term of court to be held in Swan Lake, the county seat of Turner County, in June 1876. The usual cast of characters, along with several lawyers, was present, including William Tripp from Yankton and H. A. Copeland from Vermillion. After banging the gavel, Shannon informed all those present that he was about to put the wheels of justice in motion. His groundbreaking address to the assembled members of the public "was listened to with all the attention which so creditable an effort merits." An admiring observer said, "I do not recall to have ever witnessed so impressive and interesting a . . . proceeding in a court of justice."[9] As a judge, he seldom, if ever, failed to impress a court audience.

Shannon held himself to a high standard, as though he wanted to set an example for prudent and honest behavior. In his personal affairs, guided by his Catholic faith, he was ethical and honest; no one ever accused him of being unfair or greedy. His family remained in his heart and mind throughout his busiest days on the bench. Although he was a public figure, he tried to keep his family away from the public spotlight, and even the birth of his seventh child escaped notice in the Yankton press. Charles Carroll Shannon was born in Yankton on July 27, 1876, to Ann Shannon; beyond that, little is known about the boy.[10]

Shannon seemed eager to demonstrate to people that he was more than just a judge and a man of means. In the aftermath of the great grasshopper disaster that occurred in the summer of 1874, Shannon joined William H. H. Beadle in an effort to assist those in need. The two men rode over the prairie between Yankton and Sioux Falls in the dead of the following winter to assess the need among the settlers. They made random stops at the sod homes and dugouts and bore witness to suffering families, hungry, desperate, and bearing up to the cold and the lack of food as best they could.

In Turner County, Beadle recalled his and Shannon's visit with settlers living in a dugout: "In the corner was a bed, the frame made of posts driven in the earth floor, and with ticking filled with straw for the bed. Upon it lay the wife and mother, too ill to rise." Two children, "scantily clad, were hovering over a stove, in which the fuel was hay or straw, watching hungrily their father prepare from a little milk and flour some kind of dish" for them to eat. It was a sad scene, an example of suffering that moved both Beadle and Shannon. Beadle recalled that "Judge Shannon was generous" in his donation to the poverty-stricken family. It was clear to both men that the suffering was far worse than they had expected to see, and unless aid in the form of money, food, and seed for spring planting was provided, impoverished settlers would be forced to leave Dakota, should they survive the winter. Governor John L. Pennington issued a public appeal for help, and aid associations were formed. Beadle was commissioned by the governor to go east and "gather relief in the rich centers." Through the efforts of Dakota's leaders, and with neighbors helping neighbors, the winter passed and in the warm promise of spring, a new crop was planted.[11]

Peter C. Shannon was a thoughtful and generous man in other respects. A strict Catholic, he actively supported his church in Yankton. In the summer of 1876 Shannon joined a group of fellow Catholics that came together and pledged $1,100 toward the building of a church at the northwest corner of Capital and Fifth Streets. He was selected to be the leader of the building committee. Until the construction of the church was completed, Judge Shannon and his fellow parishioners met for services in a hall over Wagner's gunsmith shop on Broadway Street. Finally, on Sunday, December 3, 1876, the first mass was celebrated in the Church of the Sacred Heart.[12]

Although he was not overtly influenced by his religious convictions when he ruled from the bench, he was of course a staunch opponent of divorce. When Rev. George Vosburgh, a charismatic preacher from New Jersey, came to Yankton seeking a divorce, he was told by knowledgeable lawyers that Judge Shannon was strongly opposed to terminating a marriage. Vosburgh, who had been tried in New Jersey and acquitted of attempted murder against his wife, was politely told that he should go to Fargo, where Judge A. H. Barnes, who was more lenient, might be inclined to grant the divorce. Vosburgh, the minister looking to become "a man without a wife," took the advice and left Yankton.[13]

Still, Judge Shannon could not avoid dealing with a divorce petition now and then. The Webster divorce case was one such matter before the second district. As a preliminary procedure, the case was referred to attorney Oliver Shannon, acting as a referee. During a heated session, Harry MacNamara, the attorney for Mr. Webster, lapsed into a tirade of nasty name calling directed at the attorney for Mrs. Webster. Since MacNamara would

Attorney Oliver Shannon ejects
Attorney Harry MacNamara from the courtroom.
Courtesy National Police Gazette.

not be silent, as ordered, Oliver Shannon aggressively stepped forward
to enforce his directive. A reporter for the *Press and Dakotaian* observed
that the court, in the person of Oliver Shannon, "placed its powerful grasp
upon the collar of the attorney for Mr. Webster." The reporter went on to
say, "parties in the room . . . aver that the feet of the attorney . . . did not
touch the floor after the muscles of the hand of the court had contracted
upon the collar of his coat." In other words, an indignant Oliver Shannon
physically ejected the offending attorney.[14]

But the case did not go away. And in due course, the Webster case was
something that Judge Shannon had to decide. About a week after Oliver

roughed up attorney MacNamara, the judge was asked to rule on a motion requesting the payment of referee's fees. During the discussion of the case, it was revealed that the petitioner, Mr. Webster, had not resided in the county the required ninety days before the filing of the petition. As such, the court held that the petition must be dismissed. That ended the matter rather quietly, and most assuredly, to the satisfaction of Judge Shannon.[15]

Although he was not an entrepreneur, Peter Shannon was connected with the Northern Pacific Railroad through his friendship with George C. Cass, president of the railroad. But he was not a speculator or a plunger, jumping from one risky venture to another. He kept a low business profile, believing that huckstering and arm-twisting were inconsistent with the dignified behavior required of a judge.

In politics he may have looked back with fondness on his antebellum preference for the Democratic Party, yet he remained a rock-ribbed Republican. He had thus far avoided political entanglements that smacked of skullduggery, and he had refrained from endorsing anyone for office. Staying free from political obligations kept his reputation intact, and it would have been hard to find a section of Dakota that disliked him. In fact he was a very popular man among Dakotans, and in 1875 the territorial legislature created Shannon County to honor the chief justice. He was also liked and appreciated in Washington, D.C. and was appointed by President Rutherford B. Hayes to a second term, commencing on April 11, 1877.[16] The oath of office was administered by Governor Pennington on November 22, 1877, during a session of the second district court at Yankton.[17]

Shannon was pleased with the reappointment, for he had found his niche as a frontier judge. His day-to-day life was immersed in the law, and his conduct as well as his court decisions were guided by the law. In short, had he not been a judge, Shannon would have been the ideal trial lawyer, for he believed that the job of an attorney was to act as a zealous advocate for his clients' rights.

Because of his palpable love of the law and his superior legal knowledge, Shannon was called upon by the governor to use his skills to revise the codified laws of the territory, a task for which he was well qualified. Since he understood the need for clarity and consistency in the law, he eagerly applied his best efforts to the project.

Apart from the state of Georgia, Dakota Territory was the first jurisdiction in America to codify all its laws, both substantive and procedural.[18] This process began in the 1860s and continued into the next decade. The legislature of 1872-73 authorized Yankton attorney C. J. B. Harris to engage in code revision, which he undertook with purpose and dedication. Harris did not produce a complete revision but his effort resulted in much that was useful. Unfortunately for Harris, he was never paid a cent for all the hours spent at his desk working for the greater good.[19] The legislature refused to accept his report, but the matter did not end there.

A major recodification project began in December 1874 when Governor Pennington, in his message to the legislature and to the people, urged the lawmakers to order a revision of the territorial codes: "the necessity for a thorough and systematic codification of the statutes of the Territory is severely felt and imperatively demanded, and I earnestly recommend that you take prompt action in this important work." The governor pointed out that the current codes were confusing, making it difficult to determine "what is and what is not in force"; as a result, he said, "justice is often delayed and sometimes altogether thwarted." He called upon the legislature to adopt a set of codes "so simple, so plain and so direct . . . that they may be readily comprehended and understood" by lay people and lawyers alike. Expressing logic and wisdom, Pennington declared that the people should not be expected to obey laws that they do not understand.[20]

Convinced by the governor's reasoning, the legislature took up the matter, passing a law calling for the review and recodification of the territorial civil and criminal codes. Under the new law, the governor was authorized to appoint a commission to do the job. Pennington wasted no time in fulfilling this duty, appointing Peter C. Shannon and his fellow justice, Granville G. Bennett, along with attorney Bartlett Tripp, to the commission.[21]

Shannon's and Tripp's qualifications were unquestioned. Bennett, too, was a good choice even though he was the junior member in terms of years in Dakota. After replacing the popular and able J. P. Kidder in the first judicial district, Bennett quietly and quickly acquired a reputation for "candor and fairness," a man with "wide legal attainments and [a] thorough comprehension of his task and position."[22]

The commission met and organized in January 1876. Selecting Shannon as chairman and attorney W. H. H. Beadle as secretary, the men went to work with a purpose. They had the full support of the legislature, which authorized the printing of 200 copies of the recodification, the job to be let to the lowest bidder and the cost not to exceed $3,500.[23]

The commissioners ignored the warning from the *Dakota Herald* whose editor insisted that Shannon and Bennett could not lawfully be members of the commission because territorial law prohibited any man who held a federal job from also holding territorial office. All four men were good lawyers and men of integrity. Therefore, had Shannon or Bennett believed that by serving on a commission they were violating territorial law, doubtless they would have withdrawn. Nor did Tripp or Beadle raise an objection. Besides, working on a special commission for a limited purpose was not like holding down the full-time position of marshal, surveyor general, governor, or other public official. It was not an "office," rather a special assignment.

Although the *Herald* snidely accused the commissioners of doing for the money, according to Beadle's *Memoirs,* the team believed they undertook their work out of a sense of duty and for "small pay," because they all had "salaries or income from other sources." Shannon, Bennett, and Tripp were each paid $800 while Beadle, the clerk, received a paltry sum of $300. The grand plan was to produce a comprehensive set of codes for the following categories: political, civil, civil procedure, probate, justice, criminal, and criminal procedure. They proceeded thoughtfully, for it was their intention to keep that which had worked, especially for local governments. Every judge and lawyer understands that legal work must be guided by precedent so the laws of other states were reviewed, with special emphasis on the codes of New York and California. Above all, they wanted the finished product to be free from anything radical or surprising.[24]

Each man worked on the revision throughout 1876 as his schedule would allow. Shannon's attention was distracted when on May 9 his youngest son became ill "near death."[25] The boy did not die, but within days of the personal crisis Judge Shannon was forced to put his pen aside and pick up the gavel to preside over an unusual criminal trial. Yankton had a firebug on the loose.

The man arrested and charged with first degree arson was George Wait, known in Yankton as Tobe Wait. Following a series of small fires in the late winter months, Wait was arrested for setting fire to the Stone block on the corner of Capital and Third Streets on April 10, 1876. His trial commenced on May 10.

Based on the condensed testimony reported in the *Press and Dakotaian,* no one saw Wait set fire to the building. But he was seen lurking near the building on the night of the fire and when arrested he had oakum (hemp), a combustible material, in his shirt. Furthermore, he was a drinker, and while in his cups was overheard saying that he had served in the Confederate army in the Civil War and was determined to retaliate against the Union by setting fires up North.

Wait's defense counsel had no evidence to present on his behalf, and after closing arguments the case was submitted to the jury. It took only fifteen minutes of deliberation for the jury to decide he was guilty of first-degree arson. The minimum sentence was ten years, but Judge Shannon sentenced him to twenty-five years in prison.[26]

The Yankton community supported the sentence, for despite no direct evidence of guilt the general consensus was that the guilty verdict was proper. Tobe Wait was just too crazy and dangerous to be allowed to go free. The *Press and Dakotaian* weighed in with an editorial: "Tobe seemed wicked from instinct. He fired buildings as a pastime" and claimed his actions were meant as "revenge for the depredations of union soldiers upon southern property." Worse yet it was believed that six fires in Yankton in the past six months were Wait's doing. It was with great satisfaction that he was hauled off to prison in Fort Madison, Iowa.[27] Had there been no law enforcement, court, or prison, a man like Wait would have been lynched.

The work of the code commission was further interrupted by the illness of Bartlett Tripp, who spent several months at his old home in Maine in an attempt to get well. There was also some friction because Shannon and Tripp did not like each other. But on the whole, the process went well, for the group was able to overcome any personality problems for the benefit of the greater good.

And yet when the body of work was presented to the legislature, there was some murmur of criticism, most of it, as could be expected, from the *Dakota Herald*. That newspaper stuck to its belief that with Shannon and Bennett on the commission the project was fatally tainted. The *Herald* complained that the commission—in Tripp's absence—cheerfully ignored the requirement that the printing of the code be awarded to the lowest bidder. The *Herald* raised some legitimate points, but it could not keep politics out of the non-partisan effort, blaming Beadle, Shannon, and Bennett—all Republicans—while holding Tripp, a Democrat, free from all suspicion. Tripp, however, made no effort to get Shannon and Bennett ejected from the commission, nor did he step aside out of a belief that the makeup of the group was illegal and that his participation would, therefore, be unethical.

The *Herald* waxed at length over the project's high cost to the public during a time of an economic downturn coupled with the great grasshopper calamity and burdensome taxes. It went on to note that many attorneys objected to the new code as inadequate or badly written. In the end the *Herald* expressed a desire that the legislature reject the new codes.[28]

Despite the objections of the only Democratic newspaper in the territory, the entire code revision was adopted by the Republican-dominated legislature in the 1877 session. While the *Herald* staff groused and grumbled, another journalist, Clement A. Lounsberry, from Bismarck had this to say: "One of our ablest and most scholarly lawyers writing on the subject says that Judge Shannon has good and just reason to congratulate himself upon his great work as Dakota's chief codifier. That code will always remain his monument."[29]

Shannon was justifiably proud of his effort and that of his fellow commissioners. In 1895 he was interviewed by Lounsberry and asked about the code revision. Alert and sharp, although getting up in years, Shannon tore into a vigorous explanation of the project: "historically, the first honor and just praise belongs to Dakota." The commission, he stated with emphasis, did not "take our codes from California." Instead, he noted, credit is due to "our old territorial assemblies" that "built well and wisely." The former judge said that there was no need to look at outside sources for creating the code of laws that became a model for future use. The work of the commission, he insisted, was done with a minimum of outside inspiration and guidance.[30]

The work of the commission is a tribute to the talent and dedication of the men who threw themselves into the project solely for the public good. They looked beyond self-interest and personal animosities, ignored the rant from the *Dakota Herald,* and performed their duty in the true spirit of public service.

CHAPTER 11

THE UNDESIRABLES: RACISM AND PROSTITUTION

The streets of Yankton, its hotels and public
places, are thronged with strangers, and new
faces are the rule wherever one goes.

Daily Press and Dakotaian
September 28, 1878

Although the residents of Dakota Territory were perhaps less class conscious than those in the East or South, the historian who examines Yankton society of the 1870s would notice its diversity and sharp division between "desirables" and "undesirables." This terminology was not used in the nineteenth century to distinguish among groups of people on the frontier, but it has certain applicability to the discussion in this book.

Desirables were those people needed by the community to make it prosper and grow. They were hard-working, church-going models of good behavior and sensible politics; they possessed good taste, sound morals, and proper manners. Newspapers were quick to showcase them, applauding their entrepreneurial spirit. Undesirables included impractical dreamers, eccentrics, "tramps," heavy drinkers, and radicals, along with people of bad or crude habits, and those lacking in honesty and proper motives. They also included those who bore the "curse" of their ethnicity. Collectively, they were a liability to the community and could not be counted on to add anything of value to it. The press left them alone unless there was a need to denounce them.

Relegated to the lowest rung of the social ladder and outside of the mainstream, the undesirables tended to socialize with those of their own kind, gathering in their own neighborhoods. Always under suspicion, they were viewed as having the potential to become outlaws. Poverty and crime kept close company. Desirables usually had money, yet a poor man might be considered desirable if he were from a favored ethnic group and could show he was working to improve his condition.

Two groups among the undesirables in Dakota Territory stand out: freed African-American slaves and prostitutes. Both represented challenges for the courts and law enforcement and other bastions of moral authority. Subject to deeply entrenched prejudices, they were considered "old sinners," yet in Yankton they were generally tolerated by the dominant class. Being an undesirable did not mean that a person could not live in Yankton; it simply meant that he or she was not wanted.

Released from the constraints of slavery, African-Americans joined others in the movement west at the end of the Civil War. But the African-American migration was slow and quiet and occurred in small numbers, largely unnoticed and unpublicized. They were met with a certain level of tolerance in Yankton and the other Dakota towns. The lukewarm welcome stood in sharp contrast to how they were greeted in Southern communities or other parts of the North. In the West people were judged less by the color of their skin and more by how they handled the challenges of frontier life. Black people in Dakota handled it all very well and white people took notice.

Yankton was one of the principal stops for steamboat traffic throughout the 1860s and 1870s. The boats hired black men to do some of the grunt work. A few of the black river men, after stopping in Yankton, liked what they saw and decided to stay and find ways to make a living. Men found employment as cooks, barbers, and waiters, while women worked as household servants and laundresses, filling these positions with competence and dependability. By 1870 the census revealed that ninety-

people were living and working in Yankton or at one or more of
￼ Dakota Territory.[1]

￼first Dakota legislature showed considerable hostility toward
African Americans when it met in 1862, during the second year of the
Civil War. Councilman Austin Cole introduced a bill "[t]o prevent persons
of color [from] residing in Dakota." It passed the Council, or upper
chamber of the legislature, by a vote of five to three. But the controversial
bill—crafted in accordance with the Republican Party's belief that
the West was to become the home for white people—was fated to fail
because the legislature adjourned before it was acted upon by the House
of Representatives.[2]

There were other expressions of hostility. Black citizens could not
rely on the Dakota press to promote racial fairness. Not outwardly or
oppressively hostile, the press was noticeably silent about black people, as
it eagerly reported the favorable exploits of the successful, public-spirited
white citizens. But when something bad occurred that involved black
people, they were in the news.

Something bad happened one Monday night in Yankton in July 1871.
The house of Elizabeth Johnson, "a colored woman," and her two female
friends, also black, were attacked by a mob of white people, who had
become outraged by the rumor that Johnson and her friends were about
to start a brothel. Between the hours of eleven o'clock and midnight,
the house at the corner of Capital and Fifth Streets was bombarded by
rocks—some about half the size of a man's head—that crashed through
the windows, battering the walls and breaking furniture.

The women screamed in terror as the assault continued with a fury,
but they were fortunately not injured by the rocks. One of the women was
heard to say, "Oh lord, teach me how to pray." Their screams attracted the
attention of several Yankton citizens who came to their rescue and stopped
the attack. They found the panic-stricken women in their night clothes,
frightened but uninjured.

Calling the incident "An Outrage," the *Yankton Press* condemned the attack in the harshest terms: "The sentiment of the community will not sustain violent measures of this character, however much it is desired to suppress bawdy houses." The *Press* boldly declared that in this instance the "prejudice" directed at the women was "more because of the complexion, than the character of the individuals." It was well known that there were houses of prostitution "occupied by white folks," and yet these places were granted immunity, while the Johnson house was attacked. This fact alone, according to the *Press*, proved that the mob was motivated by racial prejudice. The "Ku Klux" was blamed for the assault.[3]

No member of the mob was identified, and no one was ever arrested for the dangerous attack, and in time the anxiety caused by the incident subsided. In the aftermath, the black community in Yankton continued to thrive while the businesses that employed them reveled in the commercial success of the early 1870s. Work aboard the steamboats and on the levee was hard but steady, and that was what everyone—black and white together—wanted.

When it came to race relations no publicity was good publicity. But the calm was shattered by a well-publicized "shooting affray." Charles Bronson, a white man, was seriously wounded on April 10, 1875, in Yankton on Douglas Street, resulting in the arrest of Jane Proteau, a "colored" woman, also of Yankton. Though it was reported that she had booked passage on a departing steamboat, Proteau had actually been jailed and was awaiting further findings.[4]

Jane Proteau was the wife of Jerry Proteau, a hard-drinking French-Canadian trader who claimed a long and fascinating history as a Dakotan. He had left St. Louis and set out to explore the Missouri River region in 1848 in the employ of the American Fur Company. In 1854 his wanderings took him to the Black Hills in the company of Sir George Gore, an English sportsman. The renowned frontiersmen Jim Bridger was their guide. While exploring the Black Hills, Proteau claimed that he found gold in Swift Creek, scooped up handfuls of the precious metal and filled his shirt pockets. He told his story in tantalizing detail to a crowd of eager listeners in Yankton in May 1875, not long after the arrest of his wife for murder. It was also the time when gold fever was sweeping the country.[5]

Whether the Proteaus enjoyed a lawful marriage is not clear, but in 1869 they were operating a roadhouse in the Bijou Hills close to the Fort Randall military road. Since Jane was a good cook, their place was a popular stop for travelers. An entry in an 1870 census record shows that the Proteaus were living in Buffalo County with their five daughters. Very little is known about Jane Proteau, except that she was the mother of "a half dozen children" and had a "bad reputation." The 1870 Dakota census record indicates that she was from Missouri.

Charles Bronson, the victim, was a young man and "well known as an early resident of Yankton." He had been drinking heavily the day of the shooting and was later taken to his parents' home "in the upper part of the city." There he remained in critical condition until his death on the 24th.[6]

On April 28, 1875, a coroner's inquest was held to determine the cause of Bronson's death and whether a crime had been committed. A number of witnesses were questioned, among them William Kramer, the express agent for the Dakota Southern Railroad. He recalled seeing a man and woman talking and then saw the woman "snap" a pistol. It misfired and she pulled the trigger again, the bullet hitting the man in the stomach. Kramer approached the man—whom he identified as Bronson—and with the aid of another witness dragged him to "the wheeling room of the depot and left him there." Kramer said he could not tell whether the woman who pulled the trigger was "white or colored," but he believed Jane Proteau did the shooting.

J. D. Prentiss, who was with Kramer at the time of the shooting, testified that he heard "Mrs. Proteau say two or three times 'go away.'" He said Proteau was standing in the door of her house with her little girl beside her.

Another witness, Robert McCormick, had a closer view of the shooting. He heard two people arguing back and forth on the sidewalk in front of Proteau's residence. The man uttered a remark that the *Press and Dakotaian* concluded was too vulgar for publication. McCormick said Proteau told Bronson that she would shoot him if he did not leave her alone. Bronson was overheard saying that he, too, had a gun and could shoot as well as she could shoot. After he uttered the vulgar remark, she shot him in the side.

Jane Proteau's eleven-year-old daughter, Margy, present when the shooting occurred, was asked to give her version of the event. Margy said that Bronson came to the door and asked about some washing. She, too, mentioned that Bronson had made a vulgar remark, which the reporter had no qualms about repeating in his article. The little girl said that while Bronson was "stooping to pick up a rock" he called her "mama" a "black dirty bitch and said he would knock her brains out." After hearing that, Margy said her mother "got her pistol and said she would try and give him a scare." Jane fired the pistol and "he ran off a piece and came back," saying he also had a gun. Margy said her mother waited for him to shoot, while telling him repeatedly to go away. Bronson then told Jane to shoot; she fired her pistol striking him, after which he was taken away to the depot, mortally wounded.

A doctor testified as to the nature of the wound and the cause of death. The coroner's jury concluded that Charles Bronson had met his death after being shot once from a pistol by Jane Proteau at or near the doorway of her residence on Douglas Street in Yankton. Jane Proteau was jailed and the next day released after three prominent Yankton men—J. R. Sanborn, John Treadway, and Charles F. Rossteuscher—posted a $2,000 bond.[7]

Judge Peter C. Shannon was a busy public servant in the spring of 1875, with numerous cases on his calendar, among them the trial of Jane Proteau for manslaughter. If she had been worried about facing a racist judge, her fears were misplaced, for Shannon had long ago established a reputation for fairness and racial equality under the law. In 1869 Shannon publicly supported the application of a black man to become a member of the Pennsylvania bar, speaking "boldly for equal rights." The applicant, George B. Vashon, was denied in Pittsburgh, but sometime later was admitted to the bar of Washington, D.C., and Peter C. Shannon was remembered for having judged the man on his character and qualifications for practicing law, rather than on the color of his skin.[8]

Jane Proteau received the same consideration. She was treated with respect by the newspapers and not pre-judged because of her race. After a two-day trial in Yankton, the jury convicted her of second-degree manslaughter but asked for the court's mercy. While she was behind bars waiting for the sentencing date, the women of Yankton circulated a petition seeking a pardon for the newly convicted felon. Although Proteau clearly inspired a degree of sympathy, the petition was thought of in some quarters as a direct and unlawful interference with the judicial process.

At the sentencing, Judge Shannon spoke calmly, saying that a jury "composed of some of our best citizens and neighbors of the prisoner, after hearing all the evidence, had pronounced her guilty of manslaughter in the second degree." Showing that he was irked at the pardon petition, Shannon went into a short lecture about the danger of people taking action "outside the court house" based on information received from "unreliable or partisan persons." Such unwise acts, he said, "undermine the temple of justice." The judge understood that people in the community felt sorry for the defendant and her small children, but he reminded those present that sympathy for the woman who pulled the trigger was more than offset by the pain of a grieving mother who had to bury her son.

After he finished his stern lecture, Shannon sentenced Proteau to two years imprisonment. This occurred during the morning session of court, and by mid-afternoon Jane Proteau was a free woman, having received a pardon from the secretary of state and acting governor, George H. Hand, in the governor's absence.[9] After receiving one of the fastest pardons in the West, she stayed in Yankton and became a member of a "thriving black community that would develop in the 1880s."[10]

The outcome of the Proteau case gives rise to many questions. Why was Jane Proteau, a black woman, bailed out of jail by three prominent

Yankton gentlemen? What possible interest could they have had in her welfare? Did she not shoot and kill a young man from a prominent family? Further, why would the white women of the community take pity on Proteau and her plight?

All are tantalizing questions, to be sure, but without more details there are no clear answers. Perhaps the town of Yankton simply took pity on Jane Proteau, but her benefactors had nothing in common with her and most certainly did not consider her a social equal. Speculation suggests that, as a woman with a "bad reputation," at least according to the newspapers, she may have been privy to information that would embarrass several respected townspeople, so she was therefore granted assistance from the desirables to keep her from talking: a favor for a favor. If there were any such dark secrets, they were taken to many a grave, long ago.

In the middle of Judge Shannon's second term on the Dakota bench, he was called upon to preside over the case of a young black man named Lankston Cain, known familiarly as "Lank" Cain. In March 1879 Cain was arrested and charged with raping a young girl, the daughter of Mr. and Mrs. Silas C. F. Norman. The Norman family had lived in the Yankton area for several years. Mr. Norman, known as "C. F. Norman," had been a key witness in the Peter P. Wintermute murder trial in 1874.

With fury and indignation, the *Dakota Herald* reported the incident under the headline "The Negro Rape Fiend in Yankton." A "black monster" had attacked and ravished a young white girl "on the open prairie," and the Yankton newspaper made certain that its readers were exposed to all the hellish details of the terrible crime.

It was, in fact, a shocking incident, one that aroused stereotypical fears held by many white residents. Sparing no harsh words, the *Herald* dredged up biases that simmered just below the surface of racial relationships of the time. It was possible to take the black man out of the South, society concluded, but impossible to take the South and its long, tragic record, out of the black man.

As such, Lank Cain was not the "accused" or even a "suspect," he was "a black-hearted, black skinned, beastly scoundrel of a negro," according to the *Herald*. As related by the newspaper, ten-year-old Mary Jane Norman was on her way home from Sunday school about four o'clock in the afternoon. She was walking along the Bon Homme road in the direction of her parents' farm, approximately two miles west of Yankton. At "a lonely spot on the prairie," Mary said she encountered Lank Cain on horseback. He dismounted and attacked her "and proceeded to gratify his hellish, animal promptings."

In the midst of this sexual assault, Thornton W. Brisbane, Yankton County probate judge, rode by and interrupted the attack. Cain mounted up and rode toward the city. Brisbane came to the assistance of Mary Jane Norman, questioned her, and told her to go home and report the incident to her mother. Meanwhile, Brisbane went to Yankton and reported the attack to the authorities. Deputy Marshal Bates got a warrant and went to the residence of George Wilcox, at the corner of Second and Cedar Streets, where Cain was known to be staying. After some resistance, Bates arrested Cain and took him to jail.

Next, Bates and other interested parties went to the Norman residence, where they learned that Mary had not revealed to her mother any details of the alleged crime. At this point her parents were apparently not concerned, but by the time the adult conversation had ended the Normans believed the worst.

As word spread, the public rose up in anger. During the evening, groups of men gathered and spoke about "an immediate lynching," but they took no action. On the afternoon of Cain's arraignment before the justice of the peace, a large crowd milled about in the street. At some point, Norman and his daughter entered the office of the justice of the peace. She was asked to identify the man who attacked her and unhesitatingly pointed to Cain, aka Patterson. Her father then drew a pistol and took aim at the defendant's head. As Norman fired, Cain's legal counsel, Oliver Shannon, reacted. He struck Norman's arm, causing the bullet to enter Cain's leg.[11]

The *Dakota Pantagraph,* citing the *Press,* reported that Cain, age seventeen, was seated at the counsel table when Norman approached from behind, pushing his way through a crowd. He asked his daughter, "is this the nigger?" After she "replied affirmatively," Norman pulled his gun and the deflected shot struck Cain in the leg, causing a "flesh wound."[12]

The gunshot set off a "general stampede." When Sheriff Millard A. Baker seized Norman, the defendant, though wounded, ran out the back door and "flew like a streak out to Walnut Street and thence up Third" with a crowd in hot pursuit. Cain was overtaken, knocked down, and held by Charley Long, one of the pursuers. While others pressed toward Cain, Sheriff Baker forced his way into the mass and took charge of his prisoner. The crowd gave way but remained in the street all afternoon and into the evening.

According to the *Herald,* the angry crowd turned into a mob intent on breaking into the jail, seizing Cain, and hanging him without benefit of due process. But the sheriff, anticipating trouble, stationed extra guards near the jail. Although the lynch mob did not make its move, Norman "slipped into the corridor of the jail" still determined to kill Cain. Fortunately for both men, the sheriff disarmed Norman and had him returned to his home. There were no further incidents that night.[13]

As a matter of fact, few untoward incidents of any sort related to the case occurred. The anger that afflicted the community subsided as the matter worked its way through the territorial court system. Although the outrage was a reflection of racial prejudice in Dakota, it should be pointed out that had Lank Cain been an accused rapist of a white girl in the post-war South, there is little doubt that he would have been lynched.

Cain's trial was delayed due to the absence of the prosecution's key witness, Judge Brisbane. In early April Brisbane had booked passage on the steamer *Terry* bound for Fort Keogh. "When his absence became known," Judge Shannon issued a bench warrant for "his apprehension and return to Yankton to be in attendance when [he was] wanted as a witness." Brisbane was taken into custody by Sheriff Baker at Springfield and escorted to

Yankton.[14] With Brisbane at the ready, a short jury trial took place, largely ignored by the local newspapers, and Cain was found guilty of first-degree rape. On July 5, 1879, Cain was sentenced by Judge Shannon to twelve years in prison at hard labor. He could have received a life sentence.[15]

Cain's assailant, C. F. Norman, was indicted by a grand jury for shooting him. Although the act was done in the presence of several witnesses, and was at the very least an offense against the dignity of the system of due process, Norman was acquitted after a jury trial in district court.[16]

The Lankston Cain case represents the most dangerous and dramatic example of racial tension in Dakota Territory. He survived, but was justice served? The relatively light sentence indicates that Judge Shannon may have had doubts about his guilt—concerns that may have arisen from his knowledge of racism in post-Civil War America.

Serious questions remain as to the guilt or innocence of the seventeen-year-old African-American. Based on newspaper reports, it appears that Mary Jane Norman did not provide the convincing evidence. Rather, the adults who met and discussed the matter determined the evidence. Although of an age when she should have been able to describe in some detail what had transpired on that country road, she apparently did not say anything that indicated sexual assault. Perhaps the adults filled in the blanks, fabricating a rape charge out of their cultural fear of African-American men. Had Cain merely stopped to ask the girl for directions, many Yankton residents would have argued, he would have been in the wrong.

Yet with memories of the Civil War fresh in the minds of everyone, and oppressive racist laws taking root in the South, some sense of dignity and justice emerged in Dakota. The mood of the people shifted away from vengeance toward an application of the rule of law. While the charge might have been false, the outcome was at least more humane than what might have occurred in a community without a strong judicial system.

Of related interest to the Cain case is the death of Mary Jane's mother, who died in Yankton within a few weeks after the sentencing.

Two weeks prior, she had suffered a paralytic stroke from which she never recovered. But while preparing the body for burial, people noticed small signs of life as she lay in the coffin, including perspiration and suppleness of her extremities. A doctor was summoned and pronounced her dead but confirmed that he, too, noticed the unmistakable signs of life. He advised that she be left unburied until there were indications of decomposition.[17]

People in the nineteenth century lived in mortal dread of being buried alive. Faced with this possibility, the Norman family, and the community, must have suffered. Most knowledgeable persons could recall reading or hearing about a corpse suddenly returning to life at a funeral or of a premature burial in America or Europe. Was Mrs. Norman really dead or in a trance? Was she in a state of suspended animation? In any case, the family postponed the funeral.[18]

Prostitution, like racism, challenged the social structure throughout Dakota Territory. Prostitution worked its way into a community by following transportation routes and human motives. Female prostitutes came with the railroads and steamboats, some on their own and others as the victims of sex trafficking. They found work where single men were plentiful and the availability of wives was not. Once established in a city or town, "fallen women" raised the eyebrows and the ire of disapproving residents and attracted the attention of newspapers, law enforcement, and judges.

Had they quietly and discreetly provided sexual services for money, Yankton's prostitutes would have attracted much less attention. But many of the women were bold and rowdy as well as frequent and heavy drinkers. Their howling, drunken sprees in public were not uncommon, and arrests were well, and sometimes humorously, publicized.

To combat the menace posed by the growth of brothels, the Yankton city council adopted an ordinance on November 8, 1872, dealing with "disorderly houses." The ordinance was not designed to close the houses down, but rather to regulate them. Section 1 made the following activities unlawful:

> Any person who within the limits of this city, shall keep or
> maintain, or shall be an inmate of, or in any way connected
> with, or shall in any manner contribute to the support of any
> house of prostitution or other disorderly house, or shall know-
> ingly lease any building, place, lot or premises to any notorious
> prostitute, or to any other person, for the purpose of being kept
> or used as a house or place of prostitution.

Anyone who violated this ordinance was subject to a fine of $50 and a maximum of ten days in jail. People connected with "noisy" brothels that disturbed the "peace and quiet" of the city were fined $50 plus thirty days in jail. The ordinance decreed that on the first day of every month the city marshal was to report violations to a designated justice of the peace. All such persons accused would then be arrested. "All such persons" included "pimps, vagrants, or other idle of dissolute persons" and those who "indecently expose themselves to public gaze."[19]

With this ordinance, Mayor Franklin J. DeWitt and the city council had spread their nets far and wide, and soon after hauled in a large catch of people, mostly women, who appeared before a justice of peace and forked over money for fines or, if they were unable to pay, sat in jail. The steady flow of revenue was not free enterprise in its purest form, but it served to spread the wealth around. As long as business at the bagnios flourished, those who ran the unholy, but profitable, enterprises, reaped the rewards— the sex workers, themselves, and the city of Yankton.

Authorities established a routine by which women were regularly brought before a justice of the peace "to make their monthly contributions

Brothel owner Maria Briggs' gravestone,
Yankton City Cemetery.
Photo by author.

to the city treasury."[20] As in a comedy of errors, the *Press and Dakotaian*
noted that "several girls" appeared before Justice Charles F. Rossteuscher
and were assessed their "regular" fine of $20.10 each. The Yankton daily
then added that "they are among the city's most reliable taxpayers."[21]
This practice continued over a period of several years, and it would be
interesting to know how much revenue from the "sin tax" was gained in

regular "monthly assessments." Prostitution was bad behavior but good business in the territorial capital.

Some in the prostitution trade became successful businesswomen. Maria Briggs, for years a "madame" at a Yankton brothel, for example, showed skill and tenacity in running her business while dealing with the public, her customers, and the law. The exact date of her arrival in Yankton is unknown, but Briggs and her friend Belle Wilson soon became the principal providers of sexual services from their respective houses.

In May of 1877 the *Press and Dakotaian* carried a small notice that "a new house on the levee between Walnut and Cedar is being built by Maria Briggs."[22] Very soon after, though, Briggs was making headlines because of her arrest for operating a house of "ill-fame." In an important and closely observed case that went before the Dakota Supreme Court, her business became the basis for a shake-up of Yankton city government. The resulting court decision was called "The Legal Opinion Which Upset the Old Order of Things."[23]

First, Briggs was hauled up before the city justice of the peace on a charge of keeping a house of ill-fame. She pled guilty and paid a fine of $22.70 to Justice Rossteuscher. Concurrent with this action, on May 4, 1876, she was indicted by the district court, along with Belle Wilson, on the same charge.[24]

Briggs hired a Yankton attorney, S. W. Arnold, and at the district court trial she entered a plea of prior judgment. In other words, since she had just pled guilty and paid the penalty in the city court, her lawyer insisted that she could not be charged again for the same offense. But to her dismay her case went forward and she was found guilty by a jury, which recommended, however, that the fine she paid to Justice Rossteuscher be returned to her.[25]

She appealed the conviction to the Dakota Supreme Court, whose decision was published in the *Press and Dakotaian* in two parts, beginning on August 28. Arnold argued that his client should not have been subjected to another trial on the same offense. He told the court that the city justice decided that if Briggs paid the fine "it would be a bar to prosecution in district court." Justice A. H. Barnes, writing for the Supreme Court, ripped into the "so-called" city justice calling his action "high-handed" and "unwarrantable." But he said that, however inappropriate, it had no bearing on the case before the court.

Of great importance, though, was the question of how a city justice of the peace obtained his mantle of judicial power. Barnes pointed out that federal law regarding territories required that he be elected by the people of the city. This conflicted with a territorial law that allowed the mayor to appoint city justices from the roll of registered voters in a city. In this instance Rossteuscher was an appointee, and therefore not qualified to serve. An indignant Justice Barnes wrote that "he [Rossteuscher] is clothed with no judicial power or authority to act." The city of Yankton was placed on notice; it had to get busy and duly elect its city justices.

Next, Barnes turned to what he called the core issue: did the trial court err when it refused to permit the defendant, Maria Briggs, to "interpose the plea of not guilty"? Arnold contended that a not-guilty plea in district court was appropriate because by her former guilty plea in city court she had wiped the slate clean, so to speak. She could not in fact be found guilty twice for the same offense.[26] And based upon a statute enacted by the eighth session of the territorial legislature, the point was well taken. Section 13 of the criminal procedure code made the following provision: "No person can be subjected to a second prosecution for a public offense for which he has once been prosecuted and duly convicted or acquitted."[27] Unfortunately, Arnold failed to cite this criminal procedure code and never insisted that his client was being victimized by double jeopardy, a fate prohibited by the Fifth Amendment of U.S. Constitution.

Justice Barnes ignored the territorial code and the Constitution and instead focused on a statute pertaining to the right of a defendant to enter pleas. While the statute permitted a defendant to plead both not guilty and prior judgment at the same time, Maria Briggs failed to do so. Barnes wrote, "had the defendant a desire to avail herself of the two pleas, she had only to have expressed herself at the proper time." Briggs' lawyer made the mistake but she was out of luck, based on a "technicality." Chief Justice Shannon concurred in the ruling that affirmed the trial court's decision.[28]

Determined and resilient, Briggs stayed in Yankton and pursued her line of work. On March 19, 1893, she died of typhoid fever at the age of fifty-five. Her obituary was kind considering her standing in the community. Noting that Briggs was the "only remaining bagnio proprietress" in Yankton, the paper called her a "woman of kindly impulses, considerable intelligence and wide acquaintance." She left an estate of about $35,000, more than enough to mark her grave in the Yankton City Cemetery with a tall and stylish tombstone that rivals those of "respectable" people.[29]

Another case involving prostitution made its way to the Dakota Supreme Court in 1877, featuring as the aggrieved party Joseph Chartrand, also known as "French Joe." His background is unknown but he likely came to Yankton in the 1870s, along with other faceless members of the floating population of the frontier. On June 28, 1876, the *Press and Dakotaian* advised its readers that Joe Chartrand had erected a street lamp at the corner of Walnut Street and First Street, "which sheds light for the public good."[30] Since that street corner places the lamp near the levee, this could have been an oblique reference to a "red light," signifying some undesirable business activity.

In April 1877 Chartrand was charged and arraigned for keeping a house of ill-fame. He retained S. L. Spink, an experienced, skillful criminal attorney and a brilliant orator, as his legal counsel. French Joe pled not guilty and was let out on bail.[31] Thereafter, things moved rather quickly. He was convicted by a jury, based on testimony from a witness who saw him working at the house and who testified that the people who frequented the place were of "bad reputation." Judge Shannon sentenced Chartrand to nine months in the county jail, along with a fine of $200. On May 2 Spink announced that he would file an appeal because the jury verdict did "not conform to the allegations in the indictment."[32]

Shannon denied a motion for new trial and the appellate process went forward. In June the full Supreme Court met to hear arguments in the Chartrand case. Spink disputed certain jury instructions pertaining to the reputation of the business place in question, whether it qualified as a house of "ill-fame." His point was that simply to instruct the jury that "a house of ill-fame is a house of bad reputation" was ambiguous. Spink could have insisted that if this were the standard of proof, then a bank reputed to have cheated its account holders was a business with a bad reputation and therefore a house of ill-fame.

The court had no patience for Spink's parsing of words and phrases. Justice Barnes, who wrote the decision, refused to tinker with language. He took the position that a house was one of bad reputation if the people, both men and women, who were seen coming and going to and from the house, were "reputed to be of lewd and lascivious character" and that the house was "generally reputed [by the public] to be such house of ill fame." Evidence, he wrote, "tending to show the general reputation of character of the house . . . is admissible."

It was not necessary to prove any actual incidents of prostitution, for example, showing that money was exchanged for sex. Hearsay, rumor, and gossip qualified as competent evidence. According to Barnes, "acts of adultery, acts of lewdness, acts of prostitution, are not acts to which the perpetrators give publicity or notoriety." He declared that "shameless and degraded people" tend to conceal their criminal behavior, and as such, guilt can be established by one or more witnesses whose testimony brings out information, including rumor, about their secret character. If trustworthy people come to a subjective conclusion that someone is bad, the law will recognize the truth of it. And taking the gossamer logic even further, if enough "bad" people frequented a certain house, it became a house of "ill-fame." Barnes could simply have said that he did not know how to define a house of ill-fame, but he knew one when he saw it, or when it was described to him.

Given the vague and flimsy instruction and low threshold of proof, it was relatively easy for the jury to find that the house was in fact "bad" and a place of prostitution merely by listening to a witness who suggested or speculated that such activity took place. It was equally easy to find that Chartrand was "keeping the house," for he was seen there acting as a keeper and bartender. Barnes was joined in his opinion by Chief Justice Shannon and Associate Justice Granville G. Bennett, and French Joe's misdemeanor conviction was upheld.[33]

Chartrand was confined in the Yankton County jail in accordance with the sentence. But his case aroused the sympathy of the public as well as public officials, and as a result acting governor Hand issued a full pardon to the prisoner on the condition that he pay a fine and court costs. The pardon was given because the condition of the jail was so bad that Chartrand's health was placed in danger. This was backed up by physicians who inspected the jail and spoke in favor of an early release.[34]

After he was released from jail, Chartrand apparently tried to keep a low profile. He was French but he was no Cuthbert DuCharme and did not live simply to engage in bizarre or unlawful behavior in the manner of "Old Pap." No, indeed, for on March 25, 1879, Joe placed a card in the *Press and Dakotaian* announcing his intention to quit the saloon business. And to thank all his friends and patrons, he offered a free lunch at the Brewery Saloon. It was to be one last evening of conviviality.[35]

It was a kind gesture, but Joe Chartrand would never be numbered among the desirables. In fact, he continued to get in trouble with the law. In April 1879 he was found guilty of selling liquor to an Indian.[36] Eventually, he moved to Pierre where he died of diphtheria in March 1881.[37]

By the 1880s the wide-open days of the "levee mansions" were over, or at least their notoriety had become subdued. As action slowed down in Yankton, prostitutes migrated further west, to the other river town of Pierre or the mining camps of Deadwood. It was, after all, a business that thrived in frontier communities where its practitioners were considered less undesirable.

CHAPTER 12

TROUBLE MOVES WEST: GOLD IN THE BLACK HILLS

*"Rich mines of gold and silver, in a beautiful, well watered
and timbered region, is the general purport of the welcome
news that electrifies the whole country."*

Daily Press and Dakotaian
August 18, 1874

D akota Territory and its capital city suffered a double-barreled setback in the early 1870s, having been hit by the scandalous Wintermute murder trials and the great grasshopper calamity. The collapse of the national economy following the Panic of 1873 made day-to-day life even worse for struggling merchants and farmers. The stock market crashed, businesses closed, prices fell through the floor, and in some instances officials helped themselves to money from their own banks and corporations—and then vanished with their plunder.[1] The depression that followed the panic affected every part of America.

Heavily dependent on federal money, outside investment and immigration, young Dakota Territory was hit especially hard. But no part of the country was spared; in a time of a trickle-down economy, the trickle dried up. While those with means and money could ride out the storm, for others, suffering was a part of the daily fare. Children were hungry, women were scared, and men bore the look of desperation. While newspapers tried to put a positive spin on the bad economy, many of their readers lived on the desperate edge of ruin, searching for an escape from the run of bad luck, hoping that the promise of a prosperous future might be revived.

181

George A. Custer,
leader of the Black Hills Expedition of 1874.
Courtesy Library of Congress.

Proud Dakotans would have welcomed just about anything to relieve the economic pain. What they got was more than a lift. They got GOLD! In the summer of 1874 electrifying news of gold in the Black Hills hit the territorial presses. The excitement blew into other regions of the country like a raging storm out of the Northwest. Nature had opened wide revealing a new cornucopia of gleaming, glittering riches, and Dakota, a region ignored by many in the East, was soon on the lips of people all across America. The discovery of gold in the Black Hills was elixir for men who habitually had their sights set on grand possibilities and were eager to leap into the unknown, risks be damned.

While it was the well-publicized Black Hills Expedition of 1874 that confirmed the existence of gold in the Black Hills, stories had long been circulated among Dakota residents that the world's most precious metal existed in large quantities, waiting to be picked up and make fortune-hunting adventurers rich beyond their wildest dreams of avarice. And then, suddenly, there was proof—and once again the federal government was the provider. Lieutenant Colonel George Armstrong Custer's well-equipped, 1,000-man caravan—complete with Gatling guns, journalists, scientists, a son of the president, and an expert photographer—may have constituted an illegal entry on Indian land, but they went about their explorations unchallenged amidst the beautiful Black Hills scenery.

Among the men on the expedition with either mining or tracking expertise was William T. McKay, the erstwhile member of the Dakota legislature and prominent murder suspect. Acting as a "scientific miner," McKay landed a starring role in the Custer extravaganza. But McKay and fellow miner Horatio N. Ross were not "officially" part of the expedition, whose stated purpose was to conduct a reconnaissance, not to search for gold. An article in the *New York Tribune* made it clear that the expedition was scientific only, and "no miners or adventurers will . . . be allowed to accompany the expedition."[2] And yet McKay and Ross were allowed to participate. To everyone with knowledge of the expedition, they were simply "with Custer."[3]

Also with Custer was Professor Nathaniel H. Winchell, a geologist, mineralogist, and "a knowing man in the crowd." But it was said that Custer had "about as much faith in the professor's opinions as he had in the barking of his dogs." What he wanted was men who could "tell gold when they saw it," such as McKay and Ross.[4]

Another member of the Custer expedition was George Bird Grinnell, editor, author, ethnologist, and naturalist from an aristocratic eastern family. Grinnell was fascinated with the West and its rough characters

Custer's expedition winds its way through the Black Hills.
Courtesy Robert W. Kolbe Collection.

and spent considerable time talking to McKay and Ross. He also wrote about the expedition, and on the evening of July 26 he recalled hearing Ross say, "we'll lay over tomorrow and that means Mac [McKay] and I will be busy all day sinking prospect holes and shoveling dirt." The next morning Grinnell watched as McKay and Ross left camp with a pack mule and tools.[5]

McKay and Ross, the mystery men, were "said to have been worth a fortune many times as they had toes," and they knew "the names of every gulch west of the Rocky Mountains." The two veteran miners drew rapt attention as they openly searched the terrain and streams for signs of gold. McKay was heard to say, "Now, by gosh, it begins to look like something." The entire world soon read about their glittering success. A Chicago newspaper, the *Inter-Ocean*, sounded the trumpets for all to hear with news that the "Precious Dust [was] Found in the Grass under the Horses' Feet."[6]

McKay kept a journal in which he wrote the following account: "In the evening, I took a pan and pick and shovel, and went out prospecting. The first pan full was taken from the gravel and sand obtained in the bed of the creek; and on washing was found to contain one and a half or two cents, which was the first gold found in the Black Hills." McKay continued to pan downstream from his original discovery and found another three cents worth of gold. He showed it to Custer and George Forsyth, noting that "I never saw two better pleased generals in my life."[7]

According to a book penned by a pair of Black Hills pioneers, McKay found gold in Gold Run Creek, a tributary to Castle Creek. The date was July 27, 1874. His claim to being the first to find gold was disputed by Ross, who found gold in French Creek near the present-day city of Custer. Ross had the advantage of outliving his fellow prospector and was therefore able to trumpet his claim loud and long.[8]

Another writer believed that McKay and Ross experienced their "Eureka!" moment on July 30 in the "upper reaches of French Creek." There the two men "panned about $75 worth of gold." The discovery set off a "frenzy of prospecting from the troopers." One happy trooper said that "gold fever is like taking dope."[9]

T. A. Rickard, in *A History of American Mining*, also preferred that date, when the Custer expedition "halted in a natural park near the granite ramparts of Harney's Peak" and began a search for gold. Rickard contends Ross was first and that he found gold in French Creek on August 1, 1874. After the excitement subsided, a group of men sat around a campfire and divided up twenty mining claims, with Ross being awarded "the discovery" claim and his partner, McKay, receiving a claim designated as number four.[10]

Fifty years later, knowledgeable men were still debating the question, "who was first?" Luther North, a scientist who accompanied Grinnell, gave the nod to Ross: "I remember it as if it was yesterday."[11] South Dakota state historian Doane Robinson, while not as adamant, was unwilling to give all credit to Ross. He insisted that "due credit be given to the claim" of McKay as "original discoverer along with Henry [sic] N. Ross." Robinson pointed out that Custer's "official report" made no reference to Ross, but rather gave "full credit" to "Billie" McKay for "the first pan of gold sediment."[12]

In that glorious summer of 1874, the press and the public did not care who received credit for being first to discover gold, nor were they overly concerned about the details of the discovery. It was more than sufficient that gold was, indeed, among the mineral resources in the Black Hills. An authority no less than George Armstrong Custer had confirmed it.

Custer liked publicity, and the connection to the discovery of gold would be enough to keep his name in the historical spotlight for centuries. He understood that the news would set off a wave of humanity in the direction of the Black Hills, creating problems for the army. But the good far outweighed the bad, and besides, there was more to it than gold. Custer was equally enraptured with the scenery and raved about the taste of the wild raspberries.[13]

Having gained national recognition, McKay returned to Yankton and was interviewed and almost lionized by the Yankton press. The *Press and Dakotaian* explained that McKay was employed by Custer because of "his knowledge of the country and valuable experience." The notorious whiskey peddler told an eager audience that he found gold in "eight streams having their rise in the Black Hills." He was ready to start for the Black Hills again "as soon as the season will permit." Said to be a man who understood the language of the Sioux and the "Indian character," McKay had been "too long on the frontier to be caught out on the plains before grass is abundant." Like the opportunist he never ceased to be, finding gold was the formula he needed to regain his full measure of respectability.[14]

McKay talked up gold in the Black Hills with so much exuberance that people forgot about the Snake Creek lynching. He boasted about recruiting a large number of Iowa men to join him on a Black Hills expedition.[15] He told anxious listeners about a man named Antoine LeBois, who had explored the Black Hills in the mid-1850s and washed gold out of the Box Elder River.[16]

The *Press and Dakotaian* kept a watchful eye on McKay throughout the month of May 1875, although all the old suspicions seemed to have vanished. In the recent past, he was regarded as an outlaw whiskey seller, a party to a lynching, and a political adventurer. Suddenly he was "Major" W. T. McKay, and it was with pride that the Yankton daily announced that General Custer expressed a desire to have "Major McKay" accompany him on his "contemplated [second] trip to the Black Hills."[17]

The discovery of gold came when America needed an infusion of good news, and the redeemed McKay was happy to be a part of it, relishing his celebrity status. A Black Hills gold rush would provide much needed adrenalin during a time of great crisis when weary heads were bowed in hunger and stress. In cities all across America, men met to discuss and arrange for the long journey to the new promised land. An exodus of gold-crazy miners and opportunists or the just plain desperate erupted following news that gold could be picked out of the numerous streams. Or better yet, it could be gleaned from the grassroots. The "color" was gold and it was good.

Gold in the Black Hills dominated the hearts and minds of Dakotans in the summer of 1874 and throughout 1875. It was something that seemed to reach into every home, hovel, camp, hotel, and shop, giving rise to excited conversation and hastily convened meetings to consider a run for the gold. Old miners and explorers who had been to the Black Hills and returned with their scalps intact were eager to reveal their experiences and talk about others who had met with success and riches or failure and death.

Excited talk about Black Hills gold was not confined to Dakota. In the spring of 1875 Judge Peter C. Shannon and his wife traveled to St. Louis to visit one of their daughters. Upon their return to Yankton, the judge said that "wherever he stopped people were talking about the Black Hills."[18]

The nation's newspapers were in on it too, and since stories of gold increased circulation, they promoted gold fever for all it was worth. Exaggerated stories of great riches waiting to be scooped from the Black Hills' streams encouraged fortune hunters, who in turn put pressure on the federal government to extinguish the Indians' title to the land. The *Inter-Ocean*, Chicago's West-watching newspaper, declared, "It would be a sin against the country and the world to permit this region, so rich in treasure, to remain unimproved and unoccupied, merely to furnish hunting grounds for savages."[19]

Unable to ignore the clamor, Washington, D.C., was prodded into action, and during the summer of 1875, the federal government launched another Black Hills expedition. This one was to be purely scientific and was led by Walter P. Jenney of the New York School of Mines. He was accompanied by Colonel Richard I. Dodge and 400 soldiers, along with a team of scientists including seventeen geologists. Jenney confirmed Custer's claim, and soon news was circulated in the press that gold in the Black Hills could pay off the national debt.[20] This expedition, though more subdued than Custer's, nevertheless played into the public's curiosity about the Black Hills.

Reports by the "experts," along with stories from skeptics, caused interest in the Black Hills to rise and fall like the peaks and valleys of that beautiful land, but interest never subsided altogether. Men formed organizations and made plans to see the land of fabulous beauty and great wealth for themselves. Each group was brim full of enthusiasm and never lacked for members, but each time the federal government intervened, telling them to cease and desist, the groups disbanded but never lost hope. When it came to gold, the risks were always worth taking, or at least being given thoughtful consideration.

The problem the eager gold hunters faced was that of trespassing on Indian land. The Black Hills belonged to the Sioux tribes, guaranteed by the Treaty of 1868 to remain in their possession. By the terms of that treaty, the U.S. government was required to obtain the express consent of at least three-fourths of the adult male Indian population to buy or take any land from what came to be known as the Great Sioux Reservation.

Some white men, including missionaries, wanted the government to live up to its treaty obligations so as to make sure Native Americans kept the Black Hills. They sensed that the Indians would fight rather than surrender their ancestral mountain range and believed another great Indian war was in the offing, should the treaty be ignored or violated. "So what?" exclaimed the *Bismarck Tribune*, which called for a war with the Indians, believing that it would come "sooner or later."[21]

A correspondent to the *Dakota Herald* placed some blame for the dilemma on Custer, claiming the colorful colonel was trying to start a war with the Sioux. "All of us know," observed the correspondent, "that General Custer has an impatient thirst for the clash of arms and more military glory and more rank." The writer said that during the course of his 1874 excursion Custer tried to provoke an attack "by marching two days off his natural course."[22]

The Black Hills, *Paha Sapa,* are sacred to the Sioux and many other Plains peoples. White men, therefore, were forbidden to enter. The Sioux placed no intrinsic value on gold and did not reside in the Black Hills, but they went there to hunt and to hold spiritual ceremonies. They patrolled the region and there is evidence that they showed no mercy to white intruders. As far back as 1857, at a great council in the Black Hills, the tribes "resolved to execute any tribesman who revealed the existence of gold in the Hills."[23]

Most white people disapproved of the native, "pagan" religion, certainly a convenience for also disregarding the Indians' claim that the Black Hills were sacred. Had the region been smaller in area, they might have been willing to carve out a section. For example, Pipestone Quarry, a defined space in southwestern Minnesota, was accorded sacred status. The difference is that the ground in Minnesota contained stone, not gold.

The federal and territorial governments sympathized with the would-be miners, but their hands were tied because of the treaty, which was the law of the land. There was no choice but to issue orders against any proposed mining expedition. Edwin S. McCook, in his capacity as acting governor, issued one such "keep out" proclamation in April 1872, although it is highly unlikely that he favored Indian rights to the land.

Another eviction order was published on March 22, 1875. Secretary of the Interior Columbus Delano reminded those eager to mine that the land belonged to the Indians according to the Treaty of 1868, and he requested that "all persons now unlawfully in that territory . . . to leave immediately." Those who refused to leave voluntarily faced forced eviction by the army.[24]

If that order was not clear enough, Delano, in a written response to an interested party on May 7, declared the following: "You cannot be permitted by authority of the United States to enter any Indian territory, and public notice to this effect has been so frequently given as to scarcely require a repetition of this information."[25]

The orders, warnings, and notices had little impact, however, and by the spring of 1875 several groups of prospectors had entered the Hills, dodging both the Indians and the army. At mid-summer it was reported that 800 to 1,500 miners were there, and more were "coming at the rate of 20 per day and the new gulches and ravines are thickly settled."

Then on July 29, 1875, General George Crook issued a proclamation that any miner caught trespassing would not be allowed to stay. All those illegally in the Black Hills were given until August 15 to get out. The feedback from the miners was favorable, and it was reported that most intended to comply with the understanding that they could return when it was legal to do so.[26]

The anxious miners got some good news in the summer of 1875 from the U.S. attorney general. In a response to a request from Dakota U.S. Attorney William A. Pound, the nation's top law enforcement officer decreed that merely trespassing on Indian land in the Black Hills was not a punishable offense under federal law. The most the authorities could do was escort the trespassers back to ceded land.[27]

Following the edict of the attorney general, the military continued to look for miners. Troops patrolled the area between Fort Pierre and Medicine Creek, and it was announced that a temporary post would be established at Fort Laramie to aid in returning the miners to their homes. Miners began to comply with Crook's proclamation. One miner at Custer City, the first townsite in the Black Hills, seemed willing to leave as long as they were permitted to return. He called Crook's order "fair and manly."[28]

Colonel Frederick W. Benteen's cavalry rounded up forty-nine miners who were leaving their claims, temporarily, in accordance with Crook's order. William T. McKay, now called "Capt." McKay, was among the group, but during the first night on the return trip, he slipped away and returned to the Hills.[29] Having had a taste of notoriety, he wanted more and wanted it so badly that he pursued it until his death on May 27, 1884. William T. McKay, "a remarkable man . . . from . . . excellent parentage; thoroughly educated; at times possessed of a fortune" died of stomach cancer, in the county hospital in Deadwood, alone and penniless.[30]

Recognizing that it would be very difficult, if not impossible, to restrain the fevered prospector, and knowing that it would be easier and far more popular to impose another land-grabbing treaty on the Indians, the government—led by Dakota delegate J. P. Kidder—labored relentlessly on a new deal. Months before the Crook proclamation, treaty negotiations were under way. A commission was appointed and instructed to meet with the Sioux tribes to draft another treaty that would allow access to Black Hills gold.

The treaty seekers had strong support from the Yankton press and businessmen who saw a money-making opportunity of breathless proportions. An editorial in the *Press and Dakotaian* urged hard and fast work toward hammering out a treaty: "Negotiations now in progress for the purchase of the Black Hills by the government will result successfully, and that the country will soon be thrown open to occupation by the whites." The editorial speculated that occupation of the region would occur even before ratification of the treaty. A simple agreement would suffice to release all federal obligations to protect the Indians' rights and interests in the Black Hills.[31]

With or without that kind of encouragement, men continued to succumb to gold fever and disregarded both Indian rights and federal government warnings. Despite determined efforts by the army, parties entered—or re-entered—the Hills before the treaty was finalized. The rush for Black Hills gold brought new camps, string towns, and businesses to western Dakota Territory. For a short time Custer City and Hill City drew the attention of fortune hunters. Then in February 1876 those towns lost miners to the northern Black Hills, where gold was found in Whitewood and Deadwood creeks.

The excitement was felt not only in southeastern Dakota but in Minnesota and Iowa. Hotels and stores were busy greeting strangers from all over the United States, many of whom were Black Hills-bound pilgrims. While most were in possession of a good reputation, many others aroused suspicion and concern. The warm spring weather was giving rise to something much livelier than the new green grass.

In Yankton, rowdy and drunken behavior in the saloons and streets did not escape the notice of the *Press and Dakotaian*. "Yankton is full of strangers, and we are sorry to remark that some of the strangers are also full," noted the paper. The cheeky article went on to mention that "two revolvers were drawn at Sartori's Saloon and one in the Merchants Hotel. Things are getting interesting."[32]

Citizens were accustomed to dealing with the transient and unruly element, but most folks were happy to see the strangers head west. A number of young Yankton men from respectable families, including John Todd and Daniel and Oliver Shannon, Jr., also joined the mad rush in February, unwilling to wait for spring. The migration picked up as the weather got warmer. In just three days during April 1876, 280 people left Yankton for the Black Hills by "boat, stage and private conveyances."[33]

By spring of 1876 the government had given up on its efforts to keep white men out of the Black Hills. Unofficial word came west from General Philip H. Sheridan that miners on the way to the gold fields would not be stopped by the military and might even be granted protection.[34] Finally, in a letter to General Sheridan, dated May 26, 1876, General W. T. Sherman said he had conferred with President Grant and that it appeared imminent that the Black Hills would soon be opened for settlement. While he did not say that miners were welcome, he mentioned that "Indians should not be allowed to scalp or kill anybody." To address that point and to prevent Indian retaliation, Sherman ordered General Sheridan to offer military protection.[35]

The rapid changes taking place in Dakota looked good on paper and in reality. Optimism was the byword in the summer of 1876, a season of great promise and cause for celebrations throughout the land. America was in its centennial year and therefore the usual, happy Independence Day celebration would be one of profound, unadulterated joy. In Yankton, Judge and Mrs. Shannon held an open house at their mansion on Magazine

Hill, complete with a dazzling display of fireworks. It was but one of countless grand events all over America.

Then, tragedy struck a blow that put out the lights of every party. About a month after Sherman's letter to Sheridan, five companies of the Seventh Cavalry under Lieutenant Colonel Custer were destroyed by Indians at the Little Bighorn River in Montana Territory. Many of the dead had been scalped and mutilated. The disastrous battle was precipitated by Custer's carelessness, causing great embarrassment for the army. Among the public, however, the gallant figure of Custer, noted for his exploits in the Civil War, was now a hero who had died a martyr's death. The deaths of Custer and his troopers were met with hysterical calls for a war of extermination against the Indians. From coast to coast the newspapers—in a frenzied state of disbelief—pleaded for the government to launch a massive attack on the Sioux and other Plains tribes. The majority of white Americans believed it was time for a fight to the finish.

Through it all, the Black Hills persisted as an enchanted forest, a place of spectacular beauty and immense mineral riches. The presence of gold created unprecedented opportunities for businessmen and special challenges for territorial officials and courts. When it was clear to officials in Washington and Dakota that the human wave could not be stopped, efforts focused on wresting another treaty from the Sioux. The unprecedented loss of troops to an Indian "attack" provided added impetus for the federal government to take the Black Hills by treaty or by force. The American public would accept nothing less.

The Battle of the Little Bighorn did little to dampen the enthusiasm of the prospectors, adventurers, and merchants. People kept coming. The great turmoil following the convergence of a diverse mass of people, all in a mad scramble to gather up their portion of riches in the gold fields, inevitably resulted in an upsurge in crime. And it was not long before "Judge Lynch" made an appearance and claimed his first victim.

Dick Barnett of Steubenville, Ohio, went to the Black Hills, lured to the newest El Dorado as were so many others. Unfortunately, he turned horse thief—and was overtaken by a group of vigilantes about forty miles outside of Custer. Barnett was made a prisoner, and a hastily created vigilante court was convened with "the judge sitting on a pile of harness, the jury on a wagon tongue." Soon thereafter Barnett was hanging from the branch of a tree. The vigilantes marked his grave with a pine board that read, "Richard Barnett of Steubenville, Ohio. Died February 26, 1876."[36] He suffered a sad and lonely death, but he had joined the select company of those who were last seen in the Black Hills.

The action of the vigilantes was a warning that the Black Hills settlements were not waiting for the legislature in Yankton to impose law and order. On paper the area was included in the second judicial district. But the Hills were a part of the Great Sioux Reservation in accordance with the terms of the Treaty of 1868, and there was concern that the area was outside of the judicial system. Therefore, men set up courts with judges who handled property, water rights, and mining disputes, along with criminal matters. The courts adopted the California mining codes to regulate the activities of prospectors.

Although eager to have order assigned to their lives, residents of the Black Hills enjoyed the flexibility that came with setting their own rules. For example, in the spring of 1876 a deputy U.S. marshal from Yankton traveled to the Black Hills to pick up a pair of reputed outlaw whiskey dealers under an arrest warrant. On his way back to Yankton, the deputy was overtaken by a group of miners and forced to release his prisoners. The miners, of course, resented the removal of the whiskey purveyors and so intervened.[37]

The attitudes and actions of the impatient miners caught the attention of the territorial legislature, so at the 1877 session new judicial districts were drawn up. Granville G. Bennett, associate justice on the Dakota Supreme Court, was active in this endeavor and used his influence to move the first district to the western half of southern Dakota so he could hold court somewhere in the Black Hills. The second judicial district now consisted of the eastern half of southern Dakota including both Vermillion and Yankton. The third district remained essentially the same, namely, the northern half of the territory. The site of the court of the third district was moved from Fargo to Bismarck after a hard fight in the legislature, with Justice A. H. Barnes insisting that the court remain in Fargo.

The law reforming the districts was contingent, however, on approval by Congress of the new treaty with the Sioux Indians over the Black Hills. White Dakotans did not have long to wait. The treaty was ratified on February 28, 1877, thereby wresting away in dramatic fashion the Black Hills from the Sioux and confirming the revised judicial districts.

The incursions into *Paha Sapa* by miners, merchants, gamblers, and fellow travelers brought about enormous change in a relatively short period of time. The invaders obtained title to the land and along with it laws and courts necessary to run the machine. The *Deadwood Pioneer* spoke for the happy winners: "the arrival of Judge Bennett will be hailed with pleasure by every resident of the Hills."[38]

Sheridan, "a log cabin scrap of a town in the lovely valley of Spring Creek," in Pennington County, was the site of the first federal court in the Black Hills, according to the recollection of the judge's daughter, Estelline Bennett. Judge Bennett, who loved the wooded mountains, decorated his office with a "framed picture" of the log cabin where he first brought down his gavel. It remained in his office for the rest of his life.[39]

Judge Bennett recalled that the first term of court in the Black Hills was held in Sheridan on "the 4th Tuesday of May, 1877." Court was convened in a "miner's cabin with a dirt floor and a dirt roof." It was a short session for there were no cases before the court, and just as well too, for a "heavy rainstorm" accompanied by water and mud "made things very uncomfortable."[40]

Bennett's recollection was slightly at odds with an article in the *Press and Dakotaian* entitled "First Court in the Hills." The Yankton newspaper stated that the initial court session in the Black Hills was held in Deadwood on June 5, 1877. The courtroom was on the second floor of the post office building and was "a weak and flimsy affair." After the usual "Hear Ye, Hear Ye" was announced, Judge Bennett got down to business in a room full of lawyers, litigants, and spectators. It was not long, however, before "the floor was felt sensibly to be sinking." Then a "partition dividing off one corner of the jury room parted from the rafters and fell in on the crowd." Sensing danger, the judge told the sheriff to clear out the room, but "his services were not needed," for the frightened crowd rushed out on its own. The session was later continued in a nearby log cabin.[41]

Though both explanations are colorful and melodramatic, Judge Bennett should be given credit for the most accurate accounting of this comic episode of Dakota history, for after all he was there to experience it firsthand. But whether the first court session was in Deadwood or Sheridan, jurisprudence got off to a shaky, messy start.

About a year later, an incident occurred that must have reminded Black Hills residents of the antics of the miners' courts. Ben Wodsworth killed a man named McTigue over a disputed mining claim. It was reported in a Black Hills newspaper that Wodsworth escaped punishment "on the ground that he had done a good job."[42] Wodsworth's fate might have been different in the East, but it was not unusual in Deadwood.

CHAPTER 13

THE CRIME, TRIAL, AND HANGING OF JACK MCCALL

Jack McCall walked in and around directly back of his victim, and when within three feet of him raised his revolver and exclaiming, 'damn you, take that' and fired.

Daily Press and Dakotaian
August 18, 1876

O f the numerous unlawful acts committed in the Black Hills, one crime in particular rose above the many shootings and other acts of violence in Dakota Territory, rivaling the Wintermute case in national attention. In the mining town of Deadwood, a young, obscure, slovenly hot-head named John "Jack" McCall (aka Bill Sutherland) shot and killed James B. "Wild Bill" Hickok. The murder catapulted the reputation of this cavalier of the Plains to the pantheon of prominent figures of the Wild West and became the occasion for which Judge Peter C. Shannon handed down one of the most famous death sentences in American history.

When Deputy U.S. Marshal Ben C. Ash visited Deadwood in 1876, he noticed a tall, well-dressed man with long, curly hair who stood out dramatically from the prospector community. Ash thought he looked like a preacher and asked someone for his name. "Fellow from Kansas," came the reply. "They say he's killed thirty-seven men. They call him Wild Bill."[1]

Jack McCall, the man who made himself famous by shooting Wild Bill, came west from Kentucky in 1869 or 1870. He drifted into the

James Butler "Wild Bill" Hickok, murdered by
Jack McCall in Deadwood, Dakota Territory, 1876.
Courtesy South Dakota State Historical Society.

Republican River area of Nebraska and Kansas and became a buffalo
hunter. Nicknamed "Buffalo Curly," he was known as a hunter with a
"mean streak." McCall most likely came into the Black Hills a few weeks
or possibly months before the arrival of Hickok.[2] He was not well-known
in Deadwood, and one resident recalled McCall as "more of a dance hall
dude than a tough customer."[3]

Wild Bill Hickok was a celebrity long before he arrived in Deadwood
the second week of July 1876 from Cheyenne with a caravan of other

frontier personages, including his friend "Colorado" Charlie Utter, Joseph "White Eye" Anderson, and Martha "Calamity Jane" Canary, and set up a tent camp.[4] Hickok, too, came to look for gold, and though he did some prospecting, he regularly started his day with target practice followed by a stiff drink and some breakfast.[5] But as an acquaintance pointed out, Wild Bill preferred gambling to eating, so his day's work usually included playing cards in a saloon.[6]

The hastily built town of Deadwood, in a gulch of the same name, displayed an abundance of life that belied its name. The character of its people, running on energy supplied by gold, made Yankton and Sioux Falls appear tame by comparison. In an amazingly short period of time, Deadwood—and to a lesser extent, Crook City and Elizabeth City— attracted merchants, prospectors, gamblers, prostitutes, saloon men, and a variety of disreputable characters, all of them wanting to cash in on the gold rush bonanza. A panoply of the world seemed to rush in. Prices were outrageous, shootings were frequent, and gold dust was the currency. Dance halls, gambling dens, and saloons ran full blast around the clock.

There seemed to be no limit to the raucous behavior of the men and women of Deadwood, including the loud and profane Calamity Jane who "never went to bed with a penny in her pocket."[7] The absence of laws and law enforcement facilitated the outrageous conduct. Deadwood was an easy and natural fit for Hickok and his companions.

Hickok was originally from Troy Grove, La Salle County, Illinois (formerly Homer, and now a tourist attraction). Born in 1837, he went to Kansas in the 1850s to homestead. In 1861 he became involved in a shooting at Rock Creek, Nebraska, known as the McCanles Massacre. This incident, in which Hickok shot two of the three men who died, catapulted him into the top tier of western gunfighters. He also discovered that he was blessed with a fast draw and incredible accuracy, accompanied by a cool disposition in the face of danger.[8]

Having served as a Union scout during the Civil War, Hickok moved to Missouri where, unemployed, he decided to become a gambler. In a quarrel over money, he killed a man, for which he was tried and acquitted.[9] In the late 1860s and early 1870s, he worked as a deputy U.S. marshal and army guide in Kansas and Texas while his reputation as a gunfighter continued to rise, assisted by an occasional killing and dime-novel romance writers who exaggerated or invented stories about him. Life in the American West changed this mild-mannered frontiersman into the Prince of Pistoleers.

During his short stay in Deadwood, Hickok would be frequently found at a poker table plying his trade, but not always doing well. On one such occasion, on August 2, 1876, Hickok, dressed in his Prince Albert suit, was playing poker with Captain William Massie, the pilot of the Missouri River steamer *Carroll,* who had recently resigned his position and come to the Black Hills from Bismarck.[10] Carl Mann and Charlie Rich were the other two players at Hickok's table in the gambling house of Nutthall and Mann, also known as the No. 10 Saloon.[11]

Unbeknownst to Hickok, Jack McCall entered the saloon quietly and walked toward the back door. He stopped, walked back to the card table, and stealthily approached his intended victim from the back. When he was positioned about three feet from Wild Bill's head, McCall fired a shot that instantly killed the Prince of the Pistoleers.[12] The bullet entered Hickok's head near his right ear, exiting from his cheek, and striking the left wrist of Captain Massie. McCall brandished his revolver, threatening the others, and soon left the premises without encountering resistance.

Although only a few people heard the fatal shot that day in August 1876, it has nevertheless resounded throughout American history. The act immortalized both the victim and the killer, and to this day is re-enacted in Deadwood, along with the subsequent trial, for the pleasure of the curious. It was a murder with a long memory, and has brought fame and fortune to the City of Deadwood. Had Hickok been shot in Cheyenne, for example, Deadwood might not be as famous as it is today—nor would Judge Peter Shannon.

Reaction among Deadwood residents varied, depending on their like or dislike for Hickok. He was by reputation a gunfighter, and shared his company with the disreputable Calamity Jane. Some remembered that in 1872, in Kansas City, he was arrested as a vagrant "with no visible means of support."[13] Yankton resident Zack T. Sutley insisted that Hickok was not a "popular hero" but rather a "bully whom men feared but did not respect." In his memoir, Sutley insisted that writers were responsible for making Hickok into a well-known figure.[14]

News of the shocking crime worked its way through the town while the people of Deadwood dealt with McCall. After leaving No. 10 Saloon, he attempted to mount his horse, but he fell to the ground because of a loose cinch. He was captured after a short chase on foot through Deadwood and put under guard until mourners could give Wild Bill Hickok a decent burial. The deceased was buried in "the cold ground of Whitewood by kind hands" with his ivory-handled pistols and a carbine placed in his coffin.[15]

Those who liked Hickok were eager to lynch McCall—and they found a tree and rope to do the deed—when all of a sudden, a Mexican rode into town "with the head of an Indian dangling by his side." Curious men gathered around the rider, eager to learn about the killing of the Indian.[16] The bizarre sight distracted the mob and probably prevented a lynching.

Later that evening, dozens of Deadwood businessmen gathered to decide the fate of Jack McCall. The decision was to convene a "miner's court." The Black Hills were part of the second judicial district, but the area was Indian country by treaty and not subject to territorial law. As a new town, Deadwood had no county organization, hence no officials of any kind to make an arrest or conduct an examination or a trial. A judge was appointed in the person of W. L. Kuykendall, an attorney from Cheyenne with a respectable background. Colonel George May was appointed to prosecute the prisoner while Judge Miller would serve as defense counsel.

The extra-legal proceeding was conducted outdoors on Main Street, in the presence of a huge, well-armed crowd. Kuykendall recalled in his memoir that he fully expected a guilty verdict, to be followed immediately by a hanging.[17] With everyone anticipating some good theater, the prosecutor started with statements from the eye-witnesses. McCall's only defense was a brief statement that he killed Wild Bill out of fear for his life and for revenge, swearing that Hickok had killed his brother in Kansas. He insisted he had no choice but to shoot to kill, because Wild Bill could "draw and shoot" better than any other man. It was the only evidence offered by McCall at the "trial."[18]

The make-shift jury deliberated for about thirty minutes. The place selected to hear the verdict was the No. 10 Saloon, where the killing occurred. Kuykendall remembered that in front of the saloon "stood a large pine tree having a limb just right for the hanging."[19] But there would be no hanging, for the jury returned with a verdict of "not guilty," much to the surprise of the crowd that witnessed the proceeding. The large gathering of men, disappointed that there would be no hanging, started murmuring about letting "Judge Lynch" intervene and administer summary punishment.

According to a Yankton newspaper, McCall was told to mount up and get out of town—and he did not delay in making his exit.[20] John McClintock, a Deadwood resident in 1876, stated in his memoir that McCall "loitered about the city five or six days" and was not run out of town.[21] Whatever the truth, McCall's luck had been surprisingly good, for he had gambled on killing Hickok and lived to enjoy his ill-found reputation.

McCall made his way to Wyoming Territory where his streak of luck ran out. He just could not keep his mouth shut, as apparently the temptation to brag was too great. While drinking in a bar in Laramie, the snub-nosed, cross-eyed McCall recounted his tale, informing one man that "he killed Wild Bill merely because Bill snatched a card from his hand" while they were playing poker. The remarks were overheard by Colonel George May who had been tracking McCall. May found U.S. Deputy Marshal A. D. Balcombe, who went to the bar, arrested McCall for murder, and placed him in irons. McCall was taken to Omaha where he appeared before a U.S. Commissioner to determine whether there was sufficient evidence to hold him.[22]

The ruling went against McCall, so Deputy Balcombe continued on his way to Yankton with his prisoner. They stopped in Sioux City where a reporter for the *Sioux City Journal* had a look at McCall. The reporter said the young prisoner wore a "sinister expression" that "would stamp him anywhere as being a cowardly, treacherous desperado" who appeared to "gloat over the murder he was arrested for committing."[23]

Upon his arrival in Yankton on September 5, McCall was turned over to Sheriff Millard A. Baker and locked up in the U.S. jail. An object of intense curiosity, McCall was described by the *Press and Dakotaian* as "an evil looking man, young in years but apparently old in sin and is evidently a desperate character."[24] If looks alone could convict, McCall's case was hopeless.

Within a few days of being locked up, a reporter for the *Dakota Herald* was granted an interview with McCall. The prisoner showed up wearing shackled ankles and shyly introduced himself as John McCall, age twenty-five, a native of New Orleans. He admitted that Sutherland was not his true name, although he had used that alias in the past. The reporter described him as "about five feet eight inches in height, well proportioned, muscular, and a little given to adipose tissue." His face was clean-shaven except for a "light mustache" below his "pug nose," giving him a "peculiar hang-dog and malicious appearance." The reporter noted that the cross-eyed Jack McCall was not a handsome young man.

When questioned about the killing of Wild Bill, McCall lowered his head and became silent. Then he launched into a brief tirade against the newspapers of Laramie: "I made some statements while at Laramie, but they were entirely misrepresented; the newspapers published a whole lot of stuff, running me down the worst way." He refused to go into further detail except to say that he paid a Laramie lawyer $200 to represent him, "but had never seen or heard of him since." The reporter concluded his work, impressed with the fact that McCall avoided making eye-contact and that he "seemed anxious to avert our gaze, and slink away in his cell."[25]

While McCall languished behind bars, waiting for his trial, Yankton and southeastern Dakota were thrown into a state of excitement by news that two members of the notorious James-Younger Gang, from Missouri, were on the loose, having escaped from a botched bank robbery attempt in Northfield, Minnesota. The two fugitives were noted desperadoes Jesse and Frank James. They had entered Dakota Territory northeast of Sioux Falls and rode south, staying close to the Big Sioux River. Posses from Worthington, Minnesota, Sioux Falls, and Yankton combed the prairie, but the James brothers managed to avoid capture and made their way back to Missouri. Their escape denied Judge Shannon the opportunity to have dealt with this pair of outlaw luminaries.

On October 18 Jack McCall was indicted for murder after which he entered a "not guilty" plea in open court. He provided a signed statement with the names of witnesses he wanted to call on his behalf. The court, with Judge G. G. Bennett on the bench, authorized warrants for the location and production of the witnesses. Bennett also appointed counsel for the accused, after McCall stated that he had no lawyer and had no money to hire one. Oliver Shannon and G. C. Moody were named by Bennett to represent McCall. Soon after, however, Moody was excused due to another assignment and William H. H. Beadle took his place.[26]

On November 10 McCall and a fellow prisoner, Jerry McCarthy, attempted to break out of the U.S. jail. McCarthy was being held on a murder charge, having, along with John R. Carty, killed Jack Hinch, a Nevada gambler, in Gayville, a mining town in the Black Hills.[27] McCarthy was captured near Cheyenne and brought to Yankton by Wyoming U.S. Marshal W. F. Sweesy.[28]

J. H. Burdick, U.S. Marshal.
Courtesy Library of Congress.

The breakout attempt occurred when the jailer, J. B. Robinson, was preparing to lock up the prisoners for the night. He was overpowered by McCarthy. McCall and McCarthy then brutally beat the jailer and took his keys. The desperadoes broke their shackles "with the round of a chair." Unlocking the jailhouse door, they were about to step outside when they were stopped by Marshal James H. Burdick and Deputy James Bennett; with guns drawn, they forced the would-be jailbreakers back into their cells.[29] After this incident, McCall remained a well-behaved prisoner.

McCall did muddy the waters, however, when he claimed that he was paid to kill Wild Bill by John Varnes, another Deadwood gambler. The story in the *Dakota Herald* was also circulated in an eastern newspaper following McCall's trial.[30] According to this story, Varnes and Hickok had a "row" in Denver and Deadwood, and as a result, Varnes had hired McCall to avenge the wrongdoing. Acting on this information, a deputy U.S. marshal in the company of a posse rode to Deadwood but could not find the mysterious Varnes.[31]

The *Press and Dakotaian* also carried a version of the Varnes story that originated in the *Deadwood Pioneer*. The *Press and Dakotaian,* however, treated it as a "manufactured story," finding that McCall "has evinced no intention to turn state's evidence."[32] John Varnes was never mentioned at McCall's trial.

Counsel for McCall filed a motion for a continuance of the trial until the April term of court. Judge Shannon, now in charge of the case, took the motion under consideration and denied it. When he learned that his case would not be continued, McCall used "some language that wasn't very complimentary to the court."[33] Since the *Press and Dakotaian* chose not to print the language, we can only wonder what McCall said about the honorable Peter C. Shannon.

The trial of John "Jack" McCall commenced on December 4, 1876, in the U.S. District Court, Yankton, Dakota Territory, Judge Peter C. Shannon presiding. U.S. Attorney William A. Pound, a man "disposed to do his whole duty though the heavens may fall," was the prosecutor.[34] Ex-governor Andrew J. Faulk was the clerk of court. The defendant was represented by Oliver Shannon and William H. H. Beadle, appointed counsel. McCall was delivered to the sparsely populated courtroom in wrist irons, which were removed by Marshal Burdick when he reached the defense counsel table. A reporter for the *Press and Dakotaian* described McCall as a young man of about twenty-five years in age, medium height, and slender of build: "His face is one which would not recommend him to the casual observer as a man free from guilt, while his actions made it manifest that he possessed a fair amount of animal courage."[35]

McCall soon relaxed and assumed an air of confidence, chatting freely with his lawyers as if he were about to be tried for a minor offense. Later, while the examination of prospective jurors was in process, McCall showed signs of uneasiness as he closely scanned the faces of the men who would judge him. Had he known anything about courtroom history in Yankton, and the unpredictable conduct of past juries, he might have felt a glimmer of hope. With the Wintermute debacle still fresh in the public mind, all knowledgeable observers were curiously scrutinizing the men in the jury box, wondering if another bizarre result was in the offing.

The twelve jurors, who later became celebrities in their own right, were John Treadway, H. A. Dunham, William Box, George Pike, Lewis Clark, West Negus, Charles Edwards, I. N. Esmay, H. T. Mowery, Nelson Armstrong, J. A. Withie, and M. L. Winchell. The jurors were selected hurriedly out of a total of twenty-one men examined by the attorneys. Three jurors declared that they had not read anything about McCall in the newspapers.[36]

Next, the indictment was read. In form and content, the document tortured the English language. It should have—and maybe did—elicit snickers from the audience, since those present probably expected it to state simply that John McCall was charged with the murder of James B. Hickok. Instead, the indictment against Jack McCall read as follows:

> at a place in said [Indian] reservation called Deadwood . . .
> one John McCall alias Jack McCall . . . with force and arms
> in and upon one William Hickok, alias Wild Bill, feloniously,
> willfully and of his malice afore thought made an assault
> and that said John MCall [sic] with a certain revolver
> pistol, then and there charged with gunpowder and a bullet
> which said revolver pistol . . . the said John MCall [sic] in
> his right hand then and there . . . held at against the said

William Hickok . . . did shoot off and discharge . . . the
loaded bullet . . . by means of shooting off and discharging
the said revolver pistol . . . against the said Wm. Hickok as
a foresaid, did then and there feloniously and willfully and
of his malice aforethought strike and penetrate and wound
the said Wm. Hickok in and through the head of him.

It was a piece of work that only a pettifogging lawyer could love.
After that demonstration of fumbling and fractured language, the court
went into recess.

When the trial resumed in the afternoon, the courtroom was filled with
spectators, all anxious to hear the details of the great crime. Once again,
Yankton was in the national spotlight. The light of judicial scrutiny was
again focused on Judge Shannon, who had already earned the confidence
of the public, press, and bar of Dakota Territory.

The prosecution began its case with George M. Shingle, from
Cheyenne, who testified that he first met Wild Bill in 1866. On the day of
the homicide, Shingle was in Deadwood, at the No. 10 Saloon, standing
at the bar weighing gold dust while Hickok was engaged in a poker
game with "3 or 4 others sitting at the same table." The table was in the
middle of the room, facing the bar. Shingle testified that he saw McCall
enter, walk toward the back door, turn around and approach Hickok from
behind, draw his revolver and shoot when "within 3 or 4 feet of Wild Bill's
head." Shingle said that Hickok sat at the table briefly and then fell over
backwards onto the floor, dead. McCall, with gun in hand, threatened all
those present and that he (Shingle) fled the premises.

On cross-examination, Shingle stated that, to the best of his
knowledge, Hickok had killed three men, but in self-defense. He further
stated that Hickok was a "constant drinker" but was sober when the
shooting occurred. He could not state whether McCall was drunk at the
time. Shingle said he attended the trial by the miner's court but had no

knowledge of any "inducements held out to McCall to say that he had killed Wild Bill."[37]

On the whole, he made a good witness for prosecutor William Pound, who was well on his way toward getting a conviction. His next witness was Carl Mann, co-owner of the No. 10 Saloon and one of the card players at Hickok's fateful poker game. He was asked about the population of Deadwood as of August 2, 1876, to which he responded that there were "two thousand or more people." He was also asked to explain the location of other towns in the vicinity of Deadwood and their proximity to Bear Butte.

When questioned about the building where the shooting occurred, Mann was evasive. He replied that on the day of the homicide he had a house in Deadwood but went on to say, "I don't know that I should answer questions about my keeping a saloon as it may get me into trouble." Skirting the issue further, Mann stated that "there was a building there [Deadwood] which I had an interest in and I knew a man named Wild Bill. Saw both him and the defendant that day at that building."

Compared to Shingle's, Mann's testimony about the shooting was more forthright. Although Mann's was consistent with Shingle's, he offered some details about McCall that the previous witness did not reveal. Mann recalled that the day before the shooting Hickok and McCall had engaged in a poker game at his "house." Hickok emerged as the winner, but as the pot was short, Bill said to McCall, "you owe me $16.25." McCall said "yes" and left the premises. Mann stated that soon after leaving McCall returned and Hickok asked him, "did I break you?" McCall replied in the affirmative and Hickok offered him 75 cents to buy supper, but McCall spurned the offer.[38]

Cross–examination of Mann failed to elicit any testimony helpful to the defense and court adjourned for the day. The jury, having heard the bulk of the prosecution's case, was escorted from the court and sequestered.

The next day, the prosecution placed Captain William Massie in the witness chair. Massie was a reluctant witness, for when he was handed a subpoena by Deputy Marshal Ben C. Ash, the wily river boat captain stated angrily that he would not go to Yankton and testify. He argued that to do so would be disgraceful, for his daughter would then learn that he had been in a poker game where someone was killed. Ash got a bench warrant and hauled Massie from Deadwood to Yankton.[39]

Captain Massie was a veteran Missouri River boat pilot who had worked for the Coulson Packet Company and was a resident of St. Louis. He testified that at the time of the crime in question, he was present in the No. 10 Saloon, sitting opposite Hickok, when he first saw McCall. Massie was looking down at the table, with his left arm resting on the table, when McCall fired the shot that killed Wild Bill. He felt "shock and numbness" in his left wrist, looked up, and saw McCall with a pistol in his hand. McCall waved his gun at those in the bar and shouted, "Come on ye sons of bitches." Massie testified that he left the premises, not wanting to take another bullet. He testified that the doctor who examined him could not find a bullet in his wrist but that he assumed it was still there. Cross-examination failed to reveal anything that would damage Massie's credibility.[40]

Massie said nothing under oath about being shot in the wrist by McCall. Nor did he testify that after the fatal shooting he (Massie) ran out of the saloon yelling that McCall had shot him. But while he was in Yankton, Massie bragged that "the bullet that killed Wild Bill has come to town."[41] Over the years Massie capitalized on his celebrity status and made sure everyone knew that in his wrist was the bullet that killed Wild Bill.[42] It earned him a lot of free drinks.

The prosecution continued with the testimony of J. B. Robinson, who related his experiences with McCall and Jerry McCarthy, the two prisoners who assaulted him while attempting to escape from the jail. Finally, two witnesses were called whose testimony established that the crime occurred within the boundaries of Dakota Territory and, therefore, within the jurisdiction of the court. Feeling confident, the prosecution rested.[43]

The defense was then called to put on its case. Counsel stated bluntly that "there is no evidence to offer on the part of the defendant."[44] Counsel did, however, make a motion that the defendant be discharged because the prosecution failed to provide a true copy of the indictment. The matter was argued by both sides, with the defense finally admitting that it had, in fact, received a true copy of the indictment and that somehow the attorneys had merely forgotten about it.

After this weak, if not frivolous, argument by counsel for Jack McCall, the case ended. To their credit, W. H. H. Beadle and Oliver Shannon had subpoenaed witnesses from the Black Hills to testify on behalf of McCall. Deputy U.S. Marshal Charles P. Edmunds went west on horseback with subpoenas but was unable to locate the intended witnesses.[45]

The two attorneys struggled to find testimony to bolster their case. Zack T. Sutley had been asked to talk to McCall for the purpose of getting some helpful information. Sutley complied with the request but "McCall would tell me nothing that we could use in his favor."[46] The story about Hickok killing McCall's brother was never brought up by the defense.

Given that McCall's defense was nonexistent, it was an easy task for the jury to find him guilty as charged after a few hours of deliberation. At 10:15 p.m., on December 5, 1876, the jury's verdict was announced, and it was greeted with approval by Lorenzo Butler Hickok, an older brother of Wild Bill, who had been in attendance at the trial. After a nod of his head he left the court, intending to return for the sentencing phase.[47]

Sentencing of the convicted murderer Jack McCall was set for January 3, 1877. In the presence of a rapt courtroom audience, Judge Peter C. Shannon asked McCall if he had anything to say before sentence of death was pronounced. McCall spoke as though aware that he had just been given the last opportunity he would ever have to save his life. He objected to some of the trial testimony and insisted that he was drunk at the time of the shooting and had no "clear conception of the lamentable matter." McCall said he vaguely remembered going into Saloon No. 10 on the fateful day and revealed that while in the bar he simply drank more whiskey. He claimed to have known nothing about the shooting until he woke up the next morning. During his rambling explanation, he admitted that the story about Hickok shooting his brother in Kansas was a fabrication. Finally, the prisoner told the judge that Jack McCall was not his real name and that he chose it as a boy when he left home so that his parents would never know about his actions or whereabouts.

When McCall was finished, Judge Shannon began to speak. He carefully summarized the evidence against McCall and insisted that a fair trial had taken place and that the verdict of guilty was just. Next, he explained in the "most eloquent and touching language" the dangers of "the devious course and unreasonable habits of the wicked and vicious." Shannon "produced a profound feeling both with the crowd in attendance and the prisoner," and McCall appeared agitated as the judge made reference to the "tender rearing given to him by his parents in the days of his youth." When he had completed his lecture, Shannon sentenced McCall to be "hanged by the neck until you are dead." Execution was scheduled to take place on March 1, 1877, between the hours 9 a.m. and 2 p.m.[48]

His attorneys appealed the conviction, but if McCall thought that would buy him some time, he was mistaken. His appeal was on the calendar for the next session of the territorial Supreme Court for January. The arguments in favor of overturning the guilty verdict were both substantive and procedural in nature: a faulty indictment and improper and inadmissible documentary evidence that struck at the heart of jurisdiction. Jury misconduct was also brought up, the attorneys arguing that, during deliberation, the jurymen drank at saloons and had liquor available in their room at night.

The court—with Judge Shannon writing the opinion for all three justices—made short work of each point of contention, although there was no mention of drinking by the jury. Although the indictment had been poorly composed, even failing to spell the victim's name properly, the argument against it was made moot since counsel did not object to it before commencement of trial. As to the other issue, the court ruled that the reports and maps used to establish jurisdiction were properly admitted and that copies were as valid as would be the in-person testimony of the persons who conducted the actual exploration and drafted the documents. The court ruled that Deadwood was, indeed, located in Dakota Territory, and the judgment of the trial court was affirmed on January 19, 1877.

Although facing death, McCall exhibited a glimmer of optimism in his response to a letter he received from an eastern correspondent asking about the advisability for a young man to venture into the Black Hills. McCall wrote in glowing terms about the prospect of finding gold, as if he was about to make the journey himself. Then his mood turned somber, and he closed the letter by writing that because he was to be executed on the first of March he had "lost all interest in that [Black Hills] locality."[49]

McCall's last hope was for a presidential pardon or commutation of the sentence to life in prison. President Grant had been petitioned to intervene but he rejected the opportunity. The condemned prisoner was now forced to contemplate his certain death. Marshal Burdick announced in the *Press and Dakotaian* that the execution would be private, denying a number of requests that the public be allowed to attend. It would be private, the marshal argued, so as to avoid "gratifying morbid curiosity."[50]

A private hanging would be more efficiently carried out by those in charge and would probably be easier on McCall as well. But he was holding up, maintaining an uncanny sense of calm. He even penned a note to the *Press and Dakotaian* on February 21 indicating he intended to prepare an "article which I wish you to publish in your paper after my death. If you will be here the day the execution takes place, I will hand it to you. If you decline to publish it, please let me know." It was signed, "John McCall."[51]

The man whose judicial ruling caused all the speculation, curiosity, and anxiety, Peter C. Shannon, decided that a little relaxation and socializing was in order, so he invited all the members of the Dakota legislature, and other special guests, to attend a reception at his home on February 15. The highbrow gathering featured "music, refreshments and social repartee." The *Daily Press and Dakotaian* reported that Mrs. Shannon, "a lady of rare worth and intellectual attainments," graced the party with her presence, her smile, and a "pleasant word for all."[52] The gala event was a strange, even macabre, prelude to the first legal hanging in Dakota Territory.

Execution by hanging constitutes a morbid history in America with strong connections to the biblical proclamation "an eye for an eye." Up to the mid-nineteenth century, hangings were public events, often attended by large crowds of people of both sexes and all ages. The event followed a ritual, often religious in nature, starting at the jailhouse and ending at the gallows, with singing and a sermon in between. The whole town participated as if it were a civic duty. Aside from watching the final moments of a condemned person's life, spectators were called upon to contemplate their own inevitable demise. Some people believed the experience had a wholesome effect on the community.

Over time the orderly and solemn process gave way to a carnival-like event complete with food and drink vendors and jeering crowds that hurled curses and insults at the condemned prisoner. Sober minds took note. After 1860 most public executions were banned, and prisoners under a death sentence were hanged behind high walls, attended by a limited number of witnesses.[53] Dakota Territory officials had no experience with executions, although there had been lynchings aplenty. The authorities were aware that they needed to strike a balance between their desire to handle the execution with decorum and the public's fascination with ceremonial death.

The location of the impending execution of McCall was a well-kept secret in Yankton. Rumors and speculation raced through the community like a ghost on a pale horse. When three men in a wagon with "carpenter instruments and a basket of provisions" headed north of town, observers reasoned that the execution would take place in the school section. The public knew that it would not take place in the jailyard of the county court, as residents in the area had raised objection to this site, and the county commissioners ruled in their favor. Since no one saw a gallows being built in the vicinity of the U.S. courthouse, that site was also ruled out.[54]

On the night before his "taking off," McCall received a letter from his sister Mary A. McCall, living in Louisville, Kentucky. It had been sent to Marshal Burdick after Mary had read an Associated Press dispatch to the effect that the president had refused to grant a commutation of the sentence of a Jack McCall. Thinking it might be her long-lost brother, or possibly someone else with the same name, she wrote to learn the truth and included a copy of the press dispatch to prove her intentions were genuine. Mary stated that she was one of two sisters but made no mention of a brother other than Jack. McCall wrote a response to his sister that historians have never been privileged to read.

McCall's last days were occupied in reading and engaging in political discussion with other prisoners, and his final hours were spent with his spiritual adviser, Father John Daxacher, and his assistant, J. A. Curry. As they prepared McCall for death, someone dug a grave in the Catholic cemetery, about two miles north of town on the prairie. The forty-acre cemetery had been platted in October 1874[55] by Father Valentine Sommereisen, Yankton's first resident Catholic priest.[56]

Jack McCall, for whom the grave had been opened, appeared ready to endure the spectacle when his day of death dawned amid drizzle and cold. Hundreds of people were gathered in the street in front of the jailhouse, eager to accompany the marshal and his party to the gallows. The *Dakota Herald* described the gathering of curious citizens as "indeed a motley one, comprising lawyers, doctors of medicine and of divinity, reporters, ragged boys, and *demi monde*; ladies and gentlemen; Americans, Russians and of every other nationality, the grave and the gay. And in fact exactly the materials of which Yankton is composed."[57]

The place of execution no longer a secret, people on horseback, on foot, or in buggies, fine carriages, and wagons made their way slowly up Broadway, while the carriage that contained the marshal and his deputies, and another that conveyed the condemned man and his spiritual advisors, followed. The procession extended about a half-mile in length. The Yankton press was represented by reporters for the *Dakota Herald* and the *Press and Dakotaian,* as well as L. D. F. Poore representing the *New York Herald.*[58] As the solemn cortege made its way north out of town, it passed by the Catholic cemetery where McCall's grave, in the southwestern corner, was "in full view."

The long column reached the gallows at ten o'clock where another large throng of people had already gathered. The gallows had been built near the northwestern corner of the cemetery, about two miles north of downtown Yankton, and consisted of "four upright posts, 6 x 6 inches, 8 feet 10 inches apart on the ground, 15 feet 4 inches high." The drop of 7 feet 10 inches was into a box-like enclosure. McCall was escorted up the steps to the platform. He stood beneath the rope, with Father Daxacher, dressed in a white robe, at his side. Facing east toward the large and silent crowd, with his hands tied and hat removed, he showed no signs of fear.

A prayer of five minutes' duration was offered under the direction of Father Daxacher, with McCall kneeling. The noose was then placed around McCall's neck, prompting him to remark, "tie the rope tight, boys; don't let there be any mistake." At that moment, the large, silent crowd held its breath. As he stood holding a crucifix, a black cap was placed over his head, and the trap was sprung.

McCall cried out, "O God," as he dropped through the trap door to his death. The first legal execution in Dakota had been completed without delay or difficulty. Jack McCall passed quickly from life to death and into even greater infamy.

Someone in the crowd was so moved by the experience that he or she wrote a poem entitled "The Hanging of Jack McCall." As published in the *Dakota Herald*, the last four lines are as follows:

Hanging of Jack McCall, Yankton, Dakota Territory.
Courtesy Heroes of the Plains, *by J. W. Buell, 1883.*

The trap was sprung—that fatal trap
The soul from his body fled.
The dreadful debt was paid at last,
And Jack McCall was dead.[59]

McCall was buried on the prairie, at the edge of Yankton, far from his old Kentucky home. His place of rest was destined to be temporary, however, for in the summer of 1881 the bodies of McCall and others were exhumed for reburial in the new Catholic cemetery. The reburial occurred when it was discovered that Father Sommereisen had established the cemetery, illegally, on school land.[60] The grave diggers could not resist opening the coffin, whereupon they discovered that McCall had been interred with the hangman's noose around his neck.[61] His grave remains without a headstone to this day.

CHAPTER 14

ANGRY MEN AND LOADED GUNS

The victim was known to be a bad man, having frequently been engaged in shooting affairs, and it is said that he stabbed two soldiers to death in Bismarck.

Daily Press and Dakotaian
August 8, 1876

The rush of people into Dakota Territory, many drawn by the stories of gold in the Black Hills, brought trouble as sure as muddy water flowed in the Missouri River. New people meant an increase in both commerce and crime. The *Press and Dakotaian* in the territorial capitol of Yankton warned citizens to be on the lookout for the undesirables: "Yankton is full of gamblers, confidence operators and three card monte men" that prey on "greenies." The paper likened the crooks to "spiders ready to entrap the verdant Black Hillers."[1]

As the gateway to Dakota Territory, Yankton got more than its share of desperate men with loaded guns and unsavory reputations. The upriver country was still wild, and whiskey "ranches" continued to thrive. Shootings in the Black Hills occurred as frequently as new gold strikes. The young, muscular town of Deadwood was described as a place with "no sickness but plenty of funerals."[2] As such, the court calendars continued to present Judge Shannon and his fellow justices with new challenges.

Among the challenges was the murder case involving Joseph Allen, who shot and killed A. A. Nichols at Pascal's Island on the Missouri River, on November 4, 1876. Allen was arrested on the 16th at the Standing Rock

Agency. According to the *Press and Dakotaian,* Nichols was well known in Yankton and had been in Dakota long enough to be called "an old settler and pioneer."[3]

The incident was also reported in the *Dakota Herald* and apparently from a source not used by the *Press and Dakotaian.* According to the *Herald,* John Allen shot and killed Albert Nichols at Artichoke Bend on the Missouri River. Allen was brought to Yankton from the upper country by Deputy Marshal Ben C. Ash in late December of 1876.[4]

Reporting inconsistencies were common, given the unreliability of sources and inefficient information gathering practices of the time. But once the suspect arrived in Yankton, the facts began to coalesce around Joseph Allen. He was subjected to examination before City Police Justice Leonidas Congleton and then sent back to jail on a charge of murder to "await the action of a grand jury."[5]

Two more killings occurred in November both in Deadwood, and each was covered by a correspondent from the *Chicago Times.* The first took place on the night of November 17 at the Bella Union, a variety theater at No. 10 Main Street. The villain *and* the victim of the impromptu drama was Edward Shaughnessy, about thirty years old, who had arrived in Deadwood a few days previously, a passenger on a stagecoach from Cheyenne. Since then he had been seen quite frequently at the Bella Union, patronizing the bar during the day and, at night, admiring a young singer and actress named Fannie Garrettson, "a charming vocalist and comedienne." She was accompanied on stage by a banjo player named Dick Brown, about twenty-six years old. Brown was an accomplished musician and had made many friends in Deadwood with his "quiet and gentlemanly deportment."

On the day of the shooting, Shaughnessy showed up at the Bella Union and started drinking. After he made it clear that he intended to kill Brown, and possibly Garrettson, he continued to drink throughout the evening while seated near a stove, an ax, and a wood pile. During the performance, he suddenly grabbed the ax and threw it at Fannie, who, luckily, "saw the action in time to dodge the weapon in its flight and sprang affrighted behind the scenes." There were eight people on stage and all escaped being hit by the flying ax. Missing his target seemed to enrage Shaughnessy. He charged the stage and was attempting to make his way up on to it when Brown stepped out from the curtains with a pistol. He fired four shots, two of which hit Shaughnessy.[6]

A Deadwood newspaper, the *Pioneer*, confirmed that an ax was thrown "from the auditorium to the stage." Simultaneous with the tossing of the ax, a man (Shaughnessy) was seen "attempting to mount the stage." Brown emerged from the wings, and having uttered, "he has followed me long enough," fired four shots from his revolver, with two bullets hitting their target. Shaughnessy was hit in the right arm and in the right side, just above the hip.[7]

The incident was recorded in books penned by Black Hills pioneers, including Richard B. Hughes, a Deadwood journalist. Hughes wrote that throwing the ax on the stage was "little more than a drunken gesture and endangered no one."[8] Not true, according Estelline Bennett, who stated in her memoir that the ax just missed Fannie and "almost decapitated" Eugene Holman, one of the performers on stage.[9] Another pioneer memoir recalled that Shaughnessy tossed what appeared to be a bundle of letters onto the stage.[10]

Whatever it was that he tossed that night, it cost him his life. Shaughnessy lingered until the next morning. It was then revealed that Fannie had once been the mistress (or wife, according to the *Pioneer)* of Shaughnessy, who had been a conductor on the Union Pacific Railroad and had lived a respectable life until he succumbed to alcohol. Brown had recently married Fannie at the Bella Union in the presence of many witnesses. But confusion over his actual marital status was probably not a concern for Brown. He was facing murder charges, although he must have calculated that a theater full of witnesses, including those on stage, would conclude that he committed the shooting out of self-defense.[11]

On November 18 the second shooting occurred, causing the Chicago correspondent to begin his column with the old adage, "It never rains but pours." This example of gunplay lacked the glamour and bizarre nature of the Brown shooting. It was simply the result of an argument between two Deadwood men over money. The shooter was a restaurant proprietor named Edward Cook, whose place of business was on the north side of Main Street, a few doors down from the Bella Union. His victim was John Farrel, who delivered wood to citizens and businesses in order to "turn an honest dollar."

On the day of the shooting, Farrel returned "from the stampede" and "desirous of replenishing his dust bag" went to Cook's place of business to collect money owed. A mere inquiry led to sharp words and Farrel "fumbled for a weapon" while stepping outside. Cook stayed inside behind the counter. Suddenly, he heard a voice shout, "Look out, Ed!" Looking up, Cook saw a flash of light as Farrel fired his pistol. Farrel missed but Cook, returning fire, did not. The bullet hit Farrel in the chest, causing a serious wound that doctors believed would prove to be mortal. It was mortal and the shooting riled up the community and there were usual mutterings about getting a rope, but "no breach of the peace" occurred. It was just one of those incidents that made Deadwood a lively town.[12]

Notice of the Cook and Brown shootings were telegraphed to Yankton, alerting Marshal James H. Burdick of the trouble in Deadwood.[13] The city fathers of Deadwood—a town with no "official" officials—were apparently willing to turn the prisoners over to Burdick so that any trials that might result would take place in Yankton in front of Judge Shannon.

Sioux Falls, on the opposite side of the territory, experienced a November shooting as well. While the town at the falls was tame and well-behaved compared to Yankton, Bismarck, or Deadwood, it was not without a steady flow of vagabonds, gold hunters, gamblers, con artists and assorted ne'er-do-wells. Sioux Falls was still a frontier town where men gambled, indulged in liquor, and habitually carried guns, so it was probably just a matter of time before a firearm was put to deadly purpose.

The shooting occurred in the early morning hours of November 10, 1876, at C. K. "Charley" Howard's stage barn on Tenth Street. The man who pulled a trigger in anger was Alonzo V. Corson, a wild sort who had been to the Black Hills. He was related to Harry Corson who owned and managed the stylish and commodious Cataract Hotel in Sioux Falls. It was also reported that he had served two years in the Wisconsin legislature, representing La Fayette County.[14]

Corson's victim was John Van Kirk, whose mother lived in Emmetsburg, Iowa. Early in the evening, the two men were engaged in gambling in a saloon on Phillips Avenue when an argument led to a "row." As a result, the proprietor ordered Corson to leave. Corson left but stood outside and tossed several stones at the front door. Meanwhile, Van Kirk exited the saloon from the back door and walked to Howard's barn to start his day of work. Corson refused to cool off and instead went to the Williams House, a hotel. He picked up his shotgun, walked over to Howard's barn, and without a word of warning, shot and killed Van Kirk.[15]

A report of the crime in the *Press and Dakotaian* indicates that Corson and Van Kirk separated after quarreling over cards. A short time later, Corson confronted Van Kirk at the stable while the latter was hitching his team for the scheduled departure of the stagecoach from Sioux Falls to Sibley, Iowa. After another quarrel erupted, Van Kirk grabbed a pitch fork and threatened Corson with it. Corson secured a shotgun and a shell from his cousin, saying that he was going to "shoot a brant for breakfast." With another target in mind, Corson returned to the barn where he shot and killed Van Kirk, the blast nearly severing his head. Corson was seen entering the stage barn, and soon after, the shooter who had "for years borne the reputation of being a desperate man" was arrested while hiding in an outhouse.[16]

After word of the shooting spread through the small town, some Sioux Falls men began to act like those of Yankton or Deadwood. With nothing more important to do, a crowd gathered outside of the jail and commenced shouting and howling like a lynch mob. Charley Howard, one of the town's most respected citizens, intervened, and although he had lost an employee, he convinced the mob to go home. At that point Sheriff Henry Callender decided to escort the prisoner to Yankton for safe keeping.[17]

The shooting caused many, less violent Sioux Falls residents to blame whiskey and call for its eradication. Fault was laid at the feet of saloon keepers who sold alcohol, and further blame was heaped upon members of the legislature who "make laws to allow saloons to sell liquor." The tragedy was "made the text of moral lectures in the churches, on the street, and at the fireside."[18] The Corson case, which had riled up the city of Sioux Falls, would be included on the calendar of the next term of court.

Yankton marked the holiday season of 1876 with a shooting of its own, another in a long line of "shooting affrays" that seemed to plague the capital city. It was not a Merry Christmas for Frank McMahon, who was shot and seriously wounded by Charles Conrad inside the St. Charles Hotel. While churches and homes throughout Yankton were celebrating Christmas with sermons, songs, and presents, some old-fashioned gunplay occurred downtown.

McMahon and a friend, Albert Cashdollar, had been making merry during the afternoon of Christmas Day. After a few drinks to improve the "inner man," they took a stroll down Third Street. When they turned left on Capital Street at the St. Charles Hotel corner, they were confronted by Charles Conrad. An argument ensued, during which time a drunken McMahon attempted to strike Conrad who, in turn, drew his revolver and pulled the trigger. It misfired but it got McMahon's attention. While turning to run away, McMahon yelled, "don't shoot me Charley."

Charley ignored the urgent request, took aim, pulled the trigger and McMahon became the recipient of the "leaden compliments." The bullet struck McMahon in the left shoulder as he ran up the staircase inside the St. Charles Hotel. The wound failed to stop McMahon, and he continued moving with Conrad in hot pursuit. When he reached the third floor, McMahon turned to descend a stairway that led to the lobby. Just when it looked as though McMahon might escape another bullet, he was shot in the left leg by Conrad who was standing on the second floor landing.[19]

McMahon fell down in agony while Conrad merely walked to room No. 7, where he put his gun away in a "traveling bag." He had been sharing that room with a sick soldier. He had very little time to relax and reflect on his actions, for Deputy Marshal Sponsler, hearing the shots, went to the hotel, found and arrested Conrad, and escorted him to jail.

The twice-wounded McMahon was taken to the nearby office of Dr. Paddock, who examined and dressed his wounds. McMahon was then carried to his residence and, soon thereafter, to the Merchants Hotel. At this destination, McMahon was placed in the care of "the woman who caused the trouble." It was at this point that the treating physicians, the *Dakota Herald*, and law enforcement learned about the events leading up to the crime.

As it turned out, the quarrel and the shooting came about because both the shooter and his victim claimed the same woman as a spouse. The "woman," who was for all practical purposes blamed for the crime, was the niece of Conrad. A reporter for the *Herald* learned some of the lurid details of the relationship between uncle and niece. When she was only thirteen years old, he seduced her and became the father of her child. The couple was living at Ponca, Nebraska, at the time. Conrad was arrested for fathering an illegitimate child, and having been convicted of incest, served a term in the Nebraska prison.

He secured an early release and returned to the "woman" (she was never named in the *Herald* article) and supposedly married her and fathered two more children. Conrad further explained that about a year previous she had met McMahon, who convinced her to go with him to Yankton. They were living in Yankton about a month prior to the shooting. Conrad joined the couple in Yankton where both men were employed at Power's livery stable. In an attempt to mitigate the shooting of McMahon, Conrad insisted that he was the victim of harassment and intimidation. The *Herald* concluded, "we are of the opinion that both have been caught in a very bad scrape. The woman is said to be of very bad character."

Conrad was given a preliminary examination before Justice Congleton and ordered to appear before the district court at its April term. He was kept in jail due to his inability to secure release on a $2,000 bond.[20] In a case with a long history and with many twists and turns, it appears that sympathy was moving toward Conrad, as well as toward the man he shot, both having been led astray by a "woman."

Misogyny was practiced openly and shamelessly. Individual responsibility, logic, and plain facts were easily ignored when a "woman" entered the picture, even if a child of thirteen when the trouble started. Assigning blame to a woman for a man's crime was an ancient crutch that never seemed to outlive its usefulness.

As always, the law would have to sort it all out one way or another. In the Bella Union shooting, Dick Brown was cleared of all charges after Deadwood "Justice" F. B. Farnum conducted a "patient hearing of voluminous testimony." Farnum was not a real justice of the peace but Brown had no reason to be concerned. He would not be occupying a Yankton jail cell, for it was decided that he was acting in self-defense when he shot and killed Edward Shaughnessy at the Bella Union.[21] Nor was Edward Cook prosecuted for shooting John Farrel. Deadwood old-timer John McClintock simply noted in his memoirs, "nothing done about it."[22]

The Alonzo V. Corson case, arising out of the shooting death of John Van Kirk in Sioux Falls, was assigned for trial in Minnehaha County.[23] Corson's attorneys were R. F. Pettigrew from Sioux Falls and G. C. Moody from Yankton. On June 2 they applied for a continuance of the matter, arguing Corson could not get a fair trial because of "bias" on the part of Judge Shannon. After hearing arguments, Shannon assigned the case to Judge Bennett.[24]

On July 18, 1877, Corson was brought forth to stand trial in Sioux Falls before Judge Granville G. Bennett. But before a single witness was called, Corson's legal counsel told the judge that his client wanted to make a change of plea. Having previously entered a plea of not guilty to murder, Corson pled guilty to manslaughter in the first degree. Bennett accepted the plea, heard testimony pertaining to both aggravating and mitigating factors, and sentenced Corson to seven years in prison.

In Yankton, Charles Conrad had no chance to prove self-defense or argue mitigation, for he was clearly the aggressor. Frank McMahon—shot while escaping— recovered from his wounds, meaning that Conrad would not be charged with murder. Instead, he was arraigned for shooting with intent to kill. His attorney, S. L. Spink, filed a motion for a continuance that was denied and the case went to trial. A jury found him guilty of assault with intent to do bodily harm "without justifiable or excusable cause." Judge Shannon sentenced him to five years in prison at Fort Madison, Iowa.[25]

The case was appealed to the Dakota Territory Supreme Court, where Chief Justice Shannon wrote the opinion, even though he was also the trial judge. Spink raised just one error: the sentence did not fit the crime for which Conrad was convicted. Shannon looked at both the indictment and the conviction and found that while Conrad was charged with "assault with the intent to kill," a felony, he was convicted of "assault with intent to do bodily harm," a misdemeanor. Therefore, Shannon freely admitted his error: he had sentenced Conrad under the felony part of the statute.[26] The sentence was reduced to two months and, having already served eight months, Conrad was released from county jail on October 11, 1877, after nearly ten months behind bars.[27]

Clearly, the Dakota Penal Code was lenient toward acts of violence with a firearm. The jury was given a choice under the code to find Conrad guilty of a felony or misdemeanor, or even the offense of simple assault. Assuming they heard testimony about McMahon—pleading for his life, running away, and entering the hotel, with Conrad in hot pursuit, firing and hitting his victim twice—the jury had ample evidence of a felonious assault. The jurymen concluded, rather, that the defendant simply intended "to do bodily harm." They were not convinced that Conrad had murder on his mind. It was like saying that Conrad was just having a little Christmas Day fun.

There are two interesting footnotes to the Conrad case. The eyewitness, Albert Cashdollar, decided that he wanted no part in giving testimony. He was boarding an outbound steamboat when the authorities nabbed him. Cashdollar was kept in jail to insure his appearance at the trial. The other key witness and the victim, Frank McMahon, was conspicuously absent from the trial, for he had become entangled in a criminal snare of his own making. Unfortunately for McMahon, his absence may have swayed the jury away from a harsher verdict.

In his opinion, Shannon wrote that "juries do not give reasons for their verdicts."[28] He could also have said that they do not have to, for they are only asked to make a rational decision based on evidence presented at trial. And looking at the facts of the case through a twenty-first-century lens, one can only wonder about the collective reasoning of this Dakota jury. Even more curious, perhaps, is a statutory scheme that allowed a shooter such as Conrad to slide through the system with only a misdemeanor conviction.

Joseph Allen was even more fortunate than Conrad. His trial for the murder of A. A. Nichols, a "squaw man," on Pascal's Island, fifty miles up the Missouri River from Fort Sully, concluded on November 26, 1877. The prosecution was led by U.S. Attorney Hugh J. Campbell, a recent replacement for William A. Pound, who died while traveling by train from Bismarck to Yankton.[29]

At the trial it was revealed that Allen had worked for Nichols, chopping wood, an unfortunate arrangement for both men. After four days of testimony, the jury reached a verdict of not guilty. Allen's attorneys, G. C. Moody and S. A. Boyles, laid out a case of self-defense, with the skillful use of evidence that Nichols had been drinking for days prior to the crime and had quarreled and fought with Allen. They convinced the jury that Nichols was a quarrelsome and dangerous man, whose mind was corrupted to the point of frenzy by excessive consumption of alcohol. On the occasion of the shooting, both men went for their guns but Allen shot first, killing Nichols.[30]

Although these cases are typical of frontier justice for frontier crimes, the most outrageous case of criminal audacity, provoking pert commentary in the Yankton newspapers, goes to Cuthbert DuCharme, alias Papineau, a man widely renowned for his evil deeds. The old offender—known up and down the Missouri River—had been in Yankton in February in connection with his Black Hills freight business. While waiting for freight to be loaded on to his wagons, he went on a drinking spree.[31]

Papineau's propensity toward violent behavior was enhanced by alcohol. Aware of that, the *Press and Dakotaian* noted that when "Pap" was in town the "minions of the law are sure of a job." On this occasion, Papineau's drunken antics landed him in jail on February 28, 1877, on a charge of assault with intent to kill. His crime was slightly overshadowed by the hanging of Jack McCall, on March 1. If Papineau had plans to attend the hanging, he was sorely disappointed.

The man Papineau intended to kill was Henry Bradley, the proprietor of the Bradley House, a popular Yankton hotel. It was reported that DuCharme was "still laboring under the effects of bad whiskey" when he pointed his rifle at Bradley and pulled the trigger. He missed and was about to try again, but Bradley had the presence of mind to get his hands on the rifle. He took it away from Papineau, thereby saving himself serious injury or death and preventing "Old Pap" from facing a death-penalty crime.[32]

For Bradley, the Papineau incident was not the first time he had to deal with gun violence. In February 1867 he was shot and wounded by Joel M. Congdon during an altercation outside the office of W. W. Brookings in Yankton. Congdon accused Bradley of poisoning his dog, whereupon Bradley allegedly threw an ax at Congdon. The ax failed to find its target, so in retaliation Congdon shot Bradley "in the region of the short ribs," inflicting what was thought to be a fatal wound. But Bradley survived and became one of Yankton's leading citizens.[33]

Papineau, the foxy Frenchman, was indicted for assault with intent to kill Bradley and held on a $500 bond. He hired as legal counsel, the brothers Tripp, Bartlett, and William, known throughout Dakota for their criminal defense work. Papineau would need all the legal skill his attorneys could muster, for he was a dangerous man who seemed destined to hang. Sheriff Millard A. Baker escorted him to Bon Homme where he stood trial on April 28 and was found guilty as charged.[34]

The year before, Papineau was accused of stealing a mule from the Yankton Indian Agency. He was brought to Yankton for a hearing but was not charged, and "Old Pap" left town "in high glee." It was duly noted that he was quite frequently "hauled up," but he always seemed to escape "the clutches of the law."[35]

But with the Bradley case, Cuthbert DuCharme's string of luck finally ran out. He was sentenced by Judge Shannon to serve eight years in prison and on May 3, 1877, the wild man of the Missouri River frontier was taken to Fort Madison, Iowa, to begin serving his sentence. The *Press and Dakotaian* expressed the feelings of the general public with its observation that a "dangerous character has gone from our midst." The Dakota desperado was known to have killed two men since he opened his Missouri River ranch and was "strongly suspected of numerous lesser crimes."[36]

The legendary Papineau was gone but not for long. He served less than a year. On March 4, 1878, Governor Pennington pardoned him along with another prisoner, James Wilson. Papineau's pardon was supported by a large number of Dakotans including, oddly enough, "the man he attempted to kill."[37]

The governor attached a postscript to his pardon message, expressing his sincere wish that "these unfortunate men" would take a "solemn vow, before leaving the prison never to touch or taste another drop of intoxicating liquors of any kind and that they will go forth in the world again to live industrious virtuous lives."[38]

Papineau was free and doubtless had no intention of taking the governor's advice. He returned to his Missouri River domain and carried on as before. In February 1880 news worked its way to Yankton from the upriver country that "Papineau is on the rampage again" and his wife was "having a busy time keeping out of the way of his revolvers."[39] As time went on his behavior became more erratic, and Cuthbert DuCharme was eventually committed to the South Dakota State Hospital for the mentally ill in Yankton, where he died in 1903.

CHAPTER 15

"until the wolves eat the flesh from his legs": THE FIRESTEEL GANG OF HORSE THIEVES

If they succeed in capturing some of the thieves an informal funeral without mourners will be appointed, and there will be no postponement on account of weather or anything else.

Dakota Pantagraph
February 5, 1879

I n late July 1875 a young man checked into the Cataract Hotel in Sioux Falls, registering under the name of William Cheney, from Rockford, Illinois. Among his possessions were two fine horses. Exhibiting an air of confidence, Cheney said he was a detective and that he was in town to track down a gang of horse thieves. He explained that he had contacted the U.S. marshal at Yankton for help.

Not long after Cheney's arrival at the hotel, the sheriff from Pembina County, accompanied by a deputy and another man, walked into the lobby. They were on a mission, looking for a horse thief that they had tracked to Sioux Falls. Without hesitation, they confronted and arrested Cheney at gunpoint. In "a twinkling," the *Sioux Falls Independent* reported, the sheriff "adorned the fellow's wrists" with handcuffs. Accused of horse stealing, Cheney broke down, literally, and had to be picked up off the floor and helped to a chair. It seems that "his knees were too weak for his conscience."

The sheriff revealed that Cheney's real name was Martin and that he was a veteran horse thief. The two horses that Martin had with him were stolen near Big Stone Lake, far to the north of Sioux Falls. They were identified by the citizen who arrived with the sheriff and his deputy. The lawman and his fellow travelers left Sioux Falls with their prisoner, headed for Fargo.[1]

Martin had reason to be worried, for it was a long way from Sioux Falls to Fargo, and although the prairie was, for the most part, treeless, there were occasional wooded areas, so he could not be certain that he would ever see the inside of a jailhouse. Horse thieves were usually hanged and, with each tree they approached, the alleged thief was undoubtedly reminded of his possible fate. It took a lot of nerve to steal horses and more yet for a man to sit astride a horse with a rope around his neck, waiting to be "swung off." But Martin was not lynched. Handcuffed to the sheriff, after seven days and seven nights on the prairie, Martin and his captors arrived in Fargo.[2]

Horse rustling was one of the most persistent and problematic crimes facing the courts and lawmen in Dakota Territory. Plains Indians regularly stole horses from other tribes and from settlers, but within the confines of their culture it was not considered a crime, rather a custom and, for young Indian boys, a rite of passage. In Euroamerican frontier society, however, horse thievery was a criminal offense, which outraged the public and merited grave punishment, including the death penalty.

Because horses were vitally important for the mobility, safety, and security of the people on the frontier, their value was, accordingly, very high and could not always be measured in dollars and cents. If one man stole another man's horse, the thief suddenly became mobile and the victim was left alone, exposed, vulnerable, often isolated, on foot and with no other means of transportation. His life had been put at risk, so the theft was seen as attempted murder, a capital crime. Thieves understood that if caught they could expect no mercy, and many a luckless horse thief was swung from a convenient tree limb.

Despite the risk, horse rustling became an appealing alternative to honest work. Horses were often easily seized and could be quickly moved from place to place, putting distance between the thieves and the rightful owners. There was always a healthy black market for horses, with willing buyers who paid cash, no questions asked. For a reckless young man, the life of a horse thief was a life of adventure and a chance to make ready money—or die an outlaw's death.

Since the theft of a horse was such a serious matter, the pursuit of horse thieves provided the opportunity not only to right a wrong but to escape the drudgery of routine town and ranch chores. At the sound of alarm, impromptu posses would be formed and ride out in pursuit of the thieves. Sometimes horses strayed away of their own accord, but their disappearance was usually blamed on horse thieves.

One of the earliest stories of a Dakota horse thief dates back to an incident that may have occurred in 1869 or 1870 in Lincoln County. According to oral tradition, a man and his two sons, who were believed to be horse thieves, were strung up on limbs of a cottonwood tree beside the Big Sioux River, about eight miles northeast of the town of Canton. The ill-fated trio had been trying desperately to reach the Iowa border when they were captured by a group of men who had tracked the suspected thieves and found them on the west bank of the river. The chase that began several miles distant to the northwest ended with the three men buried near the hanging tree.[3]

The hanging tree is an iconic Old West image and figures in many tales of Dakota Territory. In the late 1870s, near the stagecoach station of Oakwood in Brookings County, two horse thieves were hunted down, shot up, and hanged from a tree that became known as "Dead Man's Tree."[4] Further west, in Tripp County, where ranchers had low tolerance for horse thieves, a tree near White Lake is long remembered as a hanging tree.[5]

No doubt there were many other trees across the plains where suspected outlaws met their death by strangulation, but the Rapid City "hanging tree" emerges as the ugliest tree of its kind. There, two horse thieves and a third victim, described as an innocent boy, were strung up by a lynch mob of "good cow men" on June 21, 1877.[6] The triple-lynching has forever linked Rapid City to the deaths of Curry, Allen, and Hall.

The *Press and Dakotaian* described Lewis Curry as a well-built, "slightly pock marked" twenty-eight-year-old man, known as "Rady." A. J. Allen was described as a thirty-five-year-old bearded man with a bald spot on his head. James "Kid" Hall was estimated to have been nineteen or twenty years old, of medium height with "dark complexion" and a "flat nose" that caused him to look as if he "might have negro blood." Hall was said to have come to the territory from Batavia, New York.[7]

A book published in Rapid City and written by two men with experience on the frontier took the position that Hall deserved his fate. Far from being an innocent youth, Hall was a "man of ill-repute," who had led a "disreputable life in Deadwood" and had been ordered to leave town. The hanging was, therefore, not a monstrous injustice. In fact, the two pioneer writers claimed that the triple-lynching had a "wholesome effect" and put a "damper on cattle rustling and horse stealing."[8] Was their view accurate or were they simply providing cover for the lynch mob?

The *Press and Dakotaian* took a different approach, essentially clearing Hall of horse stealing. The paper reported that Hall just happened to be riding with the thieves when about fifteen well-armed men caught them, along with four horses. Further, Curry and Allen confessed to stealing the horses at Crook City and exonerated Hall. The three men were taken to a log cabin in Rapid City and locked inside. At about three o'clock in the morning, a mob of about twenty men broke into the cabin, took them to a tree, and hanged them.[9]

Although the two older men accepted their fate, Hall begged for his life, screaming his innocence while cursing his captors. Still the mob hanged him, since turning him loose would carry the risk of being identified. Dead men (and boys) tell no tales. The three lynch mob victims were left hanging until discovered by residents of Rapid City, a ghastly spectacle in the morning light. The noose knots had been poorly tied and the three luckless men strangled to death. The lynching was a vicious and cowardly deed, which haunted the collective conscience of that community for years. Rapid City became known as a place where "stranglers" lived.

Mont Hawthorne was a twelve-year-old boy when he and his father arrived in Rapid City shortly after the lynching. Coming up from Nebraska, their wagon train was met on the edge of town by a posse with information about the hanging of three men on a hill outside of town. They also made it clear to Mont's father that it would not be healthy for anyone to ask questions about who was responsible for the lynching.

A few curious men from the wagon train ignored the advice and did some sleuthing in Rapid City. The obtuse responses they received suggested that they would be wise to forget the entire affair. Young Mont, however, was upset over the fact that a mere lad, not much older than he, riding a horse that his father bought for him, could be treated so cruelly. Mont and his father visited "Hangman's Hill," where three cut ropes, still attached to the hanging tree, lilted in the breeze. It was a horrible sight— and stayed with Mont for the rest of his life.[10]

Dakota Territory Governor John L. Pennington was also outraged, and he offered a $1,000 reward for the arrest and conviction of the persons who committed the crime. The governor called it an "atrocious murder," a crime without "apology or excuse," and a "disgrace to our civilization."[11] But no one claimed the reward and no arrests were made.

Four years later an article appeared in the *Black Hills Daily Times* reprising the ugly incident. Under the title "Coming Home to Roost," the writer reminded everyone that "the history of that night's work has remained almost a sealed book, but it is gradually leaking out." He predicted that "the men who today occupy positions of honor and trust will be called upon to prove their innocence to this most damnable outrage."[12]

No names leaked out, nor was anyone called upon to prove his innocence. Instead, the collective lie wrapped itself around the conscience of the community like a noose. As the years passed, the prevailing feeling among Rapid City pioneers was that their city labored under a curse and would not prosper until, as an old-timer was heard to say, "all them that took part in the Hangman's Hill business is dead."[13] Rapid City has more than recovered, but those who lynched Curry, Allen, and Hall remain unknown.

Incidents of horse thievery in the late 1860s and early 1870s were scarce, as were the number of good horses available to steal. Nevertheless, the courts had work. In May 1872 Joseph M. Putney was sentenced to ten months in prison after being convicted of horse theft.[14] It was a light sentence when one takes into consideration that he could have been summarily hanged had he not been subjected to justice in the territorial court in Yankton. Putney was shipped off to Fort Madison, Iowa, to serve his sentence. He was released the following February for good behavior.[15]

Putney's good behavior did not extend to his life outside of the prison walls, and his missteps continued to trip him up after returning to Yankton. As though wishing to enhance his bad reputation, Putney started a quarrel with Jim Somers, who was relaxing in a Yankton saloon. Perhaps not knowing that Somers already had a legendary appetite for violence, Putney pulled a pistol from his pocket and threatened big Jim. According to the *Dakota Herald*, Somers, "who through a desire to have an extension of time in which to better prepare to meet grim death," managed to extricate himself from the dangerous situation. Instead of killing Putney, though, Somers had him arrested, charged with assault with intent to kill.[16]

Before he could be tried for his latest crime, Putney broke out of the Yankton jail, thereby adding his name to the long list of escapees.[17] His freedom proved temporary, for in May 1873 Putney was tried on a charge of assault with intent to kill. The result was a hung jury. He was quickly retried and acquitted.[18]

But Dakota had not heard the last of Joseph M. Putney. In July 1874 the *Herald* reported that "Joe Putney is no more." He had been killed by an Indian in the "upper country and buried like a dog." In death he was denounced by the *Herald* as a drunken vagabond and felon. He had quarreled with the Indian, whose name is not mentioned in the article, and was shot dead. It was noted that "no one wanted to hang the Indian."[19]

The story of Edward DeWitt, also accused of horse theft, began in September 1874 when he arrived in Springfield from Texas, an employee of a man who brought in a herd of cattle. A friendly, likeable young man of good manners, he got a job making gloves for a Springfield merchant. He quickly became a favorite of the young ladies and was the center of attraction at local social events. Soon, however, everyone who made his acquaintance learned that there was a dark side to this tall, mustachioed man with a "prepossessing form of comely proportions."

Over the Christmas holidays, he borrowed a team of horses and drove to Yankton in an open wagon. There, he was seen "dashing around the streets with his team and lady 'friends' in gay style and high 'spirits.'" He returned to Springfield but soon after left again on a "borrowed" horse and owing one citizen $150 and others lesser amounts. For this the *Springfield Times* sounded the alarm in a front-page article, denouncing DeWitt as a "Gay and Festive Broncho [sic] youth...a Glove maker, a Love maker, Horse Thief and Confidence Swindler."[20]

About three and a half weeks after DeWitt disappeared, George Mead of Springfield received a letter from the con man postmarked Montreal, Canada. DeWitt had simply written the word "How," followed by his signature. This insolence was almost too much to bear for the staff of the *Springfield Times* and its readers. DeWitt was warned that the country of Canada, however vast, was not big enough for "his putrescent carcass."[21]

Months later DeWitt was back in Dakota, where he was arrested and charged with larceny—a charge he denied until he was identified as the thief by witnesses. At this point, "he weakened and wanted to settle the matter." He was arraigned at Bon Homme and held on bail in the amount of $500. Then it was learned that DeWitt had sold a horse stolen in Springfield that belonged to someone in Bon Homme. For this he was brought to Yankton by the Bon Homme County sheriff and lodged in jail.[22]

Unfortunately, DeWitt was not retained in the Yankton jail because "the jail keepers could not legally keep him," and he was taken back to Bon Homme and held under guard. At this point, the story becomes only more confusing. The paper reported that DeWitt had stolen another horse, this one from James Legness of Jefferson in Union County and he used that horse to pay his attorney for defending him in the Springfield case. A telegram to this effect sent Sheriff Millard A. Baker and Deputy Marshal Leeper to Bon Homme to pick up DeWitt and bring him back to "Sheriff Baker's brick and mortar box" in Yankton. DeWitt had committed multiple offenses, but some still believed that this young man could salvage his life if he "gets his feet into the path of rectitude."[23]

Someone should have explained to DeWitt the meaning of the word "rectitude," for he kept on his wayward path. Nevertheless, DeWitt was in some ways fortune's child, for although he was frequently caught, he was never lynched, and when he was behind bars, he managed to secure legal counsel.

In May1875 Edward DeWitt was brought before Judge Shannon on a *habeas corpus* hearing. The disgruntled judge was compelled to sort out the jurisdictional aspects of the case, with all of its curious twists and turns. From the bench Shannon doled out "some very whole some [sic] advice in regard to the trifling with the liberty of persons," even those as troublesome as DeWitt. The judge ruled that DeWitt "must be remanded to the authorities" in Bon Homme County or retained in Yankton under some suitable arrangement with Bon Homme County, until his alleged crimes in that county were disposed of and then, and only then, could he have his day in court in Union County.[24]

DeWitt stayed in the Yankton County jail in accordance with Judge Shannon's order, until Friday, June 11, at which time he "abandoned his situation in that institution without the consent of the jailer." Having escaped from jail, he stepped on a nail that "penetrated the full length of his foot." The painful injury compelled him to "travel a portion of the time upon his hands and knees." Then, using a hastily made crutch, DeWitt made his way east to the James River where he stole a boat near the railroad bridge. Off his feet and on the water, he floated downstream to the Missouri River where he encountered a man who attempted to make a citizen's arrest. DeWitt jumped into the water and swam to the shore, determined not to get caught. Yet he was pursued and captured by two other men, J. T. McKnight and John Robinson, at Haggins Bend on the Missouri River, opposite St. Helena, Nebraska. After a short time on the loose, DeWitt was "returned to the loving care of Sheriff Baker's turn key."[25]

But not for long. On June 17 the *Press and Dakotaian* reported with due excitement that DeWitt had again escaped from the Yankton jail. Early in the evening of the 16th, while the jailor "opened the door leading into the stairway of the main of the jail, he was seized by DeWitt," and with the assistance of another prisoner, "pushed violently to one side." The jailer quickly recovered and shoved the prisoner back into his cell, but the slippery DeWitt escaped. The jailer rushed outside and fired a couple of shots at DeWitt but missed his target. DeWitt ran through lower Yankton, hotly pursued by the jailer and other officers, eluding his pursuers. The *Press and Dakotaian* found humor in the situation, remarking that DeWitt "went off in such a hurry that he forgot to settle with his attorneys."[26]

Once again, though, DeWitt enjoyed his freedom only briefly, for he was captured and returned to Bon Homme, "where he belongs," quipped the paper. The *Press and Dakotaian* was clearly tired of keeping tabs on DeWitt, complaining that he was for too long an "expensive luxury" to

Yankton. Judge Shannon apparently shared the paper's sense of frustration with DeWitt and others who kept breaking out of the Yankton jail. He called for action, observing that the jail had to be made secure "even if the courthouse conveniences should suffer in the consequence."[27]

Shannon could have made the same complaint about the Bon Homme County jail, since DeWitt managed to escape from that small and weak "bastille" by "slipping out of his handcuffs and sliding out of a window," according to the *Springfield Times*.[28] The "irrepressible DeWitt" was "at large" once again. A man matching his description was seen near Scotland, where "a valuable horse" had been reported stolen. The author of the short article concluded that DeWitt was the thief, reflecting the public's frustration over the "veritable horse-thief DeWitt" and his uncanny ability to thwart justice for his "many crimes."[29]

It would be the last time Edward DeWitt's name appeared in a Dakota newspaper, for he evaded recapture, never again to see the inside of a Dakota jail nor to face Judge Peter Shannon. Perhaps, given his criminal proclivities, DeWitt was eventually caught, tried, and put behind the bars of a prison from which he could not escape. Maybe at long last DeWitt learned the meaning of the word "rectitude."

If DeWitt had wanted to hide in south central Dakota Territory, he could have picked no better place than the Wessington Hills, a region that over time became known as the refuge of outlaws, especially horse thieves. The Wessington Hills of Wetmore County (now Jerauld County) consist of a ridge about twenty miles in length, sloping gradually upward from south to north, terminating in a grand prominence known as Turtle Peak, or Turtle Mountain, as it was also called. Firesteel Creek, which originates on the eastern edge of the hills, flowing southeast into the James River, is another prominent feature of this part of Dakota.

Just when the name "Wessington Hills" was attached to the scenic land mass is uncertain, but according to a newspaper account the hills were named after a trapper named Wessington who was killed there by Sioux Indians. As the story goes, the trapper was working a trap line with his companions along Firesteel Creek when they were attacked and killed. Two of the victims, including Wessington, were tortured, their heads crushed by rocks, and their "intellectual faculties" scattered "all over the sides of the gulch."[30]

A group of men who visited the Wessington Hills in July 1872 had a much more pleasant experience. They were treated to a place of great natural beauty, of deep ravines and windswept peaks with breathtaking views from all directions. Leaving their camp at the foot of the hills, the adventurers climbed to the highest point. On top of the "highest mountain we found Indian graves covered with monuments of stone piled up." They also found where the Indians had "outlined on the ground with round stones the form of a huge squaw, an immense turtle, and a cross." Clearly in awe of their discovery, a member of the group wrote an account for the *Dakota Herald,* describing the "mountain" known as "Turtle Mountain, so called for the figure of the turtle thus outlined."[31] It was cause enough for sober minds to wonder silently about the great mystery of the stones arranged in the form of mosaics at the highest point of the Wessington Hills.

For horse thieves seeking refuge and a place to hide their contraband, the scenic and wondrous Hills were desirable for purposes other than hunting antelope, a species that lived there in great numbers. In these deep, heavily wooded ravines, far from towns and settlements, outlaws hid their stolen horses. One local legend relates that a posse from Huron, determined to take out the gang, rode to the Wessington Hills only to find that the thieves had vacated their "sod-walled stronghold." Someone had tipped them off.[32]

Although the Wessington Hills area was the principal focus of those interested in tracking down horse thieves, an underground stable was reputed to be located about fifteen miles west of Lake Herman in Lake County. Four horses were found there and one of the thieves was arrested in Sioux Falls.[33] This report, like others, cannot be independently verified, but it does indicate the widespread nature of the problem.

Such was the desire to identify the elusive thieves that suspicion was cast far, wide, and recklessly. Anyone found near the Wessington Hills or Firesteel Creek was suspect. Just as the land west of the James River was considered unsuitable, anyone who chose to live in this area was thought to be undesirable. The trickle of settlers into the James River Valley grew into a stream by the early 1870s, attracted by land suited to agriculture. The town of Rockport on the James River, south of present-day Mitchell, was created near a large outcropping of quartzite rock. It was the first town in the area, though it was never thought to shelter outlaws.

Reverend A. B. Smart, a Methodist Episcopalian minister from Illinois, claimed to know the origin of the infamous outlaw gangs in the Wessington Hills. In his pioneer history of Jerauld County, he states that the first organized gangs of horse thieves were created in the spring of 1874. A group of Springfield boys, having just finished a term of school, got together and decided that their future was to be adventuresome. Rather than clerk in a store or take up farming, they would become outlaws. They would "steal stock and horses and sell them, taking care to keep out of the way of the law."[34]

They formed two independent gangs but maintained contact with each other. The first gang concentrated its activity along the Missouri River in Dakota and the Niobrara River in Nebraska. This outlaw enterprise, known

Town of Firesteel, 1879.
Courtesy Mitchell Area Historical Society.

as the Niobrara Gang, was allegedly headed by Doc Middleton and later by Albert "Kid" Wade. The second gang chose for its field of operations the valleys of the James River and Firesteel Creek. This group ranged over the Wessington Hills and became known as the Firesteel Gang.

The Firesteel Gang was, allegedly, led by Starr Platt, a charge he vehemently denied. His father, Joseph Platt, along with Levi Hain, H. C. Greene, and John Head, were among the first settlers along Firesteel Creek in Davison County. The town of Firesteel was designated a post office on October 6, 1871, with Head as the postmaster. In 1874, when Davison County was organized around Firesteel, Hain was selected to be a county commissioner.[35] Although he seemed to lead an honest life, Hain accumulated an unsavory record in Dakota Territory, and throughout the 1870s his name was frequently linked to horse thievery.

By 1876, when Firesteel published a newspaper, the *Jim River Advocate,* Levi Hain was finished with the fledgling town. He had moved away and squatted on a quarter of land by the "Big Spring" on the eastern slope of the Wessington Hills, where the town of Wessington Springs was later platted. Another man, Andrew "Nick" Nicholson, had located about four miles to the north of Hain, at the entrance to a "deep gulch." Neither man engaged in any farming aside from a vegetable patch, leaving people to question how they made their living. They were suspected of being in league with the horse thieves. [36] Whether accurate or not, Levi Hain became known as "Horsethief Hain."

He apparently heard the accusation once too often for he made a trip to Yankton, where he had lived in 1866, and in a fit of anger went to the office of the *Press and Dakotaian*. In a manner described as "bulldozing," Hain told all there who would listen that he would be "damd [sic] if he was going to be called a horse thief." In response, the *Press and Dakotaian* remarked that Hain was blowing hot air in the wrong direction, for he had not been called a horse thief in its columns. But then what would one expect, asked the Yankton daily, from "a weak backed member of the human race?"[37]

There is no record of fisticuffs breaking out over the verbal exchange. But Hain was undoubtedly the kind of man who could be pushed too far, and it probably would not have been a good idea to send a reporter to the Wessington Hills for a follow-up interview. Hain and the Platts were among the many questionable characters who chose to live outside of established settlements, giving rise to suspicion about their methods and motives.

Starr Platt was perhaps more sociable than Levi Hain. According to a man interviewed by the *Press and Dakotaian*, Platt came to Dakota in 1872 and worked as a stagecoach driver on the Dakota Central Stage Company.[38] The *Dakota Pantagraph* revealed that Platt was the first justice of the peace of Hanson County (located next to Davison County), taking office on September 18, 1873.[39] He was arrested, however, for stealing cattle and brought to Yankton in September 1876.[40]

Another alleged leader of the Firesteel Gang was Hunter Claude Morgan, also known as "Red Cloud" because of his red hair. His sister, "Miss Morgan," an ethereal figure in the outlaw drama, had some connection to the gang as well. The gang operated for about thirteen years until most of the members were shot, hanged, or locked up.[41]

If, as Rev. Smart states, the horse-thief gangs originated in 1874, they must have operated quietly for about four years. They stole horses during that period, of course, but not until 1878 did the thievery reach its peak. The year 1878, when the Great Dakota Boom began, saw a major influx of immigrants into the James River Valley, north of Yankton. With families came horses, an opportunity the thieves were quick to recognize. Situated between the Indian reservations to the west and settlements to the east, the horse-thief gangs of the Wessington Hills had access to hundreds of horses.

Operating as though a secret society, members of the Firesteel Gang roamed from the Missouri River to the Iowa state line, wearing "a star hidden from the casual observer by the coat lapel."[42] A middle-aged widow known as "Mother Filkins" maintained a hideout for the thieves at her place on Firesteel Creek.[43]

The Niobrara Gang, believed to be as large as thirty-five men, was also busy with its criminal activity. By 1878 the thieves had expanded their operation to include the theft of cattle, mostly from men who had contracts with the government to provide beef for the Indian reservations. Many white Dakotans feared that Indians would retaliate against innocent settlers because of the actions of the thieves. This fear was nowhere better expressed than in the action of a grand jury from the second judicial district at Yankton. In a written plea to Judge Shannon, the grand jury asked the judge to request military intervention to protect innocent settlers from Indian retaliation for crimes carried out by "white men of a low, degraded character."[44] While Shannon did not honor the request, the authorities in Nebraska and Iowa joined together in an effort to track down members of the notorious Niobrara Gang.[45]

Other changes were in the works. By 1878 all horse thieves and other criminals arrested, tried, and convicted in Dakota Territory would no longer serve their time in Fort Madison, Iowa. In the summer of 1877, Governor John L. Pennington and Judges Shannon and Granville

G. Bennett arranged for the transfer of all Dakota prisoners to Detroit, Michigan. The new contract with the Detroit House of Corrections would result in lower incarceration costs to the territory. Although this new arrangement met with considerable criticism, some thirty prisoners were transferred under the supervision of Sheriff Millard A. Baker and U.S. Marshal James Burdick. Five prisoners were pardoned.[46]

During the time of the prison transfer, Dakota was introduced to its new U.S. marshal. John B. Raymond, a Civil War veteran and Bismarck banker and merchant, had been selected to replace Burdick.[47] The appointment brought Raymond to Dakota where he gradually rose to prominence as lawman and politician.

The U.S. marshal was still an important position, but the proliferation of new counties meant that sheriffs would assume responsibility for capturing and jailing outlaws. And since most of the outlaws were tried and sentenced in Yankton, everyone associated with law enforcement knew that the Sheriff "Ole" Baker would be making frequent trips to Detroit with more convicts.

Frank McMahon, the Christmas Day 1876 shooting victim of Charles Conrad, had positioned himself to be a Detroit-bound jailbird. When the Yankton ne'er-do-well failed to appear at Conrad's trial, the *Press and Dakotaian* suggested that McMahon had turned criminal. Having healed sufficiently, he allegedly cheated a Yankton man out of $80 and then stole a horse from, of all people, Judge Shannon. McMahon was linked to the crime after a bundle of his clothing was found near Shannon's Third Street stable. Some suggested, in jest, that McMahon used the $80 to buy a new suit of clothes, stole the horse, left his old clothes behind, and then decided not to appear at Conrad's trial because he "did not wish to return the borrowed horse at this time."[48]

Despite the humorous tone of the *Press and Dakotaian* article, Judge Shannon was not amused by this personal effrontery. On April 28, 1877, he placed the following notice in the pages of the *Sioux Valley News* of Canton:

Stolen

Yankton, April 23, 1877

On the night of the 21st inst., my horse, saddle and
bridle were stolen. The horse is a dapple gray, about
8 or 9 years old.

P. C. Shannon[49]

McMahon went into hiding after the disappearance of Shannon's
horse, prompting the law officers of Yankton and other areas to make a
concerted effort to find him. Finally, after a summer-long search, Sheriff
Baker received a telegram on September 11, 1877, informing him that
McMahon had been arrested in Council Bluffs, Iowa. Baker, the hard-
working and dedicated sheriff, immediately left Yankton to bring
McMahon back to face charges of stealing a horse that belonged to the
chief justice of the Dakota Territory Supreme Court. Shortly thereafter,
McMahon appeared before E. T. White, a justice of the peace in Yankton.
The prisoner waived preliminary examination and his bond was set at
$500.[50]

While behind bars and waiting for grand jury action, McMahon
and another prisoner, Cornelius Monroe, proposed to do what so many
prisoners did in the past: escape. They put their plan in motion while the
jailer was away eating his supper. Before he left, all the prisoners were
locked in their individual cells. But McMahon and his friend had previously
discovered that the bars that held the doors to their "dark closets" in place
could be manipulated so as to permit the two prisoners to open them. They
could then gain access to the large, central area that they occupied when
the jailer was present. A little grease on the bars cut down on the friction
and the noise. The next phase of the plan was to "dig their way through
the brick outside wall of their general apartment and escape." The scheme
was disrupted when the jailer returned. He quickly decided that McMahon
and Monroe were the "greasers." The next day Sheriff Baker adorned the
ankles of the two men with irons.[51]

A grand jury indicted McMahon for horse theft on November 17, and he remained in jail awaiting trial. Since the value of Judge Shannon's horse was undoubtedly more than twenty dollars, McMahon faced a charge of grand larceny for which the maximum penalty was five years imprisonment. And if the theft was done at night, section 587 of the Dakota penal code decreed that the offender "may be punished by imprisonment in the territorial prison not exceeding ten years."[52]

The case would normally have been assigned to Judge Shannon, but as the *Press and Dakotaian* pointed out, the chief justice was ethically bound to allow another judge to try the case. Judge Bennett would have to deal with McMahon. Shannon's participation in the case was that of a witness, since the horse in question belonged to him.[53]

Shannon was not called to testify, however, for McMahon pled guilty as charged. His only attempt to mitigate the crime was his claim that he was drunk when he stole Shannon's horse, and that he drank to ease the pain of his wounded shoulder that had not yet fully healed. Judge Bennett sentenced Frank McMahon to serve three years and six months in the Detroit House of Corrections.[54]

Did Judge Shannon ever get his horse back? Probably not, but Shannon was a busy man in the fall and winter of 1877, with enough activity to take his mind off the McMahon affair. His case calendar, which often required travel, was always full with a seemingly endless variety of miscreants to judge and punish in Dakota Territory.

CHAPTER 16

SUN GOING DOWN
ON HORSE THIEVES

Affairs in Dakota as far as outlawry and desperadoism
are concerned seem to be coming to a focus.

Daily Press and Dakotaian
May 17, 1880

"The horse crop of the valley is astonishing," wrote a reporter about farming and ranching in the James River region. The reporter for the *Press and Dakotaian* boasted that there was an average of two colts for every farm. In a land where good grass and hay were in abundance, he predicted that the area would become a leading producer of horses for the U.S. cavalry.[1] Although this was good news and worth bragging about, it was probably greeted with delight by horse thieves, whose criminal activities were the subject of numerous newspaper articles in 1878.

That summer the *Press and Dakotaian* published another story about a long and studied trip through the "valley of the Jim." When the reporter returned to Yankton, he wrote a lengthy article on his adventure, and much of it was about horse stealing. "A well-organized band of thieves has been operating in this region since early spring," causing fear among frontier families, he observed, "lest their horses or oxen may be coveted by the outlaws." The reporter's investigation revealed that outlaws "rendezvous in the Wessington Hills," and their "stolen stock is run and hid up in the timbered gulches until it can be conducted to a place of sale."

The reporter reminded his readers that the number of horses taken from "Indian country this season" numbered about 150, while the settlers "along the Jim have been compelled to contribute more than they can spare to enrich the coffers of this outlaw gang of the Wessington Hills." The bold, nocturnal raids and the shocking loss of valuable horses was the dominant topic of conversation among the settlements of Milltown, Rockport, and Firesteel. Men openly discussed taking the law into their own hands with emphasis on the "efficacy of the preventive qualities of twisted hemp."[2]

As the tension increased, there was a tendency to cast the nets of suspicion far and wide. Neighbor distrusted neighbor and in one situation a settler from Firesteel, H. C. Greene, felt it necessary to write a letter to the editor of the *Press and Dakotaian* to refute the aspersions placed upon his good character. In response to someone from Milltown, in Hutchinson County, who stamped the "horse thief" label on Firesteel men, Greene roared back against the "willful and malicious misrepresentation" that was displayed in a letter to the Yankton newspaper. While he acknowledged the gravity of the crime, Greene asked how "a horse thief differs from one who steals wholesale the character of honest individuals or communities?" Greene argued that the horse thief was "the least culpable of the two" because a horse, being property, can be replaced, but "character once gone can never be wholly recovered." The *Press and Dakotaian* offered an apology to Greene and other "worthy citizens of the upper Jim."[3]

Although many men were falsely suspected or accused of stealing horses, the fact remains that horses were disappearing on a regular basis, and the summer of 1878 promised to keep Judge Peter C. Shannon busy trying to preside over the trials of suspected horse thieves. Pressure from the public and press caused law enforcement to comb the hills and valleys with the purpose of rounding up some horse thieves. It would be unworthy of dedicated law officers and judges to allow vigilante groups to usurp legal authority. Surely, Judge Shannon was anxious to lock up a convicted horse thief or two, and woe to the guilty man who had to look up from a defendant's table toward the bench and into a pair of stern eyes looking back like a double-barreled shotgun.

Despite the number of thefts in the summer of 1878, law officers were successful in making several arrests. Two outlaws were snared along with a dozen horses. Another man was captured by Sheriff Edwin Benedict of Bon Homme County; all were lodged in the U.S. jail at Yankton, a flimsy edifice described as a "cottonwood shanty." As was expected, all three outlaws escaped, "so nobody is disappointed." They headed north toward the Wessington Hills, taking seven horses from Alfred Brown of Scotland.[4]

As noted previously, the U.S. jail at Yankton had become the subject of public derision in southeastern Dakota. In Sioux Falls, the *Dakota Pantagraph* ran an article about the arrests—and escape from jail—of Sam Smith for stealing a horse and heading for Minnesota and of Charles Dubois for "having been unlawfully in Indian country." The *Pantagraph* declared that "the [Yankton] jail has been frequently broken out of before, and is a shell from which a man needs no tools but his heels to effect [sic] an escape."[5]

Moses McGirk was another escaped outlaw. In June he was in the U.S. jail at Yankton waiting to be tried for trespassing on the Spotted Tail Indian Reservation. He had been evicted several times by agency authorities but kept returning. He was apparently enamored with an Indian woman who called him her "hubby."[6] McGirk was arrested and locked up much to the relief of exasperated agency personnel, but not for long. He "scaled a high fence" and disappeared. In light of the frequency of jail breaks, the *Dakota Herald* advised its readers to consult the jailer, Frank Bronson, "if any further information is desired on the score."[7]

Outlaw Moses McGirk (also spelled McGurk) was re-arrested for a horse stealing incident in Bon Homme County and was returned to the U.S. jail in Yankton. On the night of September 3, 1878, Sheriff Benedict and another man picked up McGirk in Yankton for the purpose of taking him to Bon Homme, a town that had recently celebrated the opening of a county jail. As they approached the bridge at Cooper Creek, a group of masked riders bolted out of the weeds, halted, and took control of the sheriff and his prisoner. They roughed up the sheriff and tied him down. Next, they turned their attention to McGirk. The vigilantes took him underneath the bridge and put a rope around his neck. With the rope attached to the "stringer of the bridge," they pulled McGirk off the ground.

Since the masked riders were more interested in getting information about McGirk's gang of thieves than they were in killing him, he was immediately lowered to the ground and allowed to confess. Having tasted death, he spilled his guts to the vigilantes who, now satisfied, rode away in possession of the names of the other outlaws. The vigilantes let it be known that "Judge Lynch" was on the job.[8] McGirk survived the hanging but was convicted of larceny and sentenced by Judge Shannon to three years in prison at Detroit, Michigan, a light sentence compared to the punishment he would have received had he not confessed to the satisfaction of his captors.[9]

Further to the west, a pair of suspected horse thieves fared far worse than McGirk. On the run with their equine contraband, they were overtaken "while attempting to cross the Cheyenne river on the Sidney road, and shot." The bodies of the unnamed outlaws were unceremoniously dumped into the river and allowed to float downstream.[10]

A Black Hills newspaper declared that there was an organized gang of horse thieves operating out of a "Robber's Roost" near the foot of Harney Peak, in a secluded, well-wooded part of the Black Hills.[11] In early July 1878 a deputy sheriff from Rapid City and "two assistants" attempted to arrest four suspected horse thieves near the Cheyenne River. But when confronted by the lawmen, the outlaws simply laughed at the threat of being arrested. Turning the game against the deputy, the thieves threatened to "plant the whole outfit on the rolling prairie." The chastened lawmen returned to Rapid City empty-handed.[12]

On September 18 the bodies of O. B. "Bean" Davis and George W. Keating were found hanging from a tree in a wooded ravine east of the town of Spearfish. Apparently asleep when their executioners found them with their contraband, the men were awakened and immediately strung up.[13] Both men were believed to have been members of the "gang of horse thieves who have been operating in the Spearfish valley and other sections of the Hills." The coroner's jury concluded that the two luckless men were hanged by parties unknown, probably the work of vigilantes.[14] The coroner was probably right.

Throughout the summer and fall of 1878, the business of taking out horse thieves kept both the law and vigilantes busy. By year's end more horse thieves had been "gobbled," with three of them facing Judge Shannon for sentencing. One of the convicted men, named John Sprague, had been captured by the victim of his crime in concert with a Dakota law officer and an Iowa farmer. The adventure began in early October when a well-dressed Sprague, acting like an ordinary customer, rented a horse and buggy from the stable of William Powers in Yankton. When Sprague failed to return, Powers set out to find him, heading east. Powers was joined in Vermillion by Clay County Sheriff G. H. McDonald. They crossed the Big Sioux River into Iowa, pushing on to LeMars. From there they went down to Sioux City, where they learned that a man with a horse and buggy matching the description of the stolen outfit was seen going in the direction of Correctionville. They exchanged their exhausted team for fresh horses at a farm and resumed their determined pursuit, with the farmer joining the chase.

Soon they were within ten miles of the thief and closing in. They managed to sneak up on Sprague while he was having dinner at a farm house. Powers and McDonald covered Sprague with their guns. He gave up without resistance and was taken to the jail in Sioux City, Iowa. He was later transferred to Yankton where he was tried and convicted. Powers and McDonald earned high praise for their gallant and unrelenting effort.[15]

In late November McDonald was involved in the arrest of two other horse thieves, aided by Sheriff Millard A. Baker and Deputy Will Hoyt of Yankton County, and the Union County Sheriff. The suspects, E. F. Kirby and James H. Carpenter, stole two horses in Yankton and started east toward the James River bridge. The victim of the crime, James M. Stone, had notified Sheriff Baker who in turn sent a telegram to the Clay County Sheriff. The law officers were soon in the hunt and the suspects were tracked down with the aid of a dog and captured along the bank of the Big Sioux River near Elk Point. Kirby and Carpenter were shuffled through the court system quite rapidly. Judge Shannon granted the prosecution's motion to reassemble the grand jury immediately, thereby expediting the trial of the men and saving the county at least $500 in boarding expenses.[16]

The suspects were quickly indicted and arraigned on charges of stealing horses, to which they pled guilty. On December 18, 1878, both Carpenter and Kirby were sentenced to serve three years and six months at hard labor in the Detroit penitentiary. Carpenter and Kirby were sent to Detroit in the company of Sprague, who, in an odd twist of fate, had been convicted by a jury of which Kirby was a member.

For many thoughtful people the long-term remedy was tougher laws. The *Dakota Herald* memorialized its discontent in an article that reviewed the "accomplishments" of the over-eager legislators and reflected on the sad state of law and order in Dakota. Among the "bills" passed were a "bill prohibiting the killing of more than seven men per day in Deadwood by means of firearms" and a "bill for the more expeditious elevating of horse thieves, road agents, moonshiners and U.S. officials."[17] The latter was a wag of the finger in the face of the legislators, reminding them that they should attend to the serious business at hand.

The year 1879 ushered in the second year of the Great Dakota Boom, which exacerbated horse thievery. There were, however, indications that the government was considering a serious crackdown. In the meantime, county sheriffs and citizen groups would remain the primary opposition to the hated "equine gobblers."

The boom brought more horses, mules, and thieves, but it also added muscle to the fight against crime. In January 1879 Jefferson P. Kidder, Dakota's outgoing delegate, introduced a bill in Congress to create a fourth judicial district and, along with it, another judge. This was a major step in the evolution of Dakota justice. Judge Shannon had been running himself ragged traveling from Yankton to Sioux Falls, Olivet, Canton, Swan Lake, Elk Point, and other sites to hold court and dispose of cases in a manner that resulted in fairness and justice. A redrawing of the districts through the addition of a fourth district and another judge would significantly lighten his case load.

Shannon got some editorial sympathy from the *Press and Dakotaian*, noting that the second district had become too large: "Since the Black Hills were declared a legal portion of Dakota, the area of labor assigned to Judge Shannon has doubled." The problem was complicated by the great influx of new people who either brought legal problems with them or became involved in litigation or crime after they arrived. "The interests of the people and regard for the physical and mental health of an overworked judge," the *Press and Dakotaian* declared, merited the creation of a fourth judicial district.[18]

In Washington, Territorial Delegate Kidder got the message. He was not re-nominated for the office of delegate; that honor went to Judge Granville G. Bennett, who went on to be elected over his Democratic opponent, Yankton attorney Bartlett Tripp. Bennett resigned his judgeship effective September 20, 1878. To fill the vacancy in the first district, President Rutherford B. Hayes, while on a visit to the northern Dakota wheat fields, appointed Yankton lawyer Gideon C. Moody to be the new associate justice on the Dakota Supreme Court.

Since arriving in Dakota in 1864, Moody, a member of the much-heralded New York immigrant party, had gained a reputation as a fine lawyer—having represented many clients, including outlaws, from an office in Yankton. Born in Cortland, New York, Moody studied law in Syracuse and moved to Indiana in 1852. He served as an officer in the Civil War from 1861 to 1864, when he resigned his commission. Moody emerged as a business and political leader in Dakota and served in the territorial legislature, including two stints as speaker of the House of Representatives.

Among those who wrote letters in support of Moody were Chief Justice Shannon, Justice Barnes, Dakota Territory governor William A. Howard, Dakota U.S. attorney Hugh J. Campbell, and former Dakota governor Newton Edmunds. Kidder also supported Moody, overcoming his earlier objection.[19] Moody received some solid newspaper support for his nomination. The *Springfield Times* called him an "able lawyer," whose appointment "no Dakotans can for a moment question."[20] Soon after his appointment, Moody was on his way to Rapid City where he opened a term of court on September 25, 1878.

Delegate Kidder wanted a third term in Congress but was not re-nominated by his fellow Republicans. A lesser man might have turned bitter and refused to take any action that would benefit the territory, but guided by his ethics, Kidder did his duty for Dakota as he saw it. His bill to create a new court was passed in the House but defeated in the Senate. Then, surprisingly, it was taken up again and passed into law effective March 3, 1879.

The new law increased the Dakota Supreme Court to four justices and added a proviso that only three were needed for a quorum. That ended the old practice of requiring the trial judge—whose decision was under appeal—to serve as a member of the Supreme Court. Thereafter, the trial judge would be excused, leaving the three other justices to handle the appeal with a fresh, unbiased look.[21]

The new act also redrew the districts. The first district consisted of all the western part of southern Dakota. The second district consisted of counties in east-central Dakota, overlapping slightly into northern Dakota. The third district remained essentially all of northern Dakota, and the new fourth district was made up of the eastern tier of counties of southern Dakota, extending slightly into northern Dakota.[22] Section six of the act declared that the fourth district "shall have no jurisdiction to try, hear, or determine any matter or cause wherein the United States is a party." All federal cases arising in the fourth district would be tried in the second district.[23]

To complete the work of Congress under the new statute, the president had to appoint a justice for the new fourth district in Vermillion. Hayes named Jefferson P. Kidder for that position, effective March 3, 1879, giving him a fourth four-year term on the Dakota Supreme Court. It was an appointment that met with the approval of the people. The new court consisted of Chief Justice Shannon and Associate Justices Barnes, Kidder, and Moody.

The changes were made in concert with the general growth of the territory and not in response to the problem of a particular crime, including horse thievery. But it was meant as a warning that the government intended to bring its resources to bear on outlaw Dakota. The sun was beginning to set on the long day of the horse thief.

For their part, settlers in the Wessington Hills were making it known that the scenic hills were not just for horse thieves. In a letter to the *Dakota Pantagraph*, a pioneer endeavored to explain the location of the hills and by whom they were being settled. He painted a descriptive word picture of the hills, the timber, and the springs. Although he admitted that the area was by reputation a rendezvous for horse thieves, he affirmed that *bona fide* settlers lived there.

Three families had found a home in the hills, including Levi Hain— still suspected of being a horse thief—and his family of seven or eight children. Others included Andy "Nick" Nicholson, who was married to one of Hain's daughters. Another man, Peter B. Barrrett, and his wife, church-going Methodists, had moved there from Wisconsin to engage in the stock-growing business. The government had established a mail route from Firesteel to the new townsite of Wessington Springs, where it opened a post office. Because of these signs of progress, the writer insisted, to "indiscriminately charge that all the horse-thieves live in the Wessington Hills is not right."[24]

In the summer of 1879 the pursuit of horse thieves became focused on the Niobrara River and Missouri River gangs. Attention was turned to a flamboyant outlaw from Texas, James B. Riley, who went by the name "Doc Middleton." While his headquarters was in Holt County, Nebraska, his marauders ranged far into Dakota, often targeting horses on the Indian reservations, including the Spotted Tail and the Red Cloud agencies. Among the members of Middleton's Niobrara Gang were Albert "Kid" Wade, John Hoyt, Andy Culbertson, and Ephriam "Eph" Weatherwax, the latter also known as the "Bon Homme County desperado."[25]

The youthful Weatherwax made news in the winter of 1876 when it was learned that he had eloped with a Bon Homme County girl named Luella Fitch. Her father was opposed to her marrying Weatherwax. But Luella was determined to wed her dashing beau, and one January night, while riding with her father in a wagon, "the girl who longed to be a bride" jumped out and vanished into the darkness.[26]

An article in the *Dakota Pantagraph,* dated July 23, 1879, provides information about Weatherwax's boss, Doc Middleton. His gang, supposedly numbering a hundred desperadoes, was blamed for stealing stock from ranchers as far away as Sturgis and Fort Meade, north of the Black Hills. Middleton was called the "Rob Roy" of outlaws, with a career compared to those of Dick Turpin or Ned Scarlet. Middleton was "born to command" and was the acknowledged chieftain of a remarkably successful group of outlaws. After appearing in Sidney, Nebraska, in March 1877, where he killed a man, Middleton had risen to the top of his craft. It was estimated that over 2,000 horses were stolen from the Sioux Indians by Middleton's gang since 1877.[27]

Middleton had a Yankton connection. One day two Yankton men were riding in the Niobrara valley when they were suddenly confronted by Middleton and his brigands. With their hands in the air, the two men were asked where they had come from. "Yankton" was the reply. Middleton told them that he was not after their horses, but since they were from Yankton, they undoubtedly had a lot of money "and we want all you got." They cleaned out the Yankton travelers and sent them on their way unharmed. The victims of the robbery were not identified, but they returned to Yankton and decided to take action against Middleton and his gang. They hired a "competent detective," and not long after he was "watching an opportunity to get his legal hands on the robber."[28]

That might be a reference to W. H. H. Llewellyn, a special agent of the federal government, acting under the authority of the U.S. attorney general. Llewellyn was sent west to "look after the violations of the acts of Congress relative to government and Indian stock." The confident agent declared in an interview that his job was to "put sugar on Mr. Middleton's tail and catch him."[29]

The quip by Llewellyn was made after the notorious Middleton was nabbed in the Niobrara country of north-central Nebraska. In late July 1879 the special agent, along with a force of fourteen men, which included soldiers and other well-armed lawmen, captured a gang member. With the reluctant assistance of that man, Llewellyn located the outlaws' camp. While his wife screamed hysterically, Middleton was shot as he tried to crawl away in the grass and, wounded, was taken into custody.[30] The authorities heaped praise on the intrepid Llewellyn, and Doc Middleton, the man whom many believed to be the most dangerous outlaw to roam Nebraska and Dakota, had now been removed from the game of horse stealing.

More Niobrara Gang members were arrested by Llewellyn but some sought to return to a legitimate way of making a living. The *Dakota*

Herald reported that two of the outlaws showed up at a Yankton store for the purpose of buying new clothes. They talked freely of life as members of Middleton's Gang and told the clothier that they were going east "to engage in more honorable and congenial occupations elsewhere."[31]

Although Middleton was behind bars, many of his men were still free. They continued to steal horses and cattle until a determined effort by vigilantes captured or killed most of the Niobrara outlaws. Among those still being pursued were Andy Culbertson and the young, dashing Ephriam Weatherwax, once referred to as "White Stockings." Both men were topics of newspaper reports in the early 1880s. In the spring of 1880, Weatherwax and Culbertson were arrested for stealing cattle and horses and locked up in Bon Homme, but they broke out of the county jail and disappeared. They stole more horses and were seen at a ranch on Pratt Creek above Fort Randall. A reward was offered for both "scamps."[32]

Weatherwax and Culbertson made headlines again when they were arrested in March 1882 and jailed in Springfield. Once again, they eluded justice. Finally, Weatherwax was captured by vigilantes during the Christmas season of 1883 and was made to "stretch hemp." His free-ranging days at an end, Weatherwax was left hanging from a tree "until the wolves ate the flesh from his legs."[33]

Further west, another notorious outlaw was captured and disposed of in haste. Cornelius "Lame Johnny" Donahue, a college-educated man from Philadelphia. A childhood injury caused him to walk with a limp, giving rise to his nickname. Despite the handicap, he became a successful horse thief in Texas. The gold rush brought him north to the Black Hills where he worked as a deputy sheriff in Custer County. He was also a bookkeeper for the Homestake Mining Company until he was recognized and "addressed as a horse thief from Texas."[34]

Johnny quit his job, disappeared, and returned to the life of an outlaw, honing his skills as a horse thief, road agent, and "bad man in general." In late June 1879, with a price on his head, Lame Johnny was arrested. While he was being transported by stagecoach to Deadwood, a party of

Lame Johnny Tree, where Cornelius "Lame Johnny" Donahue was hanged.
Courtesy 1881 Custer County Courthouse Museum.

"regulators" stopped the vehicle near Buffalo Gap. The outlaw was taken from the stage and hanged from a tree limb. The creek that flows by the hanging tree was later named, and to this day is known as, "Lame Johnny Creek."[35]

Nor was that the only lynching in far western Dakota Territory. Following a late winter storm in 1880, news reached Yankton of an old man named Wood and his son, from Deadwood, who were hanged and of two other men who were shot and killed in the Belle Fourche area after stolen stock was found in their possession.[36]

If members of the Wessington Hills or Firesteel Gang were hanged, it was done in a manner that failed to attract the attention of newspapers. Their leader, Red Cloud, "somewhat known in Yankton," was still managing the affairs of a "daring and desperate" band of thieves. In March 1880 they frightened off a work party of men "running a line for the Milwaukee road." Historically, however, the railroads usually overcame all forms of resistance, and by 1880 the government had ramped up the pressure on the pony boys who "made their hiding places in the deep ravines and high, wooded hills." The outlaws were "hindering the more rapid settlement of the territory," but the law was determined to "put an end to this condition of affairs."[37]

That was small comfort to the settlers of Wessington Hills, who felt isolated and unprotected by the law and the courts. On their own, they were not yet strong enough to move against the "strange men who mysteriously came" and disappeared. The settlers contemplated rumors of a network of horse and cattle thieves who operated from Sioux City all the way up the Missouri River with a "station somewhere in the hills." Some people believed that a well-hidden "depot or stable existed in Nicholson gulch," below Turtle Peak.[38]

Throughout the warm weather months of 1880, horses and cattle kept disappearing—and the struggling pioneers grudgingly accepted their losses. But help was on the way in the form of Reverend A. B. Smart from Illinois, who arrived at the hill country in November 1880. Smart claimed that he had a calling to venture out on the Dakota frontier and wage war against sin. He was interested in setting up a spiritual colony consisting of humble, non-drinking Christian people. He sought to impose his own moral code on his newly chosen people.

After studying maps and brochures, Smart had chosen the Wessington Hills. He had hoped to find no settlers on his promised land, preferring to start from scratch. His entourage brought medicine for snake bites but found that the only snakes in the area "were wearing boots."[39] Among the snakes, he learned, were Levi Hain and friends, so the indefatigable minister went to work. He acquainted himself with the settlers and conducted religious services for them, but the horse thieves, whom he considered anyone who did not attend his services, he confronted with the aim of rooting them out.

He and his like-minded neighbors set up what became known as the "Midland University Colony." On November 16, 1880, Smart introduced the details of his plan to the faithful. Each person who wished to become a member of the colony had to sign a contract that, among other stipulations, required members to cooperate fully in creating a Bible-based community. All recruits had to agree not to buy, manufacture, drink, or sell alcoholic beverages upon pain of being debarred from the colony.[40]

Smart was off to a good start toward advancing civil behavior in the remote but enchanting Wessington Hills. Then, after the particularly severe winter of 1880-81, the reappearance of unsavory characters stirred the settlers back into action. In the spring of 1881 the *Mitchell Capitol* reported that "an underground stable, with room for about eighty horses, was discovered in the Wessington Hills, recently." Without a word about its location, or the man or men who allegedly discovered it, the *Capitol* speculated that it was the headquarters of the Wessington Hills outlaws.[41]

In 1902, however, an account written by H. M. Travis and published in the *Monthly South Dakotan* revealed that he and three friends had set out from Mitchell in July 1880 for the purpose of exploring the Wessington Hills. Traveling north, after entering a "timbered ravine," they came upon a hideout large enough to "contain a hundred horses." Unfortunately for Travis, his claim was disputed by residents of the hills once the thieves had departed. No one was ever able to find an underground stable.[42]

Rev. Smart may have been troubled by news of the "underground stable," but he kept up a brave front in his determination to uproot the forces of evil. He knew that the presence of new settlers would tip the balance in favor of law and order, so he went to the nearby town of Mitchell in search of additional colonists. Believing in Smart's assertions, settlers moved to the Wessington Hills by the score. Many attempted to buy up claims for the colony, including Hain's land, but progress was slow in 1881. Some people found it difficult to honor their contract with Smart, leading to a disappointing number of dropouts.[43]

In the spring of 1882 horses and cattle began to disappear again, while more stories about night riders resonated throughout the settlement. Anger invited action so a group of frustrated colonists paid a visit to the wily Levi Hain and accused him of being a horse thief. After an argument, they seized "Horsethief Hain" and placed a rope around his neck. Before they could string him up, though, "Nick" Nicholson came out of Hain's house with a gun in each hand and drove off the lynch mob. The horses in question were found nearby, having apparently strayed away. Hain narrowly escaped being hanged for horses he did not steal.[44]

Finally, in the late summer of 1882, the settlers, now strong in number, felt it was time to make a serious move against the outlaws. According to historian N. J. Dunham, a suspicious young man was captured and questioned about his activities. Accused of being a horse thief, he gave a "full statement of who the thieves were, their place of rendezvous and their method of operation."[45] A Minnesota correspondent declared that the "Wessingtonites" had abducted a suspect and "strung him up till he squealed on the rest."[46] The *Press and Dakotaian* reported that gang member "Charley Williams, a cripple," was seriously wounded in an altercation with the "well armed" group of citizens.[47]

The justice of the peace issued arrest warrants for the men fingered by the tortured man, which were handed over to the constable, C. W. P. Osgood. The constable was not keen on the idea of going into the ravines and hills on his own, so he set out to gather a posse of citizens. In the meantime, the settlers, impatient with the work of the cautious constable, ventured out in a group. They confronted some armed men, and in a fire fight, shot and wounded one of their adversaries. But the supposed leader of the gang escaped.

News of the wounded man sent the settlement into a state of great excitement. The nervous constable found himself caught up in the whirlwind and was apparently ready to do his duty as a lawman. A settler,

W. I. Bateman, recruited Reverend J. G. Campbell to team up with him and the constable. The reverend grabbed his Winchester and the trio entered the gulch that, according to the captured youth, led to the lair of the outlaws.

They were soon confronted by a heavily armed man who ordered them to halt, which they did. The brave minister went forward and invited the armed man to look inside the buggy bed, where he could see several rifles and revolvers lying on the hay. Campbell convinced him to get into the buggy in order to protect his "general welfare, both here and hereafter." Seeing the small arsenal and heeding the warning of the minister, he obeyed.

The party split up and continued the search for the men named in the warrants. (The wanted men were not named in this narrative.) The search took up the entire afternoon, and when night came, Osgood and Campbell continued by starlight. After advancing about a mile, they heard "loud voices of men evidently intoxicated." Osgood recognized the voices as belonging to the men he was out to arrest. Exiting their buggy, the two men approached the drunken party, pointed their rifles at the surprised revelers, and ordered them to "throw up their hands." Taken unawares, they did as ordered, while muttering profanities at their captors.

Once they had been loaded into the buggy, the prisoners were taken to Osgood's residence, where they were kept until the following day, when they received a preliminary examination before the justice of the peace. Then, despite the dangerous work done by Campbell and Osgood, the justice released all of them for lack of any evidence that they had committed a crime of any sort. Everyone, that is, except the young man who ratted on the "gang." He "spent a long time in the jail at *Plankinton*," a new town on the Milwaukee Railroad, southeast of the Wessington Hills. Yet according to Dunham, the raid in the ravine had a salutary effect, for the "settlers were no longer molested by the desperadoes."[48]

Rev. Smart claimed that he and his people had driven out the Firesteel Gang. However, since no records or reports of arrests and convictions are extant, it is more likely that most of the gang members dispersed on their own, succumbing to pressure from civilizing influences. In 1881 the purported leader of the Firesteel Gang, Starr Platt, was known to be operating a "stock ranch" in the Wessington Hills, as reported in an article published in the *Western Bugle,* a Mitchell newspaper.[49]

Hain, Nicholson, and others left the Wessington Hills of their own accord. A triumphant Smart purchased Hain's claim for $310, after which the old suspect and Nicholson moved to Hand County.[50] In 1887 a seminary was opened in Wessington Springs, putting the final stamp of decency on an area where horse thieves once held sway. A gang member gone straight, interviewed by Rev. Smart, confessed that "we saw how others went and concluded to get out of it altogether. I am a freight conductor on the Milwaukee railroad now."[51] Like all frontiersmen, outlaws were adaptable.

The break-up of the Niobrara and Firesteel gangs and the hanging of Lame Johnny and others did not result in the immediate cessation of horse stealing, but the frontier days of open-range horse thievery were ending. With settlers entering the territory in large numbers, solicited through persuasive and often misleading railroad advertising, and with new towns popping up like prairie dogs, conditions ripe for stealing horses on a large scale eventually disappeared. Law-abiding citizens soon outnumbered outlaws like Middleton and his gang.

By the spring of 1884 the town of Wessington Springs was in full bloom. The hardy pioneers had built not only a town, but a resort, where visitors and residents alike could relax amid beautiful scenery and enjoy the spring water for its medicinal value. The town had a first-class hotel, general stores, livery stables, a weekly newspaper—and a stagecoach line, which ran to Mitchell, another booming town.

CHAPTER 17

THE DOCTOR HOLDS UP
THE STAGECOACH

*Yankton is alive with tramps, sneak thieves, bold thieves,
vagrants, fighting women and a hard crowd generally—all
members of the floating population, of course.*

Dakota Pantagraph
May 7, 1879

T he presence of the "floating population," mentioned above by
a Sioux Falls newspaper, also meant that the wheels of justice
in Yankton were turning a "hard crowd" into sullen prisoners.
Judge Peter Shannon was busy presiding over a variety of cases that added
both sparkle and shadow to the historical record, such as the stagecoach
robbery in Turner County on the Yankton Trail, which ran between the
territorial capital and the boom town of Sioux Falls. This tale of crime and
punishment in Dakota Territory reveals how settlers both longed for an
end to outlaw activity while also enjoying the spectacle.

The trail from Yankton to Sioux Falls has a long history. "There is a
good and natural wagon road from Sioux Falls to this place [Yankton],"
an article in Yankton's first newspaper observes.[1] In the summer of 1861
Governor William Jayne and Secretary of the Territory John Hutchinson
traveled over the "road" on a visit to Sioux Falls when the settlement was
still referred to as "Sioux Falls City." The trail—sometimes called the
"Old Government Trail"—was one of the main escape routes for frenzied
pioneers evacuating Sioux Falls in August 1862, following the death of
two men from an Indian raid on the townsite as part of the U.S.-Dakota
War in Minnesota.

In April 1865 Dakota Territory's second governor, Newton Edmunds, received notice that General Alfred Sully had decided to construct forts on the James River and at the falls of the Big Sioux River to insure protection throughout southern Dakota after the Dakota War of 1862 and the Indian Campaign of 1863-64.[2] Fort Dakota was duly established and with it a mail, freight, and passenger service linking Sioux Falls with Yankton was set in motion, the beginning of successful commercial transportation between the two towns.[3] Private conveyances also moved over the trail regularly throughout the 1860s and 1870s, carrying parties of excursionists from Yankton, drawn thither by the scenic beauty of the falls. Soldiers from Fort Dakota used the trail when necessary to go to Yankton.

During the ninth session of the territorial legislature, a three-man commission was created to monitor, maintain, and improve the road, including the building of bridges over streams and sloughs.[4] By the early 1870s, with improvements to the rutted trail, stagecoach service, through its many changes in ownership, was available between the two towns.

In 1879 the line was owned by William Kramer, who declared in an advertisement that it was the "Shortest, Best and Cheapest Line to Sioux Falls." A passenger could board a stage early in the morning at Yankton and arrive in Sioux Falls that evening. The ride was often rough but reliable, with stops at Marindahl, Turkey Creek, and Clay Creek, in Yankton County, Swan Lake, Finlay, and Howard in Turner County, and Wall Lake in Minnehaha County, the latter being twelve miles from Sioux Falls.[5]

Finlay was the first town established in Turner County. Situated about halfway between Yankton and Sioux Falls, it was settled in 1871 when a handful of pioneers decided to put down roots where the "Old Government Trail" crossed the Vermillion River. The first "residence" in Finlay was a cave dug into a high river bank, with a blanket for a door. It was equipped with a cook stove and cot. No one knew who had previously used the cave, but settlers speculated that it might have been a trapper's shelter or a way station for soldiers and others traveling between Fort Dakota and Yankton.[6]

Travel by stagecoach between Sioux Falls and Yankton was usually routine, but when high water destroyed bridges the journey became adventuresome, dangerous, or impossible. Usually, though, the horse-drawn coaches rambled through the scenic countryside day after day, carrying passengers who had no choice but to endure the lengthy torment. Then on the night of April 15, 1879, the stagecoach pulled into Sioux Falls and stopped outside the Cataract Hotel. Soon, a group of the curious gathered around the stagecoach to hear about an attempted robbery, the first in the history of the stage line.

The stagecoach driver, Edward Creppen, breathlessly explained to anxious listeners that Dr. John S. Parsons of Finlay had been taken into custody following his single-handed attempt to rob the stage. Parsons had been arrested by a special agent from the Chicago post office, A. B. Spurling, assisted by James Kelly, also of Chicago. Creppen said he was in on the sting and was eager to tell the story of how he became a part of a plan to thwart a robbery and unravel a dark conspiracy. The stagecoach driver's story was a bizarre muddle of speculation, half-truths, and lies.

About two weeks before the attempted robbery, Creppen related, he was approached by a mysterious group of men with designs on robbing the stagecoach of "its mail and express matter," both of which were "frequently quite valuable." Creppen pretended to be interested and, after listening to the details, agreed to go along with the plan. But later he had second thoughts and informed the post office department in Washington, D.C. Officials there, in turn, contacted agent Spurling in Chicago. According to

Creppen, the men involved in the robbery conspiracy were also members of the gang "engaged last winter in horse stealing depredations near the Wessington hills." [7]

These officials believed that an organized band of horse thieves frequently passed through Germantown Township in Turner County to get their contraband to "market." W. H. Stoddard, an early-day historian, recalled that "at dusk all was serene and quiet, the next morning a hundred horses would be seen grazing in a pasture." Then strangely, the next day, they would all be gone. [8]

These stories of horse stealing connected well with some men in Sioux Falls. Creppen provided a spark and others fanned it into flames. Anxious men started naming names. Among those accused was a man named Mellison, a man with a price on his head, who had escaped from the Yankton jail. He was declared to be more than a horse thief, for he was connected to stagecoach robberies in the Black Hills. Other men brought up the name of Starr Platt, believed by many to be a Wessington Hills horse thief. [9]

In 1931, when he published his history of Turner County, Stoddard included some anecdotal information about a mysterious gang of horse thieves. Believing it would be proper to omit Parson's name, he merely stated that a "brilliant young doctor was employed as physician and surgeon for the organization." Stoddard believed someone had tipped off federal officers, prompting them to intervene and form "a plan to break up the gang of horse thieves." To carry out the plan, they decided to entrap "the young doctor" so they could gain critical information about the others. [10]

Creppen pretended to be a part of this plan, playing the role of a gang member. He said he was forced to undergo a "Ku Klux Initiation" by the gang. "They administered to him an oath that was perfectly blood-curdling in its architecture, and made him swear on a stack of bones and with all the witchery that their cunning could devise." They warned him that, should he break the vow and inform the authorities, members of the gang would hunt him down like "sleuth hounds to the ends of the earth."

He was informed in no uncertain terms that the criminal organization that he joined was so large that he could never escape its nets of retribution. If Creppen betrayed them, he would be caught, tortured, and his heart cut out and pickled.

While he gave this account in Sioux Falls, his enrapt listeners likely wondered how Dr. Parsons could be connected to such insidious behavior. Creppen filled in the blanks, revealing that Parsons was among those who initiated him into the gang's outlaw ranks. Then he explained in detail how the robbery was planned.

A representative of the gang had informed the stagecoach driver that he should stop at Swan Lake and eat his noon meal. Members of the gang would be present and Creppen would approach them, discreetly, and make it known whether the stagecoach was carrying a sufficient amount of money and other valuables. If and when the decision was made to rob the stagecoach, Creppen would drive it to a deep ravine at Saddle Creek, near Swan Lake, where it would be waylaid by the robbers. The gang would then move on to rob the Canton and Sioux Falls stage and then retreat into hiding. Creppen seemed intent on providing these endless details to anyone willing to listen, but he had failed to inform his employer, William Kramer, who declared that he knew nothing about the crime against his business until he read about it in a newspaper.[11]

But Creppen was on a mission of his own making. He ignored his boss just as he disregarded the warning by the gang through its "initiation." Instead, he forwarded the names of some of the robbers, along with details of the robbery plan, to the postal authorities, which caused Spurling to spring into action, hoping to catch "an old offender." Spurling was called one of the most "daring and reliable men in the secret service." Having been informed of the gang's plan, he and Kelly came to Sioux Falls and checked into the Cataract Hotel. They acted under the guise of hunters who kept the hotel well supplied with wild game, as they scouted out the area southwest of Sioux Falls along the stagecoach route.

Although it is not clear whether there was a connection between the two men, Spurling did learn from Creppen that there was "swag aboard the stagecoach." He and Kelly, along with Decatur Stewart, a Turner County settler, positioned themselves in the tall grass along the ravine near Saddle Creek to await developments. They were joined by Minnehaha County Sheriff Henry Callender and a deputy, who concealed themselves on a straw pile from which they could view the road. It was believed that the robbers would send out three men on horseback ahead of the stage as it left Swan Lake in the direction of Sioux Falls. Their job was to rush the stage at the ravine and "shoot the horses and do everything to wipe out any sign of connivance between them and the driver." Spurling and his allies were, then, positioned in a manner calculated to prevent the robbers from escaping.

Leaving Swan Lake, the stagecoach carried no passengers, but at some point Dr. John S. Parsons got on board. He stayed in the coach as it made its turn off the road toward the Howard post office, near the Saddle Creek ravine. Exiting the stage, he went on foot to the ravine and waited until Creppen, having left the post office, steered his team back on the road toward the ravine. Parsons then showed himself and, with a revolver in his hand, demanded that Creppen give him the money bag. Parsons had the money bag in his hand and was reaching for the mail bag when Spurling and Kelly jumped up, covered him with their revolvers, and ordered him to throw down his weapon.

Parsons complied with "alacrity," but as he was being taken in hand by his captors, he fell into a tirade about how he was "led into the crime." Then, he suddenly quit talking and humbly admitted that the robbery was his own doing. He would not say why his "pals were absent." A taciturn Parsons, along with his captors, followed the stage into Sioux Falls where details of the robbery were revealed by Creppen to the *Dakota Pantagraph*.[12] Parsons was kept overnight at the Cataract, under guard. The next day he was taken to Yankton and lodged in the county jail.

Soon after the arrest, other territorial newspapers published articles about the shocking event. The report in the *Dakota Herald* contained information similar to that in the *Pantagraph,* except that it gave the location of the robbery about sixteen miles from Sioux Falls, where the daily stage stopped at the deep Saddle Creek ravine for water. The *Herald* also declared that "Parsons' partners in the organized gang of thieves are known, and it is expected that several other arrests will soon follow."[13] People were eager to know more about Dr. Parsons, the physician turned highwayman. And before long area newspapers obliged.

According to a Swan Lake newspaper, Parsons must have been one of the earliest residents in Turner County, for on June 29, 1876, the paper had carried a notice that "Dr. J. S. Parsons returned to Finlay after a two year absence."[14] In 1878 he was credited for performing a surgery "with great skill."[15] But at the time of his arrest, the *Herald* described Parsons as a physician who had practiced for some months at Finlay but without the benefit of "the fullest confidence and respect of his neighbors." Yet he was also not thought of as the kind of man who would resort to robbing a stagecoach.[16]

The first report from the *Press and Dakotaian* tied Parsons to the James River horse thief gang. A reporter for that newspaper noted that, although Parsons had established a medical practice at Finlay, he had been "suspected of being something higher than a hewer of wood and drawer of water for the gang of horse thieves which has made such trouble in the Jim river valley. Several stories are told of his cunning and well executed schemes for raising the wind." He had also palmed himself off as a "United States detective upon saloon keepers and others at Dell Rapids" and "different points up the valley."

Knowing little about Parsons and Creppen, the reporter took the position that the former was, indeed, a part of a larger conspiracy and that the latter's life was now in danger for "peaching" on the gang. The reporter speculated that Parsons' "pals" were very unhappy with him and that the members of the gang were likely to "see what Creppen's heart looks like when it is pickled."[17]

Such threats were not often heard in Turner County, which had been settled by hard-working, law-abiding farm folks, many of them Germans from Russia, and the merchants in Finlay and Swan Lake who depended on their patronage. There was, however, a report of a shooting near Finlay in the summer of 1879. A man shot at some barnyard chickens and the "stray shot" hit another man in the face, causing serious but accidental injury.[18]

In April 1879 Turner County's first outlaw, John S. Parsons, was arraigned before U.S. Commissioner Leonidas Congleton with his lawyer, Alfred M. Flagg, present. Flagg waived a preliminary examination and Parsons was charged with conspiracy to rob the United States mail. He was remanded to custody with bond set at $3,000. Of course, he had no money to post bond so he stayed in jail. Here was the perfect opportunity for a reporter from the *Press and Dakotaian* to conduct a lengthy and detailed interview of the sullen and contrite doctor. It was also a chance to correct a number of misconceptions and false assumptions.

The first thing the reporter did was to debunk all the blood-curdling stories then circulating about this outlaw. Parsons, he wrote, was known in Yankton as a physician practicing in Finlay, a man about thirty years of age, possessed of a good education, including medical school. He was from a respectable Pennsylvania family. The reporter did not disclose how and why he came to Dakota, but he revealed that the doctor's life in the West had been punctuated by bouts of drinking and alcoholic behavior. Whiskey and bad company, it seemed, had caused him to spiral downward into a life of shame and crime.

When asked if he had any explanation to offer for his criminal conduct, Parsons declared that he wanted to make a statement and correct several errors that were reported in the *Dakota Pantagraph*. He denied being a member of any criminal organization or had been forced to undergo a strange initiation ritual, blaming instead his drinking habit and the bad company that came with it. Parsons admitted that he had associated with many unsavory characters in several drunken episodes, and that, in so doing, he became "their tool." He said that he was unwittingly drawn into an unlawful scheme by his expanding "appetite for strong drink."

When questioned about his relationship with Creppen, the doctor said that they first became acquainted in March 1879. Creppen came to Parsons and asked to be examined for problems with his mouth, which he believed was diseased. Parsons gave him a wash to use and the two men saw each other regularly in "Lower Finlay," where Creppen would stop while working as a driver for the Yankton stage. The men started drinking together, often getting rip-roaring drunk, along with other like-minded men.

During one such spree at the Finlay stage barn, Parsons recalled, Creppen broached the subject of robbing the stagecoach. Parsons said his recollection of that discussion was hazy, claiming that he was drunk much of the time. He did remember being there with Creppen and three or four other men but denied that any type of oath had been administered, again because of drink.

A few days later Creppen mentioned to him, after offering a drink, that there would be about $800 on the stagecoach the next day. Creppen proposed a deal whereby Parsons would "rob" the stage and take the money from him, which they would later divide. He denied that anyone else, including the outlaw Mellison, was involved in the plan. Parsons' revelations shifted the burden of the con to Creppen, recalling that he (Creppen) proposed to disappear after they pulled off their crime but that Parsons could stay in Finlay and no one would be the wiser.

Parsons insisted that Creppen engaged in verbal arm twisting, but to no avail. The doctor admitted he was tempted to participate, refusing to accept the revolver Creppen offered him to use in the conspiracy. The following day, Creppen once more brought up the subject of the $800 that would be on the stage that day, bound for Sioux Falls. While Parsons continued to hesitate, he nevertheless got aboard the stagecoach with Creppen at the helm.

Parsons was questioned repeatedly about the details of his complicity in the robbery scheme. He insisted repeatedly that he resisted Creppen's overtures to commit to the plan. He told the reporter several times that he refused to touch the money or mail bag and also refused to take the revolver that was to be used in the heist. And yet he finally succumbed, though he insisted that taking on the role of an outlaw was against his will and better judgment. The interview was, on the whole, a desperate attempt to mitigate his unlawful actions and to inspire some public sympathy for a man, with decent tendencies, overcome by "strong drink."[19]

Judge Peter Shannon had considerable experience dealing with lawbreakers who blamed their bad behavior on alcohol. Within a very short time after Parsons' arrest, he impaneled a special grand jury to hear evidence and return an indictment. Parsons and his attorney appeared before the judge and without fanfare or argument entered a guilty plea.

On the day of sentencing, Parsons was permitted to present testimony in mitigation. Standing before Judge Shannon, he affirmed that his story was consistent with the interview as reported in the *Press and Dakotaian*. His attorney, Alfred M. Flagg, was also permitted to provide character testimony. Flagg said that prior to this unfortunate incident, Parsons was known in Finlay as a man of good character whose better judgment had been overcome by the frequent use of alcohol, some of it provided by Edward Creppen. In general, the community of Finlay supported Parsons, "believing that he had become ensnared in the commission of the crime by one who had a motive"—Edward Creppen, who had by now "left the country." Yet the feeling throughout Turner County was that Creppen bore equal guilt, but neither Creppen nor anyone else was named as a suspect or arrested as a conspirator.

After Parsons finished his narrative, Shannon spoke. He made it clear that he was not impressed with a plea for mercy by someone who committed a crime after voluntary intoxication. But he thought it was important to explain the dual purpose of punishing an offender: "reform the criminal and deter others from breaking the laws." Over the years, Judge Shannon, himself, had acquired a reputation as a drinker, and he knew that his peers also imbibed. But he was in no mood to be overly merciful to a man whose excessive drinking made him an outlaw. Still, he was a believer in rehabilitation, and he saw this case as an opportunity for reform and deterrence. Shannon said that he hoped a man of Parsons' intelligence would leave prison a better man—and sentenced Dr. John S. Parsons to two years imprisonment in the Detroit House of Corrections, and a $1,000 fine.[20]

Edward Creppen, for his part in the matter, received a $200 reward from the post office. This further angered Turner County citizens, who thought of him as the "bogus detective" who led Dr. Parsons into temptation. Of the two, Parsons was thought to be the better man. Popular opinion ruled that the wrong man was behind bars. The stagecoach company, too, took exception to this remuneration for its ex-employee and was, in fact, searching for Creppen, having accused him of stealing $40, but he was nowhere to be found.[21] Creppen's former employer, William Kramer, remarked, "Ed Creppen has never paid me a cent and I regard him as a scoundrel of the meanest character."[22] With the reward money in his pocket, Creppen had fled Turner County.

Dr. Parsons, perhaps seeking redemption, returned after being released from prison to take up his medical practice, but he found that Turner County had undergone substantial changes. The railroad had built a line that passed by both Swan Lake and Finlay, causing those once-promising towns to lose residents and businesses to the new town of Parker. In December 1880 Parsons placed a small notice in the *Parker New Era,* advertising his surgical skills.[23] But he did not succeed in regaining the confidence, or forgiveness, of the community, so he moved on.

On May 13, 1881, the Canton paper reported that John Parsons and James Morrisey of Parker had left Dakota for Washington Territory.[24] Far away from Dakota and the bad memories engendered by his criminal act, Dr. Parsons resumed his medical practice, got married, and conducted himself in the manner of a respected, law-abiding citizen.[25]

CHAPTER 18

INDEPENDENCE DAY MURDER AT CROW CREEK

A cruel murder was committed about twelve miles above
Crow Creek, July 4, in which George A. Landphere
was the victim.

Dakota Pantagraph
July 16, 1879

From start to finish, from the commission of the crime to the sentencing, the Parsons case—a physician who held up a stagecoach—lasted only four days. The next major criminal case to appear on the calendar of Dakota Territory Supreme Court Chief Justice Peter C. Shannon took much longer. The murder of George A. Landphere, on the Crow Creek Indian Reservation, also provided the public with a steady diet of assertion and speculation over a period of several weeks. The sensational stories were served up by eager Dakota newspapermen, some of them while Judge Shannon was taking a lengthy vacation in Pittsburgh.

On July 4, 1879, George A. Landphere was en route from Beloit, Iowa, to Crow Creek in the upriver country. He was traveling in the company of William H. Williams, George H. Cammack, and Silas F. Beebe. The four young men had plans to start a ranch at the mouth of Crow Creek where it flows into the Missouri River. While making the slow trek across the prairie, Landphere and Beebe commenced arguing, the latter having grown to dislike the former intensely. The bickering continued as the party moved west, and while encamped one night along Crow Creek, about twelve miles from its mouth, Beebe picked up his rifle and without a word to Williams or Cammack, walked over to where Landphere was sleeping and shot him in the head.

Beebe then turned to his stunned companions and said, "talk about sand, I've got it." He then ordered Cammack and Williams to help him dispose of the body, but they refused. Beebe began pulling Landphere away when he noticed that his victim was not yet dead. To apply a finishing touch to the crime, he pulled his revolver and shot Landphere again and then concealed his body in some brush by the creek. After that, Beebe took some of his victim's clothes and other items, and the three men broke camp and rode to Brule City, south of Crow Creek. Beebe said little during the ride except to tell his friends not to "peach" on him.[1]

Upon their arrival at Brule City, Cammack and Williams decided to do just that. They found Jim Somers, with whom Williams was acquainted. Somers, the erstwhile outlaw, was trying to live a respectable life as a stock farmer in Brule City, a small but lively town on the east bank of the Missouri River. Just a few months previous, a Yankton newspaper revealed that "Jim's old time reputation is gradually leaving him, sinking behind his fame as a citizen and stock raiser."[2]

Just what, if anything, Cammack and Williams knew of Somers' violent past is uncertain, but despite Beebe's warning, they related the facts of the shooting to the old sinner. After hearing them out, the man who had shot the sheriff of Yankton County in 1869 decided he was going to collar Beebe, take him to Yankton, and turn him in. While this was transpiring, Beebe was saddling his horse for a ride toward the Bijou Hills.

Somers, however, was determined that this lawbreaker should pay for his crime. He placed his hand on Beebe's shoulder and convinced him to forget about the Bijou Hills and, instead, take a seat in a buggy for a ride to Yankton. The *Press and Dakotaian* noted that "when Jim Somers gets a desperado within his clutches he is suddenly transformed into a very docile citizen."[3] At first Somers informed Beebe that he (Beebe) was wanted in Yankton for an Illinois bank robbery, but later, while the group was nearing Springfield, he revealed the murder charge. When he was questioned by Somers about the shooting, Beebe expressed guilt and remorse, saying that hanging was too good for him.[4]

When Somers' party reached Yankton, Beebe was arrested for murder and locked up. Beebe was described as a rather small man, about twenty-five years of age. He had spent much of his "dissipated" young life on the frontier and had once been a soldier stationed at Fort Laramie. Also revealed was that he was a married man and his wife worked as a cook in a Beloit hotel. Beebe's mother lived in Palo Alto, Iowa. Prior to the Crow Creek adventure, Beebe worked as stagecoach driver from Rock Rapids to Beloit. The *Press and Dakotaian* concluded that "Beebe has made a dime novel hero of himself at the sacrifice of a human life."[5]

While in jail waiting for his trial to start, Beebe was presented with an opportunity to enhance his dime novel stature. Quite unexpectedly, he was faced with a startling chance to intervene when a fellow prisoner made a desperate attempt to break out of jail. The prisoner was Mads Hanson, who had been indicted for a brutal murder committed on the west fork of the Vermillion River in Miner County. In the early evening of October 3, 1879, Hanson was on woodworking detail under the supervision of the jailer, Gus Swanson. The prisoner suddenly struck Swanson with a piece of wood, then seized the jailer, and while the two men struggled, Hanson tried to get his hands on a pistol Swanson had in his pocket. The dazed jailer called to Beebe, asking him to reach through the bars and take the pistol. Beebe was able to get the pistol and aim it at Hanson, but did not shoot. Instead, he "changed his mind and dropped the weapon."

The decision not to shoot allowed Hanson to break free from Swanson and escape into the street outside of the jail. Swanson rushed outside, yelled for help, and soon a crowd of men were chasing Hanson north along Douglas Street. He was overtaken and brought back to jail. But Hanson was resolute and in a second, more surreptitious attempt to gain his freedom he was successful.[6] Mads Hanson disappeared and was never tried for murder, but Beebe, who refused to shoot during the crisis, was destined to face justice.

The man Beebe was accused of murdering, George A. Landphere, was about twenty years old and came to Dakota from Mazomanie, Wisconsin, where his widowed mother was living. He was staying with his uncle, Albert Brown, a farmer in Union County. Brown revealed that his nephew was inexperienced and out of his element on the wild frontier. And yet the young man was eager to test himself against the frontier, having read several dime novels with their exaggerated tales about life on the Plains.

Brown blamed the dime novels for his nephew's demise. He called them a "damaging class of fiction," which ruined the lives of many boys. Under this evil influence, his nephew had fallen victim to a remorseless killer who could now say that he had "killed his man." The sad uncle also blamed himself for allowing his naive nephew to join the Crow Creek party. With a heavy heart, he contacted the authorities at Fort Thompson, asking them to find George's remains and bury them.[7]

On July 13 Mary Huntington, the mother of George Landphere, sent a letter to Justice of the Peace Leonidas Congleton, in Yankton, from Mazomanie, Wisconsin, imploring him to make certain that Silas Beebe not be allowed to escape justice. Distraught, she declared that she was not "thirsting for the blood of the criminal," but rather, her concern was "that no other mother may feel as I now do from the hands of that man." She went on to write:

> *God knows I [sic] far rather be to-day, the mother of the murdered man, than to feel that I had cradled in infancy and reared to manhood a murderer. God pity and help his poor mother. The father of George Landphere was a soldier in the war of the rebellion and died of typhoid fever in November, 1861. Since then my sorrows have been many, but this, Oh, my God! Seems more than I can bear.*

Mary wanted to be at the trial along with her brother and asked Congleton to write back with dates and details.[8]

The search for Landphere's body garnered as much news coverage as did the shooting itself. Dakota Territory newspapers had settled on Beebe's guilt: he was not a suspect, he was the murderer, and journalists, especially those from the *Press and Dakotaian,* were excitedly caught up in the adventure, including the task of finding the body. Reports filtered back to Yankton, describing the search under the scorching sun, mosquitoes "by the millions," and within sight of turkey buzzards, perched on a dead tree. The searchers sent back word of wagon tracks, an old campsite, a piece of discarded bacon, and a story of a man named Ben Arnold found hanging by his neck from a tree at Chain de Roche, near Fort Thompson.[9]

The search party, made up of curious volunteers, gave up and left the matter to the authorities. Meanwhile, Albert Brown, uncle of the deceased Landphere, with the aid of W. H. Williams, returned to Crow Creek and had no trouble finding his nephew's body, as well as the blanket he was lying on when he was shot. They did not disturb the corpse nor give it a burial. Brown was simply satisfied with the find and was willing to leave the rest up to the authorities.[10]

Finally, on the 19th, in a special dispatch to the *Press and Dakotaian,* the "official" discovery of Landphere's badly decomposed body was announced. The discovery was made by a party from Fort Thompson, led by Captain W. E. Doughtery. A prominent member of the party was Alfred Carre, a representative of the *Press and Dakotaian.* They found Landphere's body on the bank of Crow Creek, "where Beebe deposited it after the murder." It appeared to the search party that the facts, as related by Cammack and Williams, were truthful. All the evidence at the crime scene pointed toward Beebe as the murderer.

An article in the *Herald* notes that Carre had cut the head off Landphere's body and brought it back to Yankton. "What particular object Mr. Carre had," the paper asked, in severing the unfortunate victim's head from the body and bringing it to Yankton is not clear to us." Doubtless, it was also not clear to most of the citizens who were following this tragedy in the newspapers. But matters were reaching a crucial stage, and with

Beebe in jail, having waived a preliminary examination, the territory was looking forward to another sensational murder trial with the indefatigable Judge Peter C. Shannon on the bench.[11]

Beebe's lead attorney was William H. Munro, who had recently moved to Yankton with his family from Corpus Christi, Texas. He was assisted by Yankton attorney William P. Dewey, and the pair seemed to be up to the challenge of putting on a strong defense. On November 14 Munro came out swinging, with a demurrer, objecting to the jurisdiction of the court to handle the case. The motion was overruled by Shannon, and the judge asked for a plea from the defendant. Beebe replied "not guilty" in a voice described as "clear and mannerly." Munro then read a sworn statement made by his client that could best be described as shocking. It accused William H. Williams, a key prosecution witness, of killing Landphere while George H. Cammack held a gun on Beebe to prevent any interference. Munro thereby signaled to the court and prosecution the nature and direction of the defense he would present at the upcoming trial.[12] The case before Shannon would be a "he said/ they said" trial, and conviction or acquittal would come down to the issue of credibility—who had it and who did not.

The trial began on November 22, 1879. Attorney Munro launched a long, rambling opening statement, laying out a case for proving his client's innocence. A long list of witnesses promised both a lengthy trial and juicy testimony for the pleasure of the court observers. The strategy of Munro and Dewey was to prove that Williams and Cammack, the prosecution's main witnesses, each had motives for killing Landphere and, in fact, had killed him. For example, they expected witness Lafayette Somers, a brother to Marvin H. "Jim" Somers, to state under oath that Williams and Cammack said in "his presence and hearing that they had killed a horse thief on Crow Creek" and that, in so saying, they were referring to having killed Landphere.

A settler living near Firesteel was expected to testify that both Williams and Cammack entered the settler's sod house and stole clothes and guns. Landphere was with them but did not participate in the theft. Rather, he expressed regret over the incident and was heard to say that he wished he was home in Wisconsin. Munro told the jury that the testimony would tend to show that Williams and Cammack were worried that Landphere would squeal on them, which supplied a motive for murder. Unfortunately for Beebe, the name and whereabouts of the settler were unknown.

But the defense had better strategies to explore. Munro expected to prove that the pistol Jim Somers had in his possession could not have been the gun used to kill Landphere. Medical testimony would be used to explain that the hole in Landphere's skull was too big to have been caused by a bullet from the pistol in question.[13] After all, a member of the search party had noted that "the skull is badly fractured and the supposition exists that the murder was committed by more than one man."[14] Here was an opportunity for Munro to shift blame away from his client.

Munro also told the jury that he would produce evidence to refute the confession that Beebe made to Jim Somers while on the road to Yankton. Carlos L. Young of Springfield, who rode in the wagon with Beebe and Somers, was expected to testify that during the whole of the trip no confession was made.

Witnesses would testify that both Williams and Cammack had prior criminal records so as to tarnish their reputations and thereby their veracity under oath. Jim Somers would be attacked in a similar manner. His neighbors in Brule County, along with his brother Lafayette Somers, would be called to testify that his reputation "for truth and veracity" was very bad.[15] Of course, his general reputation throughout the territory had long been known as that of a violent man. Many people must have thought how brazen it would be to see Jim Somers appear in a court of law—as a witness. There was a delicious but terrible irony to it all; a man whom many thought deserved to be hanged was about to be used by the prosecution to hang another.

The trial testimony started Monday morning, November 24, 1879. U.S. Attorney Hugh J. Campbell, a fierce and determined lawyer, led the prosecution team. The first witness for the prosecution was the nineteen-year-old George H. Cammack from Dane County, Wisconsin. His testimony, for the most part, followed what had already been reported in Yankton newspapers. He tracked the small expedition from Beloit over the Firesteel road to Crow Creek in a "buckboard buggy" pulled by a team of horses. At midday the four men made camp. He said that he saw Beebe greasing his boots when, without a word, Beebe picked up his rifle and shot the sleeping Landphere. When Beebe noticed Landphere was not dead, he shot him again in the head with a revolver. Beebe wrapped a quilt around the body and hid it in some brush, by himself, after Cammack and Williams refused to assist.

The party of three then packed up, taking a quilt that Beebe believed would be incriminating evidence. (The quilt, however, was left behind.) They went to Brule City by way of Sam Coon's ranch and Red Lake. Upon their arrival at Brule City, they made camp and, at that point, Cammack and Williams decided to report the crime to Somers, but there was no testimony as to why they chose this man. The prosecution showed a rifle to Cammack which he identified as the murder weapon. He also identified the clothes and boots worn by the victim.

On cross-examination Cammack answered questions about the number and types of guns the four men had when they left Beloit. He also said they spent two nights in Sioux Falls before taking the Firesteel road to Crow Creek. Counsel for the defendant did not ask questions about the shooting itself. But the defense may have scored some points because Cammack answered many questions by saying, "I don't recall," thereby displaying a faulty memory. But he did keep a diary and did remember that the 4th of July, the day Landphere was killed, was "a nice day. I think it was a kind of nice day."[16]

In the afternoon session, Cammack was again grilled by the defense on details of the activity that followed the shooting of Landphere. In this instance his memory was quite good, as he recalled how Beebe carried the body—with blood dripping from the head—away from the wagon where the shooting occurred. He also said that Beebe scattered some dirt over the blood on the ground. The most damaging piece of testimony, though, came when Cammack said that Beebe shot Landphere—the first shot—with Williams' gun, a carbine.

The next scheduled witness for the prosecution was William H. Williams. The defense objected to his testimony because Williams had a prior conviction and served a prison term in Iowa. Judge Shannon heard arguments from both sides and ruled that Williams was competent to testify in accordance with territorial law, for he had not been convicted of perjury. Still, the witness came into court under a cloud, and the goal of the defense was to make Williams, the ex-con, the primary culprit.

On the stand Williams said he met Beebe while both were in the Anamosa, Iowa, penitentiary. As they had married sisters, they were brothers-in-law. If anything surprised the court-watchers, it was the unexpected testimony about their relationship. After this minor bombshell, Williams went on to corroborate the testimony of Cammack. He identified the murder weapon as a carbine belonging to him and stated that it was he who told Jim Somers that Beebe had shot Landphere and that an arrest was in order. Once again there was no testimony as to why Somers had been chosen to receive the bloody news and nothing to indicate his authority to make an arrest.[17]

The condensed version of the cross-examination of Williams, published in the *Press and Dakotaian,* indicates that Beebe's counsel was fishing and trying to hook something useful. If Munro and Dewey were hoping to get lucky, they were out of luck. Much of the questioning pertained to clothing that was worn, changed, or traded. Williams was not asked point blank, did you shoot Landphere? But when asked about his criminal record, he answered, without hesitation, that he had served time for forgery and had been released about two months before Beebe's prison term ended.

The prosecution was off to a good start and wanted to keep the momentum. They called Somers to the stand to seal the deal. He said his name was Marvin H. Somers and that he lived in Brule City. He testified that he had been informed of the murder by Williams and Cammack on Sunday, July 9. He had arrested Beebe but did not state his authority for doing so. Somers insisted that he did not coerce or threaten Beebe into making a confession, and, in fact, the crime was not discussed until the party reached Springfield. Somers then informed Beebe that he faced a murder charge for killing Landphere. Beebe then said, "the boys squealed on me," and began crying.

On cross-examination, Somers reinforced his prior testimony by revealing more incriminating remarks made by Beebe. He said that Beebe confessed to the killing of Landphere and that he expected to be punished. Then Beebe said, "hanging is too good for me; I ought to be burned." Strangely, at no time during cross-examination were any questions asked about Somers' violent past and his history of lawless and outrageous behavior. No attempt was made to shed light on his bad reputation. It was as though he was just an ordinary citizen, bent on doing the right thing. In fact, a short time before the trial, it was announced that Somers was a county commissioner of Brule County.[18]

Somers' testimony was followed by that of Captain W. E. Doughtery, the army officer from Fort Thompson who led the search for Landphere's body. He said that Albert Carre, a member of the party, found the body "lying in the old bed of the creek." Doughtery stated that the "skull was broken in several pieces, a bullet hole in the top and another in the temple; some of the teeth were missing." He showed the court a map he had drafted, indicating the area where the body had been found, and assured the jury that he was familiar with Crow Creek.

Under cross-examination Dougherty stated that he and his party had made a thorough examination of the area and searched for bullets but could not find any. There were several footprints visible but they were indistinct. He repeated his prior testimony about the fragmented skull, which indicated that it had been fractured by something other than a fired bullet. Dougherty ended his testimony by saying that he had procured a coffin and buried the body, minus the head. Several personal items, including the blood-stained quilt, were recovered during the search.[19]

Other important prosecution witnesses included Dr. Frank Etter, the Yankton County coroner, who said he had custody of several personal items recovered at the crime scene that belonged to Landphere, including his diary. Etter said he also received and examined the skull of Landphere. He stated from the witness chair that his examination revealed that two bullets penetrated the skull, thus corroborating the testimony of Cammack and Williams, who testified that Landphere was shot twice.

On cross-examination Etter talked about other damage to the skull. He said that a large portion of the skull near the left eye had been crushed in as if by a blunt instrument, such as a "broken gun stock." Having given the defense an opening that might cast doubt as to the cause of Landphere's death, the prosecution, on re-direct, asked Etter about the crushed skull. It was his opinion that the blow that crushed the skull could have been applied after Landphere was dead. In other words, it did not change his opinion as to the cause of death which, according to Etter, was the gunshot to the left temple. Another physician, Dr. J. W. Miller, supported Etter's findings.[20]

Three Brule City residents, Fred Hemingway, Viola Bentley, and Jane Van Meter, were called to testify. Each one of them recalled hearing Beebe talk about encountering a gang of horse thieves during their journey to Brule City. Beebe boasted about shooting and wounding one of them. That seemingly irrelevant testimony may have been elicited by the prosecution to show that Beebe made up a story about shooting a horse thief, thereby admitting that he did shoot someone, as Cammack and Williams insisted, but his target was a horse thief, not Landphere.[21]

Overall, the prosecution's case looked good, if not rock solid. The testimony of the principal witnesses held up during cross-examination; no one was impeached. There was nothing in the testimony of Cammack and Williams that remotely suggested they created a lie and stuck to it under oath. Their testimony seemed to come unencumbered. Up to this point in the trial, the defense had been merely grasping for an opening, something to exploit, but to no avail.

After several days and several witnesses, the *Press and Dakotaian* reported on December 2 that "interest in the Beebe murder trial continues unabated." The court room was packed from morning until night as the trial took on the air of great entertainment. One corner of the court was reserved for the ladies, all of whom were curious to see and hear the defendant. "In the hearts of the feminine portion of the audience he has awakened that complete sympathy," observed the newspaper, "which is always ready to go out to a man in trouble."[22]

The attorneys for Beebe would not disappoint them, and it was clear to the court observers that the defense was banking on the testimony of the defendant himself, Silas Frank Beebe. His testimony would save his neck or seal his doom.

Beebe began his testimony rather confidently. He related the details of the trek across the prairie, from Beloit to Sioux Falls, and then along the Firesteel road, describing it much in the same manner as had Williams and Cammack. The purpose of the trip, he said, was to find and locate a homestead and a timber claim. At a point where the railroad bed crossed the Firesteel road, Beebe said that Cammack, Williams, and Landphere entered a sod house and stole a number of personal items, including guns and clothing. They rushed off with their booty and, after reaching the town of Firesteel camped two nights. The party then traveled two and one-half days before reaching Crow Creek. At that point in his testimony Beebe told a story that deviated sharply from that of his two companions.

About midday at Crow Creek they unloaded their wagon, picketed their ponies, and made camp. Beebe said that his gun misfired when he tried to hit some birds and in anger broke the stock of his gun after it "kicked me on the nose." He then picked up Williams' gun to resume hunting. After about two hours, Beebe was back in camp where he "saw something was the matter." Landphere said he was sick and curled up in his quilt and went to sleep. At that point Beebe revealed what can best be called a cold-blooded murder.

Beebe said he was greasing his boots with lard when he saw Williams get up and say to Cammack, "Hank, are you ready?" Cammack replied that he was and the two men approached the sleeping Landphere. As they did so, Beebe asked, "boys, what are you going to do?" Williams replied, "you will find out." As Williams pointed a gun at Landphere's head, Cammack covered Beebe, saying, "go back and sit down or you're a dead man." Beebe did as ordered but yelled out a warning that woke up Landphere. Seeing Williams with a gun in his hand, Landphere said, "Oh! for God's sake don't kill me." Williams replied coldly, "you will die right here." He took aim and both he and Cammack fired at approximately the same time.

The defendant finished his testimony by describing their ride to Brule City, where he was arrested by Somers. He could not recall telling the story about shooting at horse thieves and denied making a confession to Somers.[23]

Beebe's testimony painted a strikingly different picture of the killing of Landphere, for he thoroughly incriminated his traveling companions, blaming them for the murder that they had blamed on him. The summary version of his testimony indicated that he was composed and consistent throughout the cross-examination. It remained to be seen, however, whose version the jury would believe. Did Williams and Cammack concoct a story to incriminate Beebe and keep their necks out of a noose? Was Beebe telling the truth, or did he weave an elaborate self-serving lie?

More questions were raised by the fact that Beebe's wife did not attend the trial, nor had she come to visit him in jail. Rumors spread that

"Beebe was jealous of Landphere" because the murdered man had shown a romantic interest in Mrs. Beebe. When asked about that, Beebe attempted to quash the rumor, saying that his wife was barely acquainted with Landphere.[24] The public had been supplied with a juicy dose of speculation to satisfy the appetite of even the most voracious rumor monger.

After a reporter for the *Press and Dakotaian* analyzed the conflicting testimony, he noted that "public opinion is about equally divided upon the guilt or innocence of Beebe, and as the public stands so the jury is liable to stand."[25] The community had just been treated to a "great legal struggle," with each faction trying to wrest from the witnesses every bit of information they could to provide the winning edge. Court observers were reminded of the historic McCall and Wintermute trials as they watched and listened to the emotionally charged testimony. Once again, a man's life was at stake. Once again, it was high drama involving lawyers and witnesses and a judge and jury—murder trial as theater.

The trial concluded after nearly two weeks of testimony. As neither side felt as though it wanted to relax its efforts, a spate of character witnesses appeared and, in a few sentences, rendered their opinion as to the reputation of Cammack, Williams, and Beebe for telling the truth. Alfred Brown, the uncle of the deceased Landphere, exhibited good character when he testified that he "had no interest in fixing guilt" on Beebe or any other party. "I wanted to know the truth," he averred, "let it strike whom it would."[26]

The closing arguments were not summarized by the *Press and Dakotaian* except to note that they were lengthy and reflected the high ability of the lawyers. When the summations were finished, Judge Shannon read the instructions to the jury, placing careful emphasis on the elements of the crime of murder, the credibility of witnesses, and the concept of "reasonable doubt." As was his practice, he was careful, patient, and meticulous in his presentation, knowing that after several days of conflicting testimony the jury had to decide a close case. He wanted to help the jury but did not want to influence their deliberations and judgment. A "reasonable doubt," he explained, "must spring from reason and the facts in evidence—not from a mere wish to acquit irrespective of the testimony. Your verdict must be a true one, according to the evidence produced."[27]

The jury began its deliberations at 11:30 in the morning on December 6, and by 4:30 that afternoon they had delivered a verdict: Silas Frank Beebe was guilty of murder. In so doing, the jury affirmed that it believed the accounts of Cammack and Williams but rejected Beebe's story. The jury also affirmed that it found credibility in the statements of Marvin H. "Jim" Somers, who testified that Beebe had freely and without coercion confessed to the crime. The weight of evidence tilted in favor of the prosecution; according to the jury, there was no "reasonable doubt" that Beebe had murdered Landphere.

Since Williams and Beebe were brothers-in-law, it would be reasonable to think that they might collude against Cammack. That Williams ignored the family connection apparently convinced the jury that he was telling the truth and that being truthful meant more to him than lying in order to acquit his brother-in-law. Since many court observers were surprised that the jury came together after a short deliberation, there was no outcry or denunciation following the verdict.

Beebe felt despondent over the verdict and remained so for several days following the jury's decision. A reporter from the *Press and Dakotaian* described him as "haggard and worn" but willing to talk freely. Beebe told the reporter that he had been visited by Mary Huntington, Landphere's mother, and that during a long talk she had revealed that it was her belief that Cammack and Williams assisted him in the murder of her son. After hearing that, the reporter could not be faulted if he left the jail thinking the prisoner was delusional.

The young, convicted murderer, waiting to be sentenced, was, indeed, struggling with feelings of disbelief. He was desperate but hopeful that some evidence in his favor might turn up or that the conviction might be overturned on appeal. He concluded the interview with these words: "'If the truth is not found out before I die, it will be found out afterwards.'"[28]

One person who was entirely satisfied with the guilty verdict was Mrs. Huntington. She was convinced that she knew the truth. In her letter sent from Iowa Falls to the *Press and Dakotaian*, dated December 15, 1879, she declared that at no time did she believe that Williams and Cammack were guilty of killing her son. The responsibility for the crime, in her mind, lay with Beebe, for whom she felt some pity, declaring that she would rather her son be dead than convicted of murder. So that her sympathy for Beebe might appear sincere to readers, she added, "Never do I wish again to feel as I did when I heard the clanking of his [Beebe's] irons as he came forward to meet me." He was not her son but she granted that he was someone's son—a young man who had lost his way—and that aroused her sense of motherly compassion.[29]

A motion for a new trial followed the jury verdict and was overruled by Judge Shannon. As expected, the decision was appealed to the Dakota Territory Supreme Court. The thrust of the defendant's challenge was that the confession made to Marvin H. Somers was improperly admitted into evidence at the trial. The court rejected this contention, explaining that "on this preliminary inquiry" the matter was raised and the "defense did not, at the time, cross-examine or offer any contradictory evidence." That issue, and others raised by the defense, was rejected by the court in its unanimous decision, upholding the verdict of guilty.[30]

While the case was under appeal to the Supreme Court, it underwent another strange twist. News reached Yankton that Marvin H. "Jim" Somers, whose testimony helped to convict Beebe, was dead. The man who had shot the sheriff of Yankton County in 1869 had, himself, been killed in

Brule City on February 13, 1880, in a shootout with his nephew, Bradley Somers, during a dispute over a wood pile. Bradley, son of Lafayette Somers, had also been killed. The Dakota desperado Jim Somers, a man who had "used the revolver on several occasions during his wild career," had died with his boots on.[31]

While Silas F. Beebe was waiting to be sentenced, on April 3, 1880, the *Press and Dakotaian* published a letter from his wife that she had sent to Sheriff Baker. At long last, Nancy S. Beebe, the mystery wife, made her presence, and her feelings, known to the public, believing it was her "duty" to "let you know my opinion in regard to the case." In a poignant letter, but without undue emotion, she explained that she was not present at the trial because she had been ill and, further, she could not afford to make the trip. Nancy insisted that Silas F. Beebe was a good and loving husband, a man who could not have committed murder. It was Williams and Cammack who lied under oath, having had plenty of time to "arrange their paths." She denied all rumors or suggestions that there was any jealousy between her husband and Landphere. She closed her letter with an apology for the "poorly written message" and without having made any reference to her husband and the death penalty that everyone was expecting to be announced.[32]

Silas Frank Beebe would remember the day of his sentencing, April 8, 1880, for the rest of his life. With Beebe seated beside his attorney, William P. Dewey, Judge Shannon asked him if he had anything to say before sentence was pronounced. Beebe said only that he was innocent and that he had been unfairly treated. Shannon replied that he had been given a "fair and impartial trial," and since he was a "stranger in the community no one had any prejudice" against him. "The people," Shannon said, "have a tender regard for human life, and a verdict of guilty, where the punishment is death, is never rendered except when formed by overwhelming testimony." Then, with the entire courtroom "standing in respectful silence," Judge Shannon sentenced Beebe to death by hanging, scheduled to take place on June 3, 1880.[33]

In sentencing Beebe, Shannon told the prisoner, and those gathered in the courtroom, that the penalty imposed was not his punishment, but rather it was "the majesty of the law . . . the awful, solemn voice of the republic that he who commits murder must die." The judge departed immediately for his chambers, overcome by emotion.[34]

Beebe showed no emotion throughout the process. He was taken back to his cell to contemplate his fate. The stress of the trial and the lengthy confinement in jail had caused his face to lose its "fullness and rounded contours." The condemned man looked "very pale," with a "pinched and unhealthy" appearance that bore the reflection of a man about to be visited by the Grim Reaper.[35]

As the hours and, then, days passed away toward Beebe's date with the gallows, Mary C. Huntington, the mother of the murdered Landphere, spoke out by way of another letter to the *Press and Dakotaian.* She expressed concern about the persistent claims made by some Yankton citizens that Cammack and Williams were somehow involved in the murder of her son, for which Beebe was soon to "suffer the penalty of law." She, too, felt "there is yet much untold which none but these three know." Why not, she suggested, charge Williams and Cammack and have a trial to get at the truth? Why not, she also proposed, question those attorneys to whom Beebe allegedly confessed? Yet despite her own personal doubts and concerns, Mrs. Huntington was not prepared to "interfere with the majesty of the law," and with a nod of sympathy to Beebe's mother, she closed, thanking the people of Yankton "for the interest they have taken in this terrible affair."[36]

The "terrible affair" was having an unsettling influence on Yankton, a town that never seemed to get a good night's sleep. Although Judge Shannon had expressed his firm belief that Beebe had received a fair trial and that the sentence of death was just and lawful, he and many others in the Yankton community were deeply troubled. There were feelings in "the minds of a considerable portion of the people of the community" that Beebe "was not alone, guilty—that his comrades Cammack and Williams" bore some responsibility. With that in mind, a commutation of sentence petition, directed to President Rutherford B. Hayes, was circulated and eagerly signed by a large number of men, including the prosecutor, Hugh J. Campbell, Judge Shannon, and Judge G. C. Moody.[37]

Then, on May 29, 1880, just a few days before the prisoner was to die on the gallows, it was announced that through "efforts of disinterested parties in this city [Yankton]" Beebe's death sentence had been commuted to life in prison by President Hayes. Because of the generosity of the president, Yankton canceled all plans for another public hanging, leaving many people relieved yet others dismayed at the state of retributive justice in Dakota Territory.

The Independence Day murder at Crow Creek persisted in the memories of those who lived through its twists and turns. In September 1881 a letter arrived at the desk of the *Press and Dakotaian* with news that one of the key trial witnesses, George H. Cammack, had died. Mary Huntington, the mother of George Landphere, had written to her "warm friends" in Yankton to inform them that both Georges were resting in the same cemetery in Mazomanie, Wisconsin, though "they met their deaths in widely distant localities, and under vastly different circumstances." The long-suffering lady closed with the quip that "there was a strange mystery connected with that murder we certainly believe." Mrs. Huntington was convinced that Cammack had taken some dark secret to his grave, a belief shared by many Dakotans.[38]

CHAPTER 19

GOVERNOR NEHEMIAH ORDWAY, OUTLAWS, AND INDIAN AGENTS

One of the most notorious outlaws in the west,
J. W. Maxwell, . . . was until recently, confined in the
jail at Yankton, D.T., where he was imprisoned for an
attempt at murder.

National Police Gazette
May 8, 1880

I n the world of politics, when someone moves down, someone else moves up. And so it was in the spring of 1880, when Dakota Territory Governor William A. Howard died while on a visit to Washington, D.C., the wheels of preferment began grinding while the curious mused over this unexpected turn of events. Attention turned to Washington in anticipation of an announcement about the next governor of Dakota.

Among those whom the territorial "exchanges" considered was Chief Justice Peter C. Shannon. The federal census of 1880 shows that a prosperous Shannon was the head of a fourteen-person household in Yankton, which included his wife, a son-in-law, granddaughter, four servants, and all his children except Sarah.[1] A newspaper editorial declared that Shannon "is spoken of as the proper man to fill the now vacant governorship . . . as a worthy successor to the lamented Governor Howard." The editor pointed to Shannon's record on the bench, noting that he was the "man who led the way to firm enforcement of the law" without "'fear, favor or oppression'" and did so despite resistance from those who felt he went too far too fast.

But it was his judicial impartiality and personal integrity that rendered him eminently qualified to be governor.[2]

It was not to be, however, for on June 24, 1880, Chief Justice Peter C. Shannon administered the oath of office to the new governor of Dakota Territory, Nehemiah G. Ordway.[3] Shannon was simply doing his duty when he swore in the new governor, but in effect he was also planting the seed that grew into a political firestorm that resulted in the removal of the

Nehemiah G. Ordway, Governor, Dakota Territory.
Courtesy Library of Congress.

territorial capital from Yankton to Bismarck and the creation of two new states. Although Shannon appeared to enjoy strong support, the ugly and divisive politics of personal attack would be a factor in toppling him from his position as chief justice of the territorial Supreme Court. And it all started with Ordway.

Nehemiah G. Ordway—the inadvertent architect of Shannon's collapse—was an experienced political hack from New Hampshire who carried with him to Dakota significant political baggage. He was a Republican and had served as sergeant-at-arms for the U.S. House of Representatives for twelve years. There was also the lingering suspicion that he knew many of the dark secrets about the great Credit Mobilier scandal that related to the financing of the Union Pacific Railroad.[4]

Ordway was a member of the New Hampshire legislature at the time he was appointed to replace the deceased Governor Howard. But unlike the thoughtful and unselfish Howard, the new governor took up his duties with the intention of profiting from his office in a manner that surpassed the worst political hacks, including former governor John A. Burbank. When Ordway arrived in Yankton aboard the evening train on June 23, he was greeted by a large delegation of citizens. The *Press and Dakotaian* was impressed: he "will have the hearty cooperation of all the people without regard to party affiliation."[5] But cooperation soon began to deteriorate, and within a few months of taking office the *Dakota Herald* declared in a long editorial that Ordway and his son, George, came to Dakota "on the make."[6] From that point until he left office, Governor Ordway was the subject of criticism that slowly but steadily increased in volume and intensity as his term lengthened.

Unfortunately, Judge Shannon leaned toward Ordway in the governor's fight against the entrenched political power in Dakota. Taking sides in a major political conflict was an unprecedented move for Shannon, and it led to undesirable consequences. At no point in his judicial career did Shannon seek the support of a political faction. As a judge he believed in avoiding even the appearance of favoritism.

The coming of Ordway neutralized that option for Shannon. It would not be possible to stand on the sidelines at a time when citizens were drawn to one side or the other of the new political divide. One was either for Ordway or against him; there was no middle ground. Besides, Shannon— like other astute men—was thinking ahead, knowing that statehood for Dakota would bring new opportunities, both political and economic. In an article about the complexities of Dakota politics, the *Press and Dakotaian* described Shannon as a dark horse, a quiet intellectual who chose his friends carefully, a man whose "education sustains the theory that he has dreams like Macbeth. He will yet be a senator."[7]

Judge Shannon may have been thinking about a Senate seat while he steadily built a reputation for hard work and accomplishment. He had been honored in 1875 when Shannon County in south central Dakota was created and named after him.[8] Also, a new town in Bon Homme County, along the Missouri River at a place called "Running Water," was named "Shannon" in honor of the judge in January of 1880.[9]

While Governor Ordway was preparing to load his political pirate ship with the spoils of office, Judge Shannon went about the business of presiding over a sizeable caseload. One of the principal cases was that of Dr. Henry F. Livingston, a Yankton man who went to Fort Thompson on the Crow Creek Indian Reservation in 1868 as a contract physician. Appointed an Indian agent in October 1870 with jurisdiction over the Crow Creek and Lower Brulé Indians, he served rather quietly through the years, building what has been referred to as an "Indian Ring."[10] Livingston and other Indian agents were the subjects of a federal investigation instigated by Secretary of the Interior Carl Schurz, who announced in 1877 that he intended to ferret out all graft and corruption from the Indian agencies and would utilize secret agents to investigate and "pounce upon" suspected crooks.

Investigating fraud and corruption by Indian agents was nothing new in America. The problem was widespread and had for so long been the subject of official scrutiny that news of another investigation was probably greeted with ennui. Investigations were frequent but prosecutions were few and convictions were even fewer, despite the overwhelming evidence pointing to guilt.[11] Although fraud at the agencies cost the government huge sums of money, there was little public outrage because there was so little regard for the rights and welfare of Indians.

Secretary Schurz's representative in Dakota was Inspector General J. H. Hammond.[12] The inspector went to work as if on a mission, visiting the Indian agencies and asking hard questions, and in due time his work resulted in an arrest. Acting on orders from federal authorities, a squad of soldiers from nearby Fort Hale descended on the Crow Creek Agency, arrested Henry F. Livingston, and confiscated his records. Hammond ordered the arrest based on evidence discovered by Captain William Dougherty, who had replaced one of Livingston's associates. The extent of the alleged fraud was staggering, causing Indian Commissioner Ezra Hayt to call Livingston "the most fraudulent agent in the history of Indian Field Service."[13]

Ordinary Dakotans disagreed. The arrest of Livingston sparked outrage among white residents who believed that a conspiracy had been hatched in Washington to remove and prosecute Indian agents accused of being a part of a fictitious "Indian Ring." In the minds of many Dakotans, the "Ring" was a fabrication, and Schurz and Hammond became two of most hated men in Dakota. It was hate with a long memory. Writing about it many years later, historian George W. Kingsbury called the prosecution of Livingston and other Indian agents a "persecution."[14]

Hammond was taken to task in a *Press and Dakotaian* editorial, accusing him of "lying without limit" and trying to prejudice the public against Livingston while placing Dakota in a bad light. The Yankton daily declared that it was not against having the matter aired out in court because a fair trial would be welcomed by the people, and everyone expected an acquittal. It was simply that Hammond was interested in creating a case where none existed, and for that he "will slide down the descending scale of public opinion so rapidly that he will never again know that he had a reputation."[15]

While the public and press together seethed over the Hammond investigations, which seemed to drag on interminably, Judge and Ann Shannon were treated to a pleasant break from the drumbeat of editorial discontent. Their daughter, Eleanor "Nellie" Shannon, who had recently completed her education in the East, got married to her beau and soldier, Major Preston Wolf, on July 10, 1878, at a Catholic ceremony in Yankton. Wolf had come to Yankton in April 1877 while serving as the private secretary to J. H. Hammond. The major was praised for the "honor of carrying off one of Yankton's brightest intellectual and social ornaments."[16]

The anticipated prosecution of Dr. Livingston finally took center stage in Yankton in January 1879. In several highly publicized and emotionally charged cases, Livingston was put on trial for fraud, forgery, counterfeiting, embezzlement, and conspiracy in connection with his duties as an Indian agent. Public sympathy—including from religious leaders—was clearly on the side of Livingston. A practicing physician in Yankton since the mid-1860s, he had worked his way into the political establishment. He was the brother-in-law of territorial secretary George H. Hand, one of the leaders in what has been called the Yankton political oligarchy.

Livingston was also aided by the persistence of racism among white residents. Because of the strong, anti-Indian bias, it was impossible for the public to view the investigation with objectivity. But Secretary Schurz was undaunted, believing he had ample evidence to convict, and he ordered U.S. Attorney Hugh J. Campbell to prosecute. In April 1879 Livingston was tried three times and was thrice acquitted. A year later, he was tried twice before Judge Shannon and was acquitted both times.[17]

In March 1880, while Livingston was undergoing trial under a seventh indictment, the doctor's attorneys turned their attack on Judge Shannon. In a startling and unprecedented move, they charged Shannon with unfairness and partiality. They presented an affidavit in open court, asking that a new judge be assigned to the case. Shannon duly noted the gravity of the charge and, rather than ruling from the bench, took the motion under consideration. Two days later, in open court, he denied the defense motion.[18] Soon after, heated testimony began anew, while outside the courthouse a late winter storm blasted much of Dakota Territory.

The Livingston trials inspired a wave of public interest reminiscent of the public fascination with the trials of Peter P. Wintermute and Jack McCall. Shannon's refusal to assign the case to another judge caused some Yankton citizens to oppose Shannon openly. At the conclusion of the Livingston trial of twenty-three days, U.S. Attorney Campbell characterized it as "'the most laborious and hotly contested case that has been tried in this territory.'"[19]

During the trials in the spring of 1880, the atmosphere in Yankton was one of raw anger and outrage at the federal government. The suicide by a Crow Creek farm laborer was blamed on the Hammond investigation. Yankton businessmen and the general public were up in arms, placing pressure on the witnesses to force the government to commit perjury, or run and hide. The unprecedented appearance of Indian witnesses, testifying under oath, was the cause of additional outbursts of disapproval.[20]

The not-guilty verdicts were greeted with cheers, along with applause in print from the territorial newspapers, although the *Dakota Herald* could not resist pointing an accusatory finger at the Yankton "Ring." But anything as emotional and catastrophic as the Livingston trials was bound to create some political casualties. Although Judge Shannon took the matter seriously—as he did every trial over which he presided—he found his popularity diminished at a time when he needed support for his reappointment to the bench. While he was an impartial judge in the Livingston trials, the public perceived his decisions favored the Indians (which was not true) and that was poisonous.

Shannon also presided over trials that involved more commonplace villains. One such malefactor was John W. "Jack" Maxwell, a "somewhat notorious outlaw" with a criminal record in Dakota, Wyoming, and other parts of the West. In Yankton he was arrested for simple assault. While behind bars, he was visited by detective W. H. H. Llewellyn, who recognized him as a member of a gang that robbed a train on the Union Pacific Railroad. Maxwell and other outlaws were also alleged to having been engaged in stagecoach robberies and "even murder," according to the *Dakota Herald.*[21] According to the *Press and Dakotaian*, three rewards were being offered for his capture, in the total amount of $2,200.[22]

Another newspaper, the *Mitchell Republican*, painted a much more dramatic picture of Maxwell, calling him "Jesse James No. 2" and characterizing him as "sharp as a steel trap." He was known throughout the West as a "road and mail robber, horse thief, and for taking his man when the business in hand required it." He had served time at Fort Laramie for horse stealing and was indicted for killing a soldier at Fort Fetterman and for robbing the U.S. mail. In Yankton he assaulted his own brother, Eben Maxwell, and for this he was turned in and locked up.[23]

The *Mitchell Republican*, however, should have done some fact checking. Maxwell did not assault his own brother, for he only claimed he had relatives in Dakota. A prosperous family named Maxwell had, for some years, been living in a community known as "Maxwell City" on the James River in Hutchinson County, and they stoutly denied any connection to the scoundrel who went by the same name.

The outlaw John W. Maxwell had for several months prior to January 1880 been living in Yankton, making his headquarters at the "parlor cigar store" on Capital Street. The place was called a "den of iniquity" by the *Press and Dakotaian* because "it breeds about as much lawlessness as any other institution in the country." The proprietress of the less-than-innocuous business was said to be the "brevet wife" of John W. Maxwell. Local law officers had been watching the place for months, hoping to arrest Maxwell, as he was "strongly suspected of numerous depredations."

When he learned that his alleged relative, John E. Maxwell, was in town at a Yankton hotel, John W. paid him a visit. Armed with an eight-inch navy colt, a smaller revolver, and a prepared speech, he forced his way into the room occupied by John E. With a gun in each hand, John W. confronted John E., informing his intended victim that when he had finished his speech he would commence firing.

According to a cheeky article in the *Press and Dakotaian* John E., "not having a taste for rhetorical exercises and having nothing special to detain him just then," jumped up and exited the room from another door. John W. "leveled his large revolver upon him and pulled the trigger." No damage was done, however, because the gun failed to fire. Meanwhile, John E. found sanctuary in another room and stayed locked inside until John W. gave up and left. Much later that night, John E. swore out a complaint against John W. and, about three o'clock in the morning, the outlaw was arrested at the "cigar parlor store" by P. C. Conway, a Yankton policeman, with the assistance of a deputy U.S. marshal.[24]

The desperado languished behind bars for some time before he joined the ranks of jail breakers. On April 11, 1880, two days after the Reading Club held a "private entertainment" at the residence of Judge Shannon, Maxwell made a brazen and noisy escape from the Yankton "bastille." Someone—believed to be his Yankton lady friend, familiarly known as "Wiggie"—may have smuggled a six-shooter into the jail. While this was later denied by jail personnel, Maxwell did indeed have a gun and used it to maximum effect. When the jailer, Frank Peterson, was in the process of moving the prisoner from his cell into the general compartment, Maxwell "placed the muzzle of a navy six-shooter" to the jailer's head, took his pistol, and ordered him into the compartment. As the prisoner had the "drop" on him, Peterson was only too ready to comply. With a gun in each hand, and the jailer behind bars with other prisoners, Maxwell disappeared.[25]

Sheriff Millard A. "Ole" Baker was away at Milltown when he was notified by a special messenger of the "jail delivery." He immediately set out for Firesteel and from there to the Wessington Hills and then to Red Lake in Brule County. Finding no trace of Maxwell, he returned to Yankton, stopping at the ranches along the Missouri River, including Papineau's establishment. Having traveled on horseback for more than one hundred miles, the hard-working and popular Sheriff Baker arrived in Yankton, an exhausted man.[26]

Not long after the great escape, the sheriff from Albany County, Wyoming Territory, appeared in Yankton with an indictment accusing Maxwell of murdering a soldier two years previously at Fort Fetterman. The *Press and Dakotaian* could not resist another tongue-in-cheek reference to the jail break, noting that "Maxwell had departed before the arrival of the officer." The sheriff also departed, empty-handed, and without taking with him the outlaw who "is as dangerous a character that ever haunted the frontier."[27] His reputation was such that Maxwell was noticed and written up in the *National Police Gazette,* a popular New York City scandal sheet that eagerly lapped up the exploits of western desperadoes.[28]

Many people believed that Maxwell would never be taken. It was suggested that he might be hiding out in the Wessington Hills with other well-armed bandits.[29] Then information came to Yankton that he was somewhere in Iowa. Detective Llewellyn rejected that idea, insisting that Maxwell, known as "Culley" or "Cully," undoubtedly went west where he had spent most of his life, "a region that he knows so well."[30]

Llewellyn was wrong—Maxwell had gone east to Iowa, where he remained for a few weeks until he was taken into custody near Cedar Rapids. He was using the alias "J. N. Scott" when he was arrested under the strangest of circumstances. Another man, named I. W. Scott, while at the Cedar Rapids post office, mistakenly opened and read a letter addressed to Maxwell under his alias. The letter contained startling information, for it revealed "information that the party, for whom it was intended [Maxwell], had committed various crimes in the region of the Black Hills country, and he had offered the jailor at Yankton, D.T., $130 for his release." The person who wrote the letter, a woman, urged Maxwell to send the money for the jailer was "hard up and needed it badly." She also warned Maxwell not to come back to Yankton or he would be killed. The startled Iowan, I. W. Scott, immediately turned the letter over to the authorities and Maxwell was found and arrested in short order and without incident.[31]

Sheriff Baker, a man accustomed to making long trips for the purpose of retrieving Dakota outlaws, went to Cedar Rapids and brought Maxwell and another fugitive back to Yankton. To make sure he behaved himself, Maxwell was chained and shackled to the floor of his cell. He expressed his disapproval of the rough treatment by threatening to kill the sheriff and his assistants if and when he had the opportunity and the means to do so.

Some believed that Maxwell had been discovered in Iowa because of clues provided in a letter from his lady friend, Wiggie, whose real name was Carrie Bankson. While she was suddenly under official scrutiny, the papers reported that Maxwell would be taken to the Black Hills if the stories of his "operations" in that region proved to be true.[32]

They were not true. Maxwell remained in Yankton, in jail. Then one day he had a visitor, in the person of Frank Howard, a government agent from Wyoming. Howard stopped at the Yankton County jail and presented a warrant for Maxwell in connection with a robbery of the U.S. mail that took place somewhere between Forts Fetterman and McKinney. Howard had been "a long time on the track of Maxwell" and was anxious to take him back to Wyoming to stand trial. Sheriff Baker was not willing to release Maxwell, noting that the county had a bill of expenses in the amount of $400 on account of the wily outlaw. Baker wanted the U.S. government to pay up. Howard contacted his superiors for instructions and that was apparently where the matter ended.[33]

Throughout the spring and summer of 1880, Maxwell endured his pre-trial jail time quietly. Then in late November excitement erupted when Charley Olsen, the jailer, spotted Maxwell "concealing some papers." Olson ordered Maxwell to turn them over to him, but the prisoner refused. The jailer entered the cell and was greeted by a blow that "peeled his nose and cut a gash under his left eye." Olson retaliated with some punches of his own, which bloodied Maxwell's face. The sullen outlaw was soon alone in his cell, bearing heavy irons, and the jailer—who apparently lost interest in the papers—had to be satisfied that Maxwell got the worst of it.[34]

In December 1880 Maxwell entered a plea of guilty to jail breaking and was tried and convicted of simple assault. Judge Shannon sentenced Maxwell to two years in prison at hard labor for the jail break and to thirty days in the county jail on the assault charge, along with a fine of $150. "He received his sentence like the hardened villain that he is," and Sheriff Baker hauled him off to Detroit.

Meanwhile, "Mademoiselle Bankson," aka Wiggie, released without bail, was waiting to be tried for assisting in the escape of Maxwell.[35] It would not be a Merry Christmas for either one of them, but for Judge Shannon ridding the territory of the desperado was a holiday gift to the entire community. Yankton had seen far too many of his ilk. The *Press and Dakotaian* promised the public that the authorities were determined to search all "places for the harboring of thieves and other lawless characters . . . to root them out and bring their keepers and abettors to the punishment they deserve."[36]

Prior to disposing of Maxwell, Judge Shannon and his wife had the pleasure of traveling to Council Bluffs, Iowa, to meet their daughter Elizabeth, whom they called Bessie. She had just completed her course of study in St. Louis and graduated with "highest honors." Bessie returned to Yankton where she was greeted by a "host of admirers," all of whom were proud of her medals and "other substantial evidence of her proficiency as a student." The Shannons were justifiably proud of Bessie.[37]

On July 2, 1880, Shannon took delivery of two yearling buffalo bulls, shipped on a steamer from the Cheyenne Indian Agency.[38] Then he went to Pierre and presided over the very first term of court in that lively, growing Missouri River city.

Pierre was about to eclipse Yankton and rival Deadwood as the favorite haven for outlaws and scofflaws who flocked to its many saloons and dance halls. Governor Ordway and his wife included Pierre on their

1880 summer tour of Dakota and were shocked at the many examples of lawless and loutish behavior. Drunken brawls and shootings made life in Pierre an adventure, especially at night. A character named "Arkansaw" shot and killed a desperado called "Texas Jack," an act that was met with popular approval because Jack was a bad man who "deserved killing."[39] It was no wonder that Pierre was called "hell's half acre" and the "Devil's headquarters for Dakota."[40]

After leaving Pierre, and traveling on to the Black Hills, Ordway addressed a crowd in Central City and, during the course of his talk, was highly critical of the lawless town that was often referred to as "East Pierre." He called the town a "disreputable place now standing on the western shore without law and without order." The town's newspaper, the *Signal*, took offense and cast some salty criticism in the direction of the governor. In response the Yankton *Press and Dakotaian* reminded the *Signal* that the "worthy executive" made the unkind remarks to call attention to the dire need for law enforcement to clamp down on the outlaws.[41] Although the Yankton daily was asking for patience and understanding, it would, in time, become the leading and most vocal critic of Governor Ordway.

Ordway was exactly correct, however, when he complained about the lawlessness in Pierre, a "rendezvous for desperadoes and blacklegs of the worst description." A Huron newspaper warned its readers that "brawls, riots and murders" were all too frequent "as to make the place a reproach to the people of the territory." But the town also claimed a law-abiding, peace-loving contingent, and these men formed a vigilance committee. The goal of the committee was to clean out the outlaw element, and, after they warned the "bulldozing gentry to leave town," they challenged Arkansaw, arguably the worst of the bunch.

Arkansaw—whose real name was Alexander McDonald Putello— apparently believed his home state of Wisconsin was too tame. So he went west to Dakota and found a place to his liking. He was not a man to be trifled with and when he learned that the vigilantes were after him, he defiantly crossed the Missouri River from Fort Pierre to Pierre at eleven o'clock in the evening, bringing fourteen friends. The brave committeemen singled out and confronted Arkansaw, telling him to leave town. His response was a couple of recklessly fired shots and a yell: "come on, you monkeys!" These were his last words, for the vigilantes "sent him a score of bullet proxies," eighteen to be exact, killing him on the spot.[42]

Judge Shannon, who had seen his share of outlaws, went to Pierre to do his duty in the Wild West town where the unexpected could erupt at any moment. And it did. While a trial was in progress, people in the audience were drawn to some noisy activity outside the courthouse. Soon they were filing out, followed by the jury, witnesses, and lawyers. Shannon, too, exited the courthouse and came in full view of the source of the excitement: two young women, both stripped to the waist, were engaged in a rousing round of fisticuffs. Shannon had been exposed to many shocking examples of bad behavior during his time in Dakota, and, sensing the only proper course of action, he discreetly adjourned court for the rest of the day.[43]

The judge quickly put the Pierre incident behind him, for he had a full slate of cases ahead of him, much of it in the counties bordering the James River. He had other matters on his mind, too, for Shannon had to concentrate on being reappointed to the territorial bench. In order for him to bring his brand of judicial skill and integrity to the outlaw town of Pierre, he needed another four-year term as judge. He was assured of his popularity with the citizens, and he was convinced that he had earned another term. And since he wanted it, he was prepared to fight for it, if necessary.

CHAPTER 20

SHANNON FIGHTS FOR REAPPOINTMENT

*Judge Shannon's backing by the stalwarts of Pennsylvania
and New York is so overwhelming that it now seems a
foregone conclusion that he will be re-nominated by
President Arthur by a large majority.*

Dakota Herald
December 10, 1881

J udge Shannon received a lukewarm endorsement from the *Dakota Herald*, a newspaper that had a negative view of all Republicans. In a long article on federal officials and their prospects for reappointment, the *Herald* stated that U.S. Attorney Campbell should be removed, along with Associate Justice G. C. Moody, who presided at Deadwood. The latter, the paper observed, was a good lawyer but not a man of good character. Moody could be removed "without injury to the people." As for Shannon, there were no complaints about his retention, and it "would be entirely satisfactory" if he stayed on the bench.[1]

A significant change took place in May 1881 when Associate Justice A. H. Barnes was replaced by Sanford A. Hudson of Janesville, Wisconsin. Hudson was appointed by President James A. Garfield on March 10, 1881, and the new justice was sworn in by Chief Justice Shannon at Yankton on May 14, 1881. Hudson then departed for Fargo with his family, arriving on May 22.[2]

Hudson was an experienced jurist with strong connections to the top echelon of Wisconsin politicians. He had served a term as mayor of

Janesville. More important, he was one of the organizers of the Republican Party and could therefore claim to have been one of the original members of the party of Abraham Lincoln.[3]

The man Hudson replaced, A. H. Barnes, left the bench a rich man and was apparently satisfied with having served two terms as an associate justice. He and his sons had agricultural and mining interests in Dakota. Judge Barnes' frugal business habits and astute political connections apparently paid dividends, for he left the bench with no regrets.

His fellow judge, G. C. Moody, became mired down in a bitter fight to retain his seat on the bench. A powerful group of Black Hills politicians wanted Moody ousted. Lawrence County officials, mostly Democrats, filed charges against Moody for misconduct over a courthouse construction controversy. While the opposing factions battled one another, supporters built two courthouses—and Moody held court in the one constructed by his friends. Upping the ante, he then accused the Lawrence County commissioners of defrauding the people of $300,000. The commissioners did manage to incite an investigation of Moody by the justice department, but the judge was completely cleared and retained his position.[4]

Shannon—who never warmed up to Moody—had his own battle to fight. Members of the Yankton bar association were anxious to find someone to take his place on the Dakota bench. Easily the most powerful and respected collection of attorneys in Dakota, they joined forces and filed charges against Shannon with the Department of Justice, claiming he was "repeatedly publicly intoxicated, and in such states of intoxication, he, at times, is abusive and insulting to members of the bar."[5]

That was just one of seven "specifications" in their arsenal. He was also accused of being "discourteous and arbitrary on the bench" and prone to taking the side of the prosecution in criminal cases, thereby prejudicing the jury. But perhaps the most damning, and certainly the most unusual, charge was Specification No. 7. It pertained to a letter addressed to U.S. Treasury Department that Shannon allegedly wrote and signed as "Henry S. Carter." This letter, dated August 17, 1876, was dredged up after apparently having been on file in Washington for many years. It was purportedly written in order to convince the treasury to audit the account of U.S. Marshal James H. Burdick in connection with a criminal case, an account that had been, in part, disallowed by Shannon.[6]

This accusation, vindictive in tone and content, was artfully, though not clearly, written and raises several questions. Why would anyone wait so long to bring up this issue? Why did Burdick not respond when the matter first came up and insist on an investigation? Why was there no outrage in August 1876? Assuming the letter was authentic, what, if anything, had the treasury done in response? Apparently, it had done nothing since Shannon was reappointed to a second term.

The specifications of misconduct were printed in the *Press and Dakotaian* on behalf of the accusers, a group of attorneys who, over the years, appeared before Judge Shannon in some of the most complex and well-publicized civil and criminal trials in the West. The signatories included S. L. Spink, president of the bar association, George H. Hand, and Bartlett Tripp. Since these were men he knew through his social and professional circles, the charges must have been hurtful. But the biggest shock came, undoubtedly, from Oliver Shannon, whose relationship to Shannon (possibly his brother) remains a mystery, and who signed the petition dated March 25, 1881.[7] It was a bitter pill to swallow, no matter the liquid used to wash it down.

Others judges, including J.P. Kidder, had survived charges of drunkenness. Although a frivolous accusation in itself, Judge Shannon must have understood the gravity of the other charges. He also knew that Dakota Territory was made up of close-knit, small cities and towns and that, over the course of two terms, he had stepped on any number of toes. Judge Shannon had spent long, hard hours in the saddle, carriage, and courtrooms throughout much of southern Dakota, and instead of being appreciated he was now in jeopardy of being fired.

The *Press and Dakotaian* might have been provoked in its opposition by an article about the John W. Maxwell case, which Shannon deemed

Solomon L. Spink, attorney opposed to
Judge Shannon's reappointment.
Courtesy Library of Congress.

prejudicial. "The circumstances connected with this [Maxwell] affair were aggravating in the extreme and should the jury find him guilty it is probable that he will receive a good sized penalty."[8] The next day Shannon launched a lengthy and stinging rebuke against "persons who are supposed to attempt to influence juries," meaning, of course, the newspapers.[9] The judge made it clear that it was one of Maxwell's attorneys who called the court's attention to the journalistic gaffe.

Taking sides in a criminal case, and making highly prejudicial remarks, was not unusual for frontier newspapers. Dispassionate reporting was of no interest to nineteenth-century journalism. Shouting and sensationalism sold newspapers. Having been called out in this public manner by Shannon, George W. Kingsbury and the staff of the *Press and Dakotaian* were undoubtedly angry. Nevertheless, they were content to allow the Yankton lawyers to handle the laboring oar.

The anti-Shannon campaign raged on throughout 1881, featuring a carnival of angry flare-ups in the territorial newspapers. The justice department was clearly unhappy with the constant bickering and finger pointing. The *National Republican*, a Washington, D.C., newspaper, reported that the "services of one officer . . . are devoted exclusively to the examination of complaints against Territorial judges."[10]

As though Judge Shannon needed another headache, the weather became a factor. The spring of 1881, following the "Winter of the Deep Snow," brought unprecedented flooding along the Missouri and other rivers. Shannon was unable to get back to Yankton to open the regular term of court. Like so many others at that time, he was trapped and isolated by forces of nature, as high waters damaged or wrecked roads, railroads, and bridges. The conditions for safe travel were beyond his control.

Shannon did, however, attend a meeting in Omaha organized for the purpose of gathering aid in the form of money and supplies for people along the Missouri River who had lost everything to the flood. Along with W. W. Brookings and others, Shannon spoke "about the destitute condition of the people."[11]

When he finally did arrive in Yankton, Shannon was forced to adjourn court, day after day, due to the lack of witnesses and jurors, still trapped by high water. On May 10 he announced that "additional" terms of court would be held commencing "forthwith."[12] Officers were sent out in search of jurors and witnesses for the prosecution.

But Judge Shannon had problems to contend with that went beyond weather conditions. On May 11 the *Press and Dakotaian* reminded its readers that "it is no secret that the attorneys who practice before the court of this district . . . prefer not to have their cases tried before Judge Shannon." The attorneys were not at all troubled by adjournments because they had, by agreement, postponed their cases to the fall term, hoping that Shannon would be replaced by a new judge.[13]

On the 12th Judge Shannon made a first and second call of the calendar but got no responses. The *Press and Dakotaian* speculated that members of the bar had "designs on fishing" until the flood waters subsided. The attorneys seemed to be "imbued with spring fever or something of that sort."[14] And so it went throughout the month of May 1881: court was opened and then adjourned due to uncooperative lawyers, missing jurors, and witnesses.

A case that finally did go to trial was that of John D. Cameron, from Sioux Falls. Cameron was a slaphappy "plunger," an uneven mixture of a pesky, self-serving gadfly and a public-spirited businessman and booster. He seemed to be everywhere at once, a veritable whirlwind of activity. The town of Cameron in McCook County was named after him. In Sioux Falls he dabbled in banking and construction, with an eye toward anything that would make money, including speculation in land. Doubtless, there were men who deemed him reckless and untrustworthy and believed it was just a matter of time before "John D." would be in trouble with the law.

Cameron was hauled into court, having been charged with inducing several settlers to submit false affidavits in connection with land claims under the Preemption Act and "procuring title to such land by false and fraudulent papers."[15] He had been indicted by a grand jury in the fall of 1880 and secured legal representation in the person of S. L. Spink. The affable Cameron was well-liked in Sioux Falls and came into court confident that he would be acquitted.

The trial sputtered for several days, but a jury was finally selected. With prosecution witnesses on hand, at long last, the testimony began. At some point early in the proceedings, Spink launched an argument to the effect that Judge Shannon had violated the Organic Act by scheduling the Cameron trial. Under the act, the governor was entitled to fix the term of court, and thereafter scheduling was in the hands of the legislature. Spink argued that the regular term had lapsed because Shannon was absent from the territory, so the judge had no power to conduct the trial.[16]

Undaunted, Shannon overruled the motion and the trial continued apace. At the conclusion of the trial, the jury was unable to reach a verdict after several days of deliberation. Cameron was at least temporarily off the hook, but significant collateral damage had been done—to the judge, not the defendant. For calling and trying the case, Shannon found his popularity slipping even further.

Following the assassination of President James A. Garfield on September 19, 1881, Yankton judges, lawyers, and politicians demonstrated a common civility. Having endured seventy-nine days of suffering, the president died and the nation went into mourning. In Yankton Shannon joined others, including Governor Ordway, in eulogizing the gallant president and Civil War general, shot down by Charles Guiteau, who had become the most reviled man in America.[17]

One attorney missing from the Garfield gathering was Solomon Spink. The man who had been leading the Yankton bar in its hard-hitting effort toward preventing Shannon from receiving a third term died on September 22, following a long struggle with malaria. Although the loss of the popular attorney caused sorrow among many of his fellow lawyers, it did nothing to diminish their interest in ridding Yankton of Peter Shannon. They found a staunch ally in the *Press and Dakotaian.*

After maintaining a respectful silence of several days, following the death of Spink, the *Press and Dakotaian* published an editorial in opposition to Judge Shannon. In mostly measured language, the editor noted the "serious nature" of the charges against the judge, which had been brought by honest and thoughtful men of "high character" who took the action as a last resort. This was not a persecution. They had proceeded, honorably, as a group, to secure "the removal of Judge Shannon." They "entered upon the unpleasant task, because they feel that they can no longer practice in his court with comfort to themselves or safety to their clients." Should Shannon get appointed to a third term, the paper warned, Yankton lawyers would be "driven from their practice or crippled in their capacity as attorneys."

Then, about mid-way through the editorial, the writer, probably none other than Kingsbury, got to the heart of the matter. Why should anyone want a man like Shannon in Yankton? In his "eight years' residence in Dakota," he "has never invested a cent in property here." Furthermore, he made most of his family purchases from eastern merchants while ignoring those of Yankton and, worst of all, it seems, he never subscribed to a local newspaper! Compare that, the editor challenged, to the lawyers and other men who "have the means and the disposition to aid materially in building up the country." Yankton could not afford to lose such men, but Shannon had to go for the good of the community.[18]

Nor was that the only shot that Kingsbury and company would take at Shannon. In another editorial the "Henry S. Carter" letter was brought up again. The late U.S. Attorney William Pound had sent a letter to the department of justice, dated October 2, 1876, condemning the Carter letter. According to Pound—whom the *Press and Dakotaian* described as the purest man that "ever crossed the boundary line of Dakota"—the Carter letter was a spiteful attempt to malign Marshal Burdick and "stab him in the dark." Pound's letter made no mention of Shannon, and Kingsbury backed away from accusing the judge of writing the Carter letter, saying only that the bar association insisted that it was written by one of his family members, "and probably at his dictation."[19]

Although the judge was under fire in Yankton, he was well-liked in Olivet, a town in Hutchinson County, where for "seven years his honor Chief Justice Shannon has visited us regularly and has faithfully and thoroughly performed the duties of the office of judge." Over time he had won the "respect and confidence of the people." A Hutchinson County newspaper, the *Menno Chronicle*, called Shannon "the perfect gentleman" and was fully in favor of his reappointment, noting that it is "the earnest desire of the people" that he continue to act as chief justice. "It would be hard to fill his place," the newspaper asserted.[20]

Elsewhere in the territory, the *Parker New Era* chimed in for Shannon, complaining that the "Yankton bar association are after Judge Shannon's scalp with increased fury." This Turner County newspaper, in a stinging rebuke, suggested that the Yankton attorneys were motivated by a desire to secure the appointment of a more pliable judge, for Shannon "does not run his court to suit the lawyers."[21]

Opposition from angry lawyers only made the hard-headed judge more determined to fight back. Shannon traveled to Pennsylvania and Washington to argue his case and shore up his support among the high-rollers in eastern political circles. In November 1881 he was interviewed in Pittsburgh for an article in the *Chicago Times,* responding to the charges against him: "that he was overbearing on the bench, he has taken undue interest in cases tried before him, has acted in a manner unworthy of a judge." But instead of addressing the charges directly, Shannon told the interviewer that the opposition was headed by the "Indian [and] land rings of Dakota, whose enemy he is." He made reference to Dr. Henry Livingston, whose trials on charges of fraud and embezzlement created a furious uproar in Dakota. Livingston and others from the "Indian ring," Shannon said, were behind the "foul conspiracy."[22]

In an interview with the *Pittsburgh Leader,* Shannon further vented his frustration at the efforts to remove him. In addition to the "Indian Ring," he mentioned the "Land Ring." He brought up the John D. Cameron case about false affidavits in connection with the filing of land claims, a trial that had resulted in a hung jury. He insisted that there "are men anxious to have upon the territorial bench a man who will be subservient to their will and not stand between them and their spoils." Shannon reiterated his belief that great frauds had been committed by Indian agents, but that he never allowed his personal beliefs "to intrude into his decisions as a judge" Finally, he disclaimed that he had senatorial ambitions that he was protecting from men who wanted to destroy him politically.[23]

But political destruction was certainly in the Yankton air. The *Press and Dakotaian* mocked Shannon's Pittsburgh interviews, insisting that he misrepresented his "affairs here in Dakota" and for that alone President Chester A. Arthur should not reappoint him. Shannon was slammed for bringing up once again the Indian and land ring scandals, clearly sore spots for the *Press and Dakotaian.* Such talk reminded everyone of the unpopular investigation by J. H. Hammond and the subsequent Livingston trials.[24] Shannon's handling of the Livingston trial, and that of John D. Cameron, would have been reason enough for strong opposition. The charges concerning conduct and attitude were just window dressing.

Continual reference to the "Indian and land rings of Dakota" brought forth an angry editorial from the *Dakota Pantagraph*, a Sioux Falls newspaper strongly opposed to Shannon. The livid editor declared, "we can scarcely write coolly in regard to such a slander as this. It makes us hot."[25] Editors were usually hot and always on the defensive, but there was something about the Indian and land ring charges that was especially infuriating to Dakotans, that to a man aroused an angry intensity. It was one thing to accuse an individual of fraud, but the use of the word "ring" implied a vast conspiracy, as though organized crime had taken root in Dakota. According to the *Pantagraph,* Judge Shannon was guilty of that sin.

In contrast to the opposition that Shannon encountered in some quarters, many of those who had little or no personal connection with the judge, such as ordinary Dakota citizens, viewed him favorably. It is worth noting that there was no popular uprising from among the general public to depose him. Among those who opposed him were individuals who were opposed on principle to office holders and speculators and their schemes. Their focus was not so much on individual cases, but rather Shannon's overall record as a judge.

Shannon could point to a sterling record as both a trial judge and a Supreme Court justice. He was absent from court only one day out of 188, while the absentee rates of the other judges were much higher, and 84% of his cases appealed to the territorial Supreme Court were affirmed. Furthermore, Shannon participated in 100% of all decisions made by the Dakota Territory Supreme Court. No other justice during his tenure on the bench could claim such high marks.[26]

Yankton Attorney William H. H. Beadle, who liked and admired Shannon, applauded the judge's time on the bench, pursuing "crime with due vigor." But he had to admit that, while Shannon was clearing "the rough elements up the river," the dedicated judge had acquired some "opposition among the bar and people" over his "forceful administration of justice."[27]

Shannon also had support from U.S. Attorney Hugh J. Campbell, who contended that, because of the impending case load of complex litigation, replacing Shannon "would injure the public interest." Shannon also mentioned that Secretary of the Interior Samuel J. Kirkwood endorsed him, along with Dakota governor Ordway, former president Grant, Illinois congressman John Logan, Maine congressman James G. Blaine, and Robert Lincoln, son of the late president. They all backed his reappointment, and he understood that President Arthur had "intimated he will be reappointed."[28]

Shannon was not the only man, however, who had ventured east to address the matter of his reappointment. Two men who opposed him, Yankton attorney R. J. Gamble and the Dakota delegate R. F. Pettigrew, went directly to President Arthur and urged him to replace Shannon. Their visit with Arthur was made because Gamble and Pettigrew learned that Shannon had widespread support and numerous endorsements, including newspapers, judges, lawyers, bankers, and businessmen in Pittsburgh and other parts of Pennsylvania.[29]

The judge's family rarely made the news, suggesting they led respectable and healthy lives. While Shannon was back East fighting for his professional life, his daughter Eleanor and her husband, Preston Wolfe, became proud parents of a ten-pound baby girl.[30] The birth of the Shannon grandchild was cause for a small notice in the *Dakota Herald* and may have relieved the judge of some of his anxiety about the future.

November came to an end and Shannon was still wondering about his reappointment. Meanwhile, others were awaiting the end of the world, as predicted by "Mother Shipton," a strange figure in the business of prophecy. A Dakota newspaper suggested wryly that "all those with plans for the future should ignore her predictions."[31] The world did not end, but Shannon's term did expire, leaving him in limbo. He sold his young buffalo to a man from the Dakota town of Webster.

Then Governor Ordway, another prognosticator, intervened, openly and strongly supporting Shannon's reappointment. In a letter to President Arthur, dated December 1, 1881, Ordway stated that he "felt constrained to differ with the delegate [R. F. Pettigrew]" who was backing the effort to remove Judge Shannon. Ordway called Shannon "an able and fearless judge," a man who deserved another term on the Dakota Supreme Court. Unfortunately for the beleaguered judge, Ordway's letter to the president concerning appointments was deemed to be an interference with the duties of the congressional delegate.[32]

Time passed and, still, there was no word from Washington about Shannon's judicial fate. The *Dakota Herald* expressed impatience with the process on December 3, saying Shannon's "prospects are good." The *Herald* maintained its coyness, however, remarking that it would be satisfied whether Shannon were retained or replaced by some other well-qualified man.

A Pittsburgh man, in the process of renewing his subscription to the *Herald,* expressed surprise that there was *any* opposition to Judge Shannon in Dakota. He mentioned Shannon's recent visit to Pittsburgh, where he met "with strong support in favor of reappointment."[33] And so it went throughout the month of December. President Arthur was in no hurry to make up his mind, while all of Dakota waited anxiously.

CHAPTER 21

DISORDER IN THE COURT:
THE KNOWLTON MURDER TRIAL

The prisoner sprang to his feet and advancing towards Judge
Shannon on the bench yelled . . . and hurled at him a volley
of epithets the most profane in the vocabulary.

Dakota Herald
December 31, 1881

Although not knowing from day to day what the future held regarding his judgeship, Chief Justice Shannon tended to court business. On December 7, 1881, Shannon was in Yankton presiding over the trial of Harvey W. Knowlton, better known as George Knowlton, who was charged with murdering David Rauck in Pierre in 1877. Both the peculiar facts of the case and the personality of the defendant rendered the trial of interest to the public.

George Knowlton, who preferred the cognomen "Rebel George," apparently had some connection with the Old South, although some believed he had ties to Wisconsin.[1] His wife was from a wealthy St. Joseph, Missouri, family; she left school, ran away, and eloped with her dashing and boisterous beau, whose life "would furnish material for a half dozen dime novels."[2]

On May 25, 1876, the *Press and Dakotaian* announced Knowlton's arrival in Dakota, saying only that H. W. Knowlton and family, from Rochelle, Illinois, were at the Merchants Hotel in Yankton. They were making preparations to settle near Finlay, in Turner County.[3] His sister,

Jennie M. Knowlton, found work as a school teacher and ran a millinery business in Finlay.[4]

But the quiet, hard life of a sod-buster was not in the cards for Knowlton. He preferred the softer life of a gambler. It was a good fit for his large physique and domineering, gregarious personality. Knowlton pursued that line of work with some success in Yankton, where he acquired a reputation as a gambler, as did so many others during the 1870s, when the capital of Dakota was earning its place as a gambling town.

A series of events starting in the spring of 1877 took Knowlton on a long, rough journey into Judge Shannon's sparsely furnished, smoke-filled courtroom, facing a murder charge. Knowlton and a friend named Mike O'Neill had established a gambling "business" in Yankton, exhibiting a penchant for the old con game called "three-card monte." They made some money fleecing unsuspecting greenhorns and Black Hills-bound pilgrims who were tempted to try their luck in a no-win card game.

Three-card monte is a simple game played with three cards placed face down on a table or box. The trick is to guess which card is the "money card," usually the queen of hearts. Simple math would suggest that a player's chances are as great as one in three. But the game is a setup, for the dealer, meaning the "monte man," cheats to make sure that no one beats the "house." Another person, a "shill," pretends to ally himself with the "mark," or the sucker, but in fact is in cahoots with the dealer. If by chance the mark picks the money card, the dealer employs a sleight-of-hand trick or other misdirection technique so that the player seldom, if ever, wins.

In the spring of 1877, Knowlton and O'Neil hired a light horse-and-buggy rig and took their racket upriver to the budding town of Pierre on the east bank of the Missouri River. Large gatherings of men going to the Black Hills were known to meet there, waiting for transportation across the river so they could continue on their way west. On April 10, 1877, Knowlton and O'Neill approached a group of travelers from Michigan, pretending to be stockmen looking for strays. Using that ruse, they were able to put the men at ease and, in a friendly manner, suggested some gambling might be just the thing to break the monotony of the camp. One man in the party was agreeable and Knowlton succeeded in taking him away from his comrades. In short order, Knowlton cleaned out the gullible man in a game of three-card monte, taking $20 and a watch.

The victim returned to his party of about fourteen men and told them what had just transpired, although he did not insist that he had been cheated. But his friends, including David Rauck, immediately suspected some kind of chicanery and set out to find the gamblers. Rauck and four others confronted Knowlton about the money and the watch. An angry verbal exchange ensued, after which Rauck sat down on a wagon tongue with his rifle on his lap, declaring that he had no fear of Knowlton. Knowlton ordered him to drop the gun, but Rauck refused, whereupon the slick gambler drew his revolver and fired a shot directly into Rauck's head, killing him on the spot.

Rauck's friends stood by apparently intimidated, for they made no attempt to avenge his death or to subdue the shooter. Knowlton made some self-serving statements about shooting Rauck out of fear for his own life. He then told the others he was willing to give himself up and started out in the direction of Yankton but, instead, headed east toward Iowa, passing through Swan Lake in Dakota. Since he was allowed to ride away to freedom, he would be a fool to surrender and subject himself to a trial, having shot and killed a man in front of several witnesses.[5]

Dakota law enforcement personnel never gave up their hunt for Knowlton. In September 1879 word filtered back to Dakota that Knowlton was the leader of a gang of "gold-brick swindlers in Chicago" and was traveling under the name "Rebel George."[6] Knowlton continued to travel in the company of Mike O'Neill, and the pair of crooks bounced around the country, visiting New York, Denver, and Chicago. Finally, with the aid of a Chicago detective agency, Knowlton was arrested in that city for "palming off a bogus gold brick."

In September 1881 Knowlton was arrested and charged with murdering David Rauck. He was escorted to Yankton by two Chicago law officers, having been indicted by a Dakota grand jury. Although he faced trail for a capital offense, Knowlton had lost none of his bravado. When he was taken to jail, he saluted Sheriff Baker. When the sheriff ignored the gesture, Knowlton said, "Well, what are you going to do with me? Take me to a hill and tie a red rag on me?"[7]

Although his gun-slinging days in Dakota were brief, the Chicago press seized the opportunity to embellish Knowlton's reputation as an outlaw. The *Inter-Ocean* announced that "Rebel George" was returned to Fort Pierre, "where he is wanted for five or six murders."[8]

But Knowlton was not taken to Fort Pierre. He was lodged in the U.S. jail in Yankton, much to his disgust. Still, he had the opportunity to get away again when three of his cellmates made a daring and successful escape from the jail. Jack Williams, John Fagan, and Dick Burr, alias Charles Roberts, one of the "Hog Ranch desperadoes," methodically and secretly removed bricks until they had created "an aperture large enough to squeeze through." With the jailer absent, and only a guard described as a "harmless sort of fellow" to stop them, they "secured an iron bar from one of the cells" and used it to increase the size of the opening. Then, as the guard simply sat and watched, the outlaws "crawled out, scaled the high fence and escaped to the timber of Smutty Bear bottom." Rebel George watched it all but refused to leave with the jail breakers.[9]

Knowlton insisted that he wanted to stand trial, and not long after the jail break, he became a model prisoner, trying to make friends with jail personnel. In the days leading up to the trial, he was all smiles as though he expected soon to be a free man.

With Knowlton on his best behavior and no other prisoners seeking to escape, there was little in the way of crime news to report except that a dog had been left overnight in the courtroom and had "proceeded to devour several legal documents" belonging to U.S. Attorney Hugh J. Campbell. That caused Judge Shannon to "lecture upon the poor [courtroom] accommodations furnished" by the United States government. The remark was apparently harsh enough for the *Press and Dakotaian* to remind its readers that the Yankton court facilities were "sufficiently luxurious" and that "the intrusion of the dog" was the sole responsibility of the federal government, as represented by his honor, the judge.[10]

The Knowlton trial soon began and the dog incident was quickly forgotten. Knowlton's smugness disappeared when he was ushered into court. He was on trial for murder, facing a death sentence by hanging, should he be convicted as charged. Hugh J. Campbell represented the government and Bartlett Tripp appeared for the defendant. Knowlton's companion Mike "Little Mike" O'Neil was brought in from Chicago and was expected to be a witness for the defense.

The defendant, the arrogant Harvey W. "George" Knowlton, was described as "a man in the prime of life, of powerful physique and a countenance indicative of a strong and determined will."[11] From his frequent, snide smiles, observers concluded that he was confident that he would be acquitted. Knowlton's wife, quiet and grim, was present in the courtroom, which was packed with people, all hoping for some excitement or some special memory to savor.

Although the government's case appeared to be strong, with Bartlett Tripp at his side, Knowlton was well represented. The first day of the proceedings was taken up with questioning members of the jury pool, and after a jury was selected the court adjourned. The next day, December 8, 1881, testimony began. Those in the courtroom expected that the parade of witnesses would provide eye-opening testimony about a frontier shooting that occurred during the peak of the Black Hills gold rush excitement. While the nation was enthralled by the trial of Charles Guiteau for assassinating President James A. Garfield, Yankton would be fully entertained by the Knowlton murder trial.

The first prosecution witness, Edwin J. Busby, testified that he was with a party of prospectors from Missouri, camped out near Pierre on April 10, 1877. He said he first met Knowlton at "a fancy house below East Pierre, about 500 yards from the river." Busby recalled that Knowlton claimed to be a stockman and that he (Knowlton) "decoyed" an old Englishman, named McKinnis, away from the camp and then cheated him out of his money and a watch. He went on to state that Rauck and others hunted Knowlton down in order to force him to return the old man's possessions. Knowlton said the old man lost them gambling and they would not be returned. Busby was present when Knowlton approached Rauck while the latter was seated on a wagon tongue with his rifle. He saw Knowlton point his pistol about "four or five inches" from Rauck's temple and pull the trigger. Immediately after the shooting, Knowlton said, "I have killed him. I thought he had his gun cocked."

On cross-examination, Busby testified in detail about the size of the miner parties and the number of weapons each one had in its possession. Tripp's questioning seemed rambling, as though he was trying to elicit some surprising testimony of benefit to his client. The only surprise on cross-examination was the revelation that, prior to shooting Rauck, Knowlton had shot at, but missed, another man named Dutch Fred. The morning session ended with the prosecution in good shape.[12]

Henry "Dutch Fred" Kreits took the stand and admitted that he, too, had lost money to Knowlton and O'Neill. But he tended to blame himself for the loss, admitting, "I love the almighty dollar pretty well and I bet on the game and lost." More important, perhaps, was his testimony about the shooting of Rauck, saying he was so close to the victim that his blood splattered on his clothes. As for Knowlton, Kreits said that the defendant mounted a black horse and rode away at top speed.[13]

Campbell was making progress with the witnesses and evidence he had at his disposal, all of which riled up Knowlton's attorney. It was known that Campbell and Tripp did not like each other, so it probably came to no one's surprise that the two lawyers engaged in verbal sparring during the trial. It started in earnest when Campbell asked for a court order excusing the defense witnesses from the courtroom until such time as they were needed to give testimony. Tripp strenuously objected to what he deemed to be prosecutorial misconduct.

Anger turned to rage and then the insults started. Campbell called Tripp a liar. "Mr. Tripp retorted by alleging in an emphatic manner," the *Press and Dakotaian* reported, "that District Attorney Campbell was a liar." Tripp accused Campbell of persecuting rather than prosecuting, causing matters to heat up even more. Finally, Judge Shannon, his patience at an end, was forced to intervene as the opposing attorneys were about to stop yelling and start fighting. Shannon "called upon the spectators to take note of the scene," scolded both lawyers, and threatened them with contempt of court.[14] All of that transpired with the jury absent from the courtroom.

Despite Shannon's admonition, the two lawyers continued their war of words. Suddenly the marshal appeared ushering the jury into the courtroom. Seeing this, Shannon shouted, "Take them out! Take them out!" The bewildered marshal "beat a hasty retreat." Then Campbell launched a ten-minute harangue against Tripp, dredging up years of bad blood between the two lawyers. Tripp's response lasted several minutes and finally trailed off into what seemed to be feelings of regret.[15] After both men had exhausted their grievances and order was restored, the prosecution rested its case.

Tripp's time had now arrived. The defense attorney's strategy was to prove that Rauck was the aggressor and, as such, Knowlton acted in self-defense by standing his ground. This tactic worked well when shootings occurred on the frontier far from law enforcement, when a man could claim his life was in danger and thereby justify the shooting of another man. Self-defense on the frontier was something that every frontiersman could understand and appreciate.

Tripp's choice for his first witness, however, was not a good choice. Charles Dilger fell asleep in the witness chair while counsel and the judge were discussing a point of contention. Sensing this mistake, Tripp woke up Dilger and asked an eager Mike O'Neill, Knowlton's partner in the three-card monte con game, to take his place. O'Neill had credibility problems, however, for he was under an indictment for accessory to murder. Still, he provided vivid testimony about the shooting, with emphasis on hard threats made by Rauck to Knowlton, causing the latter to fear for his life. According to O'Neill, Knowlton was upset after the shooting and blamed others for it: "I have killed him. I am sorry I had to do it."[16]

The next day Tripp called Dilger back to the stand. This time he was wide awake and delivered stinging testimony. Dilger recalled hearing David Rauck say that he would make Knowlton return the $20 and watch to McKinnis, and if he refused he would "shoot the dammed guts out of him." Dilger stood his ground on cross-examination, thus helping Knowlton's defense and introducing an element of doubt for the jury to ponder.[17]

Another key defense witness was Joseph E. Budd, who confirmed that Rauck made threatening remarks to Knowlton, who in turn acted fearfully and nervously. The surprise came on cross-examination when Budd was forced to admit that he was under indictment for killing a man in the Black Hills and that he would, himself, be "Exhibit A" at a murder trial in the near future.[18]

A few more witnesses came forth with somewhat repetitious testimony for the defense until, finally, after a long trial, the case was turned over to the jury. After about three hours of deliberation, the jury announced that it had reached a verdict. It was now Saturday night, December 24, 1881, and many people in Yankton were settling into their Christmas Eve ritual. And yet the courtroom was packed, all eager to hear what the jury had decided.

At about 7:30 p.m., the foreman of the jury said, "We find the defendant guilty of manslaughter." The announcement produced a brief period of "painful silence" in the courtroom. This was followed by sobbing and moaning from Mrs. Knowlton, who "leaned over the arm of her chair and gave way to the agony of her grief." The verdict and his wife's reaction were too much for the high-strung Knowlton, and he rose from his chair and took a couple of steps toward Judge Shannon. Pointing his fingers at the judge, as reported in the *Press and Dakotaian*, the newly convicted felon shouted "in tones of the wildest rage: And you are to blame for it, you bastard s--- o--- b---."

Hearing the outburst from her husband, Mrs. Knowlton "flung her arms around her husband's neck" in an effort to calm him down. Then, sensing the judge was in danger, three deputy marshals rushed forward to take Knowlton under their control. They attempted to pin his arms back, but Knowlton, a muscular man, resisted and a fierce struggle ensued. Before it was over, the court railing was smashed, chairs were overturned, one deputy had a black eye and skinned nose, having come into contact with Knowlton's fist, and "five persons came down upon the floor all in a heap."

While the deputies struggled with Knowlton and his wife, "the wildest excitement" prevailed throughout the courtroom, as the *Press and Dakotaian* recounts: "A portion of the audience rushed toward the scene of the encounter, while others had pressing business downtown. A woman fainted and Judge Shannon ran out the back door to get some water." Someone thought that Governor Ordway and his secretary were seen leaving the courtroom during the melee. A spectator, Charley Cameron, thought that Knowlton was strangling his wife while "addressing offensive language to her." That prompted Cameron to yell for someone to shoot Knowlton.

After several minutes of shocking violence and absolute chaos, Knowlton was subdued and order was restored. Knowlton was shackled and sat down in his chair while Judge Shannon completed the work of the day. He addressed the jury: "So say all of you?" To which each member replied, "Yes." After Shannon discharged the jury, Knowlton said to the judge, "and so are you," along with some profane remark that did not make the paper. Tripp made a motion for a new trial, after which Shannon, who displayed unusual patience, declared that the court was adjourned and set the sentencing for December 27, 1881. Knowlton was taken to jail and chained to the floor under heavy guard. His pitiful wife was taken to her hotel, where her cries and wails of sadness and disbelief were heard up and down the block.

This had been a Christmas Eve that would long be remembered in Yankton. While the city was accustomed to colorful and lively trials, the Knowlton trial provided the "most remarkable scene ever witnessed in a Dakota court." On the first ballot, the jury had voted seven for conviction and five for acquittal on the murder charge. The jury later found a compromise and voted unanimously in favor of the manslaughter verdict.[19]

When the time for sentencing arrived, Knowlton was in a less volatile state of mind. There were no further outbursts as Judge Shannon calmly sentenced him to ten years in prison and a $1,000 fine.[20] Knowlton's attorney made it clear that the verdict would be appealed, but a second trial of George Knowlton was not in Peter Shannon's future.

It was during the entertaining Knowlton trial that Judge Shannon received word of his replacement on the Dakota Territory Supreme Court. A few days before Christmas Eve, President Chester Arthur sent the name of Alonzo J. Edgerton of Minnesota to the Senate for approval as the new chief justice for Dakota Territory.

Edgerton had strong connections to Minnesota, going back to the early 1860s. He earned a reputation as an "Indian fighter," having served as a captain of a regiment in the U.S.-Dakota War of 1862. He was present at Mankato, in command of the guard, for the historic execution of thirty-eight Dakota Sioux warriors that took place on December 26, 1862.[21]

The news of Edgerton's appointment was cause for great celebration in the office of the *Press and Dakotaian.* On December 21, 1881, the Yankton daily gleefully ran the headline, "Chief Justice Shannon of Dakota Walks the Plank." The joy soon subsided, however, and Kingsbury and company suggested that the "past should be buried and its bitterness forgotten." While Kingsbury was pleased that Shannon had been sent packing, the editorial wished him "future success to which his abilities entitle him."[22] There was, apparently, no desire to pick the carcass.

The long, bitter fight against Shannon's reappointment, led by the Yankton bar association and other attorneys in the territory, was over, leaving a residue of both disgust and satisfaction. The *Dakota Herald* quickly stepped up to recognize the former justice, whose "nine years upon the bench have added honor and luster to his name."

Although the *Herald* was sincere, its praise of Shannon was also a jab at its Yankton rival, the *Press and Dakotaian,* the daily that strenuously opposed granting the judge another term. To drive home its point, the *Herald* exclaimed, "All might well wish that there were more of such men as Judge Shannon in public station."

The Yankton lawyers were thrilled that Shannon, or "such men" as the former judge, would not be presiding over their trials. But the "masses of people are disappointed," believing that Shannon's presence was still needed on the bench. But Shannon expressed relief that the fight was over. Citing the demands of the court schedule, he doubted that he could withstand the stress and strain "in his present physical condition." He was ready to move on.[23]

The influence of Minnesota Senator William Windom was a major factor in the ousting of Shannon. In March 1881 Windom resigned his Senate seat and accepted a cabinet position with the administration of President James A. Garfield. Edgerton was then appointed to Windom's seat in the Senate until the legislature met and either elected Edgerton to a full term or chose someone else. But President Garfield's assassination on July 2, 1881, brought Vice President Chester A. Arthur to the presidency. This unexpected turn of events meant that Windom was unemployed, since Arthur did not retain him as a member of the cabinet. But Windom was soon back in the U.S. Senate and Edgerton was out of a job—until he was named by Arthur, per Windom's recommendation, to replace Shannon.[24]

This political game of musical chairs as played by Edgerton and Windom raised suspicion to the east of Dakota Territory. It seems that a disgruntled Minnesota politician questioned the motives of the two men. So in an effort to explain the process and wash away the stain from the reputations of Edgerton and Windom, a Washington, D.C., correspondent reported that it was "several months after [Edgerton's] resignation [from the Senate] before the Dakota judgeship was offered to him, and when the offer was made it was not the result of any movement initiated by Senator Windom, but by the earnest and heartfelt efforts of prominent men of Dakota."[25]

The *Press and Dakotaian* reprinted the article to shore up support for its contention that Edgerton was a selfless and honorable man, worthy of the office of chief justice of the Dakota Supreme Court. An Ohio newspaper, however, smelled a rat and suggested that Edgerton got the job and Shannon got the boot because "Senator Windom and Delegate [R. F.] Pettigrew paid off old debts."[26]

In his waning days as a federal judge, following the verdict in the Knowlton case, Shannon was treated to a "cane presentation" by the U.S. petit jury. C. B. Valentine, from Turner County, spoke at the presentation: "The jurors in attendance upon this court desire me to express their thanks to you for your uniform kindness you have shown them . . . in the trial [Knowlton] just closed." When he was finished with his remarks, Valentine presented Shannon with a gold-headed cane, "a strong and beautiful staff" intended as a symbol of the strength of "your private and official character."

Shannon was moved by the kindness shown to him by his supporters in Turner County, which abuts Yankton County to the northeast. He rose and spoke to the group, thanking them for the noble gift that would remind him of his years on the bench. In a speech that received hearty applause, Shannon said his authority as a judge came from the people and that it was his privilege to work hard for the betterment of society and the pursuit of justice. In saying farewell to the honor of serving as chief justice, Shannon offered words of welcome to his successor, "hoping and believing that in his hands [the judgeship] will be fittingly exercised."[27] The *Press and Dakotaian* even expressed a kind word, observing that the cane, which it valued at $43, was, indeed, a handsome and generous gift.

Outwardly, Shannon appeared to accept the turn of events like the professional he was, avoiding complaint or venting his frustration. He had fought hard but he lost. When Shannon took the bench for the last time, it was simply to greet the new chief justice. After doing so, Shannon stepped down without a parting word, and Governor Ordway immediately swore in Alonzo J. Edgerton, who was equally silent. The exchange of power had been quiet and respectful, and now Peter C. Shannon could turn his attention to new opportunities.

A most unusual situation arose rather suddenly, coming from, of all people, Oliver Shannon. On January 3, 1882, just as the next murder trial was about to start, Oliver Shannon asked the court to admit the former chief justice to the bar of the Yankton district. Oliver wanted Peter to serve as his co-counsel in the trial of Brave Bear, a Sioux warrior, for a murder that occurred on the Plains in 1879. In no mood to jump back into the legal arena once removed from it, Peter Shannon declined, preferring instead to "make haste slowly."[28]

Peter Shannon and his family, however, were not planning to leave Dakota Territory. The *Herald* held out hope that Dakota would find a position for the former judge because he was too valuable a public servant to be ignored. Many citizens agreed with the *Herald,* believing that a man with his talents would serve the territory well. Even Shannon's enemy, the *Press and Dakotaian*, felt constrained to admit that he "is positively not the wickedest man in Dakota."[29]

CHAPTER 22

JUDGE SHANNON'S SHAME: THE EDMUNDS COMMISSION

*Whereas it is the policy of the Government of the United
States to provide for said Indians a permanent home where
they may live after the manner of white men.*

Proposed Agreement with the Sioux
1882–83

In the summer of 1882 George Knowlton was retried by Judge Alonzo J. Edgerton and acquitted based on self-defense. The *Press and Dakotaian* liked the verdict and used it to take another jab at Judge Shannon, informing its readers that the acquittal turned on testimony that Shannon had excluded during the first trial.[1] Knowlton and his wife immediately left Dakota to thoughts of good riddance from citizens who were tired of his bombastic and arrogant attitude. Doubtless, many people believed he was a killer who got away with murder.

Although it may have pained the former judge to see Knowlton go free, Shannon could take comfort in an interesting diversion. Some months after he stepped down from the bench, he was selected to be a member of a three-man commission whose task it would be to engage the Sioux Indians and convince them to agree to a treaty opening up the Great Sioux Reservation. The federal government's goal was to reduce the size of the reservation and force the tribes to live on smaller parcels of land as farmers.

The commission was authorized by way of an amendment to the Sundry Civil Act of August 7, 1882.[2] The amendment was supported in

337

Congress by R. F. Pettigrew, Dakota Territory's delegate to the national legislature. Pettigrew was considered an authority on Indians, since he had spent many years on the frontier, at times associating with the tribes, collecting artifacts, and learning about their culture.

On March 4, 1882, it was announced that Pettigrew had introduced a bill in Congress "empowering a commission to negotiate with the Sioux Indians." Although Pettigrew's bill failed, the issue was advanced quickly by way of the appropriation measure. In short order $10,000 was appropriated by Congress to pay the expenses of the commission, and a grand plan began to unfold. Rather than start another war with the Indians, the government—under pressure from the public to do something—decided that talking was better than shooting.

The Great Sioux Reservation, as it existed in 1882, consisted of all the land lying west of the Missouri River in present-day South Dakota, except for the Blacks Hills, for a total of 35,000 square miles, worth at least $7 million.[3] Throughout the 1860s and 1870s, when there were still thousands of acres of good land east of the Missouri for settlement, there was little or no pressure on the federal government to take more land by treaty, except for the gold-rich Black Hills, taken in 1877.

By 1882, however, Dakota found itself in the midst of a booming economy. Between 1878 and 1887 settlers claimed more than 2.4 million acres of land in Dakota.[4] Although land fever caused droves of people to exercise their rights under the Homestead Act and other federal land laws, it was railroads, politicians, and business interests that were applying the most pressure on Uncle Sam to do what he always did in the past: take more Indian land by treaty.

In addition to Peter C. Shannon, James C. Teller, of Ohio, a younger brother to Secretary of Interior Henry Teller, and Newton Edmunds, former governor of Dakota, were chosen for the commission. The trio of distinguished men were appointed effective September 15, 1882, with compensation set for each at $10 per day.[5] James C. Teller got something

Newton Edmunds, Governor of Dakota Territory
and, later, member of the Indian Commission.
Courtesy Sioux Falls Journal, *1908.*

extra out of the deal, however; he was appointed secretary of Dakota
Territory while the commission was doing its work.

Shannon was considered a good choice because of his "intelligence
and natural tact,"[6] but Newton Edmunds emerged as the leader of the
commission. He was a man of considerable experience in dealing with
the Indians and the "Indian problem." He became known as the "Treaty
Maker" for Dakota, and always seemed willing to step into the breach,
whenever an "Indian problem" arose.

About two and one-half years after his arrival in Dakota, the forceful Newton Edmunds was appointed the second governor of Dakota Territory by Abraham Lincoln. Edmunds served only one term as governor, but it was enough time for him to put his personal stamp on Dakota. Although he had political enemies, he was generally well-liked and respected. Early on, Edmunds concluded that it was useless and very costly to make war against the Sioux. It would be better, he insisted, to take a strong position, talk to them, and create treaties. He went to Washington D.C., and met with Lincoln to discuss his ideas. A great talker himself, Lincoln liked the approach and saw to it that Edmunds had enough federal funds to carry out his plans.[7]

Upon returning to Dakota, Edmunds went to work in earnest, believing, absolutely, in his ability to impose his will on the less sophisticated Indians. His determined manner made him a natural for dealing with the Sioux, and he negotiated treaties in 1865-1866, following extensive and bloody military campaigns in Dakota. The Indians listened to him while he pretended to listen to them.

The Laramie Treaty of 1868, which Edmunds did not negotiate, created the Great Sioux Reservation, which indicated that the parties intended that the huge reservation, including the Black Hills, would be permanent. Under its terms, unauthorized white citizens were forbidden to enter any part of the reservation. But since most of the land included in the treaty was believed to be a part of the "Great American Desert," and therefore essentially worthless, most Americans accepted the restrictions. But the treaty—created at Fort Laramie in far western Dakota Territory—contained a sleeper clause, destined to create problems once people were made aware that the land was not part of a desert. The clause stated that the approval of three-fourths of the male Indian population would be necessary to make any changes to the existing treaty or to establish new treaties.[8]

Between 1868 and 1882, there was no pressing need for a new treaty. The federal government had funneled large amounts of money into the Indian agencies—cash that filtered into the hands of Dakota farmers and businessmen. But with the railroads came an upsurge in the number of settlers moving into eastern Dakota, and with other markets to explore, the arrangement lost its luster. By 1882 the pressure was on and the "troublesome" Treaty of 1868 would be the focus of this commission.

Laboring toward a new treaty, Edmunds and the other commissioners were in effect advancing the federal government's policy of assimilation, adopted in the early 1860s. To assimilate meant to make Native Americans live like white men—that is to say, assimilate and isolate. It was never the intent of the government, or religious leaders, to force the natives and non-natives to actually live side by side, as friends and neighbors. Assimilation was a nice word for an ugly outcome; for all practical purposes, assimilation was another word for cultural destruction.

When Ulysses Grant became president in 1868, he initiated his own phase of the assimilation process, called the "Peace Policy,"[9] which meant, of course, peace on the white man's terms, involving a Bible and a gun. Still, Grant was sincere in his thinking and intent. He conceded that Indians were human beings, although inferior, but that they needed Christian guidance. With that in mind, he turned the management of Indian affairs over to religious organizations.

Like the president, scores of well-meaning people actually believed that the assimilation process would work if only pressed hard enough, and Grant was counting on missionaries to apply the pressure. But it was naïve to think that such fundamental change could happen quickly. What leaders on both sides learned was that assimilation, or the destruction of the Plains Indian culture, would be incremental.

The goal of Grant's Peace Policy was to clear "the Western lands for white settlement" and to usher the Indians into the circle of civilization.[10] Supported in part by reformers and religious leaders, particularly the Protestants, the policy met with stubborn opposition and neglect in Congress, which refused to appropriate money to implement it. House and Senate members were not opposed to the idea of peace, or the conversion of Indians to Euroamerican culture; rather, they did not wish to spend money to do it, even to protect white people. Some members of Congress believed that, if settlers were willing to undertake the risks associated with life on the frontier, they should also accept the consequences of their decision.

Despite congressional foot-dragging, Grant's Peace Policy had widespread public support. Thoughtful as well as selfish white men concluded that there were no alternatives. Plains Indians could not continue to live as did their ancestors. By 1880 the bison were all but extinct in Dakota Territory and, with other game scarce, circumstances would force the issue, some reasoned.

In the popular mind, Indians and buffalo were connected. There was a saying among frontiersmen that "where there's buffalo, there's Indians." For this reason the general consensus was that America would be better off without buffalo, as stated in the *Daily Press and Dakotaian*: "whatever the agency of extermination the result can be but beneficial to advancing civilization, for so long as the buffalo roam the plains, so long will the red man insist upon a nomadic life."[11] Without the bison, Indians would be faced with only two choices: assimilation or extinction.

Military leaders vacillated between supporting assimilation and advocating for outright extermination of tribal peoples. General W. T. Sherman, a Civil War hero and Grant's friend, was not opposed to fighting Indians, but he believed that peace was a more practical way of dealing with them, so long as it was strengthened by the thoughtful placement of military installations on the Great Plains.

Other military men thought the hope for peace was mere sentiment. For example, George A. Custer, also a Civil War figure, was frequently and blatantly outspoken in his low opinion of Indian rights. In an interview conducted in Ohio, just a few months before he was killed in the Little Bighorn massacre, Custer cursed the "tomfoolery of the Quakers and sentimentalists" in the East who had long stood in the way of any progress toward subduing the Indians. For Custer, the solution was clear, for "you can't civilize an Indian any more than you can teach a rooster to lay goose eggs."[12]

Although few urban Americans were as wildly outspoken in their hatred of Indians, many of those who lived on the frontier and those who sought to make a home there shared Custer's perspective. Among the latter were the three men appointed and tasked with breaking up the Great Sioux Reservation. They went about their work in confidence, buoyed by their belief in the righteousness of their cause. When one believes that a race of people is condemned because of its inherent inferiority, as in the precepts of Social Darwinism and Manifest Destiny, both current at the time, it is easy to deny them basic humanity. An Indian, according to the novelist and editor of the influential *Atlantic Monthly,* William Dean Howells, was a "hideous demon," a creature to be abhorred and driven into extinction.[13] Edmunds, Shannon, and Teller thought their work would avoid such extremes.

The commissioner of Indian affairs in Washington instructed the commission to visit the various tribes and ask whether they were interested in selling any of their Dakota Territory land.[14] But Newton Edmunds was not accustomed to ask for anything. The "Edmunds Commission," as it was called, ignored its instructions and met secretly in Yankton on October 2, 1882.[15] The result was a proposed treaty: a short but deceptive document, consisting of eight articles, designed to deceive the Indians.[16] This document sought to conceal the fact that the tribes were actually giving up land. The commission had its sights set on a region of about 16,000 square miles containing approximately 10,240,000 acres, between the Big Cheyenne River on the north and the White River on the south.[17] The rest of the reservation would remain tribal land, but it would be divided into separate entities, with great distances between the areas so as to isolate the tribes.

Newton Edmunds entered upon his duties brimming with self-confidence, backed by his understanding of Indian culture. More important, perhaps, he felt he knew which points to make in order to convince them of his way of thinking. The egotistical Edmunds was planning "a cracker and molasses treaty," meaning he would obtain their consent by plying selected leaders with gifts and feasts. Then, when he thought he had them in the palm of his hand, he would close the deal.[18]

Under the Edmunds treaty, the Indians would receive no cash in exchange for the land they were asked to surrender. Instead, as provided in article 4 of the proposed treaty, they would be offered cattle: 1,000 bulls and 25,000 cows. The animals were to be distributed proportionately, among the tribes, but the Indians were not permitted to slaughter an animal for food without first getting the consent of the department of the interior. The total value of the livestock was about $1 million. Therefore, if successful in making the treaty, the government would be getting an enormous amount of land on the cheap—about $.08 per acre.[19] Edmunds knew that the Indians would prefer cattle, since money meant very little to them.[20]

Another part of the plan, article 3, would provide parcels of land in the amount of 320 acres to heads of families to own and farm. For every minor child under the age of eighteen, the head of the family received an additional 80 acres. This was not a strong selling point, however, for individual land ownership was an alien concept to Plains Indians. Native Americans believed that ancestral land was held by the tribe for all members. No individual could claim a portion of the land for himself.

The government wanted to change this cultural precept and authorized money to cover expenses incurred by the commission, but provided no funds to pay for feasts or trinkets. To assist in facilitating their work, the commissioners requested a military escort and an interpreter. The interpreter they had in mind was the Episcopal missionary Rev. Samuel D. Hinman, who had lived among the Sioux and understood the Lakota language.[21] Hinman had also been an interpreter for the 1868 Treaty.

On October 16, 1882, with the proposed treaty drafted to their satisfaction, the commission left Yankton to meet with the tribes. No one in the public or press knew what was in the proposed treaty, and the commissioners wanted to keep it that way.[22] The three commissioners were confident in their abilities but faced one singular concern: Dakota

Territory was about to hang an Indian. The condemned man was Brave Bear, a son-in-law of Sitting Bull. Brave Bear was called a "shrewd and intelligent Indian, one of the incorrigibles," who had recently been convicted of murdering a white man in 1879.[23] The commissioners insisted that the timing was bad, for, in addition to Sitting Bull, they would have to deal with the condemned man's father and three brothers at the Standing Rock Agency. For these reasons they made a strong attempt to get the execution postponed.

President Arthur, however, would not grant an extension and Brave Bear was hanged in Yankton on November 15, 1882.[24] The commissioners did not wait for the execution. In addition to Hinman, traveling with the commissioners were Episcopal Bishop William H. Hare and Catholic Bishop Martin Marty. Both were well-known and well-respected in Dakota, and both were expected to speak on behalf of the treaty. Hare would prove to be uncooperative, but Marty was willing to argue in favor of the treaty. If more persuasion was needed, the commissioners hired "half-breeds" to pitch in.

The Swiss-born Benedictine Martin Marty came to Dakota in 1876 from the St. Meinrad Monastery in Indiana. He left a comfortable monastery life to travel as a missionary on the Plains. For three years he traveled extensively, visiting the Indian agencies and returning regularly to Indiana. On February 1, 1880, after the diocese of Dakota was established, he was ordained the first Catholic Bishop of Dakota Territory, with headquarters at Yankton. He maintained a busy travel schedule and over time acquired a good reputation among the Plains Indians, while devoting time and effort to promoting Catholicism in Dakota.

The commissioners and their entourage traveled about the territory, stopping at all the agencies, delivering glowing speeches about the glories of the new treaty and how much the Indians would benefit from it. The chiefs were told they would get separate reservations for their tribes, but they were not informed that the new agencies would be created on land they already owned.

The response varied greatly among the tribes. At Pine Ridge, Newton Edmunds was recognized by an Indian who exclaimed, "There is the man that got the Black Hills from us for nothing; get out of here!" Edmunds showed no fear or concern but merely turned the argument against the Indians and diffused the situation. He insisted that it had cost the government more money to feed and clothe the Indians as a result of the Laramie Treaty than all the gold "the white man has taken from the Black Hills."[25]

When cajoling failed, the commissioners tried coercion, threatening leaders who did not agree to the treaty to remove entire tribes far from their ancestral lands to Indian Territory.[26] The old song and dance routine had worked before, and the commission, with so much at stake, was prepared to use it or any other tactic that was likely to produce the desired result.

The work of the commissioners drew praise from the Yankton press. Although the trio had yet to meet with the upriver tribes, their apparent success at Pine Ridge and Rosebud was worthy of printed applause, for they had dealt successfully with the "worst bands." Overall, the *Press and Dakotaian* concluded, "they have succeeded so far almost beyond their expectations."[27]

Newspapers outside of Dakota were watching too, and while stopping in Sioux City to rest, Shannon was asked about the progress of the commission by a reporter for the *Sioux City Daily Journal*. Shannon's response was positive in all respects except one: the commission had not received a cent from the federal government, so each member had to pay his own expenses, trusting that they would eventually be compensated.[28]

After the Sioux City interview, the commission met in St. Paul on November 23, en route to the Standing Rock Agency by way of Bismarck. In response to questions by a reporter from the *St. Paul Pioneer Press*, Shannon talked freely and in detail about the commission's recent trip to the Pine Ridge Agency. He avoided any mention of disagreement, suspicion, or angry confrontations. Rather, the judge recalled that the treaty travelers were ushered into Pine Ridge by a mounted troop of warriors in blue uniforms, carrying the American flag. He noted that the commissioners were greeted warmly, and with dignity, by representatives of the Oglala tribe, including the principal chief, Red Cloud. The great warrior was "a fine specimen of Indian manhood and is as dignified in his deportment as a senator." They spent eight or nine days with the Oglala people, discussing "every point that could be suggested by the Government or the Indians," the newspaper reported.

Shannon declared that the Indians were eager to receive separate reservations and the promised cattle and schools. He expressed some doubt as to the willingness of the Indians to adapt to agriculture, but he was certain that they "are natural herdsmen" and would take to cattle raising "like ducks to water." He was also very pleased to inform the public that the leading men of the tribes were strongly opposed to "the admission of whiskey into the reservation."

Shannon also discussed with the *St. Paul Pioneer Press* reporter their visit to the Rosebud Agency, where he was impressed with the Brulé Sioux, noting their progress toward civilization and their eagerness for the proposed treaty. Shannon was more than pleased with the way the process had gone to date, but he cautioned that, though they had met in council with the majority of the western Sioux, they still had to meet with the more northern tribes and was, therefore, not willing to "form any conclusions as to what will be done."[29]

The treaty makers took a break for the Christmas holidays while, on December 19, 1882, Congress met amid "ugly rumors concerning the operations of the Sioux land commission."[30] No member of Congress seemed eager to deal with the matter, and the Arthur administration was mum as well. Then a Senate resolution came forth, demanding all the paperwork on the treaty. This caused a mild panic among the treaty makers, and Secretary Henry Teller wired Edmunds to get back to work and get the deal done. Finally, after more subterfuge and frantic coercion, the treaty was sent to Washington, where Teller hurriedly approved it, as did President Arthur, on February 3, 1883.[31]

But that was not the end of it. The Treaty of 1868 required that three-fourths of the Sioux male population approve and sign a new treaty. Edmunds chose to ignore the requirement, reminding his superiors in Washington that, when the Laramie Treaty was signed, no one bothered to follow the law. That an former territorial supreme court justice, known for strict adherence to the rule of law, could accept a precedent of violation is inexcusable. Peter Shannon must have known this was wrong.

The seriously flawed and incomplete treaty was, nevertheless, presented to the Senate for examination and approval, but the senators seemed to be in no hurry to take it up. Meanwhile, in Dakota the commission continued to hammer away at the recalcitrant Lower Brulés and the Crow Creek Indians, who stubbornly refused to agree to the treaty. The inability of the commissioners to convince the Lower Brulés to give in caused the Dakota press to wax pessimistic. The *Chamberlain Register* groaned that the Brulés "still hang off about the treaty." Edmunds and Shannon, however, were not willing to give in, and the latter summed up his frustration in a speech to the Lower Brulés:

> My friends and brothers, this may be the last time I will talk
> to you, and I want you to remember that you have no home,
> no boundaries marked, no land you can call your own, it is
> all in common. We have offered to give you land, mark off
> its boundaries and set iron stakes thereto. We have offered to
> give you cattle and implements to farm with, and you would
> not do it. I want you to remember that all your brothers of the
> other tribes have done it. I want you to remember when you
> see the other tribes with their lands, their cattle, and you have
> none, that we offered them to you and you would not accept.[32]

A few days later, in visiting with a *Register* reporter about the Brulés, Shannon sounded more optimistic. He had attended a church service at the Brulé Agency and was impressed with the decorum and the sermon given by an Indian missionary, Rev. Luke Walker. He insisted that the "singing was exceptionally good" and that the congregation was as "attentive as one will ever see in any white people's church."[33]

Although Shannon saw signs of religious progress, the Brulés were unrelenting in their opposition to the treaty. They held to their beliefs with great tenacity amid threats that their reservations would be closed down and their people hauled off to Indian Territory. The Lower Brulés even considered sending a delegation to Washington to appeal directly to the "Great Father." Concerned Indians made plans to sell hides in order to raise enough money to travel to Washington. Hearing of this, Shannon and Hinman both contacted Secretary Teller to request that he issue a ban on the sale of hides.[34]

At Crow Creek the commissioners fared better. White settlers had gathered at the reservation border, ready to rush in and stake out land claims. Some settlers actually crossed the line and forcefully occupied the Indians' cabins and farms. Before further violence could erupt, the Crow Creek Indians ceased their opposition and "approved" the treaty. At this point the commission deemed its work was finished.[35]

The Crow Creek incident represented the high (rather, low) mark of intimidation by the federal government and its citizens, and it convinced some members of the other tribes to sign. The Lower Brulés, however, held out to the end, refusing to give their consent—a gesture that consisted of a touch of the pen followed by the interpreter writing each "signer's" name in English. While many Americans marveled at the telephone and its impact on the technological frontier, the Edmunds Commission engaged in taking even more land from the Sioux on the geographical frontier.

But the treaty was destined to fail due to a shortage of signatures. In fact, the number of signatures was, as Standing Rock Agent James McLaughlin observed, "absurdly small in proportion to the number of Indians concerned."[36] A total of only 384 signatures had been collected.[37] Although that was sufficient for the commissioners, as time passed, the treaty, approved by Secretary Teller and President Arthur, languished in the

Senate. Meanwhile, the voices of protest from among Indian rights groups slammed Edmunds' rationale for collecting so few signatures. Finally, the Senate decreed that the proposed treaty be sent back to Dakota Territory.

Undaunted, the interior department reappointed Edmunds, Teller, and Shannon to the commission and ordered them to return to Indian country and gather the required number of signatures. Edmunds was willing to try again since he was determined to leave behind a historical legacy. Instead of going themselves, however, the commission sent out the indomitable Rev. Hinman to twist more arms. In April 1883 Hinman went at it with a passion, but at this point, the Indians were so disillusioned that his efforts proved futile. Throughout the spring and summer of 1883, he labored intensely on behalf of the treaty, meeting resistance everywhere. Chief Red Cloud led the resistance, insisting that his people refuse to sign. The execution of Brave Bear the previous year was a factor, too, especially at Standing Rock.

A desperate Hinman padded the list with names of boys under the age of eighteen, including one boy who was only three years old.[38] Historian George W. Kingsbury, a contemporary of Edmunds and his commissioners, made this observation on the fate of the treaty: "it was well understood that the Indians had now assumed a negative position toward the Edmunds agreement."[39]

People in Yankton had adopted the same opinion. Under the headline "Not Very Encouraging," the *Press and Dakotaian* blamed "Pale Faces of the East" for ruining a treaty that had started out with so much promise. The Yankton newspaper also blamed a Senate committee, consisting of Senators Henry L. Dawes, John Logan, and James D. Cameron, for intruding on the work of the Edmunds Commission. The Senate trio was criticized for turning the Indians against the treaty.[40]

Newspapers also blamed Episcopal Bishop Hare. In the article "Hare's Hair," the *Press and Dakotaian* announced that in Deadwood—where the treaty was seen as a matter of economic life or death—people were "after the Scalp Lock of the Bishop of Niobrara." In tones of respect and levity, the paper urged the bishop to withdraw his objections to the treaty and support it for the greater good. Hare and his "missionary bodies" were warned that resistance would "stop the westward march of civilization and entail upon us disappointment and disaster."[41]

For his part Newton Edmunds was not ready to give up. He, Shannon, and Hinman, along with a delegation of other prominent Dakotans, traveled to Omaha to meet with the Senate committee.[42] The treaty advocates urged the senators to accept the treaty, even though it lacked the required signatures. The senators were reminded that the Senate had accepted the Laramie Treaty "as is," without fussing over the number of signatures. The *Dakota Herald* praised Shannon for giving "the senators some pretty direct hints as to the futility of congressional interference and the harm caused thereby." Showing incredibly condescending gall, the commissioners and their political allies, eager to ignore the law, essentially scolded the senators and blamed congressional meddling and delay for the lack of a treaty.[43] For all practical purposes, the game was up and the travesty that tried to be a treaty could not be resuscitated.

The failure of the treaty was bitter medicine for white Dakotans. The principal target of public wrath was Bishop Hare, whose stubborn opposition to the treaty was seen as the main cause of its defeat. He was called an obstructionist and was "condemned by the people" for taking a position outside the mainstream. A group of Yankton Episcopalians met and adopted a resolution denouncing their bishop, while praising the "eminent services" of the commissioners and Rev. Hinman.[44]

In the final analysis, Edmunds and his colleagues had overplayed their hand and lost. It was not just the signature issue that undermined the work of Edmunds, Teller, and Shannon. The year before the commission was created, a powerful reform organization called the Indian Rights Association (IRA) had been formed in Philadelphia. At its head was Herbert Welsh, whose uncle, William Welsh, had worked on Grant's Peace Policy. Using the Edmunds treaty as an opportunity to assert itself, the IRA began making inquiries into the commission's methods.[45] Such a bold effort by an upstart group of eastern "sentimentalists," as they were called, was a shock to western sensibilities.

Criticism arose from unlikely sources. James McLaughlin of the Standing Rock Indian Agency remarked, "The whole thing was a misapprehension of the meaning of the terms of the treaty with the Sioux made in 1868."[46] He was referring to the requirement that three-fourths of the adult male Indians approve the treaty. Bishop Hare, himself, also leveled criticism at the methods of the commission and his colleague, Rev. Hinman, who emerged as a "disgraced and dishonored man."[47] Hare had suspended Hinman from his ministerial duties in 1878 on grounds of immorality. Hinman sued Hare in court, but lost the case.

In his history of Dakota Territory, published in 1915, George W. Kingsbury concluded that "certain parties" got to the Indians and convinced them not to approve the treaty unless they were "paid in cash." He believed that, had the Indians been offered cash in one-half the amount "to be expended for their benefit," they would have agreed to the land cession.[48]

But it was the lack of the required signatures and scrutiny from reform groups that proved to be fatal for the Edmunds Commission. The Senate rejected the treaty, and a Senate committee, headed by Senator Henry L. Dawes, conducted an investigation into the commission and its tactics. Testimony revealed the deceptive nature of the three commissioners, who "tried to conceal the fact that the document the leaders signed called for the cession of land." Acting through their interpreters, the commissioners told the Indian people that the one big reservation would be carved up into smaller ones. They said nothing about the "Great Father" taking the lion's share of the land.[49]

Dawes personally spoke at "every counsel" and encouraged the Indians to "talk freely." They did speak and were especially critical of Hinman. Red Cloud, for one, told the committee that "[Hinman] had "lied outrageously." Another man, Little No Heart, reminded the committee that, when the Indians gave up the Black Hills, they were promised a cow, but did not receive it. He went on to say that the Edmunds Commission "again offered the same old government cow . . . for more of their land." The Indians did, however, praise the efforts of Dawes "as the first white man who didn't want to get something from them besides words." Dawes, the Indians said, "had cleared the waters and the fish were able to see." But it was the Indians who made sure Dawes saw the light.[50] The Dawes committee offered the following observation regarding the treaty:

> It is claimed by the commission that because we took the Black Hills from these Indians in violation of the 12th article of this treaty [1868] in 1876, we have a right to violate it again and take this land also….[But] any previous violation of it is a disgrace to be shunned not a precedent to be followed.[51]

The National Indian Defence [sic] Association joined in the condemnation of the commissioners and "their pliant tools," including Rev. Hinman. Citing the 400-page Dawes report, the association condemned the treaty makers who "deceived the Indians in the most shameful manner," obtaining signatures to the treaty "by means of falsehood, treachery and threats."[52]

While no formal charges were made against the commissioners, Peter Shannon's post-supreme court career was off to a disgraceful start. The man renowned in Dakota and the nation for his integrity and ability as a trial judge and supreme court justice had fallen flat on his face. While he and his fellow commissioners were commended by many Dakota citizens for having made an effort to reach an agreement with the Sioux, historians have judged them harshly, exposing and condemning their gross dishonesty.

Shannon's legacy suffered as a result of his work on the 1882 Edmunds Commission, and it has recently been further diminished. On November 5, 2014, the residents of Shannon County, South Dakota, predominantly Native American, voted overwhelmingly in favor of changing the name of their county to "Oglala Lakota County." As a result of the referendum, state law mandates that the governor and the legislature complete the process and honor the will of the people. The name change was approved by the South Dakota Legislature in March 2015. Former Shannon County, home of the Pine Ridge Indian Reservation, is regularly ranked as having the lowest per capita income in the United States.

CHAPTER 23

THE VOICE OF WISDOM

It is the wish of the wide circle of the judge's friends and
associates, lay and professional, that he may
live long and prosper.

Pittsburgh Dispatch
Reprinted in the *Sioux Falls Press*
May 13, 1885

Bruised by his association with the discredited Edmunds Commission, Peter Shannon sought new challenges. He traveled to Bozeman, Montana, in June 1883 to investigate the official conduct and character of another judge whose career on the bench was under fire. The target of federal scrutiny was Everton J. Conger, an associate justice on the Montana Territory Supreme Court. Shannon's specific task was to investigate charges of "drunkenness and partiality in [Conger's] rulings."[1]

Judge Conger, a Civil War veteran, had been suspended on March 20, 1883, by President Chester Arthur.[2] The beleaguered judge was charged with "incompetence, neglect of duty, gambling, drunkenness and 'keeping companionship of low, vile, people.'"[3] Rather than replace Conger, however, the Department of Justice decided to send Shannon to Montana to interview Conger and submit an official report.

Conger, however, had some leverage to employ in his defense. After the assassination of President Abraham Lincoln, he was a member of the party of Union soldiers and detectives that pursued and killed the assassin,

John Wilkes Booth. When news of Booth's death exploded in the press, Conger became an instant celebrity and was awarded $15,000, his share of the reward money.

Shannon's report was thorough and somewhat sympathetic toward Conger, who insisted that his bad behavior was in the past and that his life was now one of "personal propriety and judicial usefulness." His claims apparently influenced the president to withdraw the suspension and reinstate the judge, despite the opinion of the U.S. attorney general that Conger be removed as "unfitted to administer public justice." Arthur cited "extenuating circumstances," and Conger was allowed to serve out his term of office, which expired on January 19, 1884, the day after he was reinstated. It was a gesture of sympathy by Arthur, and the decent thing to do.[4]

While Shannon was involved in the Conger investigation, the statehood movement was making its way through Dakota Territory. Admission to the Union promised full and fair representation in Congress. An otherwise logical and natural development, statehood inspired fierce arguments and political infighting on a level never before experienced in Dakota.

Although Shannon sought balance in his approach to territorial politics, even he could not avoid making his views known publicly. This was not a time for knowledgeable Dakota citizens to observe from afar. The statehood movement took on a special urgency because of another heated political issue. Governor Nehemiah Ordway had launched his "capital removal scheme."

Capital removal was not a new or even novel idea. The territory was in the midst of an economic and immigration boom. Southern Dakota had the greater population but many people were moving into northern Dakota, as well. The new cities and towns throughout the territory were gaining some regional prominence. New people became new voters, and voters meant political influence. The great distances between far-flung communities to the west and north of the capital city of Yankton were becoming a considerable inconvenience, even with the growth of railroads. The time had come to think about a centralized location for the capital.

Talk began in earnest when a bill was introduced in the territorial House of Representatives creating a capital commission, which would determine the location of the new capital.[5] The bill allowed for the creation of a nine-man commission that would travel around the territory and select a new capital site from among contending locations. It was this part of the bill—seen as an attempt at exercising naked power—that caused the greatest uproar in Dakota from men of all professions, occupations, and political persuasions. Never before in the short history of the territory had independents, Democrats, and Republicans come together so willingly in common cause. The removal bill passed both the House and Council and was quickly signed into law by Governor Ordway.

The scheme, so transparent that anyone could see through it, placed the selection of the new capital squarely in Ordway's hands. He would pick two commissioners, and the remaining seven would be selected by members of the Council, who just happened to vote in favor of capital removal. Everyone knew that they would select only those men whom Ordway could trust to follow his wishes. Ordway's opponents' saw this bill as a set-up.

The removal law required the commission to meet and organize in Yankton, but the commissioners knew full well that Yankton residents were so upset over the prospect of losing the capital by subterfuge that any meeting they might attempt would be subject to vociferous, if not violent, interruption. With this in mind, the commission came up with a plan. They would board a special train in Sioux City, and when it arrived at Yankton, it would slow down but not stop. The commissioners would "officially" meet and thereby comply with the law.

Among those Dakotans voicing their disapproval of the removalists' tactics was Judge Shannon, who expressed "indignation" in "unmeasured terms, denouncing the action of the commission as occult and tricky." Shannon and other like-minded men predicted "a storm of popular indignation" throughout the territory.[6] Shannon's outburst was especially significant because he was among the southern Dakota men who had been friendly to Ordway.

But the Ordway faction was not deterred by protest. The commission "met" on the slow-moving train on April 2, 1883. Then, with the capital "on wheels," the commission shifted into high gear and made short work of reviewing the contending sites, including Mitchell, Huron, Redfield, Frankfort, Pierre, and Ordway in southern Dakota, and Bismarck, Steele, and Odessa in northern Dakota. When the wining and dining were over, the winner was Bismarck, a choice that surprised no one.

The net effect of the triumph of the capital-removal faction was to advance the movement to divide the territory and admit southern Dakota as a state. On September 3, 1883, a Constitutional Convention was held in Sioux Falls. At this bold, historic event, the delegates drafted a constitution for the proposed state of Dakota. Shannon did not attend the convention and thereafter tended to oppose the rush toward division and admission. Though the former judge favored statehood, he preferred a more deliberate approach, which followed the law, step by step.

Shannon believed that Congress would be more likely to admit Dakota as a whole, so he supported the "One Great State" faction. For several weeks in the summer and fall of 1883, Shannon and Hugh J. Campbell, the U.S. attorney for Dakota, were locked in a duel over the matter of Dakota's admission to the Union. Their writings were published in the *Dakota Herald*, and the fiery approach both men took toward defending their respective opinions meant the reading public would be served sufficient doses of political criticism and analysis.

Campbell argued that when a territory reached a point at which it was eligible for statehood, it could, on its own, draft a constitution and establish a government, thereby becoming a state, without the consent of Congress. Shannon attacked Campbell's "states' rights" theory with great emotional and intellectual vigor. He employed his considerable legal skill while citing historic precedent and constitutional authority to show that only Congress was vested with the power to admit new states: "the people of a Territory, of their own volition, cannot resolve themselves into the corporation called a state . . . they are not a state according to the American system, and can never be such until congress, representing the national will, breathes into them the life-giving principle."[7]

The people generally conceded that Shannon, with a firm, reasoned approach, had won the debate. A mature voice of reason was needed just then, and Shannon stepped forth to provide it. It was like another pronouncement from the bench by a man who had ruled and judged many times in the past, and each time, the public usually nodded in agreement. The man who had for years passed judgment on scores of malefactors had, in effect, put himself on trial before the people.

Shannon plunged into the great statehood debate with earnest and grim determination. But aside from winning the debate with Campbell, he came up empty handed. The intellectual exercise that he pursued so relentlessly did not provide the kind of success Shannon was expecting. Although he had some popularity and support, he was for the most part ignored by leaders of the Dakota Republican Party. Shannon experienced a glimmer of optimism when he was mentioned as a possible replacement for the hated Nehemiah G. Ordway, but it faded. When Ordway left Dakota to the cheers of the masses, he was replaced by the suave Civil War veteran and journalist Gilbert A. Pierce, of Illinois.

There were, of course, substantive reasons for Shannon's inability to gain any political traction—among them, a paucity of political connections in southern Dakota. All those bridges were washed away by the raging waters of anti-Ordwayism, a turbulence that swept away not only the hated governor but all those who supported or befriended him. Almost as bad as his support for Ordway was Shannon's fight against the advocates for division and admission. It hurt him immeasurably, for it created the perception that he was against Dakota becoming a state under any and all circumstances.

News of Shannon was scarce in the mid-1880s. With the assistance of his good friend former governor Andrew J. Faulk, he was reportedly writing a history of Dakota Territory that would include, among other matters, details of settlements and Indian tribes.[8] If true, the project was never finished, or if finished, the book was never published.

Shannon seemed to retreat inwardly as time advanced and left him without office or position. He continued to command the respect of thousands of Dakotans who valued his judicial achievements and quietly admired his integrity and intellect, which towered above the average person's. For many, that outweighed his occasional support of Ordway. Could Shannon parley this popularity and appreciation into a return to power? He was never fully tempted to tap that reserve so the record is silent. Had he turned entrepreneur and been successful, the Dakota press would likely have applauded the effort. But taking on business risk was not in Shannon's mental makeup. Nor was neglect, usually sufficient punishment in Dakota. Shannon was quietly preparing to depart Dakota and leave his enemies, along with associated bad memories, behind.

In a farewell editorial in the *Sioux Falls Daily Press,* on May 13, 1885, the newspaper called Shannon "one of the ablest men who have made their homes in this territory," and noted that he had traveled back to his native state of Pennsylvania for the purpose of entering into private law practice. The *Pittsburgh Dispatch* welcomed him home, reporting that he "is as fully keen, vigorous and eloquent as he was eleven years ago when he quitted a large practice here to take his seat at the head of the Dakota bench."[9]

In his native state, Shannon, now sixty-four years of age, could cast off the ugly, political baggage he had accumulated and breathe the fresh air of new opportunity. Bringing home an enviable record of achievement, along with the prospect of living once again with old friends and colleagues, he expected acceptance and reward. He had made a name for himself on the frontier and that in itself was usually enough to make easterners take notice.

Shannon could also take satisfaction in having left the Dakota judiciary, which he had so carefully groomed over the years, on firm footing. The federal court system had grown to six districts, thereby more equitably sharing the legal business of the territory among six judges. Gone were the days and weeks of exhaustive travel that weighed heavily upon judges and court staff.

Yankton, the Missouri River city Shannon left behind, had lost the capital and all the political clout that accompanied such distinction. Still, some wanted more. When the legislature met for the first time in Bismarck in 1885, a group with ties to another town on the rise lobbied for the removal of the federal court from Yankton to Mitchell. Fortunately for Yankton, the proposal never became law.

Although the 1880s were good years for Yankton, the "Mother City" of Dakota would never again achieve prominence. Opportunity seemed to reside in Bismarck, the new capital city. Deadwood, Rapid City, Sioux Falls, Aberdeen, Grand Forks, and Fargo were attracting residents and would, over time, eclipse Yankton in population, political power, and commerce.

The Missouri River town of Pierre was also on the rise. In 1885, when Shannon left Dakota, Pierre was being considered as a possibility for the capital of the state of South Dakota, when the goal of division and admission was realized. But Pierre and Fort Pierre, on the west side of the river, were plagued by lawlessness, attracting the dredges of the frontier, drunkards, gamblers, debauchers, and killers. In other words, it had become what Yankton was in the 1860s and 1870s.

But with the coming of the railroad, and muscular efforts by its citizens, the outlaw element retreated. Then in April of 1885 Pierre suffered a setback to its emerging reputation in the form of a lynching that shocked Dakota and attracted the attention of the press from outside the territory. How could Dakota claim it was on the threshold of statehood when mob violence held sway in the very city that was being heralded as having capital pretensions?

The victim of the lynching, James H. Bell, an attorney and former New Yorker, had been arrested and jailed as a suspect in the brutal murder of Forest G. Small, also an attorney. The killing, with a hatchet, occurred out on the prairie near the town of Blunt, not far from Pierre, in December 1884.

Bell protested his innocence and insisted that he could prove that he did not commit the crime, characterized by the *Press and Dakotaian* as "cold blooded, deliberate and cowardly." But an accomplice, Ferdinand Bennett, said Bell was the killer. It was also known that there were "bad feelings between the alleged murderer and the murdered man."[10] In the dead of night, Bell was taken from the jail by a mob of about fourteen men, all "well known citizens" from the nearby town of Harold, and strung up on a flagpole by the Pierre courthouse.[11]

Angry newspapers condemned the lynch mob and demanded an investigation. Far away in Pennsylvania, Shannon would have undoubtedly concurred, but he knew from experience that an investigation of a lynching in Dakota rarely did anything except stir up some dust. For certain, he recognized the tragic irony of it all: an attorney accused of murder was lynched by a mob from a courthouse flagpole. In the gloom of a terrible miscarriage of justice, Shannon could not be faulted for thinking that it was a good time to be away from Dakota.

On November 26, 1886, an Ebensburg, Pennsylvania, newspaper, the *Cambria Freeman,* revealed that the Shannons were moving to Pittsburgh, citing "the failing health of Mrs. Shannon."[12] About a year and a half earlier, in March 1885, a newspaper had reported that she had undergone surgery that was expected to save her.[13] Then in December 1886 came the report that cancer "was gradually eating her life away," and for that reason, she moved to the town of Allegheny to be near her friends and relatives as death approached. Ann Elena Shannon died at her Fayette Street residence on December 3, 1886, and was buried in the Old Holy Name Cemetery in Ebensburg. Remembered for her "many Christian virtues," she died almost as anonymously as she had lived. Her obituary mentioned only her father, the former Pittsburgh businessman Christian Ihmsen, suggesting that her husband and children were not present at the end.[14] There was no mention of the years she spent in Dakota.

In June 1889 Peter Shannon, almost two-and-a-half years a widower, returned to Dakota as it was about to become two states, in November 1889, where he had wielded the gavel for nearly nine years. He disdained Yankton, where he had dispensed justice, and chose to live in Canton, a smaller town where he had never ceased to be liked by both the people and its newspaper, the *Sioux Valley News.* The *News* was one of the few southern Dakota newspapers that had supported Ordway. The editor of the *News,* N. C. Nash, who despised Yankton, always had a good word for the former Supreme Court Chief Justice.

Shannon had come back in time to join the statehood celebration. The tireless advocates for division and admission had, at long last, won the day. Congress had acted in the manner that Shannon had predicted, and effective February 22, 1889, four states—North and South Dakota, Montana, and Washington—were approved for admission to the Union under an omnibus bill, signed by outgoing President Grover Cleveland with an eagle feather quill. Admission to the Union was signed into law by President Benjamin Harrison on November 2, 1889.

The joys of statehood and the virtues of American citizenship were among the topics of Judge Shannon's Fourth of July oration in Canton, where Independence Day was celebrated with special vigor and happiness that year. Although he seemed to have slipped back into Dakota with little notice, his Independence Day oration was powerful, dramatic, and patriotic in tone and content: "All hail South Dakota!" In rhapsodic fashion, Shannon declared that "on this bright summer's day, fair, young South Dakota" found itself at last accepted by the Union. Moreover, "she will enter the fold through the legitimate gate of the Constitution, without threat or bluster—without ignoble barter, degrading scheme or lawless combination."[15]

Shannon seized on the occasion presented by the speech to level a solid jab at the division and admission faction and its political deal-makers, an opportunity that Shannon undoubtedly found irresistible. The oration earned the praise of the *Sioux Valley News,* but after the applause died down, Shannon seemed to disappear behind the stage curtains. He did not follow up his renewed notoriety with a role in shaping the new state government. He was not a candidate for any office, high or low, although he was invited to speak in support of the Republican ticket. At this point he was Canton's distinguished resident and nothing more.

As a legal purist, a man in love with the law, Shannon may have believed that his record on the bench and his statehood treatise were enough to get the attention and support of the people and the press, but he would be wrong. (In Dakota, the high road was usually the road to nowhere.) Instead, Shannon became something of an oracle figure, a "Voice of Wisdom" sought out when answers to difficult questions were needed. Many times someone would ask, "I wonder what Judge Shannon would say about that?"

Shannon would have witnessed a political landscape that was undergoing substantial if not radical change. The two old parties were beginning to fray along their edges. Restless men were looking for a new path to economic and political progress. The much ballyhooed Dakota Boom was over, and instead of running articles about immigration, new towns, and railroads, newspapers carried stories about such worker and agrarian movements as the Knights of Labor and Farmers' Alliance.

As reported in the *Sioux Falls Argus-Leader* in February 1890, observing that "neither of the political parties know or care" about the actual, doleful condition of the economy, discontented farmers, laborers, and their supporters had created the Independent Party. Concern over the "increase of wealth of the rich and an increase of poverty of the poor" gave rise to a wave of political protest destined to challenge the bastions of wealth and power to an extent unsurpassed by any popular movement in the past.[16]

In his realm of quiet reflection, Shannon remained silent while other, long-time Dakota residents spoke out and began to shape their political careers in the new order. He disdained participation in local politics and was seldom heard from or mentioned in the local paper. Where he might have lived in Canton at first is unknown, but he eventually took rooms at the Harlan House, a popular hotel.

Then in November he was forced out of his isolation and called upon to confront another cause for bereavement. Death took Charles Carroll Shannon, the only Dakota-born child of Peter and Ann. Charles died on November 29, 1889, and was buried in the Old Holy Name Cemetery at Ebensburg, Pennsylvania.[17] He was their youngest child, only thirteen years old at the time of his passing.

Less than a year later, Shannon was aroused from self-imposed seclusion when he accepted the invitation to speak at the Independence Day celebration of 1890, in Elk Point. The "Voice of Wisdom" delivered another outstanding oration, "simply the grandest and greatest speech ever delivered in Elk Point or any other city in the state," according to the *Elk*

Point Courier. It was, the paper declared, "the most scholarly, patriotic and thrilling address we [have] ever listened to." Those present were amazed at Shannon's oratorical skills and his knowledge of American history and politics. All agreed that Shannon had demonstrated his statesmanship and now stood in the "front rank with the leading orators of the nation."[18]

In June 1892 the *Sioux Valley News* reported that Shannon was seriously ill and preparing to leave Dakota for Pittsburgh.[19] He did not leave, and in December word came that over the past two months Shannon's health had improved, "much to the gratification of his friends." The paper announced that he was fit and able to travel and had plans to visit relatives in Pennsylvania over the holidays and then to venture south into Florida. The *Sioux Valley News* predicted that Shannon would return to Canton in the spring and resume his law practice.[20]

The "Voice of Wisdom" returned in good health but not until September 21, after a long stay in Florida and Pennsylvania, visiting the World's Fair in Chicago on his way back to South Dakota. Shannon was warmly welcomed by the *Sioux Valley News* as the "Grand Old Man" and predicted that "many years of useful service" was in Shannon's future.[21]

At age seventy-two the "Grand Old Man" resumed his quiet residence in Canton. He continued to avoid involvement in state or local politics, despite the economic and political issues arising from the depression that followed the Panic of 1893. On George Washington's birthday in 1894, Shannon resurfaced and gave a masterful lecture to a large group of Canton students, extolling the virtues and accomplishments of the "father of the country." For his effort, he was praised by the *Sioux Valley News.*[22] Conservative, patriotic themes were important to Shannon, whose speeches affirmed such values when Americans were dealing with political upheaval, as promulgated by the Populists.

In Canton, on the eve of the 1894 election, the Republicans wanted to bring out their big guns to shore up support for their candidates and slam the Populists. Who better to enunciate their party's eternal truths than the "Voice of Wisdom"? Shannon answered the call and spoke with his usual eloquence at a Bedford Hall rally, arousing the crowd while championing Republican principles. Shannon was credited for being one of the "founders of the Republican party," a significant compliment, even though only a half-truth, for in his younger days he was a stalwart Democrat. Shannon delivered a political benediction for which he received the applause of the believers, "a fit testimonial to the high esteem in which he is held by his towns-people."[23]

The election of 1894 brought good news to the Republicans as results poured in from across the nation. The party of the rich had achieved their desired gains while the unruly farmers (the "Pops") were dealt a setback in South Dakota and other states. Shannon resumed his quiet life, apparently satisfied with the status quo, while supervising the construction of a Catholic church in Canton.[24] Along with the law, politics and religion were the cultural underpinnings of Shannon's life.

Shannon settled into old age, slowed and hobbled by all the limitations that come with advancing years. He gradually retreated from the practice of law, which gave him time to reflect and think about his years in Dakota, and the many changes that time had wrought. While he valued and maintained his warm friendship with the Faulk and Burleigh families in Yankton, many of his colleagues from the territorial days had already gathered in graveyards. The Grand Old Man doubtless sensed that the specter of death was closing in on him as well. Although he fell short of reaching all of his personal goals, he must have known that the part of the West called Dakota was a better place because of Judge Shannon and his law books.

And yet, if he read the *Sioux Valley News* for November 22, 1895, the judge would have been reminded that the forces of evil were still present. In southwest North Dakota, where the Little Missouri River flows through the Badlands, "broken by ranges of hills, well-timbered," cattle ranches had for several years been thriving. But in 1895, when Frederick Jackson Turner had written about the end of the frontier in America, organized gangs of rustlers were on the prowl in the "groves and hills" of ranch country.

The newspaper reported that the ranchers had, as during territorial days, formed vigilante committees and would once again capture and hang the outlaws: "several leaders of the rustlers were lynched and the gangs forced to scatter."[25] The article reminded readers of the remedy for horse thievery in the form of a stout rope and a short drop, to which Shannon objected.

When America entered the year 1896, the country was still caught in a crippling depression. Massive unemployment and hungry families bred social discontent on an unprecedented level, inspiring a new form of politics and politician. Both a Democrat and a Populist, as a presidential candidate William Jennings Bryan had pledged to help the working-class poor even if it disrupted business as usual. His opponent, conservative Republican William McKinley, was the figurehead of corporate America, a representative of wealth and privilege. Whereas the Populists sought to harness the power of government to promote economic fairness and social justice, the Republicans insisted that no intervention was necessary.

Once again, as in 1894, the Republicans prevailed, although the Democrats and Populists, acting in concert, won enough governorships and congressional seats to give them hope for the future. It was the first and only time in American history that a third party, the Populists, nearly captured the presidency. Although defeated in 1896, their agenda was in fact, a recipe for the future and would, in time, be adopted by the progressive movement.

For Peter Shannon, the outcome of the election upheld his conservative political beliefs. At no time in America's past had the government intervened in an economic crisis to relieve the suffering of the people. Shannon and his allies wanted to make certain that nothing of the kind would happen while they were alive. Having participated in political battles from the 1840s to the 1890s, Shannon could point to an enviable record of success.

The fruits of victory from the historic campaign of 1896 were especially sweet, and once again Shannon was spoken of as a prospect for high office. In January 1897, when the South Dakota legislature met to, among other things, vote for the office of U.S. Senate, "hundreds of Republicans," according to the *Sioux Valley News,* called for Shannon to run against the incumbent, James H. Kyle, who had been elected in 1891 as an Independent. The paper, however, took exception to the draft, boasting that Shannon had "too much ability, too much honor and is altogether too well qualified for the place."[26] The U.S. Senate, according to the Canton newspaper, had been hijacked by a vile crowd of politicians (the Populists), and was therefore no place for a man of Shannon's stature. Serving in the Senate would only sully his honorable reputation at a time when the Grand Old Man should simply relax and enjoy the fruits of a lifetime of accomplishment.

CHAPTER 24

A FINAL INJUSTICE

*It was early in the 70s when the judge came to
Dakota . . . and probably no man is so familiar with the
thrilling incidents connected with the early settlements.*

The Indian Chieftan
Vinita, Indian Territory, Oklahoma
March 19, 1896

How many times Judge Shannon chose to discuss the trial of Jack McCall will never be known, but an interview conducted by the *Minneapolis Journal* in 1895 brought the ghosts of Wild Bill Hickok and his assassin out of the outlaw past and back into the headlines. At the time, Shannon was living at the Harlan House in Canton, South Dakota, and what he recalled about the shooting and the trial differs from many credible accounts. The judge observed that the makeshift miner's jury in Deadwood returned "one of the queerest verdicts that have ever been heard by anyone."

The jurymen were apparently not convinced of McCall's guilt so they decided, in an Old West sort of way, to give him a chance to get out of town. "They put him on a fast horse, filled his pockets with bread and cheese, and gave him one minute to start, after which they would kill him if they could." A number of men armed with Winchester rifles stood by ready to fire after the minute expired.

"When the word was given McCall started for his life," Shannon related. "Before the minute was up he began throwing himself rapidly from one side to the other to divert the aim of his pursers. At the end of the fateful minute the word was given and the pursuit and the fusillade began. It seemed almost incredible but he escaped."[1]

The problem with Shannon's story is not that it conflicts with other accounts of Hickok's murder and McCall's fate but that it is completely untrue—yet told by the judge who sentenced the assassin. Was he seeking attention, or was the old man simply rambling on about his exceptional past? Or was he misquoted? Sioux Falls men remembered that Shannon "used to get a crowd of congenial spirits together and pass his evenings with stories and good cheer."[2] The *Minneapolis Journal* interview seems suspiciously like one of those occasions, but it would not be the last.

It was not as a teller of tall tales that most people remembered Shannon but as the "Grand Old Man," and he began to gather unto him the honor that he so richly deserved. In the summer of 1897, the University of South Dakota, in Vermillion, conferred on him the honorary degree of LL.D.[3] It was both an emblem of respect and a reminder that he was an old man, who had, by hard work, determination, and talent, made his way into the history of his country.

In Canton Shannon was busy remodeling the Harlan House, with the goal of making it the best hotel in the state. He hired the artist Ed Shufelt to supervise the painting and papering of all the rooms in the stylish, two-story hotel. Built in 1880 the hotel had been an immediate success. A three-story brick addition, with a mansard roof and enclosed widow's walk, made it even more attractive and popular. The commodious dining room became the social center for the community. A history of Lincoln County, where Canton is located, noted that Shannon took "pardonable pride in the elegant hotel where he makes his home."[4]

In December 1897 Shannon traveled to Pittsburgh to spend the holidays with his children. While there he was interviewed by a reporter for the *Pittsburgh Leader* and was questioned about his experiences in Dakota Territory. The resulting article, reprinted in the *Sioux Valley News*, was an entertaining combination of fact and fiction.

The reporter, who met with Shannon at his hotel room, was impressed with the appearance of a robust, seventy-six-year-old man who looked fifty-five. The interview highlighted Shannon's experience as a federal judge. The reporter took pride in the fact that Shannon, a Pennsylvanian, had responsibility for an area "larger than England, Ireland, Scotland and Wales combined." The reporter noted that Shannon took the bench "as early as 6 a.m. and as late as 12 midnight." Surely Shannon spent long hours in bringing justice to Dakota, but this was a bit of an exaggeration, as were other statements: "Outlaws ruled the country before the Pittsburger [sic] went out into the wilds to administer justice. There had been murders, lynchings and raids without number." According to this account, Shannon quickly put his personal stamp on the judiciary and "only one lynching came under his notice." The reporter even credited Shannon for having made an attempt "to apprehend the lynchers but failed." Whether such a characterization of Dakota was Shannon's doing or the reporter's is open to conjecture.

As expected, the reporter raised the topic of the McCall trial. Shannon apparently did not take the liberty on this occasion to rewrite history because the reporter relates that McCall was a "notorious desperado" and the "murderer of Wild Bill, a noted scout and fighter." The reporter mentions that "it was a notable trial and its termination had a salutary effect upon the people of the territory." Through the efforts of Judge Shannon, "the desperadoes were terrorized. They had never known law before." The readers were assured that "outlawry was subdued and Dakota is as tame as a New England village."

Shannon's work on the Indian Commission of 1882 was also mentioned in the *Argus-Leader*, although the Sioux Falls paper embellished his reputation: "For three or four years the judge participated in negotiations and many a time he has laid down to rest surrounded by from 10,000 to 12,000 savages." The reporter cautioned, however, that Shannon was in no danger since "he had so won their confidence . . . that never a fear was felt for his safety."[5] Had Shannon an opportunity to correct such misconceptions, or was this another example of the imaginative creation of the West by writers and artists?

Shannon ended the interview with a good word about Canton and life in South Dakota. He confessed he was so "accustomed to the salubrious climate of the Dakotas that he feels he will have to end his days there." He told the reporter that when he left Canton, the "temperature was 18 degrees below zero . . . but it was not as cold as a temperature of 10 above in Pittsburg [sic]. I don't think I can stand the damp, foggy atmosphere of Pittsburg [sic] any more." Nevertheless, he planned to stay in the "Smoky City" until after the holidays.[6]

The judge's travel plans included a trip to California, and some weeks later, Shannon was riding the trains again, perhaps seeking a bit of sunshine and warmth for his aging bones, or just feeding his curiosity about the expanding United States. At any rate something apparently convinced him to stay away from the "salubrious" climate of South Dakota a little longer. In March 1898 the *Sioux Valley News* learned from a San Diego newspaper that "our Judge Shannon" had recently visited Mexico. He had arrived in San Diego just in time to attend a grand ball celebrating George Washington's birthday.[7] The *Los Angeles Herald* for August 29, 1898, reported that the judge was keeping busy by visiting "points of interest" in Southern California and had been doing so for quite some time.[8]

Shannon decided to stay in the small, scenic city of San Diego, by the Pacific Ocean. He took rooms at the Brewster Hotel and later at the Albemarle Hotel downtown. Little is known about his days in Southern California, but he apparently spent them alone as a man in the "fullness of years," an elegant gentleman, rich in experience, with peace in his heart, "waiting the call of the Master."[9]

One afternoon in April 1899, after living in San Diego for several months, Shannon decided to join others on a carriage ride out to Point Loma, a peninsula in the Pacific Ocean, "to witness the opening exercise of the Universal Brotherhood congress." The event was to be held at the headquarters of the Theosophical Society, then a renowned spiritual organization with an elaborate, ocean-side retreat established for people interested in studying the occult in a peaceful, communal setting. The exercise promised to be an especially illuminating event, owing to the secretive character and international reputations of the society's leaders and the beliefs they passed along to the brotherhood.

Shannon had hesitated upon receiving the invitation, but then decided to go despite the objection of W. B. Maginn, the manager of the Albemarle Hotel. He was concerned that the well-respected, elderly judge might be too frail to make the trip. Maginn decided to ride along to see to the needs of his distinguished guest.

Shannon and Maginn boarded the carriage at 2:30 p.m. on April 13 at the door of the Albemarle Hotel, joining E. D. Bates of Chicago and W. Scott of Toronto, both delegates to the congress. As the horses broke into a trot, the carriage driver accidently dropped one of the reins. This spooked the team and the horses "started on a wild run up the street," fully out of control, according to a reporter for the *San Diego Union*. Maginn jumped out at the first sign of trouble, but the others stayed in the carriage. At the southeast corner of "D" Street (now Broadway) and Second Avenue, the carriage struck a telegraph pole with a "terrible force." The violent collision caused everyone to be thrown from the carriage, with Shannon "falling on his left side in the street, several yards away."

Unconscious, the judge was taken to a nearby store and from there to his room at the Albemarle. Doctors were summoned, including Dr. Luscombe, Shannon's personal physician. He was bleeding from the nose, and those assisting him feared that his injuries were fatal. The doctor determined that he had no broken bones but had incurred serious internal injuries. Shannon regained consciousness for a short time, and then went

Pioneer Memorial Park, former Calvary Cemetery,
San Diego, California, where Peter Shannon lies buried.
Photo by author.

comatose. He was given last rites by Father Grady, and at 9:50 p.m., April 13, 1899, Peter C. Shannon was pronounced dead.[10] He may have wished to have ended his days in Canton, South Dakota, but he did not. Yet he fell victim to an accident that he more likely would have experienced on the frontier, rather than in downtown San Diego.

A funeral for the deceased judge was held at St. Joseph's Catholic Church in San Diego, attended by a large number of friends, acquaintances, and the curious. No mention was made of any family members being present. Burial was at the Calvary Cemetery in San Diego.

When word of his death reached South Dakota, the tragic event was noted in some of the state's newspapers. The Canton *Sioux Valley News* learned of Shannon's sudden and tragic death by way of a letter from H. A. Jerauld, a former Dakotan living in San Diego. Jerauld advised Newman

Grave marker for Judge Shannon,
Pioneer Memorial Park, San Diego.
Photo by author.

Nash that some months earlier the old judge had broken a shoulder and, as a result, had been confined to his hotel room. Because of the gravity of the injury, Shannon was unwilling to go back to Dakota "to try again your hard climate." Mourning the loss of a friend, Jerauld wrote that he went to the undertaker to see the body.[11]

Editor Nash, a staunch admirer and friend of Shannon, paid tribute to the deceased judge in his paper. After summarizing his life and career, Nash penned the following remark: "Judge Shannon more than any other man helped to establish law and compel its observance in Dakota."[12]

The Yankton *Press and Dakotaian* merely reprinted the obituary as published in the *San Diego Union*. The paper included no information about Shannon's career as a federal judge except to note that the "distinguished South Dakotan" had been killed in a "runaway accident."

His many contributions to the development of the territorial judiciary were thoroughly ignored as though of little or no consequence. The *Sioux Falls Argus-Leader* published a short notice of Shannon's death in San Diego and then added, "it is understood that the remains will be taken to his old home at Pittsburg, [sic] Penn., for burial."[13]

In this, the *Argus-Leader* was wrong, for Shannon's body was not returned home for burial. At the direction of his son Christian, living in Pittsburgh, his family permitted his final resting place to be among well-meaning strangers, far from his native Pennsylvania, or even South Dakota, where he had lived and worked for so many years and where any number of people would have been able to visit his grave.[14]

Little is known about Shannon's estate, although it appears that he was financially secure at the time of his death. An article in the *Omaha Daily Bee* states that he was a promoter, and possible investor, in the Superior Oil Company of Pennsylvania, a rival of Standard Oil.[15] In South Dakota, Shannon owned the Harlan House, an attractive Canton hotel. Shannon had bequeathed it to the Canton Catholic church, but it caught fire and was badly damaged in 1903.[16]

Shannon undoubtedly had assets other than the hotel at the time of his demise, surely enough to take care of the usual final expenses, including the purchase of a gravestone. But when Judge C. B. Kennedy from Canton visited San Diego with his family shortly after Shannon's death, he was astounded to find that the remains of the former Chief Justice of the Dakota Territory Supreme Court were unmarked. After considerable effort, Kennedy finally located the cemetery and with the aid of the gravedigger found Shannon's grave. Kennedy was outraged that the resting place of such a distinguished man should be neglected, not only by his children, but by his many friends and colleagues in the Dakotas.[17]

Some years later, Granville G. Bennett, who had served on the Dakota Supreme Court with Shannon, took action. In a letter dated October 28, 1907, to Doane Robinson of the South Dakota State Historical Society, Bennett called attention to what he believed was a glaring lack of respect for Shannon. Bennett was in error when he wrote that Shannon was buried in a Los Angeles cemetery, but he was correct when he declared that the grave "is not marked by so much as a head *board.*"

An angry Bennett reminded Robinson and the Society that Shannon "was a most excellent and able jurist, and rendered to our territory and state faithful and conscientious service." He felt that for those reasons the state bar of South Dakota should at the very least do something so that his last resting place was not "left in obscurity and neglect." Bennett asked that a "movement be inaugurated to have his body removed and interred at Yankton, where he lived and served so long, and a suitable monument erected to his memory."[18]

Bennett, himself, was willing to contribute money to what he believed to be a worthy cause, but he failed to inspire sufficient concern and interest among his fellow South Dakotans—and Shannon's body still lies beneath the hard dirt of San Diego. His surviving children apparently made no effort to dignify their father's life with a tombstone.

Officially dedicated in 1977, Calvary Cemetery is now a city park called Calvary Pioneer Memorial Park in the Mission Hills neighborhood of San Diego. The city moved all existing gravestones to a corner of the park, placed at a conspicuous point six large plaques with the names of those interred, and installed playground equipment and picnic tables throughout. The former neighborhood of the dead is now filled with the sounds of children and families at play—and the once hallowed earth is trod occasionally by the curious. Some visitors claim to have sensed a ghostly presence while strolling the grounds.

NOTES

Chapter 1

1   Brad Tennant, "Becoming Dakota Territory," *South Dakota History,* 43, no. 2 (summer 2013): 134, 137.

2   Wayne Fanebust, *Cavaliers of the Dakota Frontier* (Westminster, MD: Heritage Books, Inc., 2009), 230.

3   Herbert S. Schell, *History of Clay County, South Dakota* (Vermillion, SD: Clay County Historical Society, Inc., 1976), 15-16.

4   George W. Kingsbury, *History of Dakota Territory,* vol. I (Chicago: The S. J. Clarke Publishing Co., 1915), 122.

5   Ibid., 136.

6   *Abraham Lincoln, Speeches and Writings, 1859-1865* (New York: The Library of America, 1989), 290.

7   Thomas A. McMullin and David Walker, *Biographical Directory of American Territorial Governors* (Westport, CT: Meckler Publishing, 1984), 77.

8   Bernard Floyd Hyatt, "A Legal Legacy for Statehood: The Development of the Territorial Judicial System in Dakota Territory, 1861-1889" (Ph.D. diss., Texas Tech University, 1987), 55.

9   Ibid., 65.

10   *Union and Dakotaian* (Yankton), July 22, 1865.

11   Moses K. Armstrong , *Early Empire Builders of the Great West* (St. Paul: E. W. Porter, 1901), 74.

12   Hyatt, 70.

13   Richard W. Etulian, ed., *Lincoln Looks West, From the Mississippi to the Pacific* (Carbondale and Edwardsville: Southern Illinois University Press, 2010), 122.

14   George W. Kingsbury, "Dakota's First Governor," *The Monthly South Dakotan,* 1, June 1898, 1.

15   *Sioux Falls Argus-Leader,* November 12, 1906; the old landmark was demolished in 1906.

16   Hyatt, 71.

17   Earl S. Pomeroy, *The Territories and the United States 1861-1890* (Philadelphia: University of Pennsylvania Press, 1947), 35.

18   Clarence Edwin Carter, ed., *The Territorial Papers of the United States,* vol. I (Washington, DC: U.S. Government Printing Office, 1934), 8.

19   *Weekly Dakotian* (Yankton), July 20, 1861.

20   George W. Kingsbury, "Capital and Capital History of South Dakota," *South Dakota Historical Collections,* 5 (Pierre: South Dakota State Historical Society, 1910), 119.

21   *Dakota Union* (Yankton), June 21, 1864; Carter, 8.

22   Kingsbury, *History of Dakota Territory*, vol. I, 181.

23   Carter, 8.

24   Roy P. Basler, ed., *The Collected Works of Abraham Lincoln,* vol. IV (Rutgers University Press, 1953), 408.

25 *Weekly Dakotian,* August 3, 1861.

26 Armstrong, 68-69.

27 Newton Carl Abbott, *Montana in the Making*, rev. Adelia M. Price, 13th edition (Billings, MT: The Gazette Printing Co., 1964), 171.

28 Helen McCann White, ed., *Ho! For the Gold Fields, Northern Overland Wagon Trains of the 1880's* (St. Paul: Minnesota Historical Society, 1966), 18.

29 *Dakotian* (Yankton), June 17, 1862.

30 Robert Huhn Jones, *The Civil War in the Northwest, Nebraska, Wisconsin, Iowa, Minnesota and the Dakotas* (Norman: University of Oklahoma Press, 1960), 177.

31 *Dakotian,* September 15, 1862.

32 Joe E. Milner and Earle R. Forrest, *California Joe, Noted Scout and Indian Fighter* (Caldwell, ID: The Caxton Printers, 1935), 100-01.

33 Armstrong, 74.

34 Ibid., 81-82.

35 Fanebust, 344.

36 John Niven, ed., *The Salmon P. Chase Papers, Vol. I, Journals, 1829-1872* (Kent, OH: The Kent State University Press, 1993), 420.

37 Ibid., 431.

38 Robert Dollard, *Recollections of the Civil War and Going West to Grow Up With the Country* (Scotland, SD, 1906), 205.

39 *Fort Randall Independent* (Fort Randall, DT), March 29, 1866.

40 Dollard, 205.

41 Robert Dollard, *"Reminiscences of Early Pioneers," The South Dakotan, a Monthly Magazine,* VI, no. 6, October 1903, 22.

42 *Dakotian,* June 9, 1863.

43 Ibid., May 19, 1863.

44 Ibid., August 4, 1863.

45 Hyatt, 121.

46 Ibid., 119.

47 *Dakotian,* May 31, 1864; this is undoubtedly a reference to the explorations of Lt. John Mullan. See Watson Parker, *Gold in the Black Hills* (Lincoln: University of Nebraska Press, 1982), 12.

48 *Dakota Union,* June 28, 1864.

Chapter 2

1   *Dakota Herald* (Yankton), February 17, 1874.

2   M. A. DeWolfe Howe, *The Life and Labors of Bishop Hare, Apostle to the Sioux* (New York: Sturgis & Walton Co.), 1913, 63.

3   *Dakota Herald,* February 17, 1874.

4   U.S. Department of the Interior, Territorial Papers of Dakota Territory, 1861-1873, National Archives, Washington D.C.

5   Kingsbury, *History of Dakota Territory,* vol. I, 122.

6   Reneé Sansom-Flood, *Lessons from Chouteau Creek, Yankton Memories of Dakota Territorial Intrigue* (Sioux Falls, SD: Center for Western Studies, 1986), 38.

7   Reneé Sansom-Flood and Shirley A. Bernie, *Remember Your Relatives: Yankton Sioux Images, 1851-1904* (Marty, SD: Marty Indian School, 1985), 29.

8   Herbert T. Hoover, Carol Goss Hoover, and Elizabeth A. Simmons, eds., *Bon Homme County History* (Tyndall, SD: Bon Homme County Historical Society, 1994), 161. In 1880 Tackett sold out to George Trumbo, and in 1894 William Skakel and Thomas Hardwick bought the place. Skakel was an ancestor of Ethel Skakel, who married Senator Robert F. Kennedy. She visited the area in search of information on her relative but the Kennedys deny this.

9   *Atlas of Charles Mix County* (Lake Andes, SD: E. Frank Peterson, Publisher, 1906), 52.

10 *Union and Dakotaian* (Yankton), May 29, 1869.

11 Ibid., August 21, 1869.

12 Wayne Fanebust, *Tales of Dakota Territory, vol. II* (Sioux Falls, SD: Mariah Press, 1999), 45-46.

13 *Daily Press and Dakotaian* (Yankton), February 16, 1880.

14 *St. Paul Daily Globe, Dakota Edition,* January 5, 1889.

15 *Union and Dakotaian,* January 9, 1869.

16 *Chicago Republican,* rpt. in the *Union and Dakotaian,* February 23, 1867.

17 *Union and Dakotaian,* March 30, 1867.

18 Ibid., June 27, 1868.

19 Records of the U.S. District Court, 2nd District, Yankton, D.T., 1861-1873 (Bismarck: State Historical Society of North Dakota), Roll 6101, 222.

20 *Union and Dakotaian,* October 7, 1869.

21 *Daily Press and Dakotaian,* February 16, 1880.

22 Fanebust, 50-51; *Union and Dakotaian,* March 17, 1866.

23 Schell, *History of Clay County, South Dakota,* 29.

24 *Union and Dakotaian,* April 6, 1866.

25 Ibid., December 3, 1864.

26 U.S. Department of the Interior, Territorial Papers of Dakota: 1861-1873, National Archives, Washington, DC.

27 Hyatt, 94.

28 Ibid., 118.

29 *Dakotian,* August 18, 1863.

30 Hyatt, 118.

31 Howard Roberts Lamar, *Dakota Territory, 1861-1889: A Study of Frontier Politics* (New Haven and London: Yale University Press, 1956), 70.

32 *Union and Dakotaian,* May 20, 1865.

33 *Dakota Herald,* July 23, 1872.

34 *Union and Dakotaian,* July 1 & 8, 1865.

35 Kingsbury, vol. I, 182.

36 *Union and Dakotaian,* August 11, 1866.

37 *Dakotian,* December 23, 1862.

38 Hyatt, 103.

39 *Minneapolis Tribune,* January 23, 1888.

40 Edward E. Hill, *The Office of Indian Affairs, 1824-1880: Historical Sketches* (New York: Clearwater Publishing Co., 1974), 213.

41 Zack T. Sutley, *The Last Frontier* (New York: The Macmillan Co., 1930), 177-78.

42 *Dakota Herald,* June 4, 1872.

43 William H. H. Beadle, "Personal Memoirs of William Henry Harrison Beadle," *South Dakota Historical Collections*, 3 (Pierre: South Dakota State Historical Society, 1906), 115-17.

44 David A. Nichols, *Lincoln and the Indians: Civil War Policy and Politics* (Urbana; University of Illinois Press, 2000), 20.

45 Ibid.

46 Ibid.

47 *Montana Post* (Virginia City), December 21, 1867.

48 *Minneapolis Tribune,* January 23. 1888.

49 *Union and Dakotaian,* September 22, 1866.

50 James McClellan Hamilton, *History of Montana, From Wilderness to Statehood,* Merrill G. Burlingame, ed., (Portland, OR: Binford and Morts, Publishers, 1970), 273.

51 Ibid., 277.

52 Territorial Governor's Papers, "Governor Faulk's 2nd Annual Message to the Legislature of Dakota Territory," December 3, 1867, South Dakota State Historical Society, Pierre, SD.

53 John Y. Simon, ed., *The Papers of Ulysses S. Grant,* vol. 18: October 1, 1867 to June 30, 1868, (Carbondale & Edwardsville: Southern Illinois University Press, 1991), 509-10.

54 *Papers of Andrew Johnson,* vol. 14: April-August 1868, (Knoxville: University of Tennessee Press, 1999), 562.

55 *Union and Dakotaian,* March 7 and 14, 1868.

56 *Montana Post*, January 25, 1868.

Chapter 3

1   George Harrison Durand, *Joseph Ward of Dakota* (Pilgrim Press, 1913), 83.

2   J. Leonard Jennewein and Jane Boorman, eds., *Dakota Panorama,* 3ʳᵈ printing (Sioux Falls, SD: Brevet Press, 1973), 327.

3   *Union and Dakotaian,* June 5, 1869.

4   Ibid., December 19, 1868.

5   Ibid., November 3, 1866.

6   Ibid., December 5, 1866.

7   Hyatt, 96.

8   *The Union and Dakotaian,* April 10, 1869.

9   Ibid., April 24, 1869.

10   *Dakota Pantagraph* (Sioux Falls), August 6, 1879.

11   *Sioux Falls Press,* May 17, 1895.

12   Hyatt, 106.

13   John Y. Simons, ed., *The Papers of Ulysses S. Grant,* vol. 19 (Carbondale: Southern Illinois University Press, 1873), 330.

14   *Union and Dakotaian,* May 15, 1869.

15   Hyatt, 105.

16   Ibid., 98.

17   *Union and Dakotaian,* May 15, 1869.

18   Hyatt, 100.

19   Doane Robinson, *History of South Dakota,* vol. I (B. F. Bowen & Co., Publishers, 1904), 463-64.

20   Herbert S. Schell, *Dakota Territory During the Eighteen Sixties* (Vermillion: Governmental Research Bureau, University of South Dakota, 1954), 69.

21   Dollard, *Recollections of the Civil War,* 205-06.

22   Herbert S. Schell, *History of South Dakota,* 4ᵗʰ edition, rev. by John E. Miller (Pierre, SD: South Dakota State Historical Society Press, 2004), 100.

23   *Minneapolis Tribune,* January 23, 1888.

24   Hyatt, 129.

25   James S. Foster, *Outlines of History of the Territory of Dakota and Emigrant's Guide,* 1870 (Freeport, NY: Books for Libraries Press, 1971), 58.

26   *Sioux Falls Argus-Leader,* September 27, 1924.

27   *Dakota Herald,* February 13, 1872.

28   Hyatt, 129.

29   *Union and Dakotaian,* June 16, 1870.

30   Ibid., June 30, 1870.

31   Ibid., September 1, 1870.

32   Dollard, *Recollections of the Civil War,* 206.

33 Hyatt, 129-30.

34 Ibid., 131. Cowles' wife was an accomplished landscape artist with a number of sketches and paintings to her credit, including a painting of the falls of the Big Sioux River. She died in Washington, D.C., October 6, 1877.

35 *Union and Dakotaian,* August 25, 1870.

36 Robinson, 244.

37 *Union and Dakotaian,* December 1, 1870.

38 Ibid., May 19, 1870.

39 Ibid., May 26, 1870.

40 Ibid., December 15, 1870.

41 *Yankton Press,* August 16, 1871.

42 Schell, 100.

43 Clement A. Lounsberry, "Popular History of North Dakota," *North Dakota Magazine,* 3, June 1909, 1.

44 *Yankton Press,* October 25, 1871.

45 *General Laws, Memorials and Resolutions of the Territory of Dakota*, 9th Legislative Session, December 5, 1870 to January 13, 1871 (Yankton, DT: Stone & Kingsbury, Public Printers, 1870-71), 401.

46 John A. Burbank*., Message to the 9th Session of the Dakota Legislature,* Territorial Governor's Papers, December 8, 1870, South Dakota State Historical Society, Pierre, SD.

47 *Yankton Press,* December 27, 1871.

48 *General Laws, Memorials and Resolutions of the Territory of Dakota,* 9th Legislative Session, 511.

49 *Dakota Herald,* December 24, 1872.

50 *Yankton Press,* June 5, 1872.

51 Ibid., December 20, 1871.

52 *Atlas of Charles Mix County*, 53.

53 *Dakota Herald,* March 19, 1872.

54 *Yankton Press,* August 16 & 23, 1871

55 Ibid., November 20, 1872; his name was spelled various ways including Gallineau, Galenaux, Galeneaux, and Gallino.

56 Simon, 377.

57 *Dakota Herald,* May 21, 1872.

58 Hyatt, 111; *Minneapolis Tribune,* January 23, 1888.

59 *Dakota Herald,* April 15, 1873.

60 Hyatt, 135; *Yankton Press,* January 29, 1873.

61 Jennewein and Boorman, 327.

62 *Dakota Herald,* February 13, 1872.

63 John A. Burbank, *Second Biennial Address to the Legislative Assembly of Dakota Territory,* Territorial Governors' Papers, (Pierre: South Dakota State Historical Society, December 3, 1872).

64 www.mocavo.com/family-tree (Robert M. Bowers/Ihmsen Family Tree).

65 Biographical File of Peter C. Shannon, Canton, SD, newspaper clipping, South Dakota State Historical Society, Pierre, SD.

66 *Sioux Valley News,* December 20, 1895, from an article that appeared in the *Record,* November 1895, a Fargo, N.D., magazine published by Clement A. Lounsberry.

Chapter 4

1 *Sioux Falls Independent,* November 27, 1873.

2 *Dakota Republican* (Vermillion), November 3, 1870.

3 Roger Darling, *Custer's Seventh Cavalry Comes to Dakota* (Vienna, VA: Potomac-Western Press, 1988), 48.

4 *Dakota Herald,* March 18, 1873.

5 *Yankton Press,* March 19, 1873.

6 *Journal of the Executive Proceedings of the Senate of the United States of America,* 1873-1875, vol. XIX (Washington, DC: Government Printing Office, 1901), 55, 61, 72.

7 *Yankton Press,* March 26, 1873.

8 Hyatt, 210, 214, 218.

9 *Dakota Republican,* February 20, 1873.

10 Ibid., March 20, 1873.

11 *Post* (Middleburg, PA), May 25, 1871.

12 *Cambria Freeman* (Ebensburg, PA), May 27, 1871.

13 *Somerset Herald* (PA), July 31, 1872.

14 Hyatt, 221.

15 Biographical File of Peter C. Shannon, unidentified Canton, SD, newspaper.

16 *Daily Commercial-Gazette* (Pittsburgh, PA), February 18, 1873; *Pittsburgh Morning Mail,* February 18, 1873, in the *Yankton Press,* March 26, 1873.

17 Matthew Alan Gaumer, "The Catholic Apostle to the Sioux, Martin Marty and the Beginnings of the Church in Dakota Territory," *South Dakota History,* 47, no. 3: (Fall 2012): 262.

18 *Yankton Press,* April 16, 1873.

19 Ibid,. April 30, 1873.

20 Hyatt, 78.

21 *Sioux Falls Independent,* November 27, 1873.

22 *Yankton Press,* January 18, 1871.

23 Ibid., January 25, 1871.

24 Kingsbury, *History of Dakota Territory,* vol. I, 582-583.

25 *Yankton Press,* November 29, 1871.

26 Ibid., April 16, 1873.

27 *Sioux Falls Independent,* November 27, 1873.

28 Dollard, "Reminiscences of the Early Pioneers," 25.

29 *Yankton Press,* May 14, 1873.

30 Ibid., June 18, 1873.

31 Ibid., June 25 and July 9, 1873.

32 *Sioux Valley News* (Canton, DT), December 20, 1895 (in Lounsberry).

33 Hyatt, 288.

34 Ibid., 289.

35 *Sioux Falls Independent,* November 20, 1873.

36 *Yankton Press,* November 12, 1873.

37 *Dakota Herald,* December 9, 1873.

38 *Springfield Times,* December 11, 1873.

39 Hyatt, 292.

40 *Press and Dakotaian,* December 18, 1873.

41 *Dakota Herald,* January 27, 1874.

42 *Bismarck Tribune,* June 24, 1874.

43 William H. H. Beadle, "Personal Memoirs of William H. H. Beadle," *South Dakota Historical Collections,* 3 (Pierre: South Dakota State Historical Society, 1906), 142; *Daily Press and Dakotaian,* July 16, 1874.

44 *Springfield Times,* May 28, 1874.

45 *Dakota Herald,* July 7, 1874.

Chapter 5

1 *Dakota Republican,* September 26, 1872.

2 *Springfield Times,* September 26, 1872.

3 *Yankton Press,* October 2, 1872.

4 *Dakota Herald,* August 19, 1873.

5 *Springfield Times,* September 26, 1873.

6 Robert C. Athearn, *Forts of the Upper Missouri* (Lincoln and London: University of Nebraska Press, 1967), 261-62.

7 *Union and Dakotaian,* January 12, 1871.

8 *Black Hills Daily Times,* March 13, 1880.

9 Henry Van Der Pol, *On the Reservation Border: Hollanders in Douglas and Charles Mix Counties* (Stickney, SD: Argus Printers, 1969), 325-26.

10 *Union and Dakotaian,* August 15, 1868.

11 Darling, 160.

12 Kingsbury, *History of Dakota Territory,* vol. I, 538.

13 Fred M. Hans, "Diary of Fred M. Hans," *South Dakota Historical Collections*, 40 (Pierre: South Dakota State Historical Society, 1981), 52.

14 *Yankton Press*, April 10, 1872.

15 Records of the U.S. District Court, 2nd District, Yankton, DT, 1861-1873, State Historical Society of North Dakota, Bismarck, ND, Microfilm Roll 6101.

16 *Atlas of Charles Mix County*, 53.

17 *Yankton Press*, August 31. 1870.

18 *Dakota Herald*, March 26, 1872; the victim is also listed as Harry Thompson.

19 Col. Richard Cropp, "Jack Sully: The Last of the Bad Men," *Papers of the Dakota History Conference*, H. W. Blakely, ed. (Madison, SD: Dakota State College, 1981), 840.

20 Records of the U.S. District Court, 2nd District, Microfilm Roll 6102.

21 *Atlas of Charles Mix County*, 52.

22 *Springfield Times*, September 26, 1873.

23 Ibid., March 19, 1874.

24 Fred Kaufman, *Hunters of the Plains 1870's: A Historical Novel* (Aberdeen, SD: Northern Plains Press, 1975), 184.

25 *Dakota Herald*, May 5, 1874.

26 John H. Bingham and Nora V. Peters, "A Short History of Brule County," *South Dakota Historical Collections*, 23 (Pierre: South Dakota State Historical Society, 1947), 15-16. According to the 1870 Dakota Territory Census, both Holbrough and McKay were residents of Charles Mix County, but Hartert, Hirl, and Hyer are not listed.

27 William W. Blackburn, "A History of Dakota," *South Dakota Historical Collections*, 1 (Pierre: South Dakota State Historical Society, 1902), 141.

28 *Dakota Herald*, February 17, 1874.

29 *Atlas of Charles Mix County*, 52.

30 Kingsbury, vol. I, 546.

31 *Springfield Times*, May 23, 1872.

32 *Yankton Press*, December 7, 1870, and December 4, 1872.

33 Ibid., December 25, 1872.

34 John Simpson, *West River, 1850-1910: Stories From the Great Sioux Reservation* (Sioux Falls: Pine Hills Press, 2000), 97.

35 Cropp, 840.

36 *Memorial and Biographical Record* (Chicago: George A. Ogle & Co., 1897), 624.

37 *Atlas of Charles Mix County*, 52.

Chapter 6

1 *Yankton Press*, March 13, 1872.

2 *Sioux City Journal* (IA), rpt. in the *Yankton Press*, February 21, 1873.

3 *Dakota Herald*, September 23, 1873.

4   *St. Paul Pioneer* (MN), September 25, 1864.

5   *Dakota Herald,* September 23, 1873.

6   *Yankton Press,* August 16, 1871.

7   Ibid., September 27, 1871.

8   Ibid., February 21, 1872.

9   Ibid., December 4, 1872.

10 Kingsbury, *History of Dakota Territory, v*ol. I, 683.

11 *Yankton Press,* August 15, 1872.

12 *Dakota Herald,* March 19, 1872.

13 *Yankton Press,* June 5, 1872; Walled Lake was later renamed Wall Lake.

14 Ibid., July 31, 1872.

15 Ibid., September 25, 1872.

16 *Dakota Republican*, December 5, 1872.

17 *Sioux City Journal*, rpt. in the *Yankton Press,* February 21, 1872.

18 Kingsbury, vol. I, 721.

19 Andrew Jackson Faulk Papers, letter of Edwin S. McCook to Walter A. Burleigh, February 25, 1872, Yale University.

20 Thomas E. Simmons, *"*Territorial Justice Under Fire: The Trials of Peter P. Wintermute, 1873-1875*," South Dakota History,* 3, no. 2 (summer 2001), 97.

21 *Dakota Herald*, January 21, 1873.

22 Ibid., April 15, 1873.

23 *Springfield Times,* September 4, 1873.

24 *Dakota Republican,* April 24, 1873

25 Wayne Fanebust, *Echoes of November: The Life and Times of Senator R. F. Pettigrew of South Dakota,* (Freeman, SD: Pine Hill Press, 1997), 41-42.

26 *Dakota Herald,* January 7, 1873.

27 *Dakota Republican,* July 31, 1873.

28 *Yankton Press,* September 10, 1873.

29 *Springfield Times,* September 4, 1873.

30 Darling, 62.

31 *Yankton Press,* September 17, 1873.

32 Doane Robinson, ed., "Old Times Tales," *The Dakotan, A Monthly Magazine*, 5, January, February, March, 1903, 310-11.

33 *Yankton Press,* September 17, 1873.

34 *Dakota Herald,* September 16, 1873.

35 Simmons, 94.

36 *Yankton Press,* September 17, 1873.

37 *Clarksville Weekly Chronicle* (TN), September 20, 1873.

38 *Yankton Press,* September 17, 1873.

39 *Clay County Register* (Vermillion), September 18, 1873.

40 *Yankton Press,* September 17, 1873.

41 *Dakota Republican,* September 18, 1873.

42 *Sioux City Journal,* rpt. in the *Dakota Herald,* September 30, 1873.

43 *Yankton Press,* October 22, 1873.

44 Ibid., October 1, 1873; David Saville Muzzey and John A. Krout, *American History for Colleges,* rev. ed. (Ginn and Company, 1943), 454.

45 *Yankton Press,* September 17, 1873.

46 *Springfield Times,* October 30, 1873.

47 *St. Paul Press* (MN), rpt. in the *Springfield Times,* November 13, 1873.

Chapter 7

1   *Yankton Press,* November 12, 1873.

2   *Press and Dakotaian* (Yankton), November 20 1873.

3   Ibid., October 22, 1873.

4   *Dakota Republican,* July 31, 1875.

5   *Weekly Dakotian* (Yankton), June 20, 1861, and July 6, 1861.

6   *Union and Dakotaian,* May 26, 1870.

7   Robinson, "Old Time Tales," 313.

8   *Press and Dakotaian,* December 18, 1873.

9   Ibid., January 29, 1874.

10 *White River Journal* (Du Vall's Bluff, AR), rpt. in the *Springfield Times,* January 29, 1874.

11 *Dakota Herald,* January 27, 1874.

12 *Waco Daily Examiner* (TX), April 18, 1882.

13 *Daily Press and Dakotaian,* April 14, 1882.

14 *Press and Dakotaian,* February 5, 1874.

15 *Dakota Herald,* February 10, 1874.

16 *Press and Dakotaian,* March 5, 1874.

17 Ibid., April 30, 1874.

18 Ibid., April 30, 1874.

19 Allen Thorndike Rice, ed., *Reminiscences of Abraham Lincoln by Distinguished Men of His Time*, 1888 (New York: Haskell House Publishers), 1971, 639-40.

20 *Press and Dakotaian,* May 14, 1874.

21 Ibid., May 21, 1874.

22 Ibid.

23 Ibid., May 28, 1874.

24 Ibid.

25 Ibid., June 4, 1874.

26 Ibid., June 11, 1874.

27 Ibid., June 4, 1874.

28 Ibid.

29 *Dakota Herald,* June 9, 1874.

30 *Press and Dakotaian,* June 11, 1874.

31 *Sioux Falls Independent,* June 18, 1874.

32 Ibid., July 16, 1874.

Chapter 8

1 *Press and Dakotaian,* December 10, 1874.

2 *Dakota Herald,* November 4, 1873.

3 *Press and Dakotaian,* January 14, 1875.

4 *Dakota Herald,* November 17, 1874.

5 Ibid., December 15, 1874.

6 *Press and Dakotaian,* December 17, 1874.

7 Ibid., December 17, 1874; *Dakota Herald,* December 15, 1874.

8 Ibid., January 7, 1875.

9 *Dakota Herald,* December 8, 1874.

10 *Dakota Frie Presse* (Yankton), rpt. in the *Dakota Herald,* December 15, 1874.

11 *Press and Dakotaian,* January 7, 1875.

12 William M. Blackburn, "A History of Dakota," *South Dakota Historical Collections*, 1 (Pierre: South Dakota State Historical Society, 1902), 141.

13 *Bismarck Tribune,* June 16, 1875.

14 *St. Paul Daily Globe, Dakota Edition,* January 5, 1889.

15 *Press and Dakotaian,* November 5, 1874.

16 Ibid., September 24, 1874.

17 Hyatt, 184-86.

18 *Sioux Falls Independent,* October 22, 1874.

19 *Dakota Herald,* April 20, 1875.

20 *Daily Press and Dakotaian,* April 26, 1875.

21 Ibid., April 28, 1875.

22 Ibid., May 11, 1875.

23 *Yankton Press,* February 7, 1872; Dorothy Jencks, *Some Historic Homes of Yankton, D.T.,* (Yankton: Yankton County Historical Society, 1993), 51.

24 *Daily Press and Dakotaian* (Yankton), April 28, 1875.

25 Ibid., May 16, 1875.

26 Ibid., May 30, 1875.

27 Ibid., May 14 and 18, 1875.

28 *Yankton Press and Dakotan,* August 22, 1924.

29 *Daily Press and Dakotaian,* June 6, 1875.

30 Ibid., May 30, 1875.

31 Ibid., June 22, 1875.

32 Ibid., August 27, 1875.

Chapter 9

1   *Press and Dakotaian,* September 10 and 17, 1874.

2   Ibid., October 29, 1874.

3   Ibid., July 16, and 23, 1874.

4   Ibid., October 12, 1874.

5   *Dakota Herald,* October 6, 1874.

6   *Press and Dakotaian,* February 4, 1875

7   *People v. Wintermute,* 1 Dakota Reports, 61, 46 N.W. 694 [1875].

8   Hyatt, 294.

9   *Press and Dakotaian,* March 4, 1875.

10 *Bismarck Tribune,* May 19, 1875.

11 *Press and Dakotaian,* February 11, 1875.

12 *Springfield Times,* February 11, 1875.

13 *Bismarck Tribune,* rpt. in the *Dakota Republican*, March 4, 1875.

14 Hyatt, 211.

15 Ibid., 214-15, 218.

16 *Sioux Falls Independent,* February 14, 1875.

17 *Daily Press and Dakotaian,* May 7, 1875.

18 Ibid., May 9, 22, and June 8, 10 and 17, 1875.

19 Ibid., August 27- 28, 1875.

20 Ibid., September 2, 1875.

21 Kingsbury, *History of Dakota Territory,* vol. I, 743.

22 *Clay County Register,* September 3, 1875.

23 Kingsbury, vol. I, 743.

24 *Daily Press and Dakotaian,* September 4, 1875.

25 *Dakota Herald,* September 14, 1875.

26 *Corning Journal* (New York), September 16, 1875.

27 *Springfield Times,* September 23, 1875.

28 *Sioux Falls Independent,* September 23, 1875.

29 *Semi-Weekly Register* (Vermillion), September 14, 1875.

30 *Dakota Republican*, September 16, 1875.

31 Ibid., September 30, 1875.

32 *Daily Press and Dakotaian,* September 13, 1875.

33 Ibid., September 14, 1875.

34 *Dakota Republican,* September 23, 1875.

35 *Daily Press and Dakotaian,* September 17, 1875.

36 Ibid., September 14, 1875.

37 *Dakota Herald,* February 1, 1876.

38 Kingsbury, vol. I, 743.

39 Jay Robert Nash, *Almanac of World Crime* (Garden City, NY: Anchor Press/Doubleday, 1981), 122.

Chapter 10

1 Hyatt, 167.

2 J. P. Kidder Papers, Biography Folder, Kidder obituary in unidentified newspaper, South Dakota State Historical Society, Pierre, SD.

3 Fanebust, *Echoes of November,* 55.

4 *Dakota Herald,* August 31, 1875.

5 *Springfield Times,* October 28, 1875.

6 *Daily Press and Dakotaian,* June 29, 1876.

7 Dollard, *Recollections,* 207.

8 *Daily Press and Dakotaian,* June 29, 1876.

9 *Dakota Herald,* June 10, 1876.

10 www.mocavo.com/family-tree (Robert M. Bowers/Ihmsen Family).

11 Beadle, "Memoirs of General William Henry Harrison Beadle," 142-46.

12 Robert F Karolevitz, *Pioneer Church in a Pioneer City* (Aberdeen, SD: Northern Plains Press, 1971), 21-24.

13 *National Police Gazette* (New York City), April 12, 1879.

14 *Daily Press and Dakotaian,* March 12, 1879.

15 Ibid., March 20, 1879.

16 Hyatt, 207.

17 *Daily Press and Dakotaian,* November 23, 1877.

18 Robert Vogel, "Looking Back on a Century of Complete Codification of the Law," *North Dakota Law Review,* 53 (1976-1977), 225.

19 Beadle," 132-36.

20 *Daily Press and Dakotaian,* December 10, 1874.

21 Ibid., August 10, 1875.

22 *Dakota Republican,* April 1, 1875.

23 *Dakota Herald,* January 6, 1877.

24 Beadle, 131.

25 *Daily Press and Dakotaian,* May 9, 1876.

26 Ibid., May 11 and 12, 1876.

27 Ibid., May 17, 1876.

28 *Dakota Herald,* January 6, 1877.

29 Hyatt, 170-71.

30 Clement A. Lounsberry, "Popular History of North Dakota," *North Dakota Magazine,* 3, June 1909, 1-2.

Chapter 11

1 Betti C. VanEpps-Taylor, *Forgotten Lives: African Americans in South Dakota,* (Pierre: South Dakota State Historical Society Press, 2008), 54. See also VanEpps-Taylor, "African Americans," in *A New South Dakota History*, ed. Harry F. Thompson, 2nd ed. (Sioux Falls: Center for Western Studies, 2009).

2 *Council Journal of the Legislative Assembly of the Territory of Dakota* (Yankton, DT: Josiah C. Trask, Public Printer, 1862), 71, 88.

3 *Yankton Press,* July 19, 1871.

4 *Daily Press and Dakotaian,* April 27, 1875.

5 Ibid., May 2, 1875.

6 *Dakota Herald,* April 13, 1875.

7 *Daily Press and Dakotaian,* April 28 and 29, 1975.

8 *National Republican* (Washington, DC), July 23, 1869.

9 *Daily Press and Dakotaian,* June 3, 4, 7, 1875; *Dakota Herald,* June 8, 1875.

10 VanEpps-Taylor, 33.

11 *Dakota Herald,* March 15, 1879.

12 *Dakota Pantagraph,* March 12, 1879.

13 *Dakota Herald,* March 15, 1879.

14 *Daily Press and Dakotaian,* April 11, 1879.

15 *Sioux Valley News*, July 12, 1879.

16 *Daily Press and Dakotaian*, June 7, 1879.

17 *Dakota Pantagraph,* August 20, 1879.

18 The records of the Sacred Heart Cemetery in Yankton show that a Margaret Norman was buried there in 1879.

19 *The Dakota Herald,* November 12, 1872.

20 Ibid., April 14, 1874.

21 *Daily Press and Dakotaian,* June 3, 1875.

22 Ibid., May 6, 1876.

23 Ibid., August 19, 1876.

24 Ibid., May 12, 1876.

25 Ibid., June 1, 1876.

26 Ibid., August 29, 1876.

27 *General Laws, Memorials and Resolutions of the Territory of Dakota,* 8th Session of the Legislative Assembly, December 6, 1868 to January 15, 1869, (George W. Kingsbury, Public Printer, Union and Dakotaian Office), 2.

28 *Daily Press and Dakotaian,* August 30, 1876.

29 Ibid., March 20, 1893.

30 Ibid., June 28, 1876.

31 Ibid., April 27, 1877.

32 Ibid., May 3, 1877.

33 *Territory v. Chartrand,* 1 Dakota Reports, 363, 46 N.W. 583 [1877].

34 U.S. Department of the Interior, Territorial Papers: Dakota, 1863-1889, Reel 1.

35 *Daily Press and Dakotaian,* 25, 1879.

36 Ibid., April 10, 1879.

37 *Dakota Herald,* March 5, 1881.

Chapter 12

1 John F. Reiger, ed., *The Passing of the Great West: Selected Papers of George Bird Grinnell* (Norman: University of Oklahoma Press, 1985), 79.

2 *New York Tribune,* rpt. in *The Dakota Herald,* June 30, 1874.

3 Donald Jackson, *Custer's Gold, The United States Cavalry Expedition of 1874* (Lincoln: University of Nebraska Press, Bison Book, 1972), 81.

4 *Black Hills Daily Times* (Deadwood), March 13, 1880.

5 Reiger, 101.

6 *Inter-Ocean,* August 27, 1874.

7 Evan S. Connell, *Son of the Morning Star: Custer and the Little Bighorn* (San Francisco: North Point Press, 1984), 247.

8 Jesse Brown and A. M. Willard, *The Black Hills Trails: A History of the Struggles of the Pioneers in the Winning of the Black Hills,* ed. John T. Milek (Rapid City: Rapid City Journal Company, 1924), 38-39.

9 Jeffrey D. Wert, *The Controversial Life of General George Armstrong Custer* (New York: Simon & Schuster, 1996), 316.

10 T. A. Rickard, *A History of American Mining* (New York: McGraw Hill Book Co., 1932), 205-07.

11 Earl Boyce Manuscript, 1876-1899, Canton Public Library, Canton, SD (article from an unidentified South Dakota newspaper).

12 *Sioux Falls Argus-Leader,* July 12, 1924; his name was Horatio N. Ross.

13 *Dakota Herald,* August 18, 1874.

14 *Daily Press and Dakotaian,* May 7, 1875

15 Ibid., April 29, 1875.

16 Ibid., May 8, 1875.

17 Ibid., May 30, 1875.

18 *Dakota Herald,* April 6, 1875.

19 *Inter-Ocean* (Chicago), August 27, 1874.

20 Michael L. Tate, *The Frontier Army in the Settlement of the West* (Norman: University of Oklahoma Press, 1999), 11; Edward Lazarus, *Black Hills, White Justice: The Sioux Nation Versus the United States, 1775 to the Present* (New York: Harper Collins Publishers, 1991), 78.

21 Lazarus, 76.

22 *Dakota Herald,* January 5, 1875.

23 Lazarus, 73.

24 *Dakota Herald,* April 6, 1875.

25 *Daily Press and Dakotaian,* May 15, 1875.

26 Ibid., August 6, 1875.

27 *Dallas Daily Herald,* June 1, 1875.

28 *Daily Press and Dakotaian,* August 20, 1875.

29 Ibid., August 28, 1875.

30 Ibid., June 9, 1884; *Canton Advocate*, June 26, 1884.

31 *Daily Press and Dakotaian,* May 9, 1875.

32 Ibid., April 11, 1876.

33 Ibid., April 13, 1876.

34 *Dakota Herald*, February 12, 1876.

35 Ibid., May 27, 1876.

36 *Kansas City Times* (MO)*,* rpt. in the *Dakota Herald*, May 20, 1876.

37 Harry H. Anderson, "Deadwood: An Effort at Stability," *Montana: The Magazine of Western History,* 20, no, 1 (January 1970), 41.

38 *Deadwood Pioneer,* in the *Dakota Herald,* May 12, 1877.

39 Estelline Bennett, *Old Deadwood Days* (New York: J. H. Sears & Company, Inc, 1928), 37.

40 Doane Robinson, *History of South Dakota,* vol. II (Indianapolis, IN: B. F. Bowen & Co., 1904), 1124.

41 *Daily Press and Dakotaian,* June 26, 1877.

42 *Black Hills Daily Times,* June 4, 1878.

Chapter 13

1 Don Patton, "The Legend of Ben Ash," *South Dakota Historical Collections*, 23 (Pierre: South Dakota State Historical Society, 1947), 207.

2 Joseph G. Rosa, *Wild Bill Hickok: The Man and His Myth* (Lawrence: University Press of Kansas, 1996), 198.

3 Mildred Fielder, *Wild Bill and Deadwood* (New York: Bonanza Books, 1965), 86.

4 William W. Secrest, ed., *I Buried Hickok: The Memoirs of White Eye Anderson* (College Station, TX: Creative Publishing Co., 1980), 92-93.

5   James D. McLaird, *Wild Bill Hickok and Calamity Jane: Deadwood Legends* (Pierre: South Dakota State Historical Society Press, 2008), 50.

6   *St. Louis Globe-Democrat* (MO)*, rpt. in the *Dakota Herald,* September 2, 1876.

7   Doane Robinson Collection, Folder 23, letter of Doane Robinson to Joe Schulze, April 22, 1922, South Dakota State Historical Society, Pierre, SD.

8   Joseph G. Rosa, *The West of Wild Bill Hickok* (Norman: University of Oklahoma Press, 1982), 14-15.

9   Ibid., 47.

10 *Dakota Herald,* July 1, 1876.

11 Joseph G. Rosa, *They Called Him Wild Bill: The Life and Adventures of James Butler Hickok* (Norman: University of Oklahoma Press, 1964), 215.

12 *Daily Press and Dakotaian,* August 18, 1876.

13 McLaird, 41.

14 Zack T. Sutley, *The Last Frontier* (New York: The MacMillan Co., 1930), 115-16.

15 *Daily Press and Dakotaian,* August 18, 1876.

16 W. L. Kuykendall, *Frontier Days: A True Narrative of Striking Events on the Western Frontier* (J. M. and H. L. Kuykendall, Publishers, 1917), 186-87.

17 Ibid., 188.

18 Richard B. Hughes, *Pioneer Years in the Black Hills,* ed. Agnes Wright Spring (Rapid City, SD: Dakota Alpha Press, 1999), 125.

19 Kuykendall, 188.

20 *Daily Press and Dakotaian,* August 18, 1876.

21 John S. McClintock, *Pioneer Days in the Black Hills,* ed. Edward L. Senn, 1939 (Norman: University of Oklahoma Press, 2000), 111.

22 *Sioux City Daily Journal,* September 3, 1876.

23 Ibid., September 6, 1876.

24 *Daily Press and Dakotaian,* September 6, 1876.

25 *Dakota Herald,* September 9, 1876.

26 Records of the U.S. District Court, 2nd District, Yankton, DT, State Historical Society of North Dakota, Bismarck, ND, Microfilm Roll 6102.

27 McClintock, 96-97; Hughes, 116-21.

28 *Daily Press and Dakotaian,* August 19, 1876.

29 *Dakota Herald,* November 11, 1876.

30 Ibid., December 30, 1876.

31 Rosa, *Wild Bill Hickok*, 201.

32 *Daily Press and Dakotaian,* November 29, 1876.

33 Ibid., December 3, 1876.

34 *Bismarck Tribune,* June 16, 1875.

35 *Daily Press and Dakotaian,* December 5, 1876.

36 Ibid., December 5, 1876.

37 Ibid., December 5, 1876.

38 Ibid., December 5, 1876.

39 Patton, 207-08.

40 *Daily Press and Dakotaian,* December 6, 1876.

41 Patton, 208.

42 Rosa, *They Called Him Wild Bill,* 234.

43 *Daily Press and Dakotaian,* December 6, 1876.

44 Records of the U.S. District Court, 2nd District, Yankton, DT, State of North Dakota Historical Society, Bismarck, ND, Microfilm Roll 6102.

45 Robert F. Karolevitz, *Yankton: The Way it Was, Being a Collection of Historical Columns Which Appeared in the Yankton Daily Press and Dakotan,* (Freeman, SD: Pine Hill Press, 1999), 28.

46 Sutley, 116.

47 Rosa, *They Called Him Wild Bill,* 241.

48 *Dakota Herald,* January 6, 1877.

49 *Daily Press and Dakotaian,* January 24, 1877.

50 Ibid., February 15, 1877.

51 Ibid., February 28, 1877.

52 Ibid., February 20, 1877.

53 Stuart Banner, *The Death Penalty: An American History* (Cambridge, MA: Harvard University Press, 2002), 154.

54 *Daily Press and Dakotaian,* February 28, 1877.

55 *Dakota Herald,* October 13, 1874.

56 Robert F. Karolevitz, *With Faith, Hope and Tenacity: The First One Hundred Years of the Catholic Diocese of Sioux Falls 1889-1989* (Mission Hill, SD: Dakota Homestead Publishers, 1989), 13.

57 *Dakota Herald,* March 3, 1877.

58 *Daily Press and Dakotaian,* March 1, 1877.

59 *Dakota Herald,* March 17, 1877.

60 Karolevitz, 13.

61 *Daily Press and Dakotaian,* June 23, 1881.

Chapter 14

1 *Daily Press and Dakotaian,* May 15, 1877.

2 *Bismarck Tribune,* July 27, 1877.

3 *Daily Press and Dakotaian,* December 2 and 6, 1876.

4 *Dakota Herald,* December 23, 1876.

5 *Daily Press and Dakotaian,* January 10, 1877.

6 *Chicago Times,* rpt. in the *Dakota Herald*, December 9, 1876.

7 *Deadwood Pioneer*, rpt. in the *Daily Press and Dakotaian,* November 30, 1876.

8 Hughes, 83.

9 Bennett, 128.

10 Jesse Brown and A. M. Willard, *The Black Hills Trails, A History of the Struggles of the Pioneers in the Winning of the Black Hills,* ed. John T. Milek (Rapid City: Rapid City Journal Co., 1924), 348.

11 *Chicago Times*, rpt. in the *Dakota Herald,* December 9, 1876.

12 Ibid., December 9, 1876; the victim's name was also spelled "Farrell."

13 *Daily Press and Dakotaian,* December 6, 1876.

14 *Bismarck Tribune,* July 27, 1877.

15 *Sioux Falls Argus-Leader,* December 29, 1897.

16 *Daily Press and Dakotaian,* November 14, 1876.

17 *Sioux Falls Argus-Leader,* December 29, 1897.

18 *Daily Press and Dakotaian,* November 19, 1876.

19 Ibid., December 26, 1876.

20 *Dakota Herald,* December 30, 1876.

21 *Daily Press and Dakotaian,* December 7, 1876.

22 McClintock, 271.

23 *Daily Press and Dakotaian,* May 12, 1877.

24 *Swan Lake Era*, June 7, 1877.

25 *Daily Press and Dakotaian,* April 21, 27, 28, and May 1, 1877.

26 *Territory v. Conrad*, 1 Dakota Reports, 348-56, 46 N.W. 605 [1877].

27 *Daily Press and Dakotaian,* October 11, 1877.

28 *Territory v. Conrad*, 1 Dakota Reports, 354, 46 N.W. 605 [1877].

29 *Daily Press and Dakotaian,* October 19, 1877, and November 14, 1877; Pound is buried in the Yankton City Cemetery.

30 *Dakota Pantagraph,* December 5, 1877.

31 *Dakota Herald,* May 5, 1877.

32 *Daily Press and Dakotaian,* February 28, 1877.

33 *Union and Dakotaian,* February 22, 1867.

34 *Daily Press and Dakotaian,* March 21 and April 30, 1877.

35 Ibid., May 6, 1876.

36 Ibid., May 3, 1877.

37 Ibid, March 11, 1878

38 U.S. Department of Interior, Territorial Papers: Dakota, 1863-1889, Reel 1, National Archives.

39 *Daily Press and Dakotaian,* February 16, 1880

Chapter 15

1   *Sioux Falls Independent,* August 5, 1875.

2   *Daily Press and Dakotaian,* August 19, 1875.

3   *Sioux Falls Argus-Leader,* August 28, 2002.

4   Ernest V. Sutton, *A Life Worth Living* (Pasadena, CA: Trail's End Publishing Co., 1948), 101.

5   Gladys Whitehorn Jorgensen, *Before Homesteads: In Tripp County and the Rosebud* (Freeman, SD: Pine Hill Press, 1974), 90; White Lake was renamed Dog Ear Lake.

6   Dave Strain, "Jack Whipple on the Rosebud," *Papers of the 10th Annual Dakota History Conference* (Madison, SD: Dakota State College, 1979), 307.

7   *Daily Press and Dakotaian,* July 11, 1877.

8   Brown and Willard, 296.

9   *Daily Press and Dakotaian,* July 17, 1877.

10   Martha Ferguson McKeown, *Them Was the Days: An American Saga of the 70's,* (Lincoln: University of Nebraska Press, 1950), 195-96.

11   U.S. Department of the Interior, Territorial Papers: Dakota, 1863-1889, Reel 1, National Archives.

12   *Black Hills Daily Times,* June 20, 1883.

13   Robert J. Casey, *The Black Hills and Their Incredible Characters* (Indianapolis, IN: The Bobbs-Merrill Co., Inc., 1949), 35

14   *Dakota Herald,* May 21, 1872.

15   Ibid., March 4, 1873.

16   Ibid., April 8, 1873.

17   Ibid., April 29, 1873.

18   Ibid., May 6 and 13, 1873.

19   Ibid., July 21, 1874.

20   *Springfield Times,* December 31, 1874.

21   Ibid., January 25, 1875.

22   *Daily Press and Dakotaian,* May 16, 1875.

23   Ibid., May 21, 1875.

24   Ibid., May 27, 1875.

25   Ibid., June 15, 1875.

26   Ibid., June 17, 1875.

27   Ibid.

28   *Springfield Times,* July 1, 1875.

29   *Daily Press and Dakotaian,* June 30, 1875

30   *Hand County Press,* rpt. in the *Daily Press and Dakotaian,* December 20, 1882.

31   *Dakota Herald,* July 30, 1872.

32 Arthur E. Towne, *Old Prairie Days* (Otsego, MI: Otsego Union Press, 1948), 22.

33 *Moody County Enterprise* (Flandreau, DT), December 26, 1878.

34 A. B. Smart, *Outlines of Pioneer Jerauld County History* (Wessington Springs, SD: Tamblyn Printing, 1970), 6.

35 *Springfield Times,* March 12, 1874.

36 N. J. Dunham, *A History of Jerauld County South Dakota, From Earliest Settlement to January 1, 1909* (Wessington Springs, SD, 1910), 7-8.

37 *Daily Press and Dakotaian,* August 17, 1878.

38 Ibid., April 18, 1879.

39 *Dakota Pantagraph,* September 3, 1879.

40 *Daily Press and Dakotaian,* September 26, 1876.

41 Smart, 7.

42 W. H. Stoddard, *Turner County Pioneer History,* 1931 (Freeman, SD: Pine Hill Press, 1975), 82.

43 Tom Shonley, "Cattle Drives, Rustlers, and Nicholson Gulch," *9th Annual West River History Conference Papers* (Keystone, SD: Keystone Area Historical Society, 2001), 117.

44 *Daily Press and Dakotaian,* March 21, 1878.

45 *Sioux City Journal*, rpt. in the *Weekly Press and Dakotaian,* October 24, 1878.

46 *Daily Press and Dakotaian,* July 27, 1877, August 27, 1877, and September 1, 1877.

47 *Bismarck Tribune,* August 1, 1877.

48 *Daily Press and Dakotaian,* April 23 and 28, 1877.

49 *Sioux Valley News*, April 28, 1877.

50 *Daily Press and Dakotaian,* September 11 and 15, 1877.

51 Ibid., September 21, 1877.

52 *The Revised Codes of the Territory of Dakota, A. D. 1877* (Yankton: Bowen & Kingsbury, Public Printers, 1877), 811.

53 *Daily Press and Dakotaian,* November 17, 1877.

54 Ibid., December 10, 1877.

Chapter 16

1 *Daily Press and Dakotaian,* June 6, 1878.

2 *Weekly Press and Dakotaian* (Yankton), July 4, 1878.

3 Ibid., June 6, 1878.

4 *Daily Press and Dakotaian,* September 3, 1878.

5 *Dakota Pantagraph,* August 28, 1878.

6 *Daily Press and Dakotaian,* May 25, 1878.

7 *Dakota Herald,* June 15, 1878.

8 *Weekly Press and Dakotaian,* September 5, 1878; according to the *Dakota Pantagraph,* the hanging took place at the bridge on Snatch Creek.

9   *Dakota Pantagraph,* September 25, 1878.

10 *Daily Press and Dakotaian,* May 9, 1878.

11 *Black Hills Daily Times,* June 24, 1878.

12 Ibid., July 3, 1878.

13 Brown and Willard, 298.

14 *Black Hills Daily Times,* September 19, 1878.

15 *Dakota Herald,* October 5, 1878.

16 Ibid., November 30, 1878; *Daily Press and Dakotaian,* December 5, 1878.

17 *Dakota Herald,* March 1, 1879.

18 *Daily Press and Dakotaian,* May 31, 1878.

19 Hyatt, 222-23.

20 *Springfield Times,* rpt. in the *Daily Press and Dakotaian,* September 14, 1878.

21 Hyatt, 180-81.

22 Ibid., 194

23 *Dakota Pantagraph,* April 9, 1879; Hyatt, 209.

24 *Dakota Pantagraph,* February 12, 1879; this article indicates that the man who married Hain's daughter was Andy Nixon.

25 Ibid., July 23, 1879.

26 *Springfield Times,* January 20, 1875.

27 *Dakota Pantagraph,* July 23, 1879

28 *Dakota Herald,* August 2, 1879.

29 *Cameron Pioneer* (Cameron, DT), August 22, 1879.

30 *Dakota Pantagraph,* August 6, 1879; *Dakota Herald,* August 16, 1879.

31 *Dakota Herald,* August 16, 1879.

32 *Daily Press and Dakotaian,* May 4, 1880.

33 *Springfield Times*, rpt. in the *Daily Press and Dakotaian,* December 27, 1883.

34 Brown and Willard, 298-99.

35 Jessie Y. Sundstrom, ed., *Custer County History to 1876,* (Custer: Custer County Historical Society, 1977), 178; *Black Hills Daily Times,* February 27, 1883.

36 *Black Hills Daily Times,* February 24, 1880.

37 *Daily Press and Dakotaian,* May 17, 1880.

38 N. J. Dunham, *A History of Jerauld County South Dakota, From Earliest Settlement to January 1, 1909* (Wessington Springs, SD, 1910), 14.

39 Tom Shonley, "New England Influences in Dakota Territory," *12th Annual Dakota History Conference* (Madison, SD: Dakota State College, 1981), 260.

40 Ibid., 262.

41 *Mitchell Capitol*, rpt. in the *Daily Press and Dakotaian,* May 9, 1881.

42 H. M. Travis, "A Trip to Wessington Hills in 1880," *The Monthly South Dakotan,* 4, 1902, 278-79.

43 Shonley, "New England," 265.

44 Ibid., 266.

45 Dunham, 25-27.

46 *Luverne Herald* (Luverne, MN)*,* rpt. in the *Sioux Valley News*, October 6, 1882.

47 *Daily Press and Dakotaian,* September 18, 1882.

48 Dunham, 25-27.

49 *Western Bugle* (Mitchell, DT), April 9, 1881.

50 Shonley, "Cattle Drives," 120.

51 Smart, 6.

Chapter 17

1   *Weekly Dakotian*, June 27, 1861.

2   *Union and Dakotaian,* April 22, 1865.

3   Kingsbury, *History of Dakota Territory,* vol. I, 593.

4   *General Laws, Memorials and Resolutions of the Territory of Dakota*, 9th Session, December 5, 1870 to January 13, 1871 (Yankton, DT: Stone & Kingsbury, Public Printers, 1870-71), 556.

5   *Daily Press and Dakotaian,* September 3, 1879.

6   Stoddard, 47-48.

7   *Dakota Pantagraph,* April 16, 1879.

8   Stoddard, 82.

9   *Dakota Pantagraph,* April 16, 1879.

10 Stoddard, 82.

11 *Daily Press and Dakotaian,* April 12, 1879.

12 *Dakota Pantagraph,* April 16, 1879.

13 *Dakota Herald,* April 19, 1879.

14 *Swan Lake Era* (Swan Lake, DT), June 29, 1876.

15 Ibid., August 1, 1878.

16 *Dakota Herald,* April 19, 1879.

17 *Daily Press and Dakotaian,* April 12, 1879.

18 *Dakota Pantagraph,* July 30, 1879.

19 *Daily Press and Dakotaian,* April 17, 1879.

20 *Dakota Herald,* April 19, 1879; *Dakota Pantagraph,* April 23, 1879.

21 *Dakota Pantagraph,* September 3, 1879.

22 *Daily Press and Dakotaian,* June 30, 1879.

23 *Parker New Era* (Parker, DT)*,* December 11, 1880.

24 *Sioux Valley News*, May 13, 1881.

25 Stoddard, 83.

Chapter 18

1 *Daily Press and Dakotaian*, rpt. in the *Dakota Pantagraph,* July 16, 1879.

2 *Daily Press and Dakotaian,* December 21, 1878.

3 *Daily Press and Dakotaian,* rpt. in *The Dakota Pantagraph,* July 16, 1879.

4 *Daily Press and Dakotaian,* July 10, 1879.

5 Ibid., July 10, 1879.

6 Ibid., October 4, 1879.

7 *Daily Press and Dakotaian*, rpt. in the *Dakota Pantagraph,* July 16, 1879.

8 *Dakota Pantagraph,* July 23, 1879.

9 *Daily Press and Dakotaian,* July 18, 1879.

10 Ibid., July 22, 1879.

11 *Dakota Herald,* July 26, 1879. Alfred Carre was an exile, having been banished from France. A resourceful employee of the *Press and Dakotaian*, he eventually returned to France.

12 Ibid., November 15, 1879.

13 *Daily Press and Dakotaian,* November 22, 1879.

14 *Dakota Pantagraph,* July 23, 1879.

15 *Daily Press and Dakotaian,* November 22, 1879.

16 Ibid., November 24, 1879.

17 Ibid., November 25, 1879.

18 Ibid., September 24, 1879. Brule City was located along the Missouri River, south of present-day Chamberlain, South Dakota. The settlement no longer exists.

19 Ibid., November 26, 1879.

20 Ibid., November 28, 1879.

21 Ibid., November 29, 1879.

22 Ibid., December 2, 1879.

23 Ibid.

24 Ibid., December 9, 1879.

25 Ibid., December 4, 1879.

26 Ibid.

27 Ibid., December 6, 1879.

28 Ibid., December 9, 1879.

29 Ibid., rpt. in the *Sioux Valley News*, December 27, 1879.

30 *United States v. Beebe*, 2 Dakota Reports, 292, 11 N.W. 505 [1880].

31 *Dakota Herald,* February 21, 1880.

32 *Daily Press and Dakotaian,* April 3, 1880.

33 *Dakota Herald,* April 10, 1880.

34 *Canton Advocate* (Canton, DT), April 8, 1880.

35 *Daily Press and Dakotaian,* April 5, 1880.

36 Ibid., April 20, 1880.

37 Ibid., May 20, 1880.

38 Ibid., September 24, 1881.

Chapter 19

1   U.S. Federal Census, 1880.

2   *Southern Dakota Homeseeker*, rpt. in the *Daily Press and Dakotaian*, May 7, 1880.

3   *Dakota Herald,* June 26, 1880.

4   Fanebust, *Echoes of November*, 126.

5   *Daily Press and Dakotaian,* June 23, 1880.

6   *Dakota Herald,* December 11, 1880 (referencing an article in the *Press and Dakotaian*).

7   *Daily Press and Dakotaian,* September 22, 1879.

8   Virginia Driving Hawk Sneve*, South Dakota Geographic Names* (Sioux Falls, SD: Brevet Press, 1973), 32.

9   Mary Lou Livingston, *History of Running Water* (privately published, ca. 1989), 13-14. The town was never referred to as "Shannon" and was later renamed "Running Water."

10 Harry F. Thompson, ed, *A New South Dakota History*, 2nd ed. (Sioux Falls, SD: Center for Western Studies, 2009), 107-08.

11 George H. Phillips, "The Indian Ring in Dakota Territory, 1870-1890," *Selected Papers of the First Nine Dakota History Conferences, 1969-1977,* H. W. Blakely, ed., (Madison, SD: Dakota State College, 1981), 36.

12 Lamar, 182.

13 Thompson, 108.

14 Kingsbury, *History of Dakota Territory,* vol. II, 1036.

15 *Daily Press and Dakotaian,* April 28, 1878.

16 *Pittsburgh Commercial-Gazette*, rpt. in the *Indiana Progress* (Indiana, PA)*, July 18, 1878. Wolf is spelled "Wolfe" in other sources.

17 *Dakota Herald,* March 13 and April 10, 1880.

18 *Daily Press and Dakotaian,* March 9 and 11, 1880.

19 Lamar, 187.

20 Ibid., 185-88.

21 *Dakota Herald,* April 17, 1880.

22 *Weekly Press and Dakotaian,* April 15, 1880.

23 *Mitchell Republican* (Mitchell, DT), rpt. in the *Sioux Valley News*, June 21, 1883.

24 *Daily Press and Dakotaian,* January 28, 1880.

25 Ibid., April 12, 1880.

26 *Daily Press and Dakotaian,* April 17, 1880.

27 Ibid., April 14, 1880.

28 *National Police Gazette,* May 8, 1880.

29 *Daily Press and Dakotaian,* April 27, 1880

30 Ibid., May 17, 1880.

31 Ibid., May 17, 1880.

32 *Dakota Herald,* May 15 and 22, 1880; *Daily Press and Dakotaian,* May 17-18, 1880.

33 *Daily Press and Dakotaian,* May 22, 1880.

34 Ibid., November 22, 1880.

35 *Dakota Herald,* December 18, 1880.

36 *Daily Press and Dakotaian,* May 25, 1880.

37 Ibid., June 23, 1880.

38 Ibid., July 2, 1880.

39 Ibid., September 4, 1880.

40 Ibid., February 1, 1882.

41 Ibid., August 21, 1880.

42 *Huron Settler* (Huron, DT), rpt. in the *Daily Press and Dakotaian,* November 26, 1880. The *Daily Press and Dakotaian,* November 29, 1880, reported that he had been shot nineteen times.

43 Sneve, 32-33.

Chapter 20

1 *Dakota Herald,* March 19, 1881.

2 Hyatt, 211-12.

3 Ibid., 219.

4 Ibid., 228-30.

5 Ibid., 230.

6 *Daily Press and Dakotaian,* October 25, 1881.

7 Kingsbury, *History of Dakota Territory,* vol. II, 1182.

8 *Daily Press and Dakotaian,* December 1, 1880.

9 Ibid., December 2, 1880.

10 *National Republican,* November 10, 1881.

11 *Omaha Daily Bee* (NE), April 18, 1881.

12 *Daily Press and Dakotaian,* May 10, 1881.

13 Ibid., May 11, 1881.

14 Ibid., May 12, 1881.

15 Ibid., May 20, 1881.

16 Ibid., June 4, 1881.

17 Ibid., September 26, 1881.

18 Ibid., October 10, 1881.

19 Ibid., October 25, 1881.

20 *Menno Chronicle* (Menno, DT)*, rpt. in the *Dakota Herald,* September 10, 1881.

21 *Parker New Era*, rpt. in the *Daily Press and Dakotaian,* November 17, 1881.

22 *Chicago Times,* rpt. in the *Dakota Herald,* November 19, 1881.

23 *Pittsburgh Leader* (PA), rpt. in the *Daily Press and Dakotaian,* November 21, 1881.

24 *Daily Press and Dakotaian,* November 21, 1881.

25 *Dakota Pantagraph,* November 19, 1881.

26 Hyatt, 242.

27 Beadle, 208.

28 *Chicago Times*, rpt. in the *Dakota Herald,* November 19, 1881; *Worthington Advance* (Worthington, MN)*, November 17, 1881.

29 *Bismarck Tribune,* December 2, 1881.

30 *Dakota Herald,* November 19, 1881.

31 *Salem Register* (Salem, DT)*, March 25, 1881

32 Kingsbury, vol. II, 1182.

33 *Dakota Herald,* December 3, 1881.

Chapter 21

1 *Daily Press and Dakotaian,* September 20, 1881.

2 *Sioux City Daily Journal* (IA), rpt. in the *Black Hills Daily Times,* December 17, 1881.

3 *Daily Press and Dakotaian,* May 25, 1876.

4 Stoddard, 45, 217, 424.

5 *Daily Press and Dakotaian,* April 14, 1877; *Dakota Herald,* April 21, 1877.

6 *Swan Lake Era,* rpt. in the *Daily Press and Dakotaian,* September 3, 1879.

7 *Daily Press and Dakotaian,* September 15, 1881.

8 *Inter-Ocean,* rpt. in the *Daily Press and Dakotaian,* September 16, 1881.

9 *Daily Press and Dakotaian,* October 11, 1881.

10 Ibid., December 8, 1881.

11 *Dakota Herald,* December 10, 1881.

12 *Daily Press and Dakotaian,* December 8, 1881.

13 Fanebust, *Tales of Dakota Territory Vol. II,* 70-71.

14 Fanebust, 71; *Daily Press and Dakotaian,* December 14, 1881.

15 *Weekly Democratic Statesman* (Austin, TX), December 29, 1881.

16 *Daily Press and Dakotaian,* December 16, 1881.

17 Ibid., December 17, 1881.

18 Ibid., December 20-21, 1881.

19 Ibid., December 27, 1881.

20 *Dakota Herald,* December 31, 1881.

21 *Daily Press and Dakotaian,* July 1, 1882.

22 Ibid., December 21, 1881.

23 *St. Paul Daily Globe* (MN), December 25, 1881.

24 *Dakota Herald,* December 24, 1881.

25 *St. Paul Pioneer Press* (MN), rpt. in the *Daily Press and Dakotaian,* January 10, 1882.

26 *Cincinnati Commercial* (OH), rpt. in the *Daily Press and Dakotaian,* March 21, 1882.

27 *Dakota Herald,* December 31, 1881.

28 *Daily Press and Dakotaian,* January 3, 1882.

29 Ibid., March 21, 1882.

Chapter 22

1 *Daily Press and Dakotaian,* June 5, 1882.

2 James C. Olson, *Red Cloud and the Sioux Problem* (Lincoln: University of Nebraska Press, 1975), 286.

3 Donald E. Worcester, ed., *Forked Tongues and Broken Treaties* (Caldwell, ID: The Caxton Printers, 1975), 296.

4 Jeffrey Ostler, *The Plains Sioux and U.S. Colonialism from Lewis and Clark to Wounded Knee* (New York: Cambridge University Press, 2004), 217.

5 *Register of the Department of the Interior,* Washington: Government Printing Office, 1883, 122.

6 *Daily Press and Dakotaian,* September 18, 1882.

7 Joseph Ward, "Governor Newton Edmunds," *The Monthly Dakotan,* vol.1, no. 2, June 1898, 8.

8 Olson, 287.

9 Henry E. Fritz, *The Movement for Indian Assimilation, 1860-1890* (Philadelphia: University of Pennsylvania Press, 1963), 83.

10 Ibid., 135.

11 *Daily Press and Dakotaian,* November 19, 1881.

12 *Toledo Journal* (OH), rpt. in the *Sioux Falls Independent,* March 9, 1876.

13 Barry Werth, *Banquet at Delmonico's: Great Minds, the Gilded Age, and the Triumph of Evolution in America* (New York: Random House, 2009), 137.

14 George E. Hyde, *A Sioux Chronicle* (Norman: University of Oklahoma Press, 1956), 111.

15 *Daily Press and Dakotaian,* November 24, 1882.

16 Hyde, 111.

17 http://files.usgwarchives.net/sd/andreas/agency.txt, Indian Agencies, 2.

18 Hyde, 113.

19 Harry H. Anderson, "A History of the Cheyenne River Indian Reservation and its Military Post Fort Bennett, 1868-1891," *South Dakota Historical Collections*, 28 (Pierre: South Dakota State Historical Society, 1956), 486.

20 Hyde, 112.

21 *Daily Press and Dakotaian,* October 12, 1882.

22 Ibid., November 10, 1882.

23 Kingsbury, *History of Dakota Territory,* vol. II, 1204.

24 *Sioux Valley News*, November 24, 1882.

25 Frances Chamberlain Holley, *Once Their Home, or Our Legacy from the Dahkotahs* (Chicago: Donohue & Henneberry, 1890), 50-51.

26 Hyde, 118.

27 *Daily Press and Dakotaian,* November 10, 1882.

28 *Sioux City Daily Journal*, rpt. in the *Bismarck Weekly Tribune* (Bismarck, DT), November 24, 1882.

29 Kingsbury, vol. II, 1242-43; *St. Paul Pioneer Press*, rpt. in the *Daily Press and Dakotaian,* November 24, 1882.

30 Hyde, 131.

31 Ibid., 133.

32 *Chamberlain Register* (Chamberlain, DT), rpt. in the *Daily Press and Dakotaian,* February 6, 1883.

33 Ibid., February 13, 1883.

34 Hyde, 134.

35 Ibid., 136.

36 James McLaughlin, *My Friend the Indian* (Boston and N.Y: Houghton Mifflin Co., 1910), 272.

37 Hyde, 136.

38 Ostler, 221.

39 Kingsbury, vol. II, 1246.

40 *Daily Press and Dakotaian,* August 31, 1883.

41 Ibid., August 31, 1883.

42 *New York Times,* September 9, 1883.

43 *Dakota Herald,* September 15, 1883.

44 *Daily Press and Dakotaian,* November 16, 1883.

45 Ostler, 220-21.

46 *St. Paul Pioneer Press,* rpt. in the *Dakota Herald,* March 31, 1883.

47 Virginia Driving Hawk Sneve, *That They May Have Life: The Episcopal Church in South Dakota, 1859-1976* (New York: The Seabury Press, 1977), 26.

48 Kingsbury, vol. II, 1246.

49 Ostler, 219.

50 *St. Paul Pioneer Press*, rpt. in the *Sioux Valley News*, September 28, 1883.

51 Anderson, 488.

52 *The Sioux Nation and the United States, a Brief History* (Washington, DC: The National Indian Defence [sic] Association, 1891), 6.

Chapter 23

1 *Daily Press and Dakotaian*, June 16, 1883.

2 *United States Congressional Serial Set 2233,* Hathi Trust Digital Library, Expenditures of the Department of Justice, 775-76.

3 Clark, C. Spence, *Territorial Politics and Government in Montana, 1864-89* (Urbana: University of Illinois Press, 1975), 227.

4 *United States Congressional Serial Set 2233*, 776.

5 *Dakota Herald,* March 3, 1883.

6 Ibid., April 7, 1883.

7 Ibid., August 25, 1883.

8 *Bismarck Weekly Tribune,* September 19, 1884; *St. Paul Daily Globe,* August 9, 1884.

9 *Pittsburg Dispatch* (PA), rpt. in the *Sioux Falls Daily Press,* May 13, 1885.

10 *Daily Press and Dakotaian,* April 18, 1885.

11 Charles H. Burke, "Hanging of Bell," *Hughes County History* (Pierre: Museum and State Historical Office, 1927), 90-91.

12 *Cambria Freeman*, November 26, 1886.

13 *Daily Press and Dakotaian,* March 14, 1885.

14 *Cambria Freeman*, December 17, 1886.

15 *Sioux Valley News,* July 26, 1889.

16 *Sioux Falls Argus-Leader,* February 7, 1890.

17 www.mocavo.com/family-tree/Robert-M-Bowers/Ihmsen-Family /Charles-Carroll-Shannon.

18 *Elk Point Courier* (Elk Point, DT), rpt. in the *Sioux Valley News,* July 11, 1890.

19 *Sioux Valley News,* June 17, 1892.

20 Ibid., December 23, 1892.

21 Ibid., November 4, 1893.

22 Ibid., February 23, 1894.

23 Ibid., November 9, 1894.

24 Ibid., November 30, 1894.

25 Ibid., November 22, 1895.

26 Ibid., January 8, 1897.

Chapter 24

1   *Minneapolis Journal* (MN), rpt. in the *Kansas City Daily Journal* (MO), December 8, 1895.

2   "South Dakota Historical Sketches," *The Monthly South Dakotan,* 2, no. 3, July 1899, 45. The sketches were taken from northwestern newspapers.

3   *Omaha Daily Bee,* June 1, 1897.

4   *Sioux Valley News*, May 7, 1897; *The History of Lincoln County South Dakota* (Canton, SD: The Lincoln County History Committee, 1985), 35.

5   *Sioux Falls Argus-Leader,* December 13, 1897.

6   *Pittsburgh Leader*, rpt. in the *Sioux Valley News*, December 31, 1897.

7   *Sioux Valley News,* March 11, 1898.

8   *Los Angeles Herald* (CA), August 29. 1898.

9   *Sioux Valley News*, December 20, 1895, from an article in the *Record,* November 1895, a Fargo, ND, magazine published by Clement A. Lounsberry.

10 *San Diego Union* (CA), April 14, 1899; *Sioux Valley News,* April 28, 1899.

11 *Sioux Valley News,* April 28, 1899.

12 Ibid., April 21, 1899.

13 *Sioux Falls Argus-Leader,* April 14, 1899.

14 *Sioux Valley News,* April 28, 1899.

15 *Omaha Daily Bee,* May 3, 1900.

16 *Minneapolis Journal,* November 3, 1903.

17 Doane Robinson, ed., "Judge Shannon's Grave," *The South Dakotan, A Monthly Magazine,* 7, no. 5, September 1904, 10.

18 Doane Robinson Collection, Folder 8, letter from Granville G. Bennett to Doane Robinson, October 28, 1907, South Dakota State Historical Society, Pierre, SD.

SELECTIVE BIBLIOGRAPHY

Abbott, Newton Carl. *Montana in the Making.* 13th ed. rev. by Adelia M. Price. Billings, MT: The Gazette Printing Co., 1964.

Anderson, Harry H. "Deadwood: An Effort at Stability." *Montana: The Magazine of Western History,* 20, no. 1 (January 1970), 40-47.

Armstrong, Moses K. *Early Empire Builders of the Great West.* St. Paul: E. W. Porter, 1901.

Athearn, Robert C. *Forts of the Upper Missouri.* Lincoln and London: University of Nebraska Press, 1967.

Atlas of Charles Mix County. Lake Andes, SD: E. Frank Peterson, Publisher, 1906.

Banner, Stuart. *The Death Penalty: An American History.* Cambridge, MA: Harvard University Press, 2002.

Basler, Roy P., ed. *The Collected Works of Abraham Lincoln.* Vol. IV. New Brunswick, NJ: Rutgers University Press, 1953.

Beadle, William H. H. "Personal Memoirs of William H. H. Beadle, L.L.D." *South Dakota Historical Collections.* Doane Robinson, ed. 3 (Pierre: South Dakota State Historical Society, 1906), 82-246.

Bennett, Estelline. *Old Deadwood Days.* New York: J. H. Sears & Company, Inc, Publishers, 1928.

Bergeron, Paul H. *The Papers of Andrew Johnson.* Vol. 14: April-August 1868 (Knoxville: University of Tennessee Press, 1999).

Bingham, John H., and Nora V. Peters, "A Short History of Brule County," *South Dakota Historical Collections*, 23 (Pierre: South Dakota State Historical Society, 1947), 1-184.

Brown, Jesse and A. M. Willard. *The Black Hills Trails: A History of the Struggles of the Pioneers in the Winning of the Black Hills.* Edited John T. Milek. Rapid City: Rapid City Journal Company, 1924.

Burbank, John A. *Second Biennial Address to the Legislative Assembly of Dakota Territory, December 3, 1872.* Territorial Governors' Papers. South Dakota State Historical Society, Pierre, SD.

Burke, Charles H. "Hanging of Bell," *Hughes County History.* South Dakota Museum and State Historical Office, Pierre, SD, 1927.

Carter, Clarence Edwin, ed. *The Territorial Papers of the United States.* Vol. I. Washington, DC: U.S. Government Printing Office, 1934.

Casey, Robert J. *The Black Hills and Their Incredible Characters.* Indianapolis, IN: The Bobbs-Merrill Co., 1949.

Connell, Evan S. *Son of the Morning Star: Custer and the Little Bighorn.* San Francisco: North Point Press, 1984.

Council Journal of the Legislative Assembly of the Territory of Dakota. Yankton, DT: Josiah C. Trask, Public Printer, 1862.

Cropp, Richard. "Jack Sully: The Last of the Bad Men." *Papers of the 13th Dakota History Conference.* H. W. Blakely, ed. (Madison, SD: Dakota State College, 1981), 109-16.

Darling, Roger. *Custer's Seventh Cavalry Comes to Dakota.* Vienna, VA: Potomac-Western Press, 1988.

Dollard, Robert. *Recollections of the Civil War and Going West to Grow Up With the Country.* Scotland, SD: Published by the Author, 1906.

Dunham, N. J. *A History of Jerauld County South Dakota, From Earliest Settlement to January 1, 1909.* Wessington Springs, SD, 1910.

Durand, George Harrison. *Joseph Ward of Dakota.* The Pilgrim Press, 1913.

Etulian, Richard W., ed. *Lincoln Looks West: From the Mississippi to the Pacific.* Carbondale and Edwardsville: Southern Illinois University Press, 2010.

Fanebust, Wayne. *Cavaliers of the Dakota Frontier.* Westminster, MD: Heritage Books, Inc., 2009.

_____. *Echoes of November: The Life and Times of Senator R. F. Pettigrew of South Dakota.* Freeman, SD: Pine Hill Press, 1997.

_____. *Tales of Dakota Territory. Vol. II.* Sioux Falls, SD: Mariah Press, 1999.

Fielder, Mildred, *Wild Bill and Deadwood.* New York: Bonanza Books, 1965.

Foster, James S. *Outlines of History of the Territory of Dakota and Emigrant's Guide.* 1870. Freeport, NY: Books for Libraries Press, 1971.

Fritz, Henry E. Dr. *The Movement for Indian Assimilation, 1860-1890.* Philadelphia: University of Pennsylvania Press, 1963.

Gaumer, Matthew Alan. "The Catholic 'Apostle to the Sioux': Martin Marty and the Beginnings of the Church in Dakota Territory." *South Dakota History,* 42, no. 3: (Fall 2012): 256-81.

General Laws, Memorials and Resolutions of the Territory of Dakota, 8th Session of the Legislative Assembly, December 6, 1868 to January 15, 1869. Yankton, DT: George W. Kingsbury, Public Printers, 1868-1869.

General Laws, Memorials and Resolutions of the Territory of Dakota, 9th Session, December 5, 1870 to January 13, 1871. Yankton, DT: Stone and Kingsbury, Public Printers, 1870-1871.

Hamilton, James McClellan. *History of Montana: From Wilderness to Statehood.* Merrill G. Burlingame, ed., Portland, OR: Binford and Morts, Publishers, 1970.

Hans, Fred M. "Scouting for the U.S. Army, 1876-1879: The Diary of Fred M. Hans," *South Dakota Historical Collections.* Michael l. Tate, ed. 40 (Pierre: South Dakota State Historical Society, 1981), 1-174.

Hill, Edward E. *The Office of Indian Affairs, 1824-1880: Historical Sketches.* New York: Clearwater Publishing Co., 1974.

The History of Lincoln County South Dakota. Canton, SD: The Lincoln County History Committee, 1985.

Holley, Frances Chamberlain. *Once Their Home, or Our Legacy from the Dahkotahs.* Chicago: Donohue & Henneberry, 1890.

Hoover, Herbert T., Carol Goss Hoover, and Elizabeth A. Simmons, eds. *Bon Homme County History.* Tyndall, SD: Bon Homme County Historical Society, 1994.

Howe, M. A. DeWolfe. *The Life and Labors of Bishop Hare, Apostle to the Sioux.* New York: Sturgis & Walton Co., 1913.

Hughes, Richard B. *Pioneer Years in the Black Hills.* Ed. Agnes Wright Spring. Rapid City, SD: Dakota Alpha Press, 1999.

Hyatt, Bernard Floyd. "A Legal Legacy for Statehood: The Development of the Territorial Judicial System in Dakota Territory, 1861-1889" (Ph.D. diss., Texas Tech University, 1987).

Hyde, George E. *A Sioux Chronicle.* Norman: University of Oklahoma Press, 1956.

Jackson, Donald. *Custer's Gold: The United States Cavalry Expedition of 1874.* Lincoln: University of Nebraska Press, 1972.

Jencks, Dorothy. *Some Historic Homes of Yankton, D.T.* Yankton: Yankton County Historical Society, 1993.

Jennewein, J. Leonard, and Jane Boorman, eds. *Dakota Panorama.* Sioux Falls: Brevet Press, 1973.

Jones, Robert Huhn. *The Civil War in the Northwest, Nebraska, Wisconsin, Iowa, Minnesota and the Dakotas.* Norman: University of Oklahoma Press, 1960.

Jorgensen, Gladys Whitehorn. *Before Homesteads: In Tripp County and the Rosebud.* Freeman, SD: Pine Hill Press, 1974.

Journal of the Executive Proceedings of the Senate of the United States of America, 1873-1875. Vol. XIX. Washington: Government Printing Office, 1901.

Karolevitz, Robert F. *Pioneer Church in a Pioneer City.* Aberdeen, SD: Northern Plains Press, 1971.

_____. *With Faith, Hope and Tenacity: The First One Hundred Years of the Catholic Diocese of Sioux Falls 1889-1989.* Mission Hill, SD: Dakota Homestead Publishers, 1989.

_____. *Yankton: The Way it Was, Being a Collection of Historical Columns Which Appeared in the Yankton Daily Press and Dakotan.* Freeman, SD: Pine Hill Press, 1999.

Kaufman, Fred. *Hunters of the Plains 1870's: A Historical Novel.* Aberdeen, SD: Northern Plains Press, 1975.

Kingsbury, George W. "Capital and Capital History of South Dakota," *South Dakota Historical Collections*, 5 (Pierre: South Dakota State Historical Society, 1910), 113-16.

_____ *History of Dakota Territory.* Vols. I and II. Chicago: The S. J. Clarke Publishing Co., 1915.

Kuykendall, W. L. *Frontier Days: A True Narrative of Striking Events on the Western Frontier.* J. M. and H. L. Kuykendall, Publishers, 1917.

Lamar, Howard Roberts. *Dakota Territory, 1861-1889: A Study of Frontier Politics.* New Haven and London: Yale University Press, 1956.

Lazarus, Edward. *Black Hills, White Justice: The Sioux Nation Versus the United States, 1775 to the Present.* New York: Harper Collins, 1991.

Lincoln: Selected Speeches and Writings. Library of America. New York: Vintage Books, 1989.

Livingston, Mary Lou. *History of Running Water.* Privately Published, [1989].

McClintock, John S. *Pioneer Days in the Black Hills.* Ed. Edward L. Senn. 1939. Norman: University of Oklahoma Press, 2000.

McKeown, Martha Ferguson. *Them Was The Days: An American Saga of the 70's.* Lincoln: University of Nebraska Press, 1950.

McLaird, James D. *Wild Bill Hickok and Calamity Jane, Deadwood Legends.* Pierre: South Dakota State Historical Society Press, 2008.

McLaughlin, James. *My Friend the Indian.* Boston and N.Y: Houghton Mifflin Co., 1910.

McMullin, Thomas A. and David Walker. *Biographical Directory of American Territorial Governors.* Westport, CT: Meckler Publishing, 1984.

Memorial and Biographical Record. Chicago: George A. Ogle and Co., 1897.

Milner, Joe E., and Earle R. Forrest. *California Joe, Noted Scout and Indian Fighter.* Caldwell, ID: The Caxton Printers, 1935.

Muzzey, David Saville, and John A. Krout. *American History for Colleges.* Rev. Ed. Ginn and Company, 1943.

Nash, Jay Robert. *Almanac of World Crime.* Garden City, NY: Anchor Press/Doubleday, 1981.

Nichols, David A. *Lincoln and the Indians: Civil War Policy and Politics.* Urbana; University of Illinois Press, 2000.

Niven, John, ed. *The Salmon P. Chase Papers, Vol. I: Journals, 1829-1872.* Kent, OH: The Kent State University Press, 1993.

Olson, James C. *Red Cloud and the Sioux Problem.* Lincoln: University of Nebraska Press, 1975.

Ostler, Jeffrey. *The Plains Sioux and U.S. Colonialism from Lewis and Clark to Wounded Knee.* New York: Cambridge University Press, 2004.

Oyos, Lynwood E., ed. *Over a Century of Leadership: South Dakota Territorial and State Governors, 1861-1987*. Sioux Falls, SD: Center for Western Studies, 1987.

Patton, Don. "The Legend of Ben Ash." *South Dakota Historical Collections*, 23 (Pierre: South Dakota State Historical Society, 1947), 185-211.

People v. Wintermute. 1 Dakota Reports, 61, 46 N.W. 694 [1875].

Phillips, George H. "The Indian Ring in Dakota Territory, 1870-1890," *Selected Papers of the First Nine Dakota History Conferences, 1969-1977*, H. W. Blakely, ed. (Madison, SD: Dakota State College, 1981), 36-60.

Pomeroy, Earl S. *The Territories and the United States, 1861-1890*. Philadelphia: University of Pennsylvania Press, 1947.

Records of the U.S. District Court, 2nd District, Yankton, DT, 1861-1873. State Historical Society of North Dakota, Bismarck, ND.

Register of the Department of the Interior. Washington: Government Printing Office, 1883.

The Revised Codes of the Territory of Dakota, A. D. 1877. Yankton: Bowen & Kingsbury, Public Printers, 1877.

Rice, Allen Thorndike, ed. *Reminiscences of Abraham Lincoln by Distinguished Men of His Time*. 1888. New York: Haskell House Publishers, 1971.

Rickard, T. A. *A History of American Mining*. New York: McGraw Hill Book Company, 1932.

Reiger, John F., ed. *The Passing of the Great West: Selected Papers of George Bird Grinnell*. Norman: University of Oklahoma Press, 1985.

Robinson, Doane. *Encyclopedia of South Dakota*. Pierre, SD: Published by the Author, 1925.

_____. *History of South Dakota*. Vols. I and II. B. F. Bowen & Co., Publishers, 1904.

Rosa, Joseph G. *The West of Wild Bill Hickok*. Norman: University of Oklahoma Press, 1982.

_____. *They Called Him Wild Bill, The Life and Adventures of James Butler Hickok*. Norman: University of Oklahoma Press, 1964.

_____. *Wild Bill Hickok. The Man and His Myth.* Lawrence: University Press of Kansas, 1996.

Sansom-Flood, Reneé. *Lessons from Chouteau Creek: Yankton Memories of Dakota Territorial Intrigue.* Sioux Falls, SD: Center for Western Studies, 1986.

Sansom-Flood, Reneé, and Shirley A. Bernie. *Remember Your Relatives: Yankton Sioux Images, 1851-1904.* Marty, SD: Marty Indian School, 1985.

Schell, Herbert S. *History of Clay County South Dakota.* Vermillion, SD: Clay County Historical Society, 1976.

_____. *Dakota Territory During the Eighteen Sixties.* Vermillion: Governmental Research Bureau, University of South Dakota, 1954.

_____. *History of South Dakota.* 4th ed., rev. by John E. Miller. Pierre: South Dakota State Historical Society Press, 2004.

Secrest, William W., ed. *I Buried Hickok: The Memoirs of White Eye Anderson.* College Station, TX: Creative Publishing Company, 1980.

Shonley, Tom. "Cattle Drives, Rustlers, and Nicholson Gulch," *9th Annual West River History Conference Papers* (Keystone, SD: Keystone Area Historical Society, 2001).

Simon, John Y., ed. *The Papers of Ulysses S. Grant. Vol. 19: July 1, 1868-October 31, 1869.* Carbondale and Edwardsville: Southern Illinois University Press, 1991.

Simmons, Thomas E. "Territorial Justice under Fire: The Trials of Peter Wintermute, 1873–1875." *South Dakota History*, 31, no. 2 (Summer 2001): 91–112.

Simpson, John. *West River, 1850-1910: Stories From the Great Sioux Reservation.* Sioux Falls: Pine Hills Press, 2000.

The Sioux Nation and the United States, a Brief History. Washington, DC: The National Indian Defence [sic]Association, 1891.

Smart, A. B. *Outlines of Pioneer Jerauld County History.* Wessington Springs, SD: Tamblyn Printing, 1970.

Sneve, Virginia Driving Hawk. *South Dakota Geographic Names.* Sioux Falls: Brevet Press, 1973.

_____. *That They May Have Life: The Episcopal Church in South Dakota, 1859-1976.* New York: The Seabury Press, 1977.

Spence, Clark, C. *Territorial Politics and Government in Montana, 1864-89.* Urbana: University of Illinois Press, 1975.

Stoddard, W. H. *Turner County Pioneer History.* 1931. Freeman, SD: Pine Hill Press, 1975.

Sundstrom, Jessie Y., ed. *Custer County History to 1876.* Custer, SD: Custer County Historical Society, 1977.

Sutley, Zack T. *The Last Frontier.* New York: The Macmillan Co., 1930.

Sutton, Ernest V. *A Life Worth Living.* Pasadena, CA: Trail's End Publishing Co., 1948.

Tate, Michael L. *The Frontier Army in the Settlement of the West.* Norman: University of Oklahoma Press, 1999.

Tennant, Brad. "Becoming Dakota Territory: The 1861 Organic Act and the Struggle for Territorial Status." *South Dakota History,* 43, no. 2 (Summer 2013): 118-46.

Territorial Governors Papers. "Governor Faulk's 2nd Annual Message to the Legislature of Dakota Territory." December 3, 1867. South Dakota State Historical Society, Pierre, SD.

Territory v. Chartrand. 1 Dakota Reports, 363, 46 N.W. 583 [1877].

Territory v. Conrad. 1 Dakota Reports, 348-56, 46 N.W. 605 [1877].

Thompson, Harry F., ed. *A New South Dakota History.* 2nd ed. Sioux Falls, SD: Center for Western Studies, 2009.

Towne, Arthur E. *Old Prairie Days.* Otsego, MI: Otsego Union Press, 1948.

U.S. Department of the Interior. Territorial Papers of Dakota, 1861-1873. National Archives, Washington, DC.

U.S. Department of the Interior. Territorial Papers of Dakota, 1863-1889. National Archives, Washington, DC.

U.S. Federal Census, 1880.

United States v. Beebe. 2 Dakota Reports, 292, 11 N.W. 505 [1880].

Van Der Pol, Henry. *On the Reservation Border: Hollanders in Douglas and Charles Mix Counties.* Stickney, SD: Argus Printers, 1969.

VanEpps-Taylor, Betti C. *Forgotten Lives: African Americans in South Dakota.* Pierre, SD: South Dakota State Historical Society Press, 2008.

Vogel, Robert. "Looking Back on a Century of Complete Codification of the Law. *North Dakota Law Review*, 53 (1976-1977).

Wert, Jeffrey D. *The Controversial Life of General George Armstrong Custer.* New York: Simon and Schuster, 1996.

Werth, Barry. *Banquet at Delmonico's: Great Minds, the Gilded Age, and the Triumph of Evolution in America.* New York: Random House, 2009.

White, Helen McCann, ed. *Ho! For the Gold Fields: Northern Overland Wagon Trains of the 1880's.* St. Paul: Minnesota Historical Society, 1966.

Worcester, Donald E., ed. *Forked Tongues and Broken Treaties.* Caldwell, ID: The Caxton Printers, 1975.

INDEX

A

African Americans: migration of, 163–64; perception of, 164–72

Albemarle Hotel, 373–74

alcohol/whiskey: and influence on crimes, 49–51, 146, 195, 213, 223–25, 229–31; and judges, 51–52, 135–36; and Native Americans, 14–15, 19, 21, 76–78, 180, 229, 347; and typical frontier life, 49, 223

Allen, Joseph, 219–20, 229

American Creek, 21

Armstrong, Moses, 11–13, 51, 82, 91, 135–36, 151

arson, 139–40, 159–60

Arthur, Chester, 321–23, 333–34, 345, 347, 349, 355–56

Ash, Ben C., 198, 210–11, 220

Ash, Henry C., 110

assault, 131–32, 171–72, 225, 227, 230

attorney/lawyer: and contempt, 150–51; for Dakota Territory, 4, 7, 27, 34, 42, 44–45, 59, 66, 78, 191, 207, 229, 257, 286, 303–4, 312, 319, 322, 327, 330,

358; defense, 75, 78, 98, 105–6, 116, 127, 130, 178, 205, 207, 227–230, 284, 322, 329–30; for Yankton County, 98, 103, 105, 157

B

Baker, Millard, 131, 171, 204, 230, 239–40, 247–48, 254–55, 295, 306–9, 327

Bankson, Carrie (Wiggie), 306, 308–9

Bannack (town), 11

Barnes, Alanson Hamilton, 58–59, 62–63, 65, 67–70, 98, 135–36, 138–39, 148, 154, 177, 179–80, 196, 257–58, 312–13

Bartlett, Ara, 23, 26–27, 34, 39, 63

Battle of Little Bighorn, 194, 342

Bear Hill Creek, 51

Beebe, Silas, 279–297

Bennett, Granville, 140–42, 144, 148, 158–60, 180, 196–97, 205, 227, 246–47, 249, 256, 377–378

Big Sioux River, 2–4, 28, 40, 205, 234, 254–55, 269

Bijou Hills, 73, 75, 79, 166, 280

Bismarck, 70, 92, 100, 122, 161, 196, 201, 223, 229, 247, 300, 346, 358, 361

Black Hills: crimes in, 126, 198–99, 205, 219–222; trespassing in, 190–91, 193–94; and gold, 17, 51, 122–23, 165, 182–83, 185–89, 192–95, 219; settlement of, 196–97, 202, 219; and the Sioux, 50, 183, 188–94, 196

Black Hills Expedition, 122, 182–88

blackleg, 310

Black, George, 22–23

Blaine, James, 40

Bliss, Philemon, 8, 10, 13–14, 16, 26–27, 63

Bon Homme (town), 4, 8, 10, 14–15, 21, 41, 49, 64–65, 67, 75, 78, 101, 125, 230, 239–40, 252, 261

Bon Homme County, 19, 30, 50, 63, 65, 75, 78, 101, 123–24, 239, 241, 252, 259, 301

Bowdoin College, 39

Boyle, John, 29, 30–32, 39–41

Bradley, Henry, 230–31

Brave Bear, 336, 345, 350

Briggs, Maria, 175–78

Kingsbury, George W., 77, 92, 143, 302, 316, 350

Knowlton, George, 324–33, 337

L

Lame Johnny Creek, 262

Lame Johnny Tree, 262

Landphere, George, 279–80, 282–93, 295–97

Laramie County, 33–34

larceny, 50, 78–79, 125, 130, 239, 249, 253

lawyer. See attorney/ lawyer

Lincoln, Abraham, 1, 4–5, 7–8, 10, 13, 26–27, 29–32, 54, 56, 91, 106, 313, 340, 355

Lincoln, Mary Todd, 5

Lincoln, Robert, 322

Lincoln County, 63, 234, 371

Lincoln National Monument, 22, 31

Linn, Arthur, 41, 45–48, 52, 92, 100

Litchfield, Laban, 23, 34, 39, 59

Little Bighorn, Battle of, 194, 342

Llewellyn, W. H. H., 260, 305, 307

Lynch, Judge, 146, 195, 203, 253

lynching / lynch mob: of horse thieves, 235–37, 253–54, 261–62; and outlaws, 368; in Pierre, 362; in Sioux Falls, 224; stemming from slow/corrupt due process, 47; at Snake Creek, 73–75, 78–80, 122, 124–25, 187; threat of, 96–97, 171, 202, 265; in Vermillion, 24–25; in Yankton, 36–37,

M

Maxwell, John "Jack," 305–9

McCall, John "Jack" (Bill Sutherland), xii, xi, 198–199, 201–18, 230, 292, 304, 370–72

McCanles Massacre, 200

McCook, Edwin, 63, 83–85, 88–91, 93–97, 99, 103, 105, 107–15, 134–35, 142–44, 147, 190

McGirk, Moses, 252–53

McKay, William, 75–81, 122–26, 183–87, 191

McLaughlin, James, 349, 352

McMahon, Frank, 224–28, 247–49

Merchants Hotel, 70, 95, 146, 193, 225, 324

Medary (town), 2

Middleton, Doc (James Riley), 80, 244, 259–61, 267

Miner, Nelson, 24

Miner County, 281

miner/mining, 75–76, 122, 180, 183–85, 187–88, 190–98, 205, 261, 313

Minnesota, 2, 4, 13, 25, 47, 82, 86, 92, 98, 190, 192, 205, 252, 265, 268, 333–35

misogyny, 225–26

Missouri, 4, 11, 27, 75–76, 102, 166, 200, 205, 324, 328

Missouri River, 2–5, 7–8, 11, 14, 18–19, 21, 28, 30, 47, 50–51, 75–76, 78, 80–82, 88, 101, 122, 125, 129, 165, 201, 211, 219–20, 231, 240, 243, 246, 259, 263, 279–80, 229, 301, 307, 309–10, 316, 325, 338, 361, 367

Montana Territory, 2, 10, 16, 26, 32, 47, 75–76, 194, 355, 363

Moody, Gideon, 51–52, 56, 75, 78, 91, 94, 98, 105–6, 116, 124, 135–36, 142, 205, 227, 229, 256–58, 297, 312–13

Moody, James, 94

Mullen, Lieutenant, 17

Treaty of 1868, 189–90,
195, 340–41, 348
Tripp, Bartlett, 93, 98,
105–6, 116, 136, 158,
160, 230, 256, 314,
328–31
Tripp, William, 98, 106,
142, 152
Trumbull, Lyman, 5

U

Union Pacific Railroad,
33–34, 221, 300, 305
upriver country (upper
country), 16, 19, 50,
104, 219, 231, 279
U.S.-Dakota
(Minnesota) War,
12–13, 268, 333
U.S. marshal: 4, 8, 23,
34, 39, 47, 59, 66, 204,
247, 314
U.S. Supreme Court,
6, 66

V

Van Kirk, John, 223,
227
Vermillion, 4, 8, 10, 15,
24–30, 45, 62, 141–42,
144–45, 152, 196,
254, 258
Vermillion River, 4, 24,
269, 281
vigilantes, 24–25, 33,
79, 195, 251, 253–54,
261, 310–11

W

Waldron, George P., 108
Walker, John, 40
Ward, Joseph, 36
Ward, Sarah, 36
Washington, D.C., 5,
28, 31–32, 39, 55, 68,
95, 127, 135, 270, 335,
340
Washington Territory,
2, 32
Weatherwax, Ephraim
(Eph), 259, 261
Wessington Hills: area
of, 241–42; and horse
thieves, 242–46
Western Town
Company, 39–40
Whitney, Oscar, 68–69
Williams, Joseph, 8–10,
14, 27
Williams, J. Lanier, 27
Williams, William,
279–80, 283–96
Williston, Lorenzo,
8–10, 13, 15–16, 26
Windom, William,
334–35
Wintermute, Peter:
altercation with
Edwin McCook, 89,
93–97; background of,
83, 85–90; first trial,
97–99, 103–119; and
newspaper coverage:
96–97, 99, 138–40,
144–45; second trial,
135–36, 140–47; trial

legacy of, 149, 169,
181, 198, 208, 292,
304
Wixson, Eli, 4
Woodbury County,
Iowa, 19
Wyoming Territory:
area and residents of,
2, 32–35, 203, 305;
officials, 39, 105, 116,
205, 307–8

Y

Yankton: area and
residents of, 2, 4–8,
13, 16, 27, 41, 49, 57,
70, 87, 91, 93, 132,
227, 247, 305; bar
association, 52, 313,
318, 334; and crime,
23, 30, 36, 57, 95–97,
130–32, 305, 325;
court district, 27, 29,
63–64, 68–70, 336;
newspapers, 15, 17,
22, 46, 52–53, 58, 64,
69, 72, 85–86, 90,
92, 96–97, 100, 124,
318–19, 334, 346, 376;
officials, 10–11, 22,
125, 306; and outlaws,
21–22, 96, 305,
308–9; and politics,
55–56, 68–70, 89, 92,
97, 106, 318–21, 361;
and trials, 47–48,
79, 105–6, 331–33;
visitors to, 229